SHADOWPLAY

DONNA PERLMUTTER

SHADOWPLAY

The Life of
ANTONY TUDOR

VIKING

VIKING
Published by the Penguin Group
Viking Penguin, a division of Penguin Books USA Inc.,
375 Hudson Street, New York, New York 10014, U.S.A.
Penguin Books Ltd, 27 Wrights Lane, London W8 5TZ, England
Penguin Books Australia Ltd, Ringwood, Victoria, Australia
Penguin Books Canada Ltd, 2801 John Street,
Markham, Ontario, Canada L3R 1B4
Penguin Books (N.Z.) Ltd, 182–190 Wairau Road,
Auckland 10, New Zealand

Penguin Books Ltd, Registered Offices:
Harmondsworth, Middlesex, England

First published in 1991 by Viking Penguin,
a division of Penguin Books USA Inc.

1 2 3 4 5 6 7 8 9 10

Grateful acknowledgment is made to the Antony Tudor
Ballet Trust and the Estate of Antony Tudor for permission
to publish excerpts from Antony Tudor's writings
and other material from the Trust's collections.

LIBRARY OF CONGRESS CATALOGING IN PUBLICATION DATA
Perlmutter, Donna.
Shadowplay : the life of Antony Tudor / by Donna Perlmutter.
p.   cm.
ISBN 0-670-83937-X
1. Tudor, Antony, 1909–1987.   2. Choreographers—United States—
Biography.   I. Title.
GV1785.T83P47   1991
792.8'2'092—dc20   90–50785
[B]

Printed in the United States of America
Set in Bembo
Designed by Francesca Belanger

*To Jona, whose attunement
to the large issues in my life
led to this project.*

ACKNOWLEDGMENTS

Since no biography heavily dependent on anecdotal material can be written without the generosity, forbearance and memory jogging of many people, I am indebted to all who spent countless hours detailing aspects of this mercurial and brilliant man.

Several months into the project I had the good fortune to meet Sally Brayley Bliss, the estate executor and trustee of Tudor's ballets. Without her wholehearted sanction and assistance the book would not exist, nor would I have found my way to the gracious, cooperative relatives, notably: Mollie Cook, Marion Jeffrey, Madeleine May, Connaught Palmer, and Gladys Scammell. Others who were essential to piecing together the portrait include Leo Kersley, who sat with me for hours on end describing the early days at Ballet Rambert; David Nillo, who interceded on my behalf to obtain important documents; Muriel Bentley, who offered constant encouragement and Richard Beard, who painstakingly read the manuscript and offered valuable page-by-page advice.

Several trips to London brought me face to face with those from the early days: Sir Frederick Ashton, William Chappell, Angela Dukes Ellis, Sally Gilmour, Diana Gould Menuhin, Fernau Hall, Therese Langfield Horner, Gerd Larsen, Maude Lloyd, Dame Alicia Markova, Elisabeth Schooling and Dame Ninette de Valois. Telephone conversations to her South Carolina ashram put me in touch with Margaret Craske. Those interviewees associated with Tudor's return to London in 1966 include Margaret Barbieri, Anthony Dowell, Kenneth MacMillan, Antoinette Sibley, Alfreda Thorogood Wall, and David Wall. Journalists there to whom I owe thanks are Mary Clarke, Judith Cruickshank, Julie Kavanaugh, Alastair Macaulay, John Percival, Peter Williams and Ballet Rambert archivist Jane Pritchard.

For the American part of Tudor's career I thank the following: Myrna Aaron, Diana Adams, David Adams, Alicia Alonso, Gerd Andersson, Howard Barr, Pina Bausch, Edward Bigelow, Don Bradburn, Mary Burr, Betty Cage, Gladys Celeste, Cyd Charisse, Judith Colpman, Bill Como, Alfredo Corvino, Leon Danelian, Alexandra Danilova, Phillipe de Conville, Agnes de Mille, Jennifer Dunning, Scott Douglas, Alex Ewing, Mary Farkas, Eliot Feld, Celia Franca, Miriam Golden, Martha Graham, Cynthia Gregory, John Gruen, Eric Hampton, Rosella Hightower, Stuart Hodes, Judy and Stanley Holden, Marian Horosko, Lise Houlton, Hildegarde Huestis, "El" Gabriel Israel, Edith Jerell, Sirpa Jorasmaa Salatino Tepper, Maria Karnilova, Michael Kidd, Gelsey Kirkland, Earl Kraul, Arthur Laurents, Greg Lawrence, Tanaquil LeClercq, Angela Leigh, Bella Lewitzky, Ruth and Arthur Liess, Annabelle Lyon, Sam Lurie, Robert Irving, P. W. Manchester, Bruce Marks, Enrique Martinez, Gary Masters, Michael Maule, Patricia McBride, Harry Mines, James Mitchell, Joyce Moffatt, Francisco Moncion, Kathleen Moore, Yvonne Mounsey, Darlene Neel, Rudolf Nureyev, Marja Odell, Sono Osato, Charles Payne, Dorathi Bock Pierre, Tommy Rall, Janet Reed, Herbert Ross, Donald Saddler, Tony Salatino, Betty Sawyer, Richard Schafer, Jerome Schnur, Lynn Seymour, Lois Smith, Oliver Smith, Michael Smuin, Zachary Solov, Roger Stevens, Grant Strate, Maria Tallchief, John Taras, Paul Taylor, Marianna Tcherkassky, Glenn Tetley, Muriel Topaz, Paula Tracy, Michael Uthoff, Nick Vanoff, David Vaughan, Jac Venza, Gore Vidal, Edward Villella and Sallie Wilson.

To historian Robert Dallek, who lent expert guidance on biographical techniques, and dance critic Lewis Segal, whose vigilance cannot be overestimated, I offer special thanks, as well as to other writers—Janet Anderson, Clive Barnes, Ed Cray, Digby Diehl, George Dorris, Don McDonagh and Harlow Robinson—who were so helpful.

Not least were the astute suggestions given by both my editors, Joyce Engelson and Amanda Vaill. Their genuine interest in the subject spurred my own.

CONTENTS

SHADOWPLAY

Introduction

It was December 7, 1986, perhaps the most gala occasion of his life. The camera found him in a row of red plush seats. He wore the uniform of formal grandeur: black tie, tuxedo, stiff white shirt—a rarity for Antony Tudor, who until this seventy-eighth year of life had always garbed himself in the plainest, most perfunctory clothes. The evening turned out to be a paradox of sorts. Although he had chosen the name Tudor, a royal name, when he left England for America nearly half a century before, he had forfeited any chance of knighthood, and the Kennedy Center Honor being conferred on him now was as close as he would ever get to a symbol of regal esteem.

No matter. In the dance world his name inspired awe and veneration. This was the man who transformed ballet from a lambent romanticism to the equivalent of a detailed twentieth-century novel. This was the man who did not need words to lay out the specifics of yearning and conflict, pride and lust, shame and fear, tenderness and resignation—the man whose powers of observation and powers of expression led him, sui generis, to the unimagined interiors of narrative; the man who banished cliché from the stage; who seized the existing ballet vocabulary and forged from it a movement language as rich and discerning as that of Stendahl or Proust.

Fanciers of the dance called him a genius. They also ignored him. Iconoclasts like Tudor may not lend themselves to hero worship in all quarters. But, then, whoever said that profound influences come through accessible channels or go hand in hand with popularity? He gave the world a smattering of luminous ballets—no less refutable as gems than a universally loved work like *Swan Lake*.

No one before him had thought to translate specific psychological realities to the ballet stage. No one before him had thought to portray the emotional lives of ordinary people, as opposed to courtly characters and fairy-tale creatures. And certainly no one had thought to depict all this through a brand-new invention of movement, rather than the banalities of melodrama and classical mime.

Tudor also stood at the forefront in many other ways. Where so many choreographers simply plotted steps to notes, and still do, he composed in long phrases that suggest a symphonist's frame of reference. His musicality went beyond the meager measure-by-measure grasp of lesser dance-makers. He could take Schoenberg's *Verklärte Nacht,* for instance, and set it to sweeping movement as the dramatic situation dictated, as well as to inward, seemingly motionless dancescapes that honored the music's aura.

He grew up in the wake of both Freud and Diaghilev. The great thinker who penetrated the shrouds of the psyche came to London from Vienna during the 1930s, just when Tudor was beating a new balletic path that seemed to incorporate Freudian tenets. Ten years earlier, the fabled Russian impresario had donated to Tudor's sensibilities images of a magical artistic realm. From this background the young playwright of the dance would accomplish extraordinary deeds, but the dance world at large did not know him. It was George Balanchine who would enjoy recognition as the most influential choreographer of the century—reigning from the hugely successful New York City Ballet until his death in 1983. And in England the most lauded dance-maker was Sir Frederick Ashton. These were titanic peers. But their creations were not typically real people with palpable emotions. Tudor alone could claim that coup.

His ballets, starting with *Jardin aux Lilas* and *Pillar of Fire,* were—and still are—revelatory. They do not celebrate feats or stand as vehicles for virtuosic display. They hardly encourage an audience to break in with applause. But their dramatic intensity—when well-performed—can grip the onlooker the way a potent film or play or novel can.

What poetic balance, then, that on this night of tribute, the expression of Antony Tudor remained austere. Was it a mask hiding feelings he could not comfortably share? Could those feelings have included hostility or bitterness, as well as vindication for the infamous self-doubts that plagued him lifelong? One could concoct any number of scenarios to explain the gaunt face, the cold stare.

Of the six Kennedy Center honorees seated with President and Mrs. Ronald Reagan, he was the oldest, the least known to a wide public watching the special televised event: unlike the violinist Yehudi Menuhin, the singer Ray Charles, the actors Jessica Tandy and Hume Cronyn or the comedienne Lucille Ball, he made his career offstage. Whereas they all fostered love affairs with their audiences, Tudor was several steps removed from public adulation. He gave himself to the dancers, who in turn enjoyed that glory—although never in the narcissistic sense; the privilege of appearing in a Tudor ballet had nothing to do with star turns.

When, on this glittering occasion, host Walter Cronkite introduced him as "a butcher's clerk from Britain who left the old world of European dance to create a new world of American ballet," Tudor listened and watched impassively. No one could guess that the event was a keenly felt milestone, starting the

moment the Kennedy selection committee notified him. Typically sanguine, he wrote to an old dancer friend in England,
Therese Langfield Horner:

> Now, especially this year, I am being put forward as a gift
> to the dance world. I rather enjoy it, even tho' next year I may
> be relegated to the garbage heaps. But the garbage heaps have
> their value. . . .

The nomination came at what he realized was the end of his
life—a life from which he took precious little self-satisfaction.
Yet, at the start of the evening, he permitted no flicker of acknowledgment, sitting stony-faced and ramrod erect. Painfully
thin, he seemed propped up by sheer willpower. His bald pate,
his ascetic countenance gave him at once a venerable and frightening look. More than anything, however, his sovereignty came
across.

Agnes de Mille, the American choreographer who had discovered him in London and broadcast his genius across the Atlantic while both were struggling for a place in the dance realm,
narrated his story. Herself a past honoree, Tudor's stroke-afflicted
colleague had to be helped onto the stage. And as she spoke about
him the camera caught Tudor listening. There was no trace of
sympathy for her words. If anything, he looked slightly scornful.
Langfield Horner, who knew them both intimately from their
days together in England half a century earlier, speculated that
"Antony was probably on guard—no one ever knew quite what
would come out of Agnes's mouth."

"Young, bonnie and very bewildered," was how de Mille
described him, remembering back to the early thirties, going on
to talk about her colleague then "as an observer and a dreamer."
She traced his career from the beginning of American Ballet
Theatre in 1940, originally called Ballet Theatre, and mentioned
the more than twenty-six curtain calls he received for his mas-
terwork *Pillar of Fire*. She proclaimed Tudor "one of the rare

few who is permanent, immortal, a risky word in the world of dance. What he asked for was magic and he got it."

But de Mille did more than bestow accolades. Always the entertainer, she lost no opportunity here. This was a vast, elite audience before her and the national telecast boosted the number to many millions. With engaging wit, she told the story of modern ballet and then how Tudor changed the face of it. The live crowd roared with laughter. Expecting to capture his amusement or at least an inkling of pleasure, the camera cut to him. No smile lurked there—only straight, severe lines. By the time de Mille got around to saying that he was "no longer young and bonnie," he nearly glowered.

Of course he was reading a whole history of aggressive femininity and competition into de Mille's words. Friendly enemies would be a more accurate tag for their relationship. There were very few willful women he could tolerate, especially if they were ambitious and self-promoting. The personal contention between these two spanned fifty years. But there was also mutual regard for each other's talent. Tudor's taste in women friends ran to those who were intelligent, graceful, giving, empathetic and candid—all at once. So he had to relent when the lovely Margot Fonteyn followed de Mille to offer the valedictory tribute. Radiant in her satin ball gown with huge red poufs for sleeves, the British ballerina, never a Tudor specialist, uttered words that grabbed him by the heart.

"Dear Antony," she concluded, in warm, lilting tones, extending her arms up to the first ring where he sat. "We, the dancers and the public, salute you and thank you for all you've given us." So genuinely embracing was her sentiment that few could wonder at its impact on Tudor. No matter how irascible and austere he was, Fonteyn touched the wary celebrant. Hardly anything could have been so moving as the sight of this stoic visage, the chin quivering slightly, the eyes watering. He blew kisses to her. No longer frail, he rose to acknowledge the applause. He pressed his palms together against his chest and bowed his head deeply, Buddhist-style—right, then left, then nodded upward to the side galleries.

Tears for Tudor were uncommon. But not nearly so remarkable as the absence, at Kennedy Center, of Hugh Laing, for the choreographer seldom appeared anywhere without this man who had come into his life fifty-four years earlier—as an incredibly handsome West Indian from Barbados.

Where was the honoree's lover, his Doppelgänger-Muse-Soulmate, the only one with whom he shared his innermost thoughts? Had there been a fight? Was he ill? Could possessiveness, or spite, have played a part?

It's true that one is born alone and dies alone. On the most gala night of his life Tudor tasted glory alone.

Soot and Cinnamon

HE WAS BORN WILLIAM JOHN COOK on April 4, 1908. Antony Tudor would travel a vast social distance from his beginnings in Finsbury, a working-class district in London's East End. Indeed, he removed himself by a kingdom from his humble, cockney birthright; hardly any name could confer more prestige than that of Tudor.

Did it take powers of impersonation to soar so far? Undoubtedly. But it was natural for the English to impersonate others when it came to ballet. Lacking a significant native tradition in dance, they eagerly adapted themselves to Russian models and took all varieties of French, Russian and improved English names—more glamorous than their own. Marie Rambert, who came to London by way of Warsaw, had been Cyvia Rambam and then Miriam Ramberg; Alicia Markova, Lillian Alice Marks; Ninette de Valois, the Irish-born Edris Stannus; Anton Dolin, Patrick Chippindall Healey-Kay, and so on.

It was the Edwardian epoch, and an aura of positivism prevailed. Liberal politicians, returned to power with a huge majority in 1906, cast their sights to reform as an issue. In the words of the new prime minister, Henry Campbell-Bannerman, England would be "less of a pleasure ground for the rich and more of a treasure house for the nation." Yet it was also the golden age of the country weekend, of the London season, of the new business tycoon, of the Gaiety Girls (who sometimes married not tycoons but aristocrats), of the bustle and the top hat, but above all, of the golden sovereign.

William Cook seemed made for his time, ready to seize the advantage of social mobility through merit, ready to spring from the board. He would represent cultural high-diving for his parents, although their lower-middle-class tradesman level was not exactly deprived of enrichment. As he recounted, "My father could play the violin; my mother sang in an amateur way; my grandfather, I believe, played the cello. I went to one piano teacher after another, better and better ones until I got through the Beethoven sonatas, then I studied at a London music school. In fact, I like music so much I wouldn't have minded being a conductor. You know, a dictator!"

His early exposure to the theater was mainly limited to rollicking, plebeian music halls, although the staged pantomimes he saw at Christmas set his small boy's adrenaline pumping. The desire to become part of this fantasy world began incubating early. There was a show at the old Sadler's Wells Theatre, a ten-minute walk from where the four-year-old William lived on Central Street, and from this revue came a song called "Footsteps in the Snow," which hung lifelong in his memory.

It was later, at sixteen, when he visited the Marlborough Music Hall and saw a dancer he could not forget, Loie Fuller. The name eluded him at first but the image that he subsequently described for ballet historian Cyril Beaumont "of a vague figure flitting amid a golden mist of light" had made its irrevocable impact. The excitement these outings roused in him—which he kept secret at all costs—did not find encouragement from his family, especially not from Alfred Thomas Cook, who would have preferred his son to settle into a more practical pursuit or at least an occupation he understood.

As it turned out, that son, the younger of two born to Alf and Florence Ann (neé Summers), had a strong business aptitude and a strong notion of authority lurking just beneath the surface. Some even suggested that had he not made his bond with the stage, had he escaped the compelling attraction to this realm of illusion, he might, in all likelihood, have worked diligently at some managerial job, advanced to senior clerk or junior partner, married and become lord of a modest home, having someone to come in and do the rough work. It was this dream of conventional family ties that would remain missing in his life.

Nineteen hundred and twenty-four saw Will graduating from free (government-sponsored) school. This was the period prior to "11-pluses," when most youngsters did not leave for the work force or go on to higher education until fourteen. At that age he received a scholarship to the private Dame Alice Owens's School, where he stayed for the next two years, making his parents supremely happy. They had tagged him the "promising" son, the one with intellectual capacity, and thus were willing to do without his help in the butcher shop. Robert, four years older, clearly had no such academic inclinations. Besides, Alf had claimed Bob as "my son and heir," leaving Will to become his mother's boy. Traditionally, it was her prerogative to dote on and even spoil the second child. She did. And whether listening to her nostalgic reminiscences of balls she attended as a girl—anxiously waiting for her dance card to be filled—or dressing up in her clothes for the fanciful charades he played, Will identified with her.

Birthright, to some extent, was destiny in this case. Bob pleased his father endlessly. As the firstborn, he became the object of Alf's training. And for a father of that social milieu it was common to give a boy puffs on a cigarette at age four or five, to take him to cockfights—in short, to form a strong masculine bond. By the time he was a teenager Bob had become a first-rate athlete, London's champion high-diver. He was bluff and outgoing like Alf—who loved swimming and excelled at it—although never quite the same eccentric as his father.

Alf and Florrie were exact opposites. He was a man of gusto, addicted as much to the sensual pleasures of food, for instance, as to the jolly evenings at Collins Music Hall in Islington or the Finsbury Park Empire. He booked tickets every Saturday night at one or the other, always tearing about to get there on time. He loved singing along with the entertainers. So strong was this impulse and so impervious to social stricture was he that years later, when taken to see *Les Sylphides* at Covent Garden, he sang the Chopin melody aloud in the darkened theater; as Gladys Scammell, one of Will's many cousins, remembered, "Everyone in the audience turned in his direction and shushed him, but he kept on—a little more quietly after the disapproval."

Having inherited the butchery business from his father, Alf never complained, although he probably would have chosen some other trade, given the choice—as well as a different neighborhood. The East End was a vast expanse of small-scale industry, sad dereliction and growling lorries. But it put his second son practically at the doorstep of London's Theatreland, which was among the richest and most creative cosmopolitan centers of the day. Will took it in hungrily.

Whatever else Alf Cook stood to bequeath his heirs, he certainly was not intent on turning his establishment over to them if they were disinclined. Kindly and boyish, if somewhat bumbling, he would hardly set himself up as an authority figure. He was not discernibly unhappy over any aspect of his life. Indeed, his bonhomie led him to such club-oriented ventures as the Freemasons, where he became a Worshipful Master. He and Florence were surpassingly generous. When their niece Gladys, working at her father's news agency that was half outdoors, suffered near frostbite, they insisted on taking her to various homeopaths and paying the bills. "And whenever we came to Uncle's house for family gatherings there would always be a lovely cut of meat," she said. "I remember, too, how he loved rice pudding and would bring out huge bowls of it, licking the cinnamon crust from the sides."

One of four brothers who thought themselves to be descendants of the British explorer Captain James Cook, Alf was a comfortable man—with himself, with his family, with the world. He played chess, regarding it a delectable pastime, not a sober challenge of intellect. He reveled in the outdoors. He loved animals, whose slaughter, ironically, meant his livelihood. Hopelessly disengaged from practical matters, he left the serious accounting of business affairs to Florence.

She was the worrier in the family, a silent worrier—not the wringing-hands, tearing-hair variety. Her face typically betrayed no expression beyond a slight discomfort or trepidation. "Uncle was such a live wire," recalled Gladys Scammell, "that Aunt Florrie never knew what he would do next—though womanizing and drinking were not on his agenda . . . straight as a dye, he was. Always frightened of what inappropriate thing he'd do, that's why she seemed so apprehensive. For fear of being embarrassed by him."

In photographs, Florence appears stolid and graceless, unusually impassive; she seems to have no feminine consciousness of herself, or rather no appreciation of that femininity. The wooden, nearly lifeless look of her arms and legs in snapshots is startling.

The eldest of four sisters and three brothers, she was uncommonly close with the girls, but reticent in most ways, and kept to herself. Being a Summers, however, and subscribing to their matriarchal style, she made all the big family decisions. "They liked to be bosses, the Summers women," according to Gladys. In all these traits Will would reflect his mother: he would follow in her nongregarious tracks, yet he would make the big decisions.

The bond between them was strong. Although Will did not take up the manly art of hunting lions or diving off high boards— once he even backed down the ladder after finding the height not to his liking—he would later keep a football in his office at the Ballet Club and, catching a few free minutes, would run into Kensington Gardens passing it back and forth to Leo Kersley, a young dancer. But he also did "fancy needlework when we were both eleven or twelve," recalled Scammell, "fancier than I could do. My mother said, 'He should've been a girl.' " Beyond a certain age, however, nothing in his manner suggested any hint of effeminacy.

At Dame Alice Owens's school he showed exceptional apti-tude, learning enough French and German to pursue the literature of both languages, which he did—notably with Proust later, although those who knew him remembered that he always read an English translation. His inclination to be an autodidact had already begun. At the same time he acquired the bookkeeping skills that ultimately earned him a junior clerkship at Smithfield Meat Market, a huge East End wholesale house—this after several years there as an errand boy and then a cashier.

His extreme shyness had made for a difficult childhood. By now he was virtually solitary, given to daydreaming, and too old, at fourteen, to dress up in his mother's finery as he used to do and enact the grown-up scenarios of his imagination—those nascent choreographies that positively delighted him. Gone were the days when he and the next-door child, whose father owned a fish market, fashioned little dances on the giant marble slab that otherwise served as the slicing/cleaning surface.

Apart from this fertile play, Central Street was not a place Will took pleasure from. There were often unsavory characters lurking about and with his middle-class sensibilities he saw the rough street types as frightening, if not downright detestable. Occa-sionally someone would relieve himself or herself in public, a sight that branded itself on Will's memory—he would use it later, veristically in a ballet (*Undertow*).

Hating the neighborhood, he would hop on the tram at every opportunity and visit cousin Gladys and Aunt Maude, a few miles north of the Cook homestead. Most of his mother's sisters' chil-dren were girls and he was very close to the aunts, somewhat less so to the cousins.

One of the things he loved was tea dancing. "We went to the Salon Bal together," Gladys remembered. "Both of us adored ballroom dancing and he was wonderful. Curious, because Aunt

Florrie, so ungainly, simply couldn't dance and Uncle Alf had no interest."

Upon graduation from Dame Alice Owens's the sixteen-year-old Will continued to live with his family upstairs from the butcher shop in their neat but soot-stained row house on Central Street.

His parents and the other neighborhood tradespeople could be described as "very decent" or "respectable." They worried about what others thought. They sought "to keep up appearances," especially to be recognized as finer than the common sweat-laborers who comprised the neighborhood majority. But now Will had discovered this exotic world of ballet and it did not comfort Alf and Florrie. Would he lose his best opportunities? Social and financial ones? Could gallivanting around as a dancer be a prudent thing for a son to do?

Their skepticism was reasonable. But William Cook would not forget the Little Italy of Clerkenwell; he would not forget the immigrant waiters from Palermo and Pisa who, in the 1920s, could walk from their houses to the restaurants that employed them. And when he took sensual memories from here to New York, where he would ultimately live an ascetic's life—even down to a strict macrobiotic diet of grains and vegetables—it was understandable that "the fragrance of fresh prosciutto and other delectable meats" would trigger his affectionate nostalgia. And link the lingering traces of a voluptuary to his father.

By day there was his job at Smithfield—fetching mugs of tea for older clerks and helping them fill orders. By night, with the savings from his small salary, there were forays to the glittery West End, where theaters with their bright marquees heralded the magic of music and dancing and acting on the stages inside. Among these was Covent Garden, where William Cook first made his miraculous discovery of Anna Pavlova, in 1925, and then the Diaghilev Ballet.

Pavlova stood as a feminine ideal—for him and for other innocents who would look upon her as the avatar of their inspiration. Indeed the legendary Russian dancer encompassed all that was alluring in ballet. Most choreographers took as grist for their creative mill the glorification of the ballerina. "Ballet is Woman" became the dictum later of George Balanchine, but it was one that applied as well to Ashton and virtually every dance-maker for decades to come. Diaghilev, however, set off different sparks in the wide-eyed Will. Here was the art of dance framed in radiantly imaginative productions—samplings of "white" tutu ballets as well as novel extravaganzas. For these, he was prepared to "wait three hours in line on the street" and then run up the stairs like a madman, diving for a seat. He would claim that seat, bought at the cheapest price available, in an unreserved section of Covent Garden known as the "gods"—facetiously so-named because it was high enough to rank as the deities' dwelling place. Its hard, wooden, backless benches were so closely spaced that occupants had to sit up straight in order not to touch those in the rows in front and behind.

It was this exposure to Diaghilev that would signal his calling: "A choreographer—that was what I wanted to be," he remarked much later. "In those days a choreographer was a rara avis. I knew right away that was for me."

And what led him up those stairs? Before any of these revelations and before he graduated from Dame Alice Owens's he rode with his class on the top level of a double-decker tram to playing fields the school used for cricket. Along the way was a fascinating sight—"people in a horseshoe-shaped building wearing tights and doing strange things. I could see them through a window, as my seat put me in direct line with the upper-story room in which they were doing these unison things. I watched for it on the way back and sure enough they were still at it. Every time I went to the playing fields outside London with my football boots or cricket bat I'd be looking stiff-necked to see inside that room. Finally I got off the streetcar to find out what this was . . . acrobatic, tap, everything. It turned out to be a real hodge-podge. But I decided to go there for lessons, Saturdays, and rather liked this business of dancing."

The St. Pancras People's Theatre, which offered these classes in elementary ballet technique, proved useful to the budding dancer. In fact, he came to them better prepared than most—having already developed a significant knowledge of music. It was at age six that his mother had taken him to hear, coincidentally, classical music for the first time. "The dentist around the corner had a phonograph on which he played the March from *Aida* and ballet music from *Gioconda*," he remembered. "I loved the whole thing—having my baby teeth removed by this nice German man while listening to the music, his old-fashioned office with its spittoons and crank-up phonograph, and even being given a penny."

There were different kinds of music for different kinds of people, young Will discovered. On Sunday evenings when his aunties came over "they'd sing *their* songs and my father and uncles would sing *their* rowdy songs." But what he liked belonged to yet another classification—the "Pilgrim's Chorus" from Wagner's *Tannhäuser*, for instance, and "Connais-Tu le Pays?" from Thomas's *Mignon*, which he sang in the school chorus. Already, he had run a far cultural distance from his family—except his paternal grandfather who played Brahms on the cello—and the whole course of his development pointed toward the performing arts.

Surely Alfred and Florence could not be surprised over their son's clear theatrical direction. Not when they saw him going on to more advanced study of music and dance and dramatics. His attendance at St. Pancras lasted only a short time before he realized its limitations and the fact that his ambition—to become a dancer in order to learn how to create dances—required something more high-powered. So he went on to a County Council School where evening classes were given in the Cecchetti method, a program of strict classical ballet acknowledged internationally.

But the workaday world left only after-hours for the major pleasure in his life. Each step he took was an adventure that would bring him closer to finding the holy balletic grail. And by the time he made his way to a little bookshop on Charing Cross Road—having called the Imperial Society of Teachers of Dancing for a referral to professional training—he was very close indeed. The man he'd been advised to contact was Cyril W. Beaumont, London's balletomane of balletomanes, revered scribe and Boswell of the dance. Will had already acquainted himself with the bookshop, having browsed through it by the hour, admiring all the treasures he found there. Now Beaumont, the store's proprietor, was sending the nineteen-year-old seeker off to Margaret Craske. But the noted Cecchetti teacher—with whom he would indeed later study and keep up a lifelong association—had a schedule that was unworkable for him. So he took Beaumont's other referral, Marie Rambert, the woman who had been hired to coach Nijinsky.

It was because Craske's classes took place in the early part of the day, conflicting with his six A.M. to three P.M. shift at Smithfield, that William Cook turned to Rambert—but with trepidation: he was awed by her credentials, those of a highly cultured person with a far-ranging knowledge of the arts and a wealth of experience in the theater. Moreover, his coming together with her would have far greater significance than the mere agreement of study/work schedules. As in all momentous liaisons, this one seemed destined to bring out the best in each partner.

To some extent he sensed the importance of his trip to Rambert's Ladbroke Road studio, half of a bisected parish hall in the residential Notting Hill Gate, a neighborhood made up of five-story row houses. It was already winter and the end of 1928 when he entered her sanctum from the dark, cold early evening. There, with a huge pot-bellied stove radiating warmth, she held forth— this small authoritative woman in her uniform of black tights and short wraparound silk skirt, her hair pulled back into a small knot.

The scene was alluring, the personality magnetic. Nothing daunted Rambert. She barked out energetic commands in her excellent Polish-accented English. She relished the added color of her Slavic r's. She alternately yelled and whistled and laughed.

She was candid with her dancers to the point of rudeness. The onlooker stood transfixed.

Afterward he told her earnestly about his wish, to master the ballet technique. She was impressed with his quiet intensity and obvious ardor. How many other handsome young men in 1928 found their way to ballet, to begin with, and hoped, in their vanity, for a working future in this insecure and alien world? Of those, who would labor a nine-hour day and still have the drive to take difficult classes and spend hours practicing as well? Perhaps fewer than a dozen in the entire United Kingdom.

Yes, he made a major impression on her. She found his "poet's eyes" entrancing—not to mention the intelligent brow, fine features and quiet eagerness. He absorbed every scene, every lesson. Rambert attracted foundlings, aspiring dancers and choreographers who would need and value her guidance to the point of forming a dependent relationship with her. At forty, she was part *materfamilias,* part flirt—enticing her male innocents through cajolery.

Everything clicked into place. Madame invited William Cook to a performance given by her students, one that had him "bowled over with admiration." He returned for a second meeting and this time the tiny lady in her chic cloche asked him to walk her home. Suddenly the would-be danseur/choreographer had been elevated to the rank of cavalier and he conjured up visions of himself "as Prince Charming" in *The Sleeping Beauty*— a fantasy he happily indulged.

Once inside the study, with its huge fireplace, wine bar of burnished wood and gallery of antique dance prints, the talk evolved into a well-bred inquisition. The candidate recited some Shakespeare sonnets, as proof of his literary attainments, and the grande inquisitor concluded that the not-too-bad but nonetheless impermissible cockney accent would have to go. Traces of a foreign tongue might pass, but not traces of lower class.

When Rambert understood that her new disciple had very little money for tuition and that he could not attend morning classes, she turned him over to private study with her best pupils: Harold

Turner and Pearl Argyle. She also invited him, gratis, to her advanced classes. Afterward came his obligatory pas de deux with "Mim," (the nickname he was now entitled to use). It was her practice to recruit the men as *porteurs,* instruments for hoisting and balancing her in favorite lifts. William Chappell, whose primary interest was art design, recalled the time when "Fred [Ashton] and I were the two miserable boys at the studio. She nagged and nagged us to partner her. She pounced on me."

This latest *porteur* could appreciate Rambert's fantasies of being a prima ballerina. While he saw that nature had not endowed her with the proper physical prerequisites but instead short legs and unarched feet, he nevertheless played along as she gleefully sprang to his shoulder, wrapped her back around his neck and descended on the other side into a fish dive. Over and over they performed this lift and others, gaining perceptions of the difficulties so that she could better goad her students to mastery.

Many abandoned the fiercely demanding, cantankerous Mim. Her explosive manner—with its barrage of screaming, bullying and begging—was barely tolerable. The attacks were personal, although it was not really her intention to hurt people; in class dancers risked being called idiots or worse, lazy idiots—in this Rambert imitated Enrico Cecchetti, the Italian-born maestro who coached dancers in St. Petersburg at the Maryinsky Theatre and then joined Diaghilev. He ruled by insult and derogation. But no one cared that Rambert was merely following a tradition. Consequently, at one time or another, everyone was said to have hated Mim.

Despite these tactics, Rambert brought out an amazingly high degree of character and individuality in her dancers. They may not have been the smoothest technicians but they never could be accused of facelessness.

Then there was William Cook—steady, rational, astute. He knew how to contend. What's more, he recognized her as being "fantastically dynamic. However much she knew or didn't know [academically] she'd force it into you. And drove you into doing better than you could."

He could withstand her "devouring" personality, and he made the most of the considerable benefits she held out—her impeccable taste, her sense of theatrical adventure, her keen choreographic instincts.

Within a year he had developed enough stage presence and technique to set foot to board. He did so at the Scala Theatre as part of an English opera season. At this point William Cook became Antony Tudor. "He took the name 'Tudor' from Uncle Alf Summers's telephone prefix," according to cousin Gladys. His professional name—and the one that would thereafter represent him privately as well—appeared on a program for the opera *Cupid and Death* by Matthew Locke and Christopher Gibbons. But on this occasion he spelled it "Anthony," dropping the *h* only later.

It was clear to him, however, that the late start—not beginning classes until age sixteen—seriously hampered any chance of his becoming a virtuoso dancer. No matter. As Margaret Craske observed, some fifty years later: "He was bound to become the greatest ballet choreographer of our time. And that goes beyond whether he could dance well and even beyond the liability of the working-class environment he sprang from. Shakespeare wasn't so high up either."

As far as his parents knew, their diligent son seemed a good prospect for advancement—in business. So when Uncle Alf Summers, Florence's brother, offered to take Will into the assessors and surveyors firm that he owned, the Cooks prevailed on their second-born to accept this job of higher salary and prestige. "There was enough browbeating that I did go," he recalled, knowing that the rise in status would mean being saddled now with regular hours and having no free afternoons. The new position would seriously interfere with the more important business of his life, classes at Rambert's studio.

Alf Summers had no heirs and understandably wanted to leave his business to a family member. His sister's boy seemed the perfect choice, being both smart and industrious. But not long after he began, remembered Gladys, "Will told me he didn't like Uncle Alf's aggressiveness. I always thought of him as mild mannered, but that was away from the office, Will said. Everytime he saw Uncle coming in the front door, he'd duck out the back." It wasn't as though there'd be nothing to do. Covent Garden was only three minutes away.

What the inherited position did for him was hasten his break from an ordinary workaday existence. A complete absorption into the world of ballet could take place only with his full-time pursuit of it. Fortuitously, the time was right for Antony Tudor to come forward.

Rambert was about to launch a ballet company. First there had been assorted little studio performances. Then, with her own choreography and that of a certain Frederick Ashton—also a student, but two years ahead of Tudor—she booked the Lyric Opera House on February 25, 1930, for a matinee, returning with what she called the Rambert Dancers for a full two-week summer season.

Meanwhile Madame Rambert's husband, Ashley Dukes, followed his instincts for real estate and purchased the church hall adjoining their house in Notting Hill Gate; it became the Mercury Theatre, home of the Ballet Club. He was a playwright and his interest in theater dovetailed with his wife's ambitions. In fact, Rambert had her husband's taste for works in the literary, dramatic mold as opposed to the decorative, lighthearted ones that typified most ballet. Consequently, she and Tudor were a good match, just as Ashton and Ninette de Valois—the other grande dame of British ballet—suited each other in their eventual long-term association.

Given all this activity—the establishment of a site, the Mercury Theatre; the formation of a permanent company, the Ballet Club; and a schedule that would entail four seasons of three weeks each—Tudor saw his opportunity. Rambert needed every kind of assistance and he was the young man to provide it, both as aide-de-camp and a potential bearer of creative gifts. "I did cut a good deal with her," he said. "Otherwise the amount I would have owed over the years was five hundred pounds. And I insisted on a two-year guarantee, with the stipulation that I would have a chance during that time of making a first ballet."

But Rambert might have gotten the better part of the bargain, as it turned out. "Antony was the dogsbody and a stage manager at the same time," recalled Leo Kersley, a Clerkenwell confrere who joined the Ballet Club in 1934. "Because he could do everything, Mim took advantage of him. But he certainly wasn't abused. He seemed too smart for that. Rather it was a quid pro quo arrangement. Each benefited greatly."

In exchange for £2 a week, the man Agnes de Mille called "a young, friendly drudge" painted scenery, served as stagehand and electrician, took charge of lighting, served little hot sausages at intermission to go with the fine wines Ashley Dukes selected, provided piano accompaniment for Mim's classes, partnered ballerinas, taught beginning students, kept the books, danced in performances and "arranged dances." Talk about apprenticeship. What's more, he learned everything Mim and Ashley could teach him—not just through his ears and eyes but virtually his pores.

As part of the bargain, he lived on the premises—in what Rambert's daughter, Angela Dukes Ellis, called "a hovel, a room that was ten by four feet, just big enough for a cot and a washbasin." Being on hand at all times, he was able to absorb and take part in everything.

Momentous things happened for Tudor over the next nine years. Incredible though it seemed, he would create two of his enduring masterpieces—*Jardin aux Lilas* in 1936 and *Dark Elegies* in 1937—here in Notting Hill Gate for Rambert. Not many knew it at the time but ballet history was made with their advent. Everything that Tudor was to become over the rest of his life happened in microcosm in his late twenties with this tiny enterprise and this tiny tyrant of an impresaria at the beginning of modern British ballet.

Genesis

As WAS TRUE in the flowering of other cultural eras, British ballet reflected a coalescence of sensibilities in society and the arts. London, a decade after the turn of the century, got its first glimpses of the Russians: a small company headed by Anna Pavlova and Mikhail Mordkin played the Palace Theatre, followed by Tamara Karsavina and Georges Rosay (a former classmate of Nijinsky's from St. Petersburg) at the Coliseum. These events served as a catalyst at a time when all elements were prime for response.

A year later, in 1911, Serge Diaghilev's Ballets Russes began regular London seasons. Not only did the company's mastermind draw the intelligentsia to his performances of ballets, he also absorbed the local talent into his enterprise—foraging at the schools of Craske, Rambert, de Valois.

Because Diaghilev was an elite scavenger, one whose hunger for artistic finery impelled his constant quest, he managed to bring the Russo-Polish dancer, Rambert, together with Nijinsky in 1913. He knew that her knowledge of Dalcroze's eurythmics—a system linking movement to rhythm—could help his protegé-star penetrate Stravinsky's metrically complex *Le Sacre du Printemps*.

In all ways Diaghilev wielded a powerful influence. Indeed, he was a stimulant in the fertile London atmosphere and reaped its rewards for nearly two decades. Besides Rambert and de Valois, who, herself, had danced as a soloist from 1923 to 1925 with the Ballets Russes, there were those Diaghilev plucked from the local vine—among them, Markova and Dolin—who went on to illustrious performing careers.

Few were secure in their ordinary British identity. So the names were routinely changed—some Russified or Francized and some (from the younger generation) merely theatricalized. For all their historical significance, however, the ranks of English dancers, choreographers and designers were incredibly small. That Tudor and Ashton—comprising, together with Balanchine, the major choreographic forces in twentieth-century ballet—both evolved from this speck of turf is astonishing. All three were in the theater together, albeit on opposite sides of the footlights.

In 1929, Diaghilev died. Creditors who had been lurking in the wings seized what they could of his heavily mortgaged sets and costumes. Afterward, the splendid Ballets Russes was nothing but picked-over rubble. The dancers scattered and the extravagant showcase of collaboration ceased to exist.

To help fill the void left by Diaghilev the Camargo Society was established in October 1930. It drew at first on the efforts of Ashton, Craske, Dolin and Karsavina, as well as those of Rambert and de Valois. Its treasurer was none other than the celebrated economist John Maynard Keynes, husband of Diaghilev's former ballerina, Lydia Lopokova and then deputy on the Supreme Economic Council and a member of the British Committee of Finance.

One year later, de Valois seconded Rambert's company debut and began operation of her Vic-Wells Ballet at the new Sadler's

Wells Theatre in Islington. Thus did the two grandes dames of British ballet oversee its birth.

These were the pioneer days as well as the era of economic depression. In the wake of America's stock market crash, a surge of unemployment swept over all of England. Conditions started going bad, in fact, in the early twenties, a few years after the World War I armistice. Every third family was at some time in receipt of the "weekly seven and six" dole—seven shillings and sixpence. Even while Tudor was still a teenager, two and a half million were out of work. So his decision to disinherit himself from his uncle's thriving firm not only shocked Rambert, it left her in awe. Indeed, this indifference to fortune in the face of creative satisfaction never deserted him. "We were all quite agog with what he gave up," said William Chappell. "The degree of his enterprise was positively astounding."

Given the economic climate, one would not expect high-powered operations in the performing arts. There were no unions then, certainly no specialized jobs, and very little in the way of wages. Especially when it came to a fledgling venture like the one at Ladbroke Road, the rule was makeshift production materials and shoestring budgets. But the willingness and excitement were palpable, to say nothing of the extraordinary talent. Rambert, notoriously stingy, had a true need to be so; otherwise no ballet company could evolve from her meager resources. Where it counted, though, in her tireless enthusiasm and total engagement, she was more than generous. Whether working like all the furies on a performance to be given under her own aegis or acting as agent for one of her dancers, she held nothing back. A prospective employer would call to engage the beauteous Pearl Argyle for a show or for Antony to choreograph a play interlude and she would put husband Ashley on the phone to finalize the negotiation. Harumphing in his loftiest British tones, he would lend snobbish hauteur to the proceedings, which always upped the ante.

· · · · ·

The returns from working with Rambert came in high artistic attainment, however improbable it might have seemed under these haphazard conditions. Experience cost nothing, after all. It was a commodity easily obtained from the seventy-plus performances logged by the Ballet Club and Camargo Society members in the first year.

Meanwhile, the de Valois enterprise offered its personnel nearly respectable salaries, better commercial opportunities and a larger stage. As a result a number of dancers and choreographers were lured away from Rambert, although they often worked piecemeal for both establishments at the same time. Of the two, Rambert ended up struggling against greater adversity; this was yet another resemblance she and Tudor shared. The converse was true with de Valois and Ashton, who would become her choreographer laureate.

Being the daughter of an Anglo-Irish squire, de Valois saw herself as a proper lady, comfortably reticent in the English manner and happy to set that same and sane example for others. Behind her reserve, however, was a lust for empire-building that would know no surcease until every significant dancer and choreographer whose greatness she recognized had been brought to her domain.

Tudor was not one of them—partly because she did not classify his ballets as audience-pleasers, partly because "she could not understand what they were about," according to dancer Maude Lloyd, and partly because her operation was not large enough to champion another choreographer besides Ashton. Years later, she would suffer a penalty for her myopia; it came in the form of constant barbs and accusations from the London press. "They never stopped their outrage," de Valois said. "They never stopped screaming, 'How could you have let that genius get away? This country produced only two. He was one of them. And you permitted him to leave!' "

Rambert could not have been more different from de Valois. A Polish Jew who would as soon throw a tantrum as sniff a flower, she raced to the edge of artistic invention. If anyone ever

wore the avant-garde banner proudly it was Madame Rambert—
not just in art but social politics also. She was an early feminist
and joined the fray by throwing away her corset; she rallied to
every libertarian cause, including "free love," although she had
no desire to practice it herself. What was artistically glib or just
fashionably decorative didn't interest her. The classics, yes. But
disposable fluff, no. After all, Stanislavsky was her heritage. And,
like Diaghilev, she had an instinct for the creative or intellectual
spark—the spark she herself lacked but which could be divined
in others.

Utterly open, uninhibited and given to sharing her observations, she thought nothing of targeting a critic in the audience,
plopping down next to him and singing into his ear the praises
of her dancers onstage. John Percival of *The Times* of London
recalled how Mim would point out to him someone's gifts in
performance "and then, in a preposterous turnabout, jump up
and announce that she had to rush backstage to scold so-and-so
for not getting this or that right."

It was into this frenzied atmosphere that the quiet Tudor was
thrown. And while he absorbed the best of what his marvelously
mad little despot had to offer, he placed limits on how close she
could come. He knew all about reserve—firsthand, from his
mother. Moreover, he brought along his own defensiveness from
Central Street and used it as a barricade against vulnerability.
That vulnerability had much to do with the social distance between his feverishly artistic present and the mundane reality of
his past. But it was also a relic of his shy, friendless, solitary,
dreamy childhood. He could not abandon those old ways at a
given signal. Not surprisingly, they lasted a lifetime.

There was little to cling to. He had broken away from the
family, a natural parting common to adolescents. All his interest
now centered itself in the ballet world. Peripherally there were
concerts at Queen's Hall, browsing through music along Far-
ringdon Street, with its stalls similar to those lining the Seine in
Paris, attending avant-garde plays by Wedekind, the German

Expressionist. Not only did Antony subscribe to a wholly different frame of cultural reference from that of the Cook-Summers clan, but his coming of age naturally brought with it a generational gap.

The same independence of spirit that led him to snap his tenuous ties to Smithfield applied at the Ballet Club. Here, no matter how admiring of Rambert he might have been at first, he would need to fend her off—personally, and ultimately, artistically. Otherwise, he wholeheartedly embraced this world so foreign to his own. Here, at last, was something he could belong to. The bustling activity of classes, costume-sewing and scenery-building took his concentrated attention throughout the week. And on Sunday—in the beginning Sunday was the only day of rehearsals since most of the dancers had to support themselves through the week in jobs elsewhere—the pace was exhausting.

From early in the morning right up to the nine o'clock curtain that night the company rehearsed the ballets to be presented. No one merely marked steps, so as to save strength and vitality for the audience. Each person danced full out. Mim oversaw everything and scrutinized the last detail. Because the stage was so tiny—eighteen feet of proscenium arch and no deeper than it was wide—the slightest nuance of a gesture could project any lingering insincerity or doubt of purpose.

By other standards the actual theater, which seated 120, looked like a place to stage puppet shows, not to frame lifesize humans moving through space. Dancers had to leap high rather than let their momentum carry them horizontally into the shallow wings—or risk crashing against the walls. But there was a relatively large rehearsal hall, which had a ceiling gridded with heavy oak and high little squares of window that let in dim shafts of light.

Apart from the practical experience Antony gained, there was Ashley Dukes's association with T. S. Eliot and W. H. Auden and Louis MacNeice—which thrust him into the thick of London's literary world. It was here, after all, at the "Merc," that

Murder in the Cathedral had its first theater performance. The Dukes's stronghold became a favorite meeting place of the Bloomsbury group, headed by Virginia and Leonard Woolf.

Keynes—a leading figure in this loose association of intellectuals devoted to reforming or confounding post-Edwardian society—was a charter member of the Ballet Club. In fact, the "Bloomsberries" took up the call of *savoir vivre* as expressed in G. E. Moore's *Principia Ethica* and applied it to Rambert's cause. "The enjoyment of beautiful objects . . . the creation and enjoyment of aesthetic experience," which became their creed, was in marked contrast to the public philosophy of the nineteenth century. Those thinkers who comprised the Victorian galaxy—Bentham, Mill and Spencer—went the way of their Utilitarianism. The succeeding attitude was one that defined "as the most valuable those things we can know or imagine, certain states of consciousness roughly described as the pleasures of human intercourse." Tudor would hear the call and practice it in excelcis.

And the Ballet Club exemplified this new philosophy. Its Print Room, doubling as a wine cellar—Ashley's passion was his vintage bottled grape—featured a gallery for Rambert's fine collection of Romantic ballet prints. After performances on Sunday night company members mingled there with London's artistic elite. As the reputation of Mim's little enterprise grew, the audience multiplied—forcing her to perch at the back of the theater on her shooting stick, so that every one of the 120 seats could be sold.

As Agnes de Mille noted: Antony "watched everything with remembering eyes and drank his tea quietly wrapped in dreams." Who could know what dreams he dreamed? But surely those rapt silences embodied more than fantasies of thundering ovations and grand proscenium triumphs. There was a whole realm of unrequited yearning to work out in his ballets. Now he had the means to explore it.

3

Different Muses

Prince Charming was not what Antony aspired to be—despite the rare ecstatic notion of himself as *danseur noble* early on. It didn't matter that Rambert recruited him as her practice partner following class. That was a rite of passage "all the new boys were subject to." Although he did not make his real ambition known to her until their contract talks in 1930, apparently he realized, even from the first, that what engaged him was the challenge of making ballets.

For the majority of youthful beholders, though, the attraction to ballet is closely connected to the performer's sheer exhibitionism—his or her pleasure in technical brilliance and soaring freedom. More than any other of the performing arts, it invites the onlooker to admire the body in its essential physicality and bravura display.

Ashton, for instance, had the modest ambition to be "the world's greatest dancer," taking up the craft of choreography only because it was foisted on him, because Rambert would not rest until he provided her with some dances.

But although he did discharge his fair share of partnering duties and assume small roles as they were assigned to him by Rambert, Tudor (according to Cyril Beaumont) "had conceived the unusual ambition of wishing to compose ballets himself."

It's hardly difficult to understand his predilection. For one thing, he was not an exhibitionist—just the opposite. The spontaneity, innocence, openness, need for instant gratification and almost childlike desire for approval that mark the best showoffs were qualities he lacked. Not as much as his mother did; compared to her he was downright gregarious. But his attempt to master a physical self-consciousness could take him only so far.

By his own admission Antony had "a slight reserve." It was a characteristic that he could trace directly from himself to a role such as that of the repressed but passionate Caroline in *Jardin aux Lilas,* his ballet of 1936; it illuminated a whole mode of social constriction as applied to affairs of the heart.

What he did connect to was the idea of movement design as theater, an intriguing theater in which he did not have to rely on words to convey human essences or, crucially, reveal himself.

But more than others, he depended on literary sources for his dance dramas. In the very first ballet he choreographed, *Cross-Garter'd,* he turned to Shakespeare's *Twelfth Night.* While still a member of St. Pancras, a small church group that put on plays, he won the role of Malvolio for an amateur production of the Bard's comedy. As was his wont, the man who would become one of "Mim's little geniuses" carefully mapped out his idea for the ballet before bringing it to her, "wanting to play it safe" on this momentous occasion.

The plot follows what he may have perceived to be his own story to that point: a foolishly presumptuous man, William Cook, sets out to conquer and claim as his own the ever-elusive muse. Was the muse his art, or Mim herself, as the judge of his efforts? Was it a more prestigious social class from which he felt the discomfort of exclusion?

Astutely, he created a role for himself that did not expose what he lacked as a technician. Since his strength lay in characterization—in this case, Malvolio's inane vanity—that is exactly what he portrayed. The other main character, Olivia, was danced by Maude Lloyd and in their pas de deux he demonstrated not only a special understanding of partnering but how to express in the choreography her emotional resistance to him. His Malvolio, then, came across as pompous and self-ridiculing.

It was with the flourish of a great undertaking that the debutant choreographer created his ballet. Just prior to this, Antony, now so-called even by the Cooks, was about to celebrate his twenty-third birthday. Ever-generous, Alf gave his son money for a trip to Florence. Arriving there, he sat on the banks of the Arno, "absorbed the northern Italian atmosphere and wrote down half the ballet on a notepad." Once back in London, he discovered that at least one aspect of the scholarly mission had been a fiasco. "I got my dancers together and taught them the steps I'd carefully composed. It was a disaster and I had to start all over again from scratch. Needless to say, I never resorted to this method again. The whole thing has to come right out of the body. Then and there."

His methods did not prove fruitless, however, when it came to the Frescobaldi score, which he discovered while browsing in a secondhand music store. This time the source was a book of Italian organ music from the Renaissance period. It fit *Cross-Garter'd* to a T—being Italian, in keeping with Shakespeare's characters and contemporaneous with the playwright as well.

But for the costume designs he consulted Rambert, telling her that they must also belong to the Renaissance. As they sat in her library discussing the matter she said, "I've got it," and pulled out a book of designs by Ludovico Burnacini, which suited Tudor perfectly. He studied them carefully before rehearsals began so that he "would know from the shape of the skirt and bodice how the movements would be affected, even down to a hand gesture."

Cross-Garter'd was hardly the work of a dilettante. Nor did it resemble some of the scattershot enthusiasms or improvisations common to the hectic assembling of ballets in Notting Hill Gate. Rather, it was the first demonstration of what would characterize his lifelong effort: a meticulous and thoughtful searching out of truth through drama.

At the time that Tudor created the piece—it premiered at the Ballet Club on November 12, 1931—he was obviously subordinate to Fred Ashton. Not only was Ashton his senior in every way, but the difference between them in matters of social class proved great. Tudor had attended the free school in grimy Finsbury—to age fourteen—along with all the other underprivileged neighborhood children, while Ashton's education took place at an exclusive public school.

Distinguishing between himself and Tudor in those early years Ashton said half a century later, "I never had any concern about my social background, coming from the upper middle class. All of it was quite comfortable. For Antony, though, it was a preoccupying issue, something he seemed keenly aware of." In this regard, Tudor shared little common past experience with most of the dancers and artists who comprised the Ballet Club.

Of course, the Rambert enterprise was not exactly a refuge for rich aristocrats. Most of Tudor's peers—Prudence Hyman, Frank Staff, Elisabeth Schooling, Walter Gore, Pearl Argyle, Maude Lloyd, William Chappell, Peggy Van Praagh, Harold Turner—came from more modest backgrounds, nonetheless the shameful resonances of Central Street had to weigh heavily.

But at least the atmosphere was informal—a reality the world over in rehearsal halls and dance companies. Moreover, everyone at the Ladbroke Road studio suffered shoulder to shoulder. The dressing rooms were "shiveringly cold," according to the wealthy Diana Gould, who would later marry violinist Yehudi Menuhin. "We shuddered into our practice clothes, still damp from the day before. And then after class and between rehearsals we went across the road to Lyons Mermaid House for lumps of cheese and buns and black coffee. I was always struck that the connoisseurs—Diaghilev included—came to see us, wretched, starving, frozen creatures that we were."

Hopeful and buoyed by his inclusion into this circle of "art ballet," Tudor learned quickly how to capitalize on his talent. He also developed a certain diffident manner that served to protect him from whatever inferiority he may have felt. It is likely, however, that this mask of diffidence existed before he ever met Rambert.

By most accounts he was a quiet, thoughtful, unrevealing person. "A monkish man," said Gould, "a complete introvert. He lived in an extraordinary icebox." But those who were close to him held another view, although until Hugh Laing appeared on the scene he was not known to have any flagrantly overt love affairs.

Maude Lloyd, who joined Rambert in 1925, remembered the first day she returned to class, having been gone several years to live with her family in South Africa and teach ballet there. "It was 1930," said Lloyd, "and I spied a handsome young man at the end of the barre. He gave me a long look and said: 'You must be Maude from Capetown.'" Mim had told him, in advance, of the "Beautiful Maude," who would be his dancer, the choreographer's instrument.

Not only did she represent a feminine ideal to him—a serenely lyrical, poetic dancer rather than one who exulted in bravura feats—but she remained his affectionate friend over the next fifty-seven years.

As they both encountered his choreography for the first time—*Cross-Garter'd*—she had no idea of his intention: "to write a ballet" based on the few steps they put together backstage in Manchester while on tour. Initially, she even found the movements to feel "uncomfortable"—how telling that the man who felt such great discomfort would create in his work that same quality. But by the time Tudor had been given Rambert's official go-ahead and they were working fully on the project Maude had become entirely appreciative of his innovations.

So had the critics and established choreographers attending the premiere. Leonide Massine, for instance, one of Diaghilev's favorite dance-makers, was in the audience for this opening of the

Ballet Club's second season. And when he came backstage to pronounce his judgment, Rambert had to pay heed. Tudor recalled the words of praise: "This boy has great talent. You've got to give him lots of chances." And that's all the earnest innovator ever professed to want, "just to make a ballet good enough that I'm asked to do another."

Curiously, Rambert didn't grant *Cross-Garter'd* her sanction in the autobiography *Quicksilver,* summing it up as "not good," but a work that "showed sufficient talent to justify its inclusion" on the bill.

It surely is no coincidence that Ashton, who turned out fashionable and engaging ballets with great ease, became the fairhaired boy. Not only did he inspire tremendous confidence in Rambert, whose own self-doubt quotient belied her controlling nature, but she took inordinate pride in him over the course of his long, prolific career.

Tudor, less accessible as a human being—in fact, at the other extreme of the charming, good-humored Ashton—and certainly less conventional as a creator, rarely drew the kind of rock-solid support from company directors that might make him feel secure and wholly embraced. Without an Ashton halo, however, he risked being tagged as a distrustful outsider, a trait that, if not overcome, might forever color his relationships with patrons.

Of *Cross-Garter'd* Cyril Beaumont wrote that Tudor "had obviously tried to work out his ideas in his own way. The result was a workmanlike little ballet which impressed by its obvious sincerity, while the dances and mime really did express the story. The steps were simple, the mime simple, but it was all done in the lusty spirit of the text."

That lusty spirit hardly seemed the kind of thing to come from "a monkish man," yet it did recall Antony's father and he went on to create several ballets in this vein. Among them were *Judgment of Paris* and *Gallant Assembly,* whose seduction scene for herself and Tudor Agnes de Mille described as "the most obscene bit of nonsense in the literature of ballet and one of the funniest."

In fact, it may have seemed scandalous then but Therese Langfield remembered that "apart from the men goosing the girls it wasn't all that bawdy—deliciously suggestive, but not so bawdy." Much later there would be *Knight Errant,* also in the ribald mode. Antony was nothing if not a personality of contradictions.

Although Maude Lloyd became a constant in his ballets, there were other dancers comprising his little circle as he went on to create *Mr. Roll's Quadrilles, Lysistrata, Pavane pour une Infante Défunte* and *Atalanta of the East.* Alicia Markova, who danced both for Rambert and de Valois at the Vic-Wells when she wasn't appearing elsewhere with Anton Dolin, took the leading role in *Lysistrata* and found the experience unusual for her own reasons.

"I was used to dancing either the very sophisticated things for Diaghilev or the classics," she recalled, "but what did Antony want me to do? Why, play something so mundane as a wife with a baby. It was unimaginable to me."

The scenario, suggested by Dukes, was based on Aristophanes' comedy about wives striking against war by withholding their matrimonial duties until arms were laid down. It had just the sort of intrigue between characters that appealed to Tudor and an underlying theme of seriousness as well. A review in the *Observer* confirms why he jumped at the opportunity to stage it: "Mr. Tudor has taken what he wanted from Aristophanes and makes good fun of the plight of the Athenian veterans whose war-weary wives, refusing any longer to treat their husbands as heroes or to make their homes fit for heroes to live in, drop the passive connubial resistance with violence." *Lysistrata* was an outlet for Tudor's fascination with role-playing, and his delight in seeing conformity overturned and authority questioned; as Margaret Craske recalled, "Antony always wanted to be the leader. He didn't like bowing to others, no matter who they were."

Another notice published in the same paper praised Tudor for "locking out all high-brow pretentiousness in order to charm and amuse." He was not one to put on airs, to clothe himself in creative finery he didn't wear naturally—although he would seem to have had more reason than most to do so. Rather, he contradicted the writer's assessment; his goal orientation had little to do with audience-pleasing. If anything he had to be reminded by Rambert to play to the audience when dreaming up his scenarios.

Whatever the rivalry between Ashton and Tudor—as their respective careers grew and they came to be known as England's two greatest choreographers—"they were as close as any two blokes could be," said Leo Kersley, about the early days at Rambert. And given ballet critic and historian Richard Buckle's observation of Ashton, that "he had a regrettable tendency to fall in love," it was believed by a few on the scene that some sort of love relationship existed between these handsome, lanky men, both of them smitten by Pavlova, both of them indebted to Diaghilev, both of them striving to make a mark in the utterly absorbing world of ballet.

But it didn't take long for their artistic paths to diverge. Looking back to 1931 years later, Ashton summed up the striking personality differences between them: "Antony was serious, while I was frivolous and light and superficial. I suppose that's why I didn't like *Cross-Garter'd,* which seemed to me too theatrical and slow and portentous. The first ballet of his that I really admired was *Jardin.*"

It's hardly surprising that Ashton did not relate to his competitor's works. One evening at the refectory table in the Dukes's Campden Hill house, Fred turned down *Lysistrata*—Ashley had offered it to him first. Antony was only second choice. But with this ballet he established, for himself as performer, the typecasting that was to continue from then on. Here, he danced the husband of the title character. And although it's true that the men in this scenario were all husbands of the Athenian protagonists, it was an identity—head of the household—that stuck. Tudor was forever intrigued by relationships between people and the dynamic that determines who gets what, why and how. Over and over his themes dealt with love and sex and the complications therein.

In nearly all his ballets Tudor danced the mature man—married, sometimes patriarchal, wise, understanding or stoic. This was his ego ideal. He recreated himself onstage in the image of how he would be in the best of all possible worlds—a man calmly assured that he could take his place in society as a wholesome and admired representative of it.

But one month after *Lysistrata* had its premiere, Hugh Skinner, later to be known as Hugh Laing, arrived on the scene—precluding such an outcome. An extraordinarily handsome twenty-one-year-old, he had golden skin, coal-black hair and pale green eyes. The sculptural planes of his face—high cheekbones, a perfectly symmetrical square of jaw with a cleft in the chin and a broad, straight brow—qualified him as a matinee idol.

Like Tudor—and Ashton—he came late to dancing. He had made his way from Barbados, in the British West Indies, to attend art school and develop his talent for painting and design. Given the atmosphere in London at the time, the richness of collaboration among composers, librettists, choreographers and artists, it's no wonder Laing discovered Rambert.

First he was a student at the Grosvenor School of Art, where he met his teacher's wife, the dancer Helen Wingrave. Enormously impressed with Hugh, she asked him to take part in a production she was staging at the Ruby Peeler School. He liked the assignment as she explained it: merely to "stand about and look beautiful." But at the first rehearsal he found something awakened in him—the urge to move around, to enact a mood or an idea. He ended up begging to try a few dance steps.

Wingrave agreed to give him dance lessons. Since her husband, Hugh's art teacher, Iain McNaib, was a supporting member of the Ballet Club, she took him to Rambert—understanding that he was determined now to become a dancer, not a painter.

But Hugh Laing just might have found his way to Rambert regardless, as her Sunday soirées attracted the elite among London's arts society as well as those eager to stake out their own claim as creative or performing artists. Managers of commercial theaters also came—for the purpose of raiding Rambert's ranks. It was April 13, 1932, when Laing first entered the domain of Rambert. Again, there were not many young men in the whole British Commonwealth who would seek out ballet. Its rigors

imposed hardship as well as actual technical barriers to the late-
comer. Its social stigma proved even more off-putting than its
physical difficulty. Possibly, however, the world of "art dance"
also beckoned as a haven to those men already destined to find
their sexual preferences outside the pale of the majority.

Hardly quiet or closed off as Tudor tended to be, Hugh was
spontaneity itself. Reticence had no place in his temperament.
No sooner did an emotion rise up in him than it burst forth.
This being the case, he never adapted well to the mold of student.
He lacked patience and self-discipline. Whenever confronted with
frustration he threw tantrums. The simple obstacles to learning
how to move the body in the unnatural ways that classical ballet
dictated found in him little tolerance. What's more, he brooded
over his temporary failures. The moment of defeat did not spin
away in the next activity. It stayed. It dogged him.

But he had attributes that were enormously prized: a grasp of
drama, a magnetic presence onstage, an uncanny intuition of how
to make every gesture count. And he had what many called
"impeccable taste"—all of these being traits that Tudor valued
highly.

In the course of the next year the two began an intimate, all-
encompassing relationship. Each seemed to be indispensable to
the other—artistically and personally. The masterworks that Tudor was to produce all came following Laing's appearance on the
scene. But no one can know whether these would have materialized regardless, nor whether Tudor might have enjoyed—in
his life—a less obstructed path without Laing.

4

●

A Dream Role

THE DAY HUGH SKINNER LAING had his first and decisive interview with Rambert was the same day Antony laid eyes on him. In fact, the acquisitive impresaria conducted her examination of the new candidate in the very Ladbroke Road studio where she and Antony had exchanged their momentous vows.

It was April and the nip had gone from the air. The fat stove in the corner did not need to serve as the same beacon of warmth for Hugh as it had for Antony. Neither did the same literary inquisition take place, for here was a vital, springy young man— more interested in engaging Rambert on a sensory level than locking souls with her. At any rate, they did not rival each other reciting Milton and Shakespeare since he was not so well versed.

It was Antony's job, as unofficial secretary, to receive and chat with the visitors until Rambert was ready, and then usher them into her studio—thus he became the first person Hugh would meet at the Ballet Club. All during the session Antony was just outside the door. So Rambert took the opportunity to draw him into the appraisal.

"Have you ever seen a *plié* like this?" she asked, cueing Hugh to stand up and execute the deep knee bend with feet and hips turned outward. Not understanding the rudiments of classical ballet, never having had a single authoritative lesson, he scooped down without worrying about alignment or holding his chest high and his shoulders low.

Tudor recalled Laing "bouncing his bottom on the floor." But that hardly deterred the two appraisers. What they saw was a gleaming uncut diamond. Both offered extravagant compliments on his physical beauty and prime condition. Hugh inherited a new mentor in Rambert. She, in turn, proudly displayed him before her budding choreographer, as a gift to his imagination. Little did she know.

Rambert had Hugh remove his shoes so they could both gaze on his strong feet. As Tudor remarked many years later a child-hood spent "climbing trees and living in the sea" had given Laing a "fabulous body."

True, he lacked the early training so crucial to achieving high skill as a technician, but he showed a keen aptitude. And what he ultimately couldn't conquer in terms of sheer fluency, he certainly compensated for in theatrical persuasiveness and poetic projection.

"I was as mad about him," said Antony of Hugh, "as Mim was." What followed from that moment was a crash campaign to forge his new identity. Rambert put him into both her advanced class and a beginners' class at the same time. She guided him personally and with unrelenting zeal. It was no longer a matter of how strong his own drive was. She took over completely—keeping him in class up to seven hours a day.

At least part of the urgency to train Laing came from need. Rambert simply didn't have enough male dancers as partners for her girls. So when a late-starter boasting the right body and instincts stood at the door he was regularly invited inside.

Also, back in those days when Rambert's company had just graduated from being called the Marie Rambert Dancers to the Ballet Club—Ballet Rambert was yet to establish itself as the rightful and lasting name—dancers were more likely to be artists and designers or even actors than gymnasts and baton-twirlers. Technique, obviously, did not rank as the be-all and end-all of performance life. Especially when it came to the new ballets being written. They were as much dependent on the performer's sensibility for the work's tone and intent as his facility at doing the steps.

So it was from the realm of fine arts that candidates for the dance materialized. And as Tudor himself noted, the Ballet Club had "a very well-brought-up audience, very West-End, very Kensingtonian, very good class, quite elite."

For the nine momentous years from 1931 to 1940 there was hardly any person of consequence to London ballet remaining outside the pale of Rambert's establishment—as dancer, designer or painter.

In this fertile atmosphere it was Laing who became central to Tudor. The process of creating ballets is the stuff of constant interaction; it involves a working intimacy. A dancer who can intuit what the choreographer is trying to deliver—and help him in that crucial quest—is not only the truest collaborator, but the most significant element of all. And that is what Hugh came to represent for Antony—as they would soon perform together works mirroring aspects of their real-life personalities.

Perhaps nothing enlivens a creative relationship more than a dancer who nearly jumps out of his body to impress a choreographer. When Tudor saw such a rare display he sat characteristically stock-still, mute and upright—savouring the exquisite moment, his eyes glittering with pleasure, his adrenaline surging. That, no doubt, summed up the first encounter with Hugh, whom he saw as one who "would kill for anything he believed in." And Hugh would come to believe in Antony as no one else ever had or ever would.

In December 1932, Antony made a curious little ballet, *Adam and Eve,* for the Camargo Society, with Prudence Hyman and Anton Dolin in the title roles. Although the stellar dancer never did anything onstage so lewd as the movements devised for him here, he was known to enjoy the experience—and the near nudity—so much that he asked to have the ballet, fig leaves and all, revived for him.

The fact that Antony ferreted out this aspect of Dolin's stage personality confirms the intuition he had about those who became his dancers. For they were never just dancers. They were people first. And that possibility of manipulating them, based on knowing them, was what fired his creativity.

In *Adam and Eve,* moreover, Antony seemed to spell out his momentous relationship with Hugh—it had begun eight months earlier—by casting himself as the Serpent, a nefarious activist, a provocateur. Although any who knew him recognized Antony as a relationship engineer (Gore Vidal would later point out: "Tudor was the master of gamesmanship. . . . He saw everyone around him as pawns"), his most common persona within a scenario was the wise patriarch—sometimes judgmental, sometimes compassionate.

But in *Adam and Eve,* the Serpent, who, in this libretto, is blessed with a Guardian Angel, seduces the God-send behind a tree. If Antony recognized in Hugh that instant ally, confidant and helpmate, he apparently also noted his own overwhelming attraction to—and thus seduction of—this Adonis. After all, he was in the dominant position of master, as teacher and choreographer. He represented the authority figure and so could command his willing disciple. Of the many guru/disciple liaisons he would enjoy throughout his career, only this one was overtly sexual.

And here Antony permitted an intimacy forbidden to others. Almost from the start, Hugh tended to his new mentor, to his insecurities, and guided him unerringly in artistic matters. By the time they got to *Atalanta of the East,* which Antony choreographed in April of 1933, he had reverted to type, though, casting himself as the benign King. Hugh's role, Vikram, the lovesick swain, *was* that romantically involving personality, and the combination of his handsomeness and charisma made him as alluring to audiences as he was to the creator of the ballet. Antony may not have known it but the work presaged his later embrace of Zen Buddhism, with its libretto adapted from a Greek legend.

Atalanta also pointed the way to a futuristic vision. Tudor had seen Mary Wigman and Harald Kreutzberg and Kurt Jooss, those paragons of German Expressionism. Already, the force of modern dance was upon him. Critic Arnold Haskell cited the work as "a striking example of research into entirely new material, not yet fully assimilated and translated into ballet. Poses are there, the style is fine, but it is heavy and lacking in movement. For all that, I find these three works (including *Cross-Garter'd* and *Lysistrata*) amongst the most interesting yet produced by an Englishman."

But *Atalanta* was, in the words of John Percival, "a resounding flop with most of the Ballet Club audience." Antony had tried to commission a score that would suggest the same Javanese elements he used as dance figurations. Unlike Ashton, who was commonly accused of being a slave to fashion, Tudor strove for an ideal of *Gesamtkunstwerk,* an integrated totality of art, and looked in this case for music befitting the Eastern motif. He found none, so the program credits "eastern airs arranged by Szanto and Seelig." According to critical consensus the score severely detracted from the ballet.

Mixed critical notices did not discourage his habit of foraging for new experiences, however. And now he had Hugh as a coadventurer. Nor did he miss an opportunity to improve himself. During his years in Ladbroke Road he managed regular visits to Margaret Craske, whose teaching was the very model of Cecchetti exactitude—calm, orderly, precise.

When Antony realized that Hugh needed something more than could be learned from his own and Rambert's classes, he brought him to Craske. She spent an entire private lesson with Hugh, doing only *pliés*, but concluded, years later, that he was "too difficult . . . for Antony and for me." Her remark, meant both in a general and particular sense, was said with a great sigh. Indeed, it took in the whole span of Tudor's and Laing's relationship as she would come to know it over half a century.

5

Partners

ONE YEAR FROM THE DAY he took his first class at the Ballet Club, Hugh sent "Madame Rambert" a thank-you letter—posted April 13, 1933, from 45 Holland Park Mews. The script, in green ink on lavender paper, was large, practiced and distinctive. The message had both charm and effusion, describing feelings of great tenderness and sentimentality for a day that avowedly began the happiest time of his life.

When he handed out a compliment or expressed gratitude it was with unabashed candor. Nothing complicated about Hugh. Nor did he shy away from acknowledging himself and Antony as a couple, and how the Ballet Club, Rambert and Tudor, in combination, had led him to a taste of heaven on earth. Nor did he withhold judgment of his writing performance. In a mingling of pride and self-consciousness he actually apologized, with exclamation marks, for his theatrical instincts: green ink and lavender paper.

. . . . .

It was shortly after Hugh arrived at Rambert's doorstep that Antony moved out of the tiny cell he had occupied in Ladbroke Road and they went off to live together. While he seldom talked about his ballets to anyone—almost as though the talk might magically dilute his inspiration, almost as though he wanted to savor privately his creative schema—Hugh was the exception.

There was an inviolable trust between them, on the one hand, and an explosive battle always brewing, on the other. Tudor had developed the fine art of needling, of "trying it on" to see how much he could get away with. He knew exactly what caustic remark to make and where to aim it. Moreover, Hugh was an easy target. His piercing outcry and retaliative call to arms would have put a stop to this war tactic in any but the perversely engaged.

"One late afternoon," Ashton recalled, "I heard them having a furious row. It was frightening. 'There goes our dinner plan,' I said to myself. Surely they could not digest food together after that kind of bloodletting. But a half hour later, it quieted down and Hugh and Antony were behaving as if nothing had happened. We all went out together and not a word was mentioned."

Inspired by Hugh's warlike rages, Antony gave him his first prominent role as the Mortal in "Mars," a section of the 1934 *Planets*. It was this stridently expressionistic work—with influences traceable to Jooss's *The Green Table* and Nijinsky's *Le Sacre du Printemps*—that illustrated the creative excitement between them and the depth of Tudor's insights. As the critic David Vaughan aptly pointed out, "the Mortal's conflict was as much within himself as with an external enemy."

As bitter as the quarrels between Antony and Hugh were it was folly to intervene. "Especially when the dogs were the subject," said Kersley. "They were besotted over the dogs, like parents over children. When just Antony was in a rage, only an amusing remark would come out, but from Hugh there were colossal fire burnings. And they just loved watching each other react. Antony was only too delighted to see Hugh go up in the air about something unimportant and Hugh was fascinated to see something catastrophic happen to Antony. Then he would make an outrageously witty remark. Other times they just sat and giggled. Hugh was a great teller of funny stories—so filthy you could curl up. His favorites were the ones about Little Audrey."

This small heroine, the subject of popular jokes at the time, was a minisadist. Her antics, often dirty, positively tickled Hugh. Backstage, just before performances, he would tell the latest saga of Little Audrey. "She and her brother went up in a plane," recounted Kersley, according to Hugh. "The plan was to jump out and pull the cord after counting to ten. Lovely. But as she watched him go, she knew he couldn't count that high. And little Audrey laughed and laughed. Hugh convulsed telling it."

There was great camaraderie among those Rambert assembled at her Mercury Theatre. Not only because the company was small, with each member having a vested interest in the common cause, but also because there was no strict division of labor. There couldn't be. Just keeping the operation going meant that everyone had to pitch in. Often the existing costumes and sets were used for new ballets. In the process, some historically valuable flats were painted over to make new decor.

Although Tudor's manifold contributions exceeded those of the others, hardly anyone performed just one function. They all sewed costumes, for instance, or made wigs, and people like Chappell and Hugh Stevenson danced as well as designed.

Laing did everyone's makeup. "Gorgeously," according to Leo Kersley. "He was like a mum." They "all snacked together," remembered Ashton. And they went to the movies as the workload permitted, to see pictures starring Pearl White, a Tudor favorite. But seldom was anything systematized. Because there were no unions rehearsals did not have to be cut off at the timekeeper's signal. Often, after supper, they would return to the theater or to the nearby flat Antony and Hugh shared in Holland Mews and there rehearse for several more hours. By that time the last bus had come and gone. Whoever couldn't get home simply stayed overnight.

The flat, two rooms over a garage, "was smelly," recalled Therese Langfield Horner. "There were the fumes from the cars and the odors from their dogs, Gito and Tobias. Hugh put down newspapers for them because he and Antony were gone all day. The decor was early orange crate. Poor Mrs. Cook. She came to tea one day and seemed very upset to see her son serving on the orange crates. He refused the money she offered because it was important, this identity of the starving artist. All of us at the B-Club shared it." Leo Kersley concurred, remembering "how much care went into selecting just the right orange crates. . . . They were a point of pride among us."

In all matters, Hugh and Antony worked as a team. They formed a united front, for instance, against Rambert. While she helped every would-be artist and dancer who came begging, she also had a knack for alienating those who would sit at her feet and promise the greatest loyalty. Inevitably, Rambert lost most of the people she valued highly. Despite her generous—no, unceasing—outlay of energy in spurring the creativity of others, she also ended up earning their enmity.

Yet Antony would remember the unfettered optimism of those days spent under her aegis and the wealth of experience he gained there.

Some forty years later he wrote:

Dearest Mim,
   Constantly I ponder the good fortune that fell upon Fred and myself to find ourselves in your magnetic field. I don't know with any precision what we inherited from you, but it seems to have included staying power to a most beneficial degree.
   And some of the other things—it is such guesswork—Audacity? Patience? Tolerance? Not particularly. More probably a being made more sensitive to our instincts & the abilities to see & smell out the right.
   Well, thank you. And it is nice to know that the two of us old-timers still bounce & keep your flag flying. I look forward

with a hope to see you again soon, with another little pilgrimage
to your abode.

Love, Antony.

In turn, what the impresaria admired and came to appreciate
in Tudor—beyond his inventiveness—was the thoughtful approach he brought to everything and his remarkable powers of
organization. These were qualities that compensated for her own
usual frazzled state, but as Leo Kersley pointed out, "Rambert
was a born Romantic and Antony was the intellectual. Ultimately, they were doomed to conflict."

In the beginning, however, the crucial balance of acolyte and
master was easy to maintain and their relationship had a certain
harmony to it. In classes, Tudor was never cowed by Mim, nor
did her usual castigations fall on the boys. She was a flirt, after
all, "a terrific vamp and very feminine," according to dance critic
John Percival, and that made her dealings with them less depre-
cating. Besides, there were enough girls—hopelessly vulnerable
to her outbursts—to punish, and even praise on occasion.

Ashley Dukes, on the other hand, was not always perceived as
a faithful Ballet Club supporter. "He thought us all mad," said
Chappell, "including Mim." De Mille, for one, saw him as
"pompous, aloof and amused," a belles lettres snob who looked
down on ballet as a somewhat vulgar physical art. And his attitude toward homosexuality, as a reviled persuasion, was in line
with the commonly held one. When Antony made his first ballet,
Cross-Garter'd, Angela Dukes Ellis remembered her father's exclamation on seeing it: "Oh. So that's what they do." According
to Kersley, "Ashley was always up against the homosexual barrier—he couldn't get his plays produced because it was a closed
club that controlled the situation and he was not a member in
good standing." As for Antony, he once again had to experience
disapproval from an authority figure—modified by the mutual
regard each had for the other's reasoning powers and intellect.

Nevertheless, Dukes prospected avidly for Rambert via his

theatrical involvements and in this way pushed her to start doing some choreography herself. Whenever a play required incidental dancing he acted as his wife's agent and brought her together with the producer. He provided the very impetus that led to the establishment of the Marie Rambert Dancers.

Unfortunately, Antony did not have such a partner, one who stood as an authority in the art world, one with clout, one who commanded respect among the intelligentsia. Instead, he had a cantankerous youth as helpmate, a beautiful boy whose childish tantrums could hardly be of much political assistance. Not then nor ever did Tudor maneuver his career with craft or savoir faire. He would never employ an agent of any sort. He was a stranger to the world of mutual back-scratching and diplomatic relations. Unlike Ashton, whose easygoing charm and amiability attracted sponsors, Tudor struggled alone.

No small reason for this came from his need to stay hidden. As Chappell said, "From the very beginning Antony played it close to the vest." Because of his lack of freedom to bargain openly and to stand up and with assurance to ask for what he deserved he followed his inclination to retreat. Whatever the degree of self-contempt he may have brought with him from Central Street, it did not sift away in Ladbroke Road. And when he formed his personal alliance with Hugh, he opened the door to a compounded denigration.

"Antony's family never accepted Hugh," said Maude Lloyd. "Or his homosexuality." What's more, she never saw Tudor's parents attending any of the Ballet Club performances. For all intents and purposes he cut himself off from the past when he resolved to enter the ballet world—a decision prompted, perhaps, by parental disapproval of his chosen lifestyle. However, the Cooks finally did come to terms with their son's and Hugh's relationship. As Tudor's sister-in-law Mollie recalled: "They lived through two world wars on Central Street. They were people with enough heart to be accepting." Lloyd remembered Mrs. Cook as "a dear woman" and even received a letter from her, dated 1950, thanking her son's friend for being so kind and helpful to him.

By contrast, Hugh's parents did come to the Mercury Theatre—all the way from Barbados—and "sat there watching rehearsals like two little round muffins," according to Diana Gould, who guessed their quietly middle-class origins. Apparently, they subsidized their son, for he was always able to buy the things he needed. Antony, on the other hand, accepted no support from his family. He rarely had more than a few shillings in his pocket. He lived like a pauper, not just because that was his circumstance but also out of some vague identity as a monk or holy man. Not to be discounted was his father's frugality, a trait Antony would share, knowingly, with pride.

Frank Staff and others cast in the later Tudor ballets often said they "were going to Vespers" as a metaphor for attending his rehearsals of *Jardin aux Lilas.* When Antony and Hugh moved from Holland Mews to a house in Chiswick where it was possible to give classes, he took on a new epithet: "Jesus of British Grove." Yet he was more inclined than most to pixilated humor and didn't mind thumbing his nose when the moment permitted.

In the spring of 1935 came *The Descent of Hebe,* less ambitious overall, but a musical achievement that far surpassed anything Tudor had done previously. In Ernest Bloch's B-minor Concerto Grosso, he found a contemporary score dealing with the Baroque form—a particularly compelling piece of music and one that invited the choreographer to represent its structure. Tudor did exactly that, according to Fernau Hall, and with all the brilliance of Balanchine's *Concerto Barocco,* but six years earlier. What he divined, in the fugal finale, was a way to make the viewer "see the music and hear the dancing"—as surely as did Balanchine, for whom the phrase was coined.

Rambert regarded the ballet as "something altogether ravishing," and, according to writer Mary Clarke, regaled her friends with like descriptions, closing her eyes in ecstasy.

Once again, he was dealing with characters removed from his

time and place. *Cross-Garter'd* went back to Shakespeare; *Lysistrata* to Greek antiquity; *Adam and Eve,* the Bible; *Atalanta,* Indian myth; *The Planets,* the cosmos; and here, in *Hebe,* more Greek antiquity. Specifically, love as it is affected by the power of authority.

It's not difficult to see the same themes—seduction, shame, banishment, retribution—being repeated again and again by Tudor. Or why this particular story appealed to him. Serving his god, the arts, he had to do penance for "stumbling and spilling the nectar," the dramatic upshot of *Hebe.*

Its resolution came with the promise of other rewards, rewards that made the sacrifice of Olympus palatable. Maybe love (Hugh) and art on earth (the stringent, inadequate Ballet Club) offered him compensation enough for the unattainable goal.

6

In His Own Right

DURING THE MID TO LATE 1930s, the period of most concentrated creativity in Tudor's life, he also enjoyed the closest associations he would ever know. And not just with Laing, although their relationship seemed to inspire his productivity. It was a mutual labor of love that he and others in "the B-Club" devoted themselves to. Ashley Dukes referred later to those days in Notting Hill Gate as "*nostalgie de coterie*." It was a time that stirred affection in their hearts—a time whose spirit and action yielded ballets with an integral aesthetic. Moreso, perhaps, than with other choreographers, Tudor's intimacy with the dancers and their faith in him became the impetus for new works.

Most of his experiences prior to joining Rambert were solitary; now he had Hugh and Maude and the others to accompany him for evenings at Covent Garden or the Adelphi or wherever his curiosity took them. He didn't join Therese Langfield Horner and Leo Kersley as they handed out copies of *The Daily Worker* at Underground exits—unlike them, he wasn't a devoté of communism or any political system, although he sympathized with the cause, especially in 1936 and 1937 when the Spanish civil war drew many new members to the party. Sometimes he and his cohorts would go to the Speakers' Corner in Hyde Park to hear the rant of colorful amateur orators. Sometimes they came out to watch what Kersley called "the saber-rattling that went on as Fascist groups marched through the Jewish quarter, trying to stir things up." Therese and Antony shared a deep interest in theology; she said that "he was a Zen Buddhist even then, long before he formally embraced the Eastern body of thought."

Whatever the dreams he dreamed, his most private fantasies took shape only in conjunction with others. A few dance-makers may be able to write the work out and then slip it on the dancers like a costume, but most need full-fledged cocreators. And for Antony the dynamics of their offstage relationships provided idealized scenarios for his ballets. The happiest of these was the triangle script, one he played out with himself, Hugh and Maude Lloyd. Partly because she lived alone at first and had no nearby family (her parents were in faraway South Africa), Maude eagerly spent whatever leisure time she had with "the boys." They loved being in her company. She was beautiful and intelligent and "well brought up," in Antony's estimate. She made a fine showpiece. Escorting her in public brought them an alluring respectability they would not otherwise have had. And they took a genuine pleasure in her.

Antony adored Maude. Her softness and feminine modesty were a foil for his virile powers of manipulation. "It was the hidden passion he saw in her," recalled Angela Dukes Ellis, explaining his attraction to Maude. Also, the absolute willingness to be his instrument, to experiment by the hour with different solutions to choreographic problems and then the next day watch him discard all the hard work in preference to something "that better expressed what he wanted," Maude said.

When they were not laboring in the theater, they played. "Sundays in the park or down to the flea markets," remembered

Lloyd, "where Hugh and Antony bought sad, little, dying dogs. Lunch together always and to the cinema. Once we saw a marvelous Russian movie [*The Road to Life,* 1931, directed by Nikolai Ekk] about a boys' school and building a railway line. The boy died and Hugh and Antony cried."

For all his explosive fury, Hugh was very compassionate, easily moved to tears. But Antony buried his feelings. "Hugh at once would see the underlying horror of something and say: 'Ant'ny, can't you see it?' And then he would soften," recalled Therese. Whatever his vulnerability, he defended it with a sardonic veneer. The difference in their personalities showed in the diverse ways Hugh and Antony related to Maude in their real-life pas de trois.

What transpired between Hugh and Maude was spontaneously physical. He loved picking her up and carrying her at the end of a long hike through the park when she was exhausted. He was openly affectionate. "He kissed me a lot and flirted outrageously," she volunteered years later. Antony, on the other hand, matched her own reserve and tentativeness. He engaged her verbally—in teasing, titillating mind games, seducing her with his wit, "always trying to shock me with naughty jokes." This was a penchant, the risqué comment, the sexual pun he indulged lifelong; it stood as his interactional trademark.

He would translate their roles to the stage in *Jardin aux Lilas,* casting himself as the domineering figure, Maude as the sacrificial one, and Hugh as the swept-away lover.

But when it came to the rapturous worship of women Antony did not prefer a flesh-and-blood girl. Rather, he turned to the great Russian ballerina, Olga Spessivtseva, and actress Madeleine Carroll. Fernau Hall said Antony "mooned over them like a lap dog." They were both beyond his reach. He saw Spessivtseva when she danced for the Camargo Society starting in 1932 and found her to be the physical embodiment of perfection, "the greatest dancer of all," John Taras remembered his saying. On the night of her last performance he spent every penny he had to buy a wreath of white orchids as a parting gift. And Carroll, also extremely lovely, was a member of the Ballet Club, someone he worshiped from afar. Later he choreographed dances for her play, *The Toy Cart.*

Fixating on an idealized female—the diva, the *ballerina assoluta*—was and is common to the cultured gay sensibility. And Tudor's preference for such theatrical paragons as Luise Rainer and Simone Simon, along with their balletic counterparts Spessivtseva and Pavlova, exemplified his exquisite taste. Drawn, along with his peers, to render them sexually unthreatening through adulation, he was able to transcend such glorifications. As a result, the women in Tudor ballets were multidimensional in the deepest sense.

These were full, enriching times for him. Not only did he see a steady growth of his works under the Rambert aegis, but there were also incidental ballets he made for stage plays and between 1933 and 1935 he had even worked on a limited basis for de Valois at her Vic-Wells Ballet, dancing mostly small roles and teaching boys' classes.

The recurring themes of those scenarios say much about the universe he saw or wished for or struggled against. *Paramour,* like *Adam and Eve,* and works yet to come—*Gallant Assembly, Judgment of Paris,* and *Knight Errant*—involved seduction as a dramatic crux. *Undertow* and *Pillar of Fire* would also use sexual conflict as a test point for the story's resolution.

What Tudor missed, increasingly, was Rambert's deepest faith. For all her artistic elitism, she could not persuade the innovative choreographer that she stood firmly behind him. "She never really understood Antony's ballets," said Maude. When they scored a success she swooned along with the audiences and critics—but he needed her *unconditional* belief to sustain him as he groped toward maturity, and her applause for his experimental forays. Without that security, he grew more distrustful of her and let the chasm between them widen.

Nor was Rambert able to give him—or anyone—the breathing space so essential for remaining whole. Somehow she managed to suck up all the oxygen and even devour the Mercury's inhabitants. It was not in her nature to allow freestanding artists. She tended to forsake the already autonomous talent for that which had not yet developed.

What Tudor did extract from her, however, was a nod to perfectionism. She preached it and he practiced it, with a vengeance. "Never accept the first solution," she used to say. For Ashton, this advice did not prove difficult to carry out. Just as quickly as he thought up one combination of steps, he could think up another. No strain. But for Tudor it might have been a push in the wrong direction. He was already hypercritical and conscientious. So much depended on the quality of the work he produced—just to meet his own standards. Now came the burden of even greater compulsivity.

He was certainly not alone in bearing Rambert's influence with discomfort. Just the average rehearsal brought bouts of hair-tearing and teeth-gnashing, especially when a season was being prepared. "Hardly a day went by without Madame clashing with a choreographer, designer, dancer or just the class pianist," wrote Peggy van Praagh in her memoirs. "There were rows. There were tears. Constantly there were scenes—and always someone being driven to distraction about something." But it was the boys who stood the hardest battering, simply by virtue of their having to bear Rambert's denigrations and assaults stoically. The greater their resistance the harsher her goadings. "They were much more warped about Mim than the girls who could break down and cry, and thus flee the studio in tears," Kersley explained. "By the time they'd had their little weep—and little laugh—and come back, she was on to someone else." Billy Chappell agreed and thought that "Antony, especially, found her too strong and controlling. But things were always stirred up. There was more uproar in that little company than in the whole Diaghilev operation," he said.

The toll taken on Rambert was perhaps greater than that on her company. When she couldn't get any satisfaction in the studio she next vented her wretchedness and rage on Ashley, only quieting down, according to Mary Clarke, by memorizing poetry or standing on her head—literally. When she came back downstairs, "contrite and on her best behavior," the injured would get up and return to work. "Rambert could do for you," said one dancer "what ten years of hard living couldn't. You endured misery and knew exaltation; you experienced every kind of emotion; you knew artistic death and the miracle of survival."

Antony was among the knowing. Like the others, he took the best of what she gave her dancers, even to the last corps member. She made time to see each person individually, to guarantee, said Maude, that "every finger placing was just so." Much as her attention was appreciated, the beneficiaries had all they could do to simply get away from her, for she was prepared to spend more hours than existed on supervision.

Often, after a class and then a rehearsal and then some coaching, Maude would arrive home and, climbing the stairs, would hear the phone ringing. "It would be Mim saying, 'Ah, but I did want to tell you . . .' I'd put the phone on the bed and Andrée Howard and I would hear her voice coming out and we'd say, 'No, *you* pick it up.' We were exhausted. She would walk you to the bus after class in order to tell you more about what you could improve. You would always see her, this tiny figure, holding onto someone's arm and walking with them while they were saying, 'Well, I have to go now.' She would be holding onto Ashton's or Tudor's arm, to tell him more and more what she thought, and I dare say this is when she criticized the ballets."

By the end of 1935, a year that saw Antony doing only one major ballet for Rambert, *The Descent of Hebe,* Madame and her choreographer entered a period of accelerated hostilities. Ironically, it was over *Jardin aux Lilas* that the greatest furor arose. This was his first masterpiece; perhaps she sensed something great in the making, and the prospect of his artistic independence scared her. Although she took utmost pride in the ballets spawned at her breeding ground—she once told Diana Gould proudly that she "produced choreographers, not dancers"—there was a more intense need to hover and censor than before. The more firmly rooted Antony's ideas for the ballet, the greater her fear of being dispensable. Would he demote her to agent status? To being a mere custodian of the premises? Would she become an outsider, playing no part in the essential creation of this artwork she sensed to be especially important?

Hugh had declared all-out war with Mim by now. Like a sleek, wetted-down panther he would emerge from their skirmishes in a flush of triumph—leaving her behind "lying prostrate on the floor and suffering palpitations," according to Maude. Ever faithful and ameliorating, she would, on those occasions, rush in and minister to the felled *materfamilias*. And Hugh, in addition to all the other superbly dramatic ploys of his vendetta mode, would resort to blackmail. Waiting until the day before a performance, he would threaten not to appear unless Mim met his demand of the moment. Sometimes he would leave a message saying that he was unreachable. And finally, when Hugh and Antony had a phone installed, they kept the number from her. Enraged on discovering their skullduggery, she railed at them. But Hugh cut her off, hollering: "If you ever call that number I will lay hands on you."

At the climax of one of their infamous cat fights, with voices shrilly ascending, "hers in resourceful European English, his in Barbadian . . . he rushed up the stairs at the side of the stage and out onto the dressing room balcony, slamming the door behind him. The glass shattered frighteningly. Ashley Dukes, two blocks away in Notting Hill High Street, heard the crash and cried out, 'My God, Hugh's got Mim!' and ran as hard as he could to save her."

Nothing gave Antony greater satisfaction than to see his alter ego act out with gut-thumping ferocity the very impulses he either denied himself or had lost altogether in childhood. Perhaps it was at his repressed mother's side that he had learned how to disconnect from feelings. But locking arms with Hugh brought a surge of delight. What better vicarious thrills than these Hugh-Mim *scenas?* While he still had to endure his own little confrontations with her, it was left for Hugh to land the mortal blows.

Their conflicts escalated in exact proportion to Antony's blooming as an independent artist. Clearly, he no longer needed

Rambert as a mentor. Nor could she confine the creativity she had nurtured. It now grew beyond her control, a critically threatening development. He was bursting with ideas, one after another. He brought to her the plan and music for *Dark Elegies,* but she waved him aside saying that he lacked the life experience to deal with the subject of death.

He also had plotted what would have been a full-length ballet—one based on the Kalevala, a Finnish epic that he wanted to set to a patchwork of Sibelius music, two hours' worth. It would have been the first English evening-long work, appearing ten years before Ashton's *Cinderella.* Theater dates did not open up, however. Nor was there an alternate stage big enough for the production. Tudor's ballet never materialized.

Besides the masterworks he was envisioning and composing, Antony was attracting some of Rambert's students away from Notting Hill Gate to his British Grove studio in Chiswick, a west London suburb redolent with literary and artistic associations. The relatively large house he shared with Hugh had a good-sized studio that enabled him to give classes. Hugh, who would always assume the housekeeping and decorating duties no matter where they lived, was also an avid collector. His many forays to the Caledonian Market brought enough pieces to furnish the glass greenhouse-styled place. It had a practice room upstairs and, like the flat in Holland Mews, was alive with the smells of their untrained dogs, Gito and Tobias.

Setting himself up as Rambert's competitor hardly improved his relationship with her. True, she could not be bettered as a teacher of theatrical conviction. Those who benefited from it say that she accomplished small miracles in the classroom. But what Antony offered was revelatory—an in-depth analysis of the dramatic meaning of movement. Nothing was done as a rote exercise or merely for the sake of its beauty—rather as a believable essence of the human condition. Consequently, he appealed to the dancers who were sensitive to his aesthetic. The same as those he cast in his ballets. The ones who came to be known as his disciples. The ones who followed their "Jesus of British Grove."

7

○

Lilac Scents

MIDWAY THROUGH THE DECADE the gap between Ashton and Tudor had narrowed. One's reputation no longer far overshadowed the other's so that the geniality between them turned to what Chappell called "bristling, sideways glances." Envy, suspiciousness and jealousy were easily on hand when either dance-maker caught sight of his rival's success.

Ashton, now looking for bigger opportunities, exited the Ballet Club in the fall of 1935. And just three months later Tudor put his *Jardin aux Lilas* on the tiny Mercury Theatre stage. Obviously, the knowledge that the mantle of chief choreographer had been passed to him intensified his creative focus and lent that sense of authority he came to crave. While it's seldom possible to determine whether an action is inevitable for a host of other reasons or as a consequence of some particular incident, it is safe to say that Tudor's star was on the ascendancy with some help from Ashton's departure.

At that point, his head was teeming with ideas. True, the Kalevala fell by the wayside and *Dark Elegies* had to be postponed. But neither of these blighted hopes took energy away from *Jardin*. And so strong was Tudor's aesthetic intuition that he basically discarded the original story he had chosen by the Finnish writer, Aino Kallas, in favor of a self-devised one truer to the issues that fascinated him: the politics of love as laid down in the Edwardian era, its licenses and taboos, but most of all, the pathos and frustration generated within the characters.

For Tudor was intrigued less by social injustice, arbitrariness and corruption than by how individual victims struggled in the grip of these phenomena. His approach was intellectual, like that of a photographer who knows exactly how to set the scene so that its expressive details project a certain mood or emotion. As Leo Kersley has said, "Antony was madly curious about people, he was like so many little boys always experimenting. Trying tactics out on this one and that one."

But no matter how detached he was as a creator, he knew at the deepest level of himself the precise anguish of his characters. He had to. One does not mold images of truth without being on close terms with it. And the truth could not be acknowledged anywhere else in his life so he stamped it into the ballets.

The Kallas story dealt with a crisis of class codes: the sexual privilege of feudal lords over their vassals, otherwise known as the *droit du seigneur*—and in this case, a bride murdering the lord of the manor as he, not the bridegroom, is about to indulge his first-night rights with her. But Antony was more interested in projecting the poetic tone and mood of his characters' interior states than in detailing such high melodrama. The designer Hugh Stevenson helped in this—one day, early in the rehearsal period, he brought a French poem by an unknown poet, one whose aura and title Antony immediately responded to; Stevenson recited it quietly and in that moment gave the force of inspiration to his colleague's ballet.

As a result Antony scrapped the tale of murder and updated the scenario to the nineteenth century, where social restrictions were no less harsh but far more insidious. By refocusing the story line so that it implied sexual taboo as well as sexual privilege he also brought it closer to home.

At the same time, setting the story back to the late Victorian or early Edwardian era—rather than staging it as a contemporary piece—was a stroke of genius. For it was then in English history that social conventions were imposed with a rigorous, thwarting hypocrisy. Also it provided the necessary distance to fictionalize his own situation. But the fact that everything about *Jardin* is French, including the title and music—Chausson's *Poème*—doesn't negate its strongly English character. Nothing provides a better foil for the stifling atmosphere of repression than the nocturnal languor of a moonlit lilac garden.

The overrefinement and pomposity of the epoch made a perfect frame for the type of constraint that the *Jardin* characters personified. With this ballet he perfected the use of small, naturalistic gestures and sent them soaring to theatrical heights. Each seemingly unimportant detail of placement—an arm locked stiffly behind the heroine's back to telegraph her tension—loomed as a thing of great moment.

The only vestige of the Kallas story that remained was the forced betrothal of Caroline to an unloving opportunist. Their *mariage de convenance* became the blade that severed two sets of lovers from each other—as tellingly drawn as a skilled scenarist's. "For the first time in the twentieth century," wrote Fernau Hall, "a choreographer succeeded in emulating the achievements of good dramatists, novelists and film directors." Besides conjuring Stendhal and Proust and Chekhov—whose works he studied and admired—Tudor also sought to represent in *Jardin* the ideas of Henri Bergson, the French philosopher who believed that reality exists only as ever-changing intuition, not as the consequence of finite physical laws. Hall maintains that Tudor "adapted to ballet Bergsonian ideas about time, memory, consciousness and determinism in the same way that Proust adapted them to the novel."

On the one hand what he sought to do was revolutionary; in 1935 few choreographers besides Tudor attempted to focus the subtle complexities of human interaction, indeed to charge them with the entire dramatic thrust. On the other hand, his personal investment in the terms of a so-called psychological ballet was paramount.

Antony deeply understood the silent anguish of the ballet's heroine, Caroline. He had been there. He knew that she could not act on her desire—marry the man she loved—for her family had chosen another bridegroom, one who could benefit its fortunes. Nor could *he* "marry" Hugh, who would remain forbidden to him, both by society and the law. The practice of homosexuality, even the intent to practice it, was illegal and punishable as a crime. Indeed, it did not become decriminalized in Great Britain until 1967.

The role he took himself, The Man She Must Marry, satisfied several needs. It allowed him to identify with the aggressor—to be the cold, domineering, willful man he enjoyed impersonating and the harsh, depriving husband who looks upon his bride as a purchased object. In his own words, Caroline's betrothed is "a bossy sort of character. If he turns his head it's almost with a disapproval of everything that's going on around him. And if he looks at her, it's because she belongs to him. And if he takes her, it's a possessive hand. And if he turns her, he turns her possessively, 'Here you come, my girl.' If he gives an arm, it's demanding that she should take it. He never asks. He tells."

By following his fictive instincts and becoming the aggressor, he relieved himself of the pain of victimization; in art comes release. Nothing hurts The Man She Must Marry because he is invulnerable. He hurts others. Not only that, the role carries with it society's approbation. Tudor presumably took a vicarious pleasure in portraying the powerful, wealthy, heterosexual male—all the things denied him offstage.

For Hugh's role as Caroline's lover, Antony looked to the real-life Laing. "Desperately in love, enthusiastic, not crafty in any way," according to Tudor's own description. "I think he's so open he has no quirks of any kind. Whereas my part has nothing but quirks." In his view Hugh epitomized the lover. He was ardent, direct, extravagant in his passion. Over and over he cast Hugh as the compleat Romantic. He saw himself, however, as complex and ambivalent, a mass of conflicting emotions. Not to be taken lightly, either, is Antony's role as the spoiler: the husband-to-be robs Hugh of Caroline, his great heterosexual hope. Later, in the course of their lives, Antony would indulge Hugh with what always seemed guilty compensation. There would apparently be instances where he thought that, but for him, Hugh might opt for the so-called straight path. It's little wonder, given these elements, that *Jardin* sprang so powerfully from his imagination. Still, finding a way to translate this deeply felt scenario into such gripping choreographic pictures remains something to marvel at.

Maude Lloyd danced Caroline, with Tudor indicating that the character must be "well-bred," a young woman who does what is expected even when doing so crushes her to the quick. "She always holds herself correctly, shoulders down," he explained, whereas the mistress of her fiancé (An Episode in His Past) is comparatively flamboyant and assertive. She balances Caroline's unquestioning obedience but also conforms to the prescribed social code of the occasion.

Since ambience counted for so much in this vividly surreal dream of a work, Tudor surrounded the four principals with party guests. They came and went, amplifying the environment in detail fragments, but never disturbing the exquisite economy of construction. From these he built a mood mosaic, a context for the story's dramatic crux.

Equally important to him as the smallest gestural detail was the depiction of time flow in *Jardin*. Fernau Hall likens it to the device Proust used in *À la Recherche du Temps Perdu,* noting that several times the action slows down to emphasize the meaning of a gesture. At the ballet's climax—the startling moment when Caroline realizes she will never see Her Lover again—Tudor freeze-frames the scene. Only Caroline, casting a final desperate glance at the others, keeps moving. Rambert, who ended up bitterly opposing the work, was struck by Tudor's ingenious device: "At the height of the drama the movement froze and the music continued alone for several bars. It made you hold your breath."

Analyzing the connection Tudor made to Proust, Agnes de Mille wrote: "Embraces and filigrees of arm movements, faint rubbings-out, like little sighings or half-heard exclamations, seemingly whispered in the air, are never mere decorations but evocations and echoes. . . . Each physical statement sets up a rippling of contrary suggestions, and each step is wreathed with doubts, regrets, aspirations, until the dancers seem literally to be moving through the human mind."

Throughout the whole rehearsal period there was a sense of imminent artistic breakthrough and Rambert made a point of frequently dropping in. She was alarmed at the idea of floor-length Edwardian gowns. "Is it going to be all right?" she asked the dancer Elisabeth Schooling, who stood watching at the side. Assurances meant little. Her skepticism only mounted. Finally, she ended up pleading for visitation rights. "Oh, Antony," she would entreat him with her outstretched hands clasped in prayer and her voice rising as she bargained and wheedled, "please let me come and watch." But her disapproval became so clear and so annoying that Antony and his dancers made a pact: whenever Mim entered, the rehearsal would come to a complete stop; no one would do or say a thing until she left. Aware that her presence was unwelcome and that she was perceived as the enemy, she became even more resentful.

As the premiere drew closer, tension mounted—not over the performance but Rambert's anger. Arguments raged daily. But Tudor was implacable. He moved headlong into production and at one point started spraying lilac scent around the stage area, intent on bringing the dancers every last drop of the scene's atmosphere. At the Thursday dress rehearsal and with only half the ballet finished Rambert started screaming at him: "I will not have theese feelthy thing in my theater." What she saw onstage, said Kersley, was "a large piece of chaos from this comparative nobody. She carried on and jumped up and down. But he didn't want to play the usual games and have fancy arguments. The more excited she got the more he turned a deaf ear. They all thought she would shout herself out and go away or hoped she would, but no. Ordinarily they could stop for the day and next morning, with Hugh there as mediator, end up kissing each other and making some silly, idiotic concession like putting the ballet second on the program instead of third."

But this time was different. With the premiere scheduled for Sunday there was no moment to lose. So Antony dug his heels in and prepared an ultimatum: to relieve her of the objectionable ballet—but only after the premiere. He argued that it had been announced and not presenting it would prove a public embarrassment. She refused to consider his claim. He told her to go fetch Ashley for corroboration, and in the roughly half hour it took to go home and get him, Antony moved the rehearsal ahead in a frenzy of speed. When Ashley turned up he asked, in his most urbane and clerical manner, for the choreographer's point of view, having to shush Mim to hear it. "Quite right," he said, agreeing with Antony's assessment that he was entitled to have his ballet performed. What's more, he could sue for breach of promise if she did not allow it.

Temporarily defeated, she agreed to uphold her end but insisted on the right to denounce *Jardin*—in a curtain speech upon its conclusion. "Oh, yes, that's fine, lovely, you do that," said Antony, while Ashley stood shuffling, with a look on his face that cried, "Oh, that mad woman of mine."

For the next three days Antony went at his rehearsals "hammer and tongs," as Kersley put it, "perhaps because he was expecting a verbal embarrassment from Mim." Everyone came Sunday, not necessarily to see *Jardin,* but to witness this denunciation. Throughout the sixteen minutes of its performance she hopped from one side of the theater to the other, sat a moment here and a moment there on her shooting stick. She had to gather her courage for the speech because in those days she was unaccustomed to public speaking. But there would be satisfaction in having her say and regaining her rightful control of artistic decisions. She practiced the speech throughout the performance.

When the curtain rang down and the audience roared its approval, she stood in furious astonishment. Over the years, the world has marveled at this ballet—staged by no fewer than twenty-five companies. In the wake of its acclaim, Rambert wore *Jardin* as proudly as any other lapel pin in her small jewel collection. Both Ashton and Balanchine would later admit to wishing they had created it.

Despite the admiration she now professed for *Jardin*, Mim's support for Antony's projects must have seemed tenuous at best. Why, then, did he stay on with her in the wake of his new success? The answer suggests, in part, that he was drawn to fellow underdogs. Rambert was definitely one, and Hugh another. They stood as a fraternity of self-doubters. Despite the strong profile all three projected—each in a different way—there was a terrific appetite for defeat, almost a will for it.

Nevertheless, Antony made the effort to improve his lot. At the time when he was coming to terms with his need for greater opportunity he pleaded his case to Ninette de Valois. Since she ran a company that could accommodate the ballets he was planning, it made sense to appeal to her. What's more, he had the perfect opportunity to discuss a new arrangement with her, as his limited contract with the Vic-Wells was about to expire. Their meeting constituted a turning point of sorts.

De Valois turned him down flatly. "I couldn't do otherwise," she said. "With Ashton and myself as choreographers I didn't need another one. What I needed was a virtuoso dancer. I had just signed Robert Helpmann, who didn't fill that gap, so I had to take Harold Turner, who was a marvelous technician and could do justice to the classics."

In the course of de Valois's conversation with Tudor, she told him that he needed more professional experience in how large companies function, that he "should join de Basil [Ballets Russes] for a year or two and then talk with me again." Tudor responded to her advice with typical skepticism, she remembered, and then asked, "How do I know you will hire me after getting this experience?"

"You have only my word," she answered.

Apparently, he did not put much stock in it. Or he may have felt that in the end de Valois did not appreciate his ballets and was simply making excuses for not accepting him into the Vic-Wells. Most observers on the scene believed that her tastes ran counter to Tudor's. If Rambert had difficulty understanding his ballets, de Valois was even harder put. Her company characteristically veered in the direction of spectacle rather than experiment. It was audience-pleasers that she sought out for her stage, not profound or revolutionary undertakings.

"I don't think Antony belonged to the theater," said de Valois, trying to account for the differences in their aesthetic. "But I mean that as a compliment. He was an intellectual. I came from the professional stage, where strong technique was the very basis of performance. Rambert came from Dalcroze and eurythmics. She was well informed and had fine taste but had never been a real pro. Antony grew up in her image."

After the *Jardin* premiere, however, de Valois eagerly rang Tudor and asked him to stage the ballet for Vic-Wells. He refused, shrewdly looking to the future and the possibility of forming his own company. According to Kersley, he had no desire to let someone else bask in his reflected glory.

Ashton, too, claimed *Jardin,* as "my kind of ballet"—although he didn't put much value on Tudor's works in general. Together, de Valois and her resident choreographer formed their own British bastion of establishment ballet. Tudor realized that he had no alternative at this time but to stay with Rambert and wring the best he could from the situation.

Meanwhile he had the satisfaction of artistic success. With *Jardin,* which won him many fans and served notice of the most theatrically profound English choreography to date, Tudor could weather other setbacks. He had moved the boundary further than any before him. He created the first ballet whose characters could mirror all the repression and ambivalence and conflict any auteur might strive for—earning it, and others to follow, the label, "psychological ballet." No other dance-maker had even attempted so remarkable a feat.

Sangfroid

THERE WERE SEVERAL Antony Tudors. One was the intellectual progressive—working within the idiom of classical ballet but inventing a new and profound language. Another, just having given up the post of Mercury Theatre factotum in 1936, was Antony Tudor for hire—arranger of dances for stage plays, opera, revues, experimental television, and musicals.

As he moved farther and farther from the Central Street of William Cook, new identities—even new voices—were called for.

Who would it be? The bloke from EC1 or the arts sophisticate with a high-tilt accent?

For the latter he adopted a chichi style of speech—often beginning statements with "I say." While speaking before a camera in 1959, for instance, in a documentary entitled "Modern Ballet," his voice took on an exaggerated English lilt and the sort of emphatic enunciation that he did not commonly use. Here was Antony Tudor in a performance that not only showed him to be extraordinarily outgoing, but contradicted the image of the terse and cryptic character he sometimes cultivated. His words spilled out in a fluent, articulate stream. He could have passed for a most poetic scholar.

Such transformations were not considered unusual in England. As Maude Lloyd rightly pointed out: "Lords marry chorus girls and change them into ladies." And as Diana Gould said, "England is a breeding country. And although it takes two generations to make a gentleman, the idea of class barriers here is a misconception. Especially after World War I when the aristocracy were reduced to paupers and there was great social flux. Anyone with ambition automatically cleansed his accent."

But when he took free-lance work as a stage manager for shows in the West End—a job at which he was eminently practiced, Leo Kersley recalled that "Antony spoke the richest cockney to the crews. They adored it and this man who seemed just like any other stage manager to them. We both learned to speak proper English, but always could turn it off and on." To whatever degree Antony remained conscious of the speech of his new identity, he evidently also kept careful guard that only what he chose to reveal would be revealed. He was ever in control of both his image and his feelings—not forgetting the words of his early mentor on the subject. In a letter to Rambert, dated 1979, he closed with a reference to her helpful admonition:

"It was on another visit to the library that you recited much English poetry and in the very nicest way led me to understand that my cockney accent was 'not the thing.' "

Once the recommendation was made he took himself to what he called "a specialist on Harley Street [who was] very expensive." Antony went on to explain how this "diction doctor" had him choose an article from the editorial page of *The Times* of London and read it over and over "until it made sense." Following that, "he had to correct my vowels." The elocution lessons he had taken some years previously "were awful" and apparently didn't help him as an amateur actor.

The letter reflects Tudor in his mellow old age, a time when he no longer harbored resentment toward Rambert. But at a bustling and energetic twenty-eight, he quite naturally saw her as an obstacle to his ambition. It was partly for this reason and partly because he needed to earn a better living than she could pay him that Antony looked beyond the Ballet Club for additional jobs.

He didn't have to look hard, as it turned out. Not least among the offers was one from the Royal Opera House in Covent Garden, then under the artistic direction and baton of Sir Thomas Beecham. After Antony's first success there, contributing the dances for Rossini's *La Cenerentola,* in May 1935, he went on to create other ballets for the company and brought a select group from the Ballet Club to perform them. Although the assignments called on his skills, the genre of opera ballet is not exactly grist for a great choreographer's mill. All he does is fashion some decorative movements around the singing statues who take the spotlight. It requires a certain craft but hardly challenges one's creativity. Yet many significant dance-makers—Balanchine among them—have supported themselves over the thin times working in this often unrewarding capacity.

During that same summer season Antony also devised dances for the *Carmen* production. And one day when the rehearsal pianist did not show up, he simply plunked himself down at the keyboard and accompanied his dancers—"keeping one eye on stage while sight-reading the score," remembered Kersley, who was elected as page turner. "He didn't want to waste his rehearsal time so he did both—played and directed.

"Midway through, in walks Sir Thomas, himself, who watched unseen for quite some time. Finally he said, 'Well, I can't do as well as you my boy, but I can give you a hand. One of them works.' [Beecham's left hand was afflicted by a strange muscle condition.] Antony happily agreed. And there he was, playing three hands with the great Sir Thomas, who took an instant liking to him. Both of them enjoyed joking around and in fact used humor as a cover-up for what they didn't want known about themselves personally."

Otherwise, his ploy was aloofness—an image of cool disdain mingled with piercing wit so studiedly indifferent as to be inappropriate. One day at the Ballet Club he entered the studio announcing that the Mercury's secretary had just done himself in. "I say, where do you suppose the janitor found Colin this morning?" Tudor reportedly asked, with something approaching mild amusement. "Sitting with his head in the oven, quite dead. It did give him a turn."

It seems not only perverse, but impossible, that the same person who created *Jardin* would be prone to such monumental sangfroid. More likely, the response served to protect him against the horror of what had happened. As it turned out, "Antony disliked Colin," remembered Therese Langfield Horner. "He was a social climber, sort of dishonest in that way. And he tried to hide his homosexuality by marrying one of the girls. But when his wife found him in bed with a man his fantasy fell apart. I think it precipitated the suicide." So Antony had good reason to step over the body. He must have sensed Colin's despair—and been goaded toward speaking as an aggressor. But even this role was only a defensive posture. As Agnes de Mille wrote: "Again and again in his work I began to sense a tenderness, compassion, love and grief that may have been beyond the power of any other contemporary choreographer or stage director."

Tudor's ballets redeemed his otherwise sealed-off self, but they did not have easy births. For the act of recreating these emotional interiors forced him to confront their existence as well as his self-worth. Maude Lloyd remembered "the agonies he went through in writing his ballets. There were long periods when nothing came to him and he would stand there thinking and cracking his knuckles, cracking his knuckles. They made a terrible noise. But we all knew he was extraordinary, that nothing like Antony had ever happened before in the world of dance. So we endured with him. And when we would work out a pas de deux or a solo and think with relief that we'd come a little distance closer to accomplishment, the next day he would discard what was done and start all over again. It wasn't quite right, not precisely the thing that expressed what he had in mind."

Sometimes they rehearsed in the basement of the Mercury Theatre. The studio there had no mirrors and its ceilings were so low that lifts could not always be negotiated. Even with these handicaps Maude remembered that the work Antony did "was marvelous." He never discussed any of it with her, however, or the others. The first time she acted as his instrument—it was backstage while Rambert's dancers were touring Manchester—he did not tell her that the combination of steps he was figuring out were for *Cross-Garter'd.* Whatever he had in mind and was striving for, it remained his secret—to be shared only with Hugh.

And Hugh played the most significant role in this process. It was he alone who ministered to Antony during his creative tribulations—those times when, witnessing the choreographer's despair and self-doubt, he reached out, the only one with the permission to do so and say: "Yes, you can do it, Ant'ny. That's good. That's good. Go ahead." Maude recalled that Antony would then reply, 'No, I can't' "—the extent of his complaints.

From the earliest point in their relationship, Hugh was "the Guardian Angel"—except when he turned on Antony and raged at him. His flair for offstage dramatizations helped in significant ways. When Antony and Rambert deadlocked on some point about a rehearsal or the casting of a ballet, for instance, Hugh went as emissary—sometimes a kindly one, sometimes menacing—in order to bring about movement. Invariably, he accomplished the mission. Poor Rambert never knew that at least part of the mayhem Hugh threatened was playacting. Angela Dukes Ellis said that her mother "was always terrified that he would pull a knife." Because Hugh was so willing a henchman, or rather a Little Audrey, Antony didn't mind using him thus. Besides, the vicarious pleasure of these enactments merely fired Antony's incentive. The pact between the wronged citizen and his ombudsman had very deep roots.

Antony sent out the word on Hugh's polar reactions. Sometimes he would describe him as "self-destructive" and other times vouch for his "instincts of self-preservation." But Hugh was always on the verge of violence. The slightest thing set him off. Repeatedly, he would threaten to throw himself from the studio's high window. Billy Chappell remembered how "he would peel off his tights in a rage and jump on the stove fender," readying himself for the next leap up and the much-promised death dive. Or "race up to the roof next to nude in a pouring rain." Suicide was forever imminent. Those who observed this behavior from a distance had trouble believing its depth—one dancer said that Hugh could be as devastated by a mosquito bite as a broken heart.

The few others who developed a close relationship with him years later saw Antony's bewildered adjunct as a person of great sincerity. "His emotions were larger than life," said Betty Cage, an administrator at New York City Ballet. For better or worse, this was the person with whom Antony formed his elemental bond. Was he the overwhelming detriment some say? Was he the troubled but vitalizing force, without which little of Tudor's greatness would have emerged? Observers line up on both sides of the question.

But there's no argument that he altered the course of a life and a career. For Hugh bolstered Antony's grandiosity, which was the counterpart of nearly crippling self-doubt. "Hugh was the whip to scourge him on," wrote de Mille. "He was the gadfly, Shakespearean in his undiluted determination that Antony should become famous, and that he, Hugh, should become the great interpreter of Antony's works." It was only later, after his immigration to America, that anyone called him "Tudor." Had Hugh tried it with the B-Clubbers "he would've been laughed out of the room," according to Kersley. Across the ocean it was a different matter. And Hugh took advantage. He seized on the effects of using the last name only—as de Mille observed, "the way one speaks of 'Verdi' or 'Michelangelo' . . . the established great 'Tudor'—a name in the floor of Westminster Abbey."

On the other hand, Antony was quick to read lack of regard into the merest suggestion. Once he turned on his trusted friend, Maude, misunderstanding a comment she made and punishing her for it. This was the same Maude who lent herself ceaselessly, "to be sensitive to the slightest intonation" of the steps he squeezed out. Hardly anyone could be more loyal.

But one day during a feverishly busy period at the Ballet Club, when Tudor's late arrivals to rehearsal threw off the dancers' schedules, she was elected to speak to him about his tardiness. After all, they did have to get from Notting Hill to their jobs in Theatreland. Little did she anticipate the furor her request would set off. In angry retaliation he dashed off a note "discharging me from my role," said Lloyd, "and giving as a reason that I was too grand to really want to dance in one of his lowly ballets."

The following letter to Rambert, written the very week of this incident, explains both a physical problem that brought him late to rehearsals, but, more important, the heady elation of grandiose dreams come true:

Dearest Mim,

I am sorry I could not get to the photograph call but the dentist passed me through purgatory in one afternoon with four stoppings, and I finally escaped him very late with an aching jaw and twenty minutes to get to a dinner appointment. I worked a little earlier in the afternoon and actually thrill in myself with the movement for "Lempo." I suppose it is what one calls the awakening of an artist. I do most sincerely pray so.

Tomorrow morning again is a stage rehearsal with rostrums at the Old Vic and I must be there changed at eleven o'clock. So, if you can be at the Club at 10:30 I would thank your goodness. And I will telephone you immediately after this rehearsal (before lunch) about the part of the monk. Surely Susan could manage the lighting. She knows our switchboard and the cues perfectly.

With much love,
Antony

This, for Rene's record, will be the fifth class at which you have relieved me this term. Already almost a week.

In the midst of a packed calendar—one that had him teaching, performing, running lightboards, rehearsing and composing new work—he begged off some of the assignments and knew enough to kiss his benefactor's hand for her help. He also tasted the sweetness of creative affirmation. How ardently he longed for it.

9

The Irresistible Other

ALTHOUGH THEY HAD THEIR FAVORITES, other choreographers worked happily with any number of dancers. Massine, Ashton, Fokine, Balanchine—all of them looked essentially for stellar technicians possessed of quality and élan.

But Tudor the interiorscape put a far greater creative burden both on himself and those he chose to inhabit his ballets than did his peers. Beautiful movement for its own sake meant little to him. He needed his ballets to be allegories—the kind that could resonate with real yearning, conflict, resignation. To get this required him to tap the dancers' own resources.

Being a disciple or "a Tudor dancer," as would be the case in America, required the willingness to risk exposure in the extreme—to show one's own vulnerability, for instance, not some gestural cliché that symbolizes the condition. It also meant having the capacity to give oneself up to the obsessive perfectionism that defined Tudor's work style. Maude Lloyd could and did meet the qualifications; another worshiper was Peggy van Praagh—similarly giving, even slavish.

Their dedication went not only beyond the norm, it made ballets like *Jardin* possible. Ashton could create another lovely work with a different cast. But Tudor could make a *Jardin* only with dancers on speaking terms with the characters' sensitivities. Caroline's despair could not be poignant without the crushing social repression that Maude dredged up from the well of her own experience. She knew that Caroline would not flinch publicly no matter what awful thing befell her. Composure and grace were involuntary, no matter the passion. Antony reveled in the agony of such constraint, being intimate with it himself. "The reticence in *Jardin* is something that people wouldn't understand today," observed Maude, half a century later. "Not dancers, not anyone in our culture."

And van Praagh comprehended why Antony "would insist on every movement being performed in just the way he wanted, and would spend hours exactly fitting a dancer to his conception of the whole. Usually he chose difficult music and would not accept the slightest variation from his interpretation." Without doubt there were artistic gains to be had in this fastidiousness of process. But the need to control everything also proved a creative restriction. To the degree that Antony could not feel true self-worth he imposed rigid systems on those he could dominate.

There's little doubt that van Praagh's complete trust and openness were invaluable to his sense of progress. Her selfless attitude, the capacity to take on any amount of work with patience and pleasure shone like a beacon of affirmation in these unknown waters.

It was a two-way stream, however. The women in Tudor's ballets were multifaceted, creatures of every mood and nuance. He empathized with them in the most intimate ways. He elaborated on those moods and nuances. Guided by a deep knowledge of how they might react to each situation and inspired to create the kind of poetic equivalent—unique and economical—that could telegraph a state of mind, he reached out beyond ballet's limited realm. He found not just a whole new narrative form but a whole new body of material to narrate.

Needless to say, women were central to him—as they were to most ballet choreographers of the day. Whereas Ashton and Balanchine were often satisfied to know the individual dancer—how she moves, what she can do that some other cannot—he fed on her psychodynamics. It was the human behavior game that he played so expertly, plotting each interactional gambit and then exiting after the move. Antony was ever the self-conscious outsider in this regard, except, of course, for his bonding with Hugh. He lacked the ease with people to sustain contact over long periods.

"The things he said to us," remembered Maude, "were all lighthearted quips. We were keenly aware that he had innermost thoughts—he thought those thoughts even in our presence—but he never expressed them, except in his ballets, and we never asked what they were." Moreover, Leo Kersley said that Antony reminded him "of a brilliant physicist, sitting back and observing the scene, watching everyone and drawing his own conclusions." Maude, who spent so much time with Antony and Hugh, found it curious to note how hidden he kept himself since, in her eyes, they were all peers. Less so for Alicia Markova, who remembered "that the world was a difficult place for Antony. Even during the good times—those long evenings we spent together as a group with Hugh cooking something wonderful and all of us sitting around till two in the morning. He was outside the group, just observing. He related only one way. Some found it strange or arrogant or rude. But I thought he was just being Antony."

In classes and rehearsals it was a different matter. Here he had the intimacy not possible elsewhere. Here he was the master, the one in charge. Here there were no social barriers. He was free "to pick anyone's brains who had any," according to Kersley. He could step over the line of politesse with impunity. Offstage he did somewhat the same, but it was not quite like conducting the whole show. In the studio he could legitimately probe some-one's personal feelings. Socially, he was limited to teasing and quipping.

Those who comprised the hand-picked group were totally amenable to Tudor's sardonic little exchanges. Furthermore, be-cause he already knew them so well, as people, he didn't have to go through the emotional undressing process that proved so frightening to dancers he would later encounter in the United States. Contrary to some accounts, Tudor could often get sec-tions of his ballets together without spending agonized, inordi-nately long amounts of time on them. In *Jardin,* for instance, he set himself the task of devising new movement every time the musical theme repeated itself, so as not to fall in step with the composer's melodic obsession. "I wanted to present it in a dif-ferent choreographic form, so it wouldn't ape itself," Tudor recalled, many years later. And he explained how the freeze-frame moment "came out of desperation," that, finally, he "could think of nothing else to do. It was a Zen moment." But it was also the logical option to follow all the other variations. There was simply no need to find another motif when the frozen image could do more, at that point, than anything else. "It came out of having discarded all the possibilities," he said, explaining his concept of the spare dance image, a thing of stripped-down, economic power. Tudor knew the meaning of the Bauhaus axiom "Less is More."

So thoroughly was his life embedded in his work and vice versa that even on the occasional weekends he spent away from British Grove, he would experiment with steps for a planned ballet. Once, in the summer of 1934, he and Hugh visited Ram-bert and her family at their beach house in Dymchurch. Angela Dukes Ellis remembered the weekend. She was age eight and Antony had her try some of the dance motifs he was working on then for *The Planets.* But what came to mind more clearly than the steps she tried out for him was "the horrendous row that he and Hugh had with my parents. Mother had put them in separate rooms. It was the proper thing and she thought that it would be all right. But it wasn't. What a big drama. The screaming and hollering didn't stop until Hugh and Antony settled into the same room."

In view of Ashley's hostility to homosexuals and Rambert's covertly moralistic attitude it's surprising that the weekend guests would insist on sharing quarters. For even with the looser codes that governed theater people, intolerance was great on the part of many English. Later, variations on standard sexual preference would even become fashionable. But not in the 1930s. As Diana Gould pointed out, "The English have always practiced hypocrisy to do with sex." The Oscar Wilde case had left an imprint that still burned. And not until 1987, as John Percival observed, could Sir John Gielgud freely state for a newspaper interview that he shared a flat with his male friend. So for Antony and Hugh to take such courageous action and insist on their human rights was quite remarkable.

Tudor did not go in for flamboyant behavior of any kind. He went so far as to suggest that the roles he fashioned for himself were functionally simple because "I wasn't secure about being able to entertain an audience as a dancer." The estrangement and discomfort he often felt socially invaded his stage persona as well. Generally, he could not exult in the act of dancing because any act of physicality was a mirror of self-expression—something to be devoutly avoided. He knew this from experience as a choreographer. He knew this as a tenet of his art. Paradoxically, his performances were splendid. And Kersley remembered how "Antony jumped around and jigged about, shaking the old bones to see if he could do it." Once engaged, he did not hold back anything, although the very structure of his self-styled characters reflected the stoicism he used as a mask.

"I made [The Man She Must Marry in *Jardin,* The Friend in *Pillar,* and so on] for myself, usually the role that was central to the story. These are not the best parts, but without me there is no ballet. It's essential in my ballets to get inside of the skin, so you're not acting a part but actually in the role, conveying it to the audience and *conveying it to yourself* at the same time."

What he performed onstage was as much as Tudor could reveal about himself—not an inconsiderable body of testimony. Nevertheless, the character he defined over and over was not the one with palpable yearnings. He left that to the others, dancers (and people) with the freedom to show their feelings. For Tudor could only participate vicariously. He had to be the observer, the voyeur—not the protagonist, rather the puppeteer. As he has said, "Each of the dancers in the ballets was part of myself. I think I knew who Caroline was, who Her Lover was, who the despised woman was. I carried them all within me somewhere."

Yet not too close. Better for Hugh, so naturally a creature of sexual fervor, to portray those unabashed emotions. Meanwhile dancers were, though perhaps less then than now, "notoriously bisexual," according to Peter Williams, editor of the periodical *Dance and Dancers*. "But not Tudor. Nor Ashton, who was terrified at the knowledge of his being gay. It was an awful thing then." While Antony was a figure so many women dancers looked up to and dreamed of marrying—even de Mille admitting to having "a crush on him"—he had nothing sexually to do with any of them. Fernau Hall remembered seeing de Mille rush up to him following a performance "and kiss him passionately on the mouth. He stood impassive, his eyes glazing over."

Gould speculated that "anyone so self-absorbed, quiet and ascetic as Antony wouldn't be obsessed with sex. If it weren't for Hugh, he might never have been awakened." P. W. Manchester pondered the same question. "For all we know it could happen to anyone. Perhaps in each man's life there is one other who represents that irresistible other, that fatal attraction. Who knows what different course things might have taken had these two never crossed paths." But Kersley insisted that "Antony didn't have a seven-year itch, he had a seven-minute itch—and acted on it."

Hugh, while bound to the single most important relationship, was gregarious. And having already won Tudor he went on to enjoy whoever else appealed to him. He admired beautiful women openly, for instance. "He would hold me by the shoulders," Gould recalled, "and say: 'You have the most beautiful shape I've ever seen.' "

Just as Tudor stood back and made only verbal contact, Hugh was perpetually hurling himself into physical situations—threatening violence to Rambert, lavishing affectionate embraces on Maude, on Diana. Tudor and Hugh were Apollo and Dionysius, opposites. Apollo conceived his landmark ballets by way of high intellect and reason, filling them deep with the residue of unexpressed feeling. Dionysius threw himself passionately into every scene, both onstage and off.

Hugh was the child and Antony the parent. Hugh needed to be placated, indulged, soothed, stroked, rewarded, admired—persuaded that he was lovable. He needed declarations of love. Antony was the authority figure, whose sense of relating to people came from controlling them. Younger dancers called upon him for help and looked up to him. In light of this the infatuations were not surprising. "I fell in love with him," admitted Therese Langfield Horner. "He was my teacher and that relationship made me feel very close to him." But, of course, nothing tangible beyond her infatuation ever developed. The most he felt for her, she said, was a fondness. When Langfield unwittingly became pregnant by a man outside the company it was Antony who helped her through the crisis. Again, playing the patriarchal role, he offered to break the news to her mother, and, indeed, won gratitude all around for interceding. "I was so distraught. Running around threatening to topple an armoire on myself to cause a miscarriage. By calming both of us and taking the sting from my mother Antony showed a great compassion—although his offhanded manner would have looked like indifference to an outsider. But I think the indifference was just a facade. He just never felt free to show tenderness."

Some of that vulnerability Tudor channeled into his ballets—notably, at this point, the one that would become *Dark Elegies*. He had begun working on it several years earlier, after attending a concert in Queen's Hall and hearing Mahler's *Das Lied von der Erde*. "I thought it was the greatest piece of music I had ever heard. And I was going to use it. And I knew that I must use Mahler but obviously this work was impossible [scored for augmented orchestra]. So I went to find out what other things he had composed that were available. And I came to a piano reduction of the *Kindertotenlieder* for baritone."

Mahler had died in 1911. Almost immediately his music fell out of favor and performances of it were rare. It wasn't until the late 1950s, when Leonard Bernstein championed the mammoth symphonies—symphonies bespeaking twentieth-century angst and alienation—that a true resurgence began. Tudor was not just a vigilant surveyor of the arts, he was ahead of his time. Nobody listened to Mahler in the mid-1930s.

Immediately upon finding these songs for the death of children he had gathered together "some nondescript little girls" and went down to the basement one morning to start on a dance for the third song. He completed some of it but when Rambert heard about the theme she asked him to postpone the ballet.

Now, however, in the winter of 1936, he and Hugh attended an exhibition of Nadia Benois's paintings. She was the niece of the Russian artist and designer Alexandre Benois (and later would become the mother of actor Peter Ustinov). Here before them was a canvas whose mood and tone captured the essence of what would be known as *Dark Elegies*. Here staring back at them was the backcloth for the Mahler ballet. They returned to Ladbroke Road with singular enthusiasm and roused Rambert to come and see the painting. Impressed with their choice of Benois, an artist she already admired, Rambert changed her mind about the Mahler ballet: she heartily approved the plan after seeing a few movements.

A Finale and a Prelude

Dark Elegies stands alone among the Tudor ballets. It steps away from the passion and repression, yearning and deprivation of *Jardin*. It leaves behind those transference elements that rise up from love fantasies and become hyperreal distillations of ancient cravings. Whereas Chausson's solo violin unfurls a certain grandeur in its melancholy, Mahler's song cycle leads down the path to pathos—an exquisite pathos lined with the calm of resignation. So keenly did Tudor respond to the score and its unthinkable message—the death of one's children—that he was thrust into an entirely different choreographic world. He turned his back on *Jardin*'s nocturnal party with bare-shouldered women wearing plumes in their hair, for an *Elegies* plain with peasants locking arms and circling some untold grief as if to exorcise it.

Although Tudor had experimented with a new movement vocabulary before—*Atalanta of the East* featured Javanese motifs, *The Planets,* angular semaphores—here he made an even bolder entrance into the contemporary realm. Martha Graham herself would proclaim *Elegies* to be "the first ballet to invade modern dance."

This was a work that conjured mood just as strongly as *Jardin,* albeit a mood worlds away from that moonlit garden. It bypassed any particular narrative, having no plot, nor even much of a progression. Solos surround a pas de deux, while those who are not dancing quietly watch at the sidelines or intermingle. The singer sits onstage on a bench. The atmosphere is that of a contemplative ritual. Anything more ornate would contradict the score's simplicity.

Dark Elegies is the closest thing to an abstract ballet Tudor made, until years later with the 1975 *The Leaves Are Fading.* The decor, a lakeside setting that implies death by drowning, provides clues. Significantly, Tudor went beyond trying to mime Friedrich Rückert's lyric poetry—so gorgeously set by Mahler. His instinct to let the songs convey all feeling and make the choreography reflect the same chastened, noble sorrow could not have been sounder. Nor did he have it within him to vulgarize the music with hyperphysical movement. Rather, he strove for a universal message. But while Tudor's musical source was Germanic, the expressive mode seemed to be English. As de Mille wrote, "his native land was a point of view, not a place of birth."

Tudor was nothing if not an Ericksonian, that sort of self-actualized person whose creative force moves inexorably to gather and assimilate all in its wake. So for this ode to the communal sharing of grief he used fragments derived from tap dancing (but not specifically identifiable as such), Irish folk dance, accents from the German modern school of Mary Wigman and Kurt Jooss, oddly oblique balletic alignments. The gestalt—Mahler's unmuscled surrender to peace born of deep aching, Tudor's sublime expression of loss and supplication, and Benois's darkly simple outlines of a barren lakeside—conspired to put *Elegies* in a category all its own. As Fernau Hall observed, this work was to the London Ballet, which Tudor would soon found, what Chekhov's *The Three Sisters* was to the Moscow Art Theatre.

The ballet came more easily to Tudor than others did. Maude Lloyd remembered creating her pas de deux with him: "We went down to a small basement studio which had no mirror, where he couldn't even lift me without my knocking my head on the roof. It was written very quickly; he didn't alter anything." Without a mirror, they had no idea what it looked like. But when they returned to the main studio and performed it for designer Nadia Benois and Rambert the response was ecstasy. Benois decided instantly on the costumes: just what Lloyd was wearing—a black leotard and kerchief, to which she would add a peasant skirt. No further adornments. And Antony strictly forbade any makeup. Nor did he allow anyone "to pull faces or express emotion." The feeling was to be encoded in the movement. Simplicity would define grief.

No one in the cast—which also included Peggy van Praagh, Walter Gore and Hugh Laing, of course—ever heard from Antony an explanation of intent. The mood of the musical settings sufficed. Not even a translation from the German text was needed. But the rehearsals went at a hellish pace toward the end. On the afternoon of the premiere de Mille saw the whole thing assembled for the first time, with "the last five minutes unfinished. The fifth song was completed at eight o'clock in dressing gowns while the curtain was held and Mahler's publisher sat in the wings to see that the ballet met his official approval." Twenty minutes of work and Antony put the last touches to the scene that concluded with Hugh's solo. As Mahler biographer Deryck Cooke wrote, this "last song describes the storm that raged on the day of the funeral, the violent grief of the heart-broken father." Again, Antony's typecasting brought Hugh to the most explosive role in a ballet marked, paradoxically, by its outlawing of emotional explosion. It was Hugh who would rage against the enemy: a "howling gale" that took the children.

But that evening he had to appear first in another ballet. Afterward, while waiting for his entrance in *Dark Elegies,* he watched the Maude-Antony duet from the wings and became mesmerized. The upshot was that he forgot his solo. Having learned it so hastily and amid so much hysteria and without a rehearsal, this came as no surprise. Frantic, he ran around just before his entrance asking Maude and the others: "What do I do next? What do I do next?" Antony recalled that Hugh "became demented." He went on and simply improvised the steps he could not remember. When he found a familiar cue in the music, "he threw himself on the floor with such abandon that he practically broke his back. And he got the most marvelous reviews the next day. But, thinking he had ruined my ballet, he left the theater afterward and walked along the Embankment in a total depression. Actually, he had saved it, sort of."

So. Antony credited Hugh for rave notices even without being able to remember the solo. He could do no wrong. After all, he was the Guardian Angel. As for *Dark Elegies,* it proved the hit of the company's West End season that 1937—February 19—at the Duchess Theatre.

Indeed, of the dozen ballets presented that winter, five—including *Elegies*—were Tudor's. Clearly Rambert was dependent on his continuation at Ladbroke Road, even though she had a backlog of Ashton works and such new choreographers coming up through the ranks as Andrée Howard and Walter Gore. But bitterness had begun to roil between them and their battles grew increasingly nasty. His departure was inevitable.

He had been gearing for such a break over a period of at least two years. Although he said nothing, the idea became more potent with each victory, each gain in confidence.

And now Rambert provided him with the excuse.

He had a ballet in mind for the B-Club: a spoof on vainglorious ballerinas, complete with a title, *Gala Performance,* and music, selections by Prokofiev. Under normal circumstances he would simply have presented the idea to his boss. Instead "Antony brooded on it and brooded on it," recalled Kersley. "And then one day he screwed up his courage, got the records together and went in to see Mim. She nixed it—couldn't see its value—and afterward he was very low. I tried to joke him along but he wasn't even listening. Finally, he took the records, rather than filing them, and left. I do believe that's when his company began."

By this time "Jesus of British Grove" boasted disciples who would gladly leave the fold with him—regardless of his poor prospects. They put their faith in his genius. Confirmation came from the small but devoted throng of London literati that turned out for all Tudor performances. What better commodity for a fledgling troupe than a choreographer who appealed so to the arbiters of elite taste? So it was that Maude Lloyd, Peggy van Praagh, Hugh Stevenson, Therese Langfield Horner, Charlotte Bidmead and Margaret Braithwaite—as well as Hugh Laing, of course—gave notice to Rambert, and Antony, with Agnes de Mille as codirector, began operation of his Dance Theatre.

This partnership seemed an unlikely one. He hadn't much cared for de Mille's manner during *Elegies* rehearsals, having been accustomed to Maude, Peggy and Therese; they not only accepted him on faith but were attuned to his artistic sensibilities. Nor did he like her open doubts about how he could possibly carry on without counting beats—most choreographers teach their dancers the steps by counting out the music; neither Tudor nor Ashton resorted to this. And often when Aggie would press Hugh and Antony to rehearse something with her, they would hang back until she had exhausted her patience and would simply leave. One particularly hot Sunday at the British Grove headquarters, with no one in the group susceptible to her urgings, they all watched as she worked herself to a foam, exiting in a huff. "Now we can all breathe," Antony said to the others.

He did, however, regard her professionally with enormous respect; how he perceived her on an emotional level was entirely different. Apart from the solo he made for de Mille in *Elegies,* he cast her as an unattractive, grabby shrew/whore. In *Gallant Assembly,* a satiric romp in which a group of sophisticates tries to seduce an innocent young couple, she dances what *The Dancing Times*'s critic Lawrence Gowing described as "the part of an ineffectual old maid. . . . Her rapt obliviousness gives the impression of eccentricity and a habitually self-sufficient air; moreover, the movements suggest a spider's spinning and so the latent mood of cunning desire. Later she finds a man, tries her utmost to win him, and, repelled at last by the beauty who commands his affections, returns to her pathetic motif of rotating hands." Therese Langfield Horner, who later danced Agnes's role, remembered the piece for its "wonderful sense of Moliére, its aristocrats who hide, under their fastidious manners, the most lewd and depraved instincts."

The other role Tudor devised for de Mille would be that of a prostitute in *Judgment of Paris*. Based on the fable of the Trojan prince, Paris, it traces a mythical contest among Venus, Minerva and Juno. Tudor satirically retained the goddesses' names while personifying the three women as prostitutes. Weary and downtrodden, they compete for their prey, a drunken denizen of the café. The tinny, hard-hearted nihilism of Kurt Weill's music—excerpts from *Threepenny Opera*—complemented the tone of Tudor's seamy essay, and encouraged comparisons to a Toulouse-Lautrec cartoon or an acidic sketch à la George Grosz.

Unfortunately, the budget had to be short-term. Within a few months, though, he could count on other resources. It was 1937 and he had attracted the notice of two experimentalists in the infant field of television: Stephen Thomas and Willem Bate. "They were very advanced and rather intellectual," remembered Maude. "Both were great admirers of Tudor and they used to get us up there [at the BBC], doing pas de deux and little ballets very often. We became the king and queen of television for a few years. It kept us in bread and butter because they paid us properly. We got ten pounds for one performance and fifteen pounds when we repeated it in the evenings because there were no videos at that time."

The best known of these innovative works was his *Fugue for Four Cameras,* a solo for Maude that merged a quartet of views of her. The last staging Rambert managed to drag from Antony was the ten-minute *Suite of Airs,* which he originally did for television and supervised at the Mercury for its premiere there on May 16.

Hugh Laing, whose small fund from his family had been in place from the beginning, was able to add further to the household income by doing fashion illustrations for *The Sunday Times* of London. According to Kersley these drawings had "understandable value to the couture houses, being so attractive that heavy sales resulted from Hugh's persuasive pen."

The mood in British Grove was buoyant. Saddled no more with Rambert's restrictions and interventions, Antony and his disciples could race into new ventures without the furtive maneuvers so necessary before. And in reaction to the strictest standards of thrift that had been imposed under Mim—getting new pointe shoes and good costumes was a real departure from the norm—Tudor and de Mille flew out to buy relatively extravagant production materials for Dance Theatre. Silk tights were not the least of these heady purchases.

The company's inaugural performances, a week-long season at Oxford, took place in June. But in their zeal for freedom from Rambert and with a runaway sense of omnipotence, they gave scant thought to business strategies. The agenda featured Tudor's recognized masterpieces—*Jardin aux Lilas* and *Dark Elegies*—along with *The Descent of Hebe* and *Gallant Assembly,* the new ballet created for the engagement with designs by Stevenson. De Mille contributed her best concert pieces. In a rush of exhilaration they bought new scenery and costumes for the repertory works.

Because they plunged heedlessly into the contract, getting neither any kind of sponsorship nor box office guarantee—the worst of all scenarios came to pass. It was examination week at the university—which explained why the Playhouse Theatre had an opening, and why the students could hardly take note of anything extracurricular. As a result, the company played to a near-empty house every night.

One of the few opening night commuters from London was Rambert. Just as she perpetually rattled doorknobs and peered through windows to glimpse the creative surprises Tudor and his cohorts were hatching on her premises, she could not suppress her curiosity now. After all, Dance Theatre might very well end up as the competition. And if, by some fluke, it failed, then whatever haughty disdain she might feel on such a discovery would be well worth the trouble of a train ride. Surely the sea of empty theater seats gave her some satisfaction. Nor could she have been unhappy to report later to Agnes that the Tudor-de Mille experiment was "a very wasteful clashing of styles."

Rambert's verdict was at odds with that of *The Dancing Times*'s critic, Lawrence Gowing. His notice, which appeared July 1937, advised the public "not to dismiss Dance Theatre's debut as promising—English ballet has received too many blows from that polite blunt instrument." Rather, he let it be known that the Oxford season "has given a brilliant taste of what any who with-hold their support are likely to miss."

But there were difficulties ahead, not least with the partnership of Tudor and de Mille. Aching to escape Rambert all this time, Antony would not find it easy to work with another intense, willful, opinionated and challenging woman.

Financially, the Oxford season had been a flop, and as a test of temperamental compatibility it proved that Tudor and de Mille had no future together. So ended the brave, perhaps rash, experiment.

For the next year he had no platform for creating new ballets— other than a single commission from de Mille (*Judgment of Paris* for performances at the Westminster Theatre) and the television work. It was this that put food on the table and provided some small artistic satisfaction. De Mille speculated on "what those long months of hopeless idleness and neglect cost a man of his tornado ambitions."

But it's more likely that the fallout seeded Tudor's quick-to-thrive ambivalence and that the "tornado ambitions" were little more than de Mille's own projections. Dreams, yes. But he was not ever a man of "tornado" ambitions. No one with so many misgivings could be. At any rate, he had few prospects during those twelve months. Even the fairly steady flow of free-lance opera ballets and musicals fell out of the picture.

The one thing he knew with certainty was that he could not

go forward without funding. There could be no further enterprise without the rental fees for a theater, salaries for the dancers and a budget for production costs. Teaching ballet classes was hardly the answer; it brought a mere pittance. These were painful times. Painful in a different way from those he had known with Rambert. But, ultimately, he was not daunted. He would have his company. The moment would arrive.

Dogfights

FROM THE TIME HE WAS A TEENAGER Antony had learned the by-ways of reform education, England's attempt to bring parity to the underprivileged. At the City Literary Institute, a London County Council School that offered night classes, he polished his French and German. He may not have come by his cultural enlightenment via birthright as his betters had, but he didn't suffer ignorance as a result of "growing up within the sound of Bow Bells." Now, facing the enforced idleness (and penury) brought on by the failure of Dance Theatre, he found himself returning to the familiar institutions of adult learning.

One of them was Morley College, once a part of the Old Vic in the south of London near Westminster, another in Hampstead Gardens, the London suburb, and a third, Toynbee Hall, in the seamy section of Whitechapel. It was run as an Oxford Settlement by the university's recent graduates, who were bent on intro-ducing higher life to the lower orders; to this end they put heartfelt energy. There were lectures on everything from accounting to zoology, with generous samplings of drama and literature as well.

Shortly after the demise of his first company, Tudor got himself on the autumn syllabus to give ballet lectures at Morley College, which operated with many of the same guidelines as Toynbee. This had to be a novel experience—inasmuch as he was no longer William Cook, a soft-spoken cockney seeking to improve himself, but Antony Tudor, noted choreographer, addressing and instructing, rather than sitting among, the audience.

Making a mark in the world of ballet may have been his goal. But he must have secretly gloated over his transformation from student to teacher and how the latter suited him. Antony savored words and pithy phrases. He felt comfortable relying on them. What's more, he loved acting, which allowed him to take great enjoyment enunciating his newfound upper-class speech.

Little about ballet was known by the general public back in 1938; audiences for Tudor's lecture/demonstrations were comprised of neophytes who regarded this exotic performing art as something strange, possibly even associating it with a kind of intellectualism. He acknowledged none of this. And rather than boring his auditors with a history of the dance, he tried to bring living examples of how choreography and music relate to life experience, real or fancied. This same creative, rather than academic, approach characterized his teaching lifelong.

As he told a group of dance students many years later, "I used to have my audience write down a time of day, a situation, a locale—mountain, beach, city, street—a person. And then I would make up a dance from these clues. I might get a duck on a frozen pond in mid-July in New Zealand. And then invent something right there on the spot. Making dances is not a problem. Anyone can do it, at least on a primitive basis. But this set of twelve lectures was enormously popular, if I say so myself."

Another East End teaching prospect turned up at the rebuilt Toynbee Hall, which boasted a 400-seat theater. It didn't take him long to imagine how he could put it to use. With several important theatrical figures already on the Toynbee board, Tyrone Guthrie for one, the possibility of staging ballets there seemed good. Antony managed to get approval for a season of fortnightly performances at the theater, starting in December of 1938. It was now June. He rounded up his dancers and, adding Hugh's legacy from the Skinners to his own small savings, was able to put the brand-new London Ballet into operation.

This development was as important to Antony as it was to Hugh. The past year had been one that saw him "all but beating his head on the bricks of British Grove," wrote de Mille, noting that although Antony might not be publicly recognized as yet, he no doubt would be one day; "whereas nobody foretold very much for Hugh. He alternately raged and consoled." Without the stage, Hugh ceased to exist in a deeply satisfying way. No doubt he would gladly have gone into debt to finance Tudor's company. Now both of them had something tangible to foster.

But it was the worst of times for launching the London Ballet, with Adolf Hitler casting a shadow over Europe. "We were the mad English," explained Kersley. "Imagine putting up a company against the echo of gunshots." The piece of paper that Prime Minister Neville Chamberlain waved so cheerily before his countrymen on returning from Munich—his appeasement policy— was a meek symbol of bravado, only a stopgap measure. For any thinking person realized that time alone stood between peace and conflict. Indeed, the Germans were to march into Prague, Czechoslovakia's capital, six months after their madman of a leader promised not to do so. Chamberlain then guaranteed Poland's sovereignty, an even more impossible threat to back up, given England's meager resources.

It came as no surprise, then, that people were scattering by the last months of 1938. Aliens cleared out of England as the country prepared for war. None of that seemed to matter, however, to the new dance company as rehearsals for the December 5 debut got under way. A. V. Coton, the commentator-critic who volunteered to act as publicity/business manager for the fledgling troupe and thus had an inside view, described the atmosphere:

"Even when the Munich crisis filled everyone with terror and despair, the keynote of conversation amongst the dancers was not the gruesome possibility of air-raids but their concern that 'even if war came' the season would take place somehow, somewhere. Many of the dancers were working in films, cabaret, other ballet companies, so that rehearsals were intermittent affairs, mostly exhausting Saturday morning and Sunday all day sessions."

These were not the only hardships. Toynbee was a private theater, which meant that it had no ready audience because it offered no regular attractions. And because it was new, no administrative system had been put in place. As Coton reported, the company had to recruit "willing amateurs" to fill the jobs of lighting and scene changing, box office and clerical. "Neither Toynbee Hall nor Antony Tudor could have afforded to pay for the services of the twenty-odd persons necessary. No ballet company faced its last week of rehearsals with so many stones unturned, so many avenues unexplored."

What money they could lay their hands on went to sets, costumes and music parts. In addition were the theater rental and performance fees for dancers and musicians. As Coton observed:

The complexities were harassing. . . . Dancers cut meals and tore over to the other side of London between rehearsals in order to fit costumes. Painters worked furiously, silently, on the scene floor and suddenly stopped for lack of materials; then it would be found that no shop within miles could supply what was needed. The focal point towards which all activities converged was the theatre, but no private office or separate telephone existed in the theater for the exclusive use of the company.

Somehow the last nightmare week ended. Tudor's big following at the evening institutes where he taught and lectured, and the avant garde of keen ballet-goers, were all *au fait* with what was developing. At 8 P.M. that fifth day in the last month of 1938, every disengaged dancer in London, most of the musical and theatrical press, the gossip columnists, and what appeared to be about a thousand ardent ballet-goers filled the immaculate plush chairs or stood jammed in a tight phalanx at the back of the stalls. Ballet had come to the East End, not as an act of patronage to the East Enders, but for good practical reasons. . . .

The dancers were nervous but controlled. Backstage was seething with scene-shifters, assistant electricians, amateur dressers, friends. Disconsolate followers of the dancers, who had got hopelessly lost on the way, kept on arriving almost up to the final curtain.

There was no room anywhere in the theatre and they waited in a huddled knot peering through a small window in one of the wing doors which gave a view across part of the backcloth, on which now and then a leg in arabesque or a detached arm would be visible. Long after the last curtain, everyone stayed on discussing the performance, all dazed by the fact that such professional—in the best sense of the word—results had been achieved in this so unprofessional theatre.

Having spent the past fifteen months patiently and quietly waiting for this moment, Antony forged ahead on cue. For he had every reason to be confident that the effort would establish him, that he had the wherewithal to sustain his own company. Between the repertory he had amassed and dancers who could make artistic capital from it the only thing wanting was an on-going financial support system.

Still, he managed—not least because the sense of community and camaraderie reinforced his faith. Meanwhile there was sweet success to taste, even if he had to grudgingly relent on the designation, London Ballet. From his point of view such a name was presumptuous. After all, the great modern city of London comprised 4 million people, as of 1900; it was the biggest metropolis in the world and the first to develop in the industrial age. Who was he to appoint himself its ballet arbiter?

For the first bill Tudor programmed *Jardin aux Lilas* as the dramatic centerpiece, surrounding it with the premiere of *Gala Per-*

formance, his mocking account of rival ballerinas, *Judgment of Paris,* and *Gallant Assembly.* He always considered *Jardin* to be the most popular and admired of his works, rightly. The others, cast in all grades of satire, were the most recent. These, together with the best of his earlier ballets—*The Planets, The Descent of Hebe, Jardin* and *Dark Elegies,* would comprise the repertory base.

Jasper Howlett, writing in *The Dancing Times* and clearly indicating her preference for Ashton over Tudor, nevertheless gave the company its highest and most snobbish approbation: "Anyone who sees the London Ballet must wish it well. Its fortnightly programmes continue, and it is assuredly worth a visit to the wilds of Whitechapel, and that is saying a good deal."

She singled out *Gala Performance* (over *Jardin* and *Elegies*) for praise, arguing that "humor in dancing has proved, so far, the most successful medium of nationalistic expression . . . and that this entirely delightful ballet, in which the foibles of three rival ballerinas are wittily caricatured, gives ample scope for technical brilliance."

Maude Lloyd, Peggy van Praagh and Gerd Larsen portrayed the competitors. Lloyd was the Milanese ballerina, Larsen the *étoile* from the Paris Opera and van Praagh the Muscovite. Tudor and Laing were cavaliers. Hugh Stevenson, whose contract called for him to design all new productions for the company, created his most lavish decor in this assignment.

What Tudor strove for was hardly the kind of slapstick into which this sly and most subtly sardonic portrait has subsequently disintegrated. Originally, he wanted no caricature at all. The dancers were never told it would be funny or to expect laughs. They simply tried to do the difficult technique represented in each national style of ballet as best they could, emphasizing just a small gesture or two at the end. The self-indulgence and conceit of these stars was to project as a symptom of a very real tradition, not as a clown act. And the extravagant set and costumes that Tudor drew from Stevenson served a dramatic function, although, considering the ragtag budget, these took a severe and almost perverse toll on the finances.

Indeed, Rambert—eager to see how her protegé would fare, naturally was among the audience opening night—commented on the expense specifically. When the curtain opened on *Gala Performance,* the ballet she rejected for her own company, she was heard to exclaim, "Oh, it's far too overdressed."

There was nothing tentative in Tudor's approach. Here he was, the social critic, the outsider, staring hard at the mores of ballet society and the ridiculously exaggerated exponents of that society. As much as he adored the Russian Spessivtseva and the various exemplars representing the Italian school and the giddy French ingenues from the Paris Opera Ballet—which played London in 1934—he saw something to identify with and scorn in their licensed narcissism. But, more important, he saw something eminently mockable. And the diabolic wit with which he dispatched strangers was also on tap for those close to him. Nothing brought him greater pleasure than uncovering another's foibles. Or seeing that person publicly humiliated.

He referred to his sense of humor as "perverted," knowing that he did not find the things that other people laughed at funny. Yet his keen instinct for humor rarely failed him theatrically. He knew, for instance, that a bad performance of *Gala* could be likened to "a funeral service" because when "people think they are funny, they are not. Chaplin knew that." Humor is dead serious business, he was saying.

So as Tudor began work on *Gala Performance* he let certain images dominate the choreography. His trio of feminine "ideals" would be represented as national symbols. For La Reine de la Danse he envisioned "the towers of the Kremlin with an eagle emblazoned there and that famous Russian barbarity, which would take its form from the wildly extreme arms. Man eating."

His picture of La Déesse de la Danse came from the Forum and other Italian monuments. For her characterization he thought of "the grandeur and the fact that everything is immemorial. And when she slowly takes her arm up it's as though she can go on growing forever, 'til she's there and you know nothing can ever push her over. And she's cold. She's made of stone, rather." Whereas La Fille de Terpsichore came to exist as "only a frou-frou, petticoats." His emphasis on jumps, very much a trademark of the Parisians, sprang from the musical impulse, not a conscious element.

What *was* conscious, the powerful emblems of the Russian queen and the Italian goddess, shows Tudor's world as a ma-triarchy. The strong, controlling figures in his life were women. But it was time for him to break free of them, if he could. His triumph with the spunky London Ballet was a first step.

In short order, Tudor would leave. It was summer of 1939, the performances at Toynbee Hall drew to a close, and he took his little band of dancers off to Covent Garden under contract to do more opera ballets. Dancers, musicians—just some of the mad English—went about their business, oblivious to the RAF's prac-tice dogfights gleaming in the halcyon sky. Meanwhile Antony let Maude, Peggy and the others know very little about his plans for the fall, only that such plans did exist. What they couldn't guess were his negotiations with an Australian wool tycoon named Harold Van Thal Rubin, the new proprietor of the Arts Theatre Club. Throughout June and July he and Tudor had spent long sessions together reviewing every shilling spent on every production of the London Ballet, trying to forecast expenses for the company's upkeep.

A notice in *The Dancing Times* announced that the London Ballet would begin its autumn season on October 23, "with performances every Monday evening and probably a Saturday matinee once a month." It went on to say that "Walter Gore has joined the company as choreographer and will produce a work. . . . Antony Tudor himself plans to produce a new ballet early in the season, to Schoenberg's *Verklärte Nacht*."

At the same time an invitation to Antony from one Richard Pleasant arrived at British Grove, postmarked New York City. This was the second communication, the first having been re-ceived during the early part of the winter. Would he be interested in staging some of his works for a new American company that, as managing director, Pleasant was seeing to, one called Ballet Theatre?

Whatever way he might have handled the offer under normal circumstances can only be guessed. But when the rumblings of World War II finally erupted into a declaration on Sunday, September 3, all bets were off. The theaters shut down the following day. Any artistic enterprise in the near future was doomed. The Tudor-Rubin partnership faded to a far-off prospect, putting a different cast on the second inquiry from America.

Now it seemed more attractive. What matter that Ashton had been first choice and turned down the offer. Antony and Hugh were adventurers. They loved the idea of traveling to unknown places. This was a chance to cross the Atlantic, see New York, mount *Jardin aux Lilas,* and possibly *Gala Performance.* Peggy and Maude and Walter would be on hand for the London Ballet, just in case war was actually averted. Maybe it would be good to give up, temporarily, all the aggravation of running a company, pinching pennies, worrying about every last detail and instead enjoy the luxury of being a high-status import, just staging a ballet or two and possibly conquering a new world.

Tudor signed the contract with Ballet Theatre. The following week Therese and Peggy installed themselves at British Grove—to wash and iron Hugh's and Antony's clothes. There was no time to spare. With all the hatches being battened down only one more boat would ship out and they would have to be on it or forfeit the chance altogether. No one spoke of friendship and yet this intimate act said something. Nor was there mention of endings or new beginnings or even the war. As Therese said, "The talk was full of quips and jokes." On September 10, 1939, the SS *Washington* set sail from Southampton with its precious cargo: Antony, Hugh and Andrée Howard, another choreographer from Ballet Rambert. An era, perhaps the most creative era for Tudor, ended.

12

Tale of Two Cities

THE NOT-SO-CALM SEA on this soon-to-be prosperous voyage hardly foretold the schism to come between Tudor and his country. To leave England during wartime might have been an excusable breach of loyalty had he returned within a decent interval. But as this migration proved permanent—he and Hugh never took up residence again in Great Britain—it was impossible for Antony to eradicate the mark of a deserter.

Hugh, meanwhile, was happy for the opportunity to trade on his British identity in America. If he never returned to England there would be nothing lost. After all, Londoners saw him as a downgraded West Indian, a tag he preferred to escape. But to Americans, an English accent carried a certain cachet; it brought him the illusion of greater culture and education than he actually possessed.

For Antony, New York would be an exhilarating fresh start. The New York dance scene was almost on a par with London's.

In both cities the birth of ballet was a 1930s phenomenon. It came in the wake of Serge Diaghilev's Ballets Russes, the upstart prodigal that split off from the Imperial Ballet in St. Petersburg and splashed its way across a new frontier, far from the Maryinsky Theatre. The company made only a few token visits to U.S. shores, starting in 1916, while it played nearly two decades of regular Western European seasons.

But six years before its American debut, Otto Kahn, director of the Metropolitan Opera, saw the Ballets Russes in Paris and brought its star, Anna Pavlova, and her partner Mikhail Mordkin to New York for a month's engagement. Their Gotham debut took place following a scheduled performance of Massenet's *Werther* and went on into the early morning hours. It was an instant revelation. Pavlova turned out to be an extraordinary emissary; her calling card launched the Met in the ballet business.

The small ballet public got its early indoctrination piecemeal and not always with fully professional stagings. But just as had happened in London, audiences embraced this new-age ballet, defined by Michel Fokine via his *Scheherazade, Les Sylphides* and *Petrouchka*. The expansion went on with Nijinsky, when the Diaghilev company presented not only its legendary male dancer but his avant-garde choreography for *L'Après-Midi d'un Faune.*

He made a huge impact on American audiences, given his small number of performances. So did Pavlova, of course, traveling all around the country as an indefatigable pioneer.

New York held out a certain appeal to disaffected Russians. Adolph Bolm, who followed Diaghilev out of the Maryinsky Theatre and, after resigning from the Ballets Russes as premier dancer and choreographer also partnered Pavlova on her American tours, was one such. From among these primary creators in the New York community, however, emerged another Russian immigrant, Sol Hurok. In 1933, four years after the death of Diaghilev, came this powerhouse who would capitalize not only on his affinity for the performing arts but also twenty-five years' experience in taking America's cultural pulse. He was, in effect, an arts promoter. He made marketing history with his Barnum

& Bailey style and brought ballet to the masses. Using as publicity bait the three delectable, barely teenaged wonders known as his "baby ballerinas"—Irina Baronova, Tatiana Riabouchinska and Tamara Toumanova—he swept through the land with Colonel de Basil's Ballet Russe de Monte Carlo, a remnant of Diaghilev's company for which many of the same St. Petersburg expatriates, notably George Balanchine and Leonide Massine, now toiled.

While Hurok waged a campaign of unabashed sensationalisms and superlatives to promote his Russian import, Lincoln Kirstein, the Harvard-educated scion of a New England department-store family, had managed to lure Balanchine away from the Ballet Russe (after its second season the name changed to singular form). The tall, introverted, ungainly scholar who dubbed himself "a Renaissance man" had gone to Europe looking for ballet big game—a taste cultivated by his exposure to Nijinsky lore. Electrified by photographs and tales of the phenomenal dancer and transformed into an unremitting balletomane, Kirstein would not rest until he could set up his own lair.

He was of a certain ilk—wealthy, gentrified, Ivy League aesthetes fatally attracted to ballet and, specifically, its practitioners, who personified physical beauty and elegant exhibitionism. All that perfect musculature made up a visual feast whose allure was compounded by musical poetry and theatrical magic. Kirstein had much in common with Richard Pleasant, the Princeton architect and founding director of Ballet Theatre, who had sent out the call to Antony Tudor and others. And then there was Charles Payne, a Yale lawyer who functioned as the troupe's executive manager and later its archivist.

These men were not exactly hands-on impresarios like Diaghilev, but they had a positively born-again fervor for ballet. They were powerful voyeurs, informed fans, even brilliant commentators. Yes, they wanted to see their chosen performing art flourish. More than that, they wanted to come as close to possessing it as possible. But they bore little resemblance to their European predecessors, Diaghilev, Ninette de Valois and Marie Rambert, who grew up inside the dance world. These men, after being smitten at a later age but in much the same way as Tudor and Ashton had been—as spectators in the audience—never strained at the barre; they contented themselves with gripping the armrests of their theater seats and, beyond that, acting as benevolent eminences and administrators.

Kirstein would come to champion a single hero—George Balanchine, a sophisticate with grace and panache in addition to his exceptional gifts as a choreographer. Around him Kirstein would build and help fund the American Ballet, which next bore the title Ballet Society and finally became the New York City Ballet. But Pleasant's aesthetic was comprehensive. It embraced not just the Russian classics—*Swan Lake* and other tutu ballets—but the post–Imperial genre, of which Fokine was the major exponent, as well as the emerging native variety of choreography and the English, courtesy of Tudor and Andrée Howard.

Pleasant had abandoned architecture for lack of prospects in post–Depression 1932 and began representing Hollywood artists. Then came an invitation that would change his life: Mikhail Mordkin—now in the throes of expanding a school-and-recital enterprise as administered by Rudolf Orthwine, a businessman who saw his rightful place in the theater—asked him to come to New York and manage the school-turned-company. Pleasant agreed. One of its advanced students was Lucia Chase and by 1937, the year the Mordkin Ballet was established, this wealthy, young New England widow was bankrolling the venture as well as dancing principal roles.

A year later Orthwine and Pleasant realized that it was time to lay down more professional designs. They took the next step, after staging the quintessential romantic classic *Giselle* and Mordkin's sprightly *La Fille mal Gardée,* and formed a new organization called Ballet Theatre. Pleasant was named managing director and Orthwine president. This new company could no longer reflect the name of a single person, certainly not Mordkin's. True, he had been a star at the Bolshoi and briefly danced with the Diaghilev company. But he wasn't their man.

Maria Karnilova, a dancer who later went on to Broadway

fame, was on hand for the transformation of the Mordkin Ballet to Ballet Theatre (later called American Ballet Theatre). "Lucia paid for everything," recalled Karnilova, whose Russian parentage put her on the inside language track with Mordkin. "Even when it was just a school and the performances were not altogether professional, he used to flatter Lucia and promise her every opportunity. 'If you pay for my school I'll make you a ballerina,' he said. 'You'll get to dance *Giselle.*' "

But Chase preferred to throw in her considerable chips for a grand venture, forfeiting her leading roles in the process. She and Pleasant realized that Mordkin was not essential to their ambitions for a company, one on a par with the Ballet Russe. So they wrested from him what remaining control he had. With Pleasant's brains and Chase's money and a strategy for amassing an eclectic repertory—Russian, English, American—they hardly needed Mordkin. By then he was no longer young enough to dance, his choreography was unremarkable and there were no other assets he could claim, apart from his excellence as a ballet master. He certainly lacked the authority, in their minds, to lead Ballet Theatre.

"I felt sorry for him," said Karnilova, remembering "how badly they treated him. But he never protested. He used to bring a little windup Mickey Mouse to class and shoot it with a toy gun he would pull out. 'Gangsters, gangsters,' he hollered. Everyone thought him mad, but not so. This was his way of telling us they were all gangsters robbing him.

"It was a sleazy thing to do, squeeze Mordkin out. After all, he was from the same, illustrious era of Fokine. Possibly, Fokine had something to do with it." But Karnilova, who was among the dancers for Ballet Theatre's inaugural season, thought Pleasant's plans were "brilliant." It was his idea, she said, to collect as many well-known choreographers and dancers as possible, forging from these an American tradition as well as showcasing the preeminent Franco-Russian style that Diaghilev had popularized and including the Anglo-Diaghilev connection. Prominent among that wing was Frederick Ashton.

But the successful British dance-maker had already visited New York in 1933, when commissioned to choreograph the Virgil Thomson/Gertrude Stein *Four Saints in Three Acts,* a modern *opera buffa*. At that time he explored possibilities and said he "had many offers to stay and work in America." Ashton even recalled that he met with dance critic John Martin and asked for advice. "He told me not to stay here. That this country was occupied with Martha Graham and her brand of barefoot dance. That the public would not be interested in what I had to offer.

"Some years later I met Lucia Chase. But I didn't take to her as a person. In retrospect, it occurred to me that she had no vision like Ninette, that she was always looking for a flash in the pan and wanted success above all else. Meanwhile I had the Royal Ballet, which could absorb my failures. Not so at Ballet Theatre. There was no infrastructure. If you were out of sight as a choreographer, you were out of mind."

Ashton had good instincts for survival.

Meanwhile Agnes de Mille, who had returned to New York at the first hint of war and was a recognized figure at home, consoled Pleasant with word about one Antony Tudor. No one had heard of him, but Agnes persuaded the director that her recommendation was one that would put the new company far beyond the place Ashton might take it. Many years later, however, she remembered a remark made by "a boy at the Ballet Club" who disagreed with her. "Antony won't last six months," had been the dancer's far-from-prescient words.

Tudor's arrival in New York was a thrilling moment for him. The last theater in which he had staged his ballets (excluding the opera ballets at Covent Garden) was Toynbee Hall, the little 400-seat community center, far from the glittery sophistication of the West End. Now he was preparing to put three of his major ballets onto Radio City Music Hall's glamorous Center Theatre stage in a house with 3,500 seats. An intrepid publicity campaign preceding the company's debut hailed it as "The greatest collaboration in ballet history."

There were to be eleven choreographers, including Michel

Fokine, who would come out of retirement to supervise revivals of his own works, eighty-five dancers, twenty-one ballets, among them six world and five American premieres. A souvenir program touted the company as standing for "the best that is traditional, the best that is contemporary and, inevitably, the best that is controversial." The prevailing attitude was to spare no expense and worry about the future later.

This would be an assemblage of stellar figures. If the object was big-scale ballet, which had never been locally produced before except as ad hoc stagings here and there, then Pleasant, Chase and Orthwine were out to do it. Dance historian Selma Jeanne Cohen extolled the company as "a full-fledged organization, recovering the past with reverence and laying a groundwork for the future with courage. It was big enough to encompass the Russian greats and democratic enough to let a coryphée from the Bronx reach for stardom."

For Tudor the undertaking was on a par with the Diaghilev seasons that had so enthralled him. And now he was being given equal status with Fokine, the choreographer who had inspired a wide-eyed William Cook to cast his lot with the dance-making profession.

It was Fokine's *Les Sylphides* that had awakened in Antony the intuition of ballet as something other than stylized decorativeness in motion. He saw that a choreographer could be a poet, one who created mood from movement and music, one who delved into the particulars of emotion. It was hard to believe that he would be giving company classes, along with Fokine and Anton Dolin and Adolph Bolm and Eugene Loring (the only American among them). Curiously, he had caught up with his hero. As Tudor was always quick to notice, time and progress, or lack thereof, had a way of closing gaps between people. The hierarchy changed and thus the relationships altered.

He and Hugh settled into rooms at the Windsor Hotel on West Fifty-eighth Street. Apart from Andrée Howard, Dolin and Markova, they knew no one, but the Windsor was home away from home to many Brits. The days of Antony's coterie were over for now. But with the bustle and excitement of preparing Ballet Theatre's inaugural season his temporary disorientation seemed unimportant. He was, after all, in the cultural capital of North America.

When Lucia Chase called the dancers together for the first time she wanted to impress on them what was in store. "Several famous choreographers and dancers from England have been engaged," she said. They recognized the names Dolin and Markova, but not Tudor, Laing or Andrée Howard. Nevertheless, it was taken on faith that all were equally famous. From this moment Antony ceased to be simply a peer. Those who accompanied him from London would continue to address him by his first name, of course. But to the American dancers he was "Mr. Tudor."

Miriam Golden remembered "the strangeness of those first rehearsals and classes" with the famous foreigners. "We were in awe," she says. "They looked at us and we looked at them. There was no familiarity. They were trying to assess us. We were trying to impress them. But we were scared because we knew these classes with Fokine and Dolin and Tudor and Loring were like auditions and we wanted to be chosen for their ballets."

It didn't take long for Tudor to establish the same kind of cult following among American dancers as he did among the English. On January 15 the company gave its premiere of *Jardin aux Lilas*. Again, he treated his cast to Stanislavsky "method" aids—spraying lilac scent around the stage to give the dancers a sensual whiff of the still, night air, as heavy with stifled yearnings and furtive encounters as with floral fragrance.

But this time Tudor had to enlarge the cast in order to accommodate the relatively huge dimensions of the Center Theatre stage, and he accomplished this without destroying the work's intimacy or focus.

The audience went wild at the premiere. Primed by its exposure to Martha Graham and the high-minded seriousness of modern dance and somewhat weary, even then, of the Russian glitz being spread in the name of ballet, these enlightened New

Yorkers took the full measure of *Jardin*. So did the critics. Of its American premiere *The New York Times*'s John Martin wrote: "With sure and simple strokes his choreography projects haste in leisure, turbulence in ordered calm, mute desperation and constraint. . . . Tudor belongs to the extremely small fellowship of choreographers who can take hold of the academic tradition and bend it to their uses instead of being taken hold of by it and bent to its uses."

Here was a work that honored the title Ballet Theatre, indeed, defined it. Here was an example of classic dance that, instead of pandering to spectacle, took a progressive approach—appealing to the head and the heart as profoundly and originally as the other, more respected art forms. As *The New York Times*'s Clive Barnes would later write: "The man, the time and the place came together like an explosion."

But there was an irony here. No matter the acclaim for Tudor, Ballet Theatre fostered eclecticism above all else. So the choreographer, who, for personal reasons, needed a director's undivided attention, was not to find it. Only Balanchine and Ashton, in their respective patron saints Kirstein and de Valois, would bask in such beneficence.

Swanning Around

THE PAST WAS PROLOGUE as far as relationships went—this prince across the waters would follow two parallel courses simultaneously. One involved the dancers, starry-eyed ingenues with whom he had his way, and the other involved the strong, dominant women who always seemed to be.challenging his authority.

Starting with the American premiere of *Judgment of Paris,* January 22 of that inaugural 1940 season, Tudor clearly pegged Lucia Chase as a replacement for Marie Rambert—awarding her one of the prostitute roles. And once again he could cast his friendly enemy Agnes de Mille, commissioner of this piece whose scenario Hugh had supplied. For Antony and Hugh, de Mille epitomized the manipulative woman. This was her ballet. But it could also stand for Rambert and Margaret Craske, their first teachers and sponsors—women who, like de Mille and Chase, took a contentious stance, women they contemptuously ridiculed.

Antony's role here (as before) was the victim/customer—neither the antagonist nor the kindly sage. Conversely, Hugh was cast as the nefarious figure, the whores' accomplice/bartender, pitting himself against Antony—even robbing him, in effect raping him.

Tudor's description of the scene tells perhaps too much about his feelings for the new impresaria: "I get drunker and drunker until I'm almost reeling. And then when she [Chase] gets up to dance I say, 'Take her away.' But she keeps coming to my table and looking at me. And each time I get a wave of disgust. I wish she'd sit down where she belongs. But she comes again. . . . The trouble is she had to make enough money that evening 'cause her mother hadn't eaten a crust of bread in weeks and she had to try and get a penny from somewhere. She didn't get it out of me."

When it came to the underlings, those who bowed down before him, Tudor hardly softened. They were prepared to meet whatever demands he might make. Why? Because in the three months of rehearsals he had inspired them so—with his ballets, with his classes and rehearsals. Muriel Bentley remembered her first impression. "We were watching him demonstrate the Russian ballerina in *Gala*. He walked on, doing her entrance. His back was facing us. We saw only his back. But he said more with his back than most dancers do with their faces. It was just one little passage but all her arrogance and flashiness was there."

His reputation within the company grew practically overnight. As a result dancers went to great lengths trying to get into his classes or anywhere close to him. This supply-and-demand ratio worked to his advantage. Leo Kersley reported, from a visit, that Tudor "was a different sort of bird in America, one given to swanning around. But, then, that was the role foisted on him." The truth is he loved being sought after and delighted in making his club an exclusive one. Those who weren't cast in his ballets did not give up usually, but tried sneaking into rehearsals. Jerome Robbins remembers "hanging around on the off chance of getting into a Tudor ballet," which he finally did.

"*Mister* Tudor" was the mode of address—partly because he was so sharp-tongued, quietly flinging his brilliant insults, and partly because he was so formidably English and held himself in so inaccessible a way, and partly because the dancers were just plain awestruck. It was also "Mr. Fokine," in deference to his age and fame. Only later, as the first generation of Ballet Theatre dancers moved with Tudor through the decade, did they drop the "Mister"—those who were on familiar enough terms.

In England it was Antony and Hugh, spoken as though a hyphenate. Privately they sometimes called each other "Bugs." Tudor often referred to himself and Hugh as "Darby and Joan," typifying a cozy English couple of old marrieds. Where one went, so did the other. Nothing changed in New York, except that the hyphenate became "Tudor and Hugh"—as if to denote importance for one and mere dancer status for the other. But if dancers were and are called by their first names partly because they remain identified as youthful, rather than fully mature, then Hugh certainly offered no contradiction in terms. He held on to his petulance. Childish behavior had always served him well. In fact, his tendency to fly into tantrums at Ballet Theatre was as great as at the Ballet Club and over the years he would even lash out physically at the meek and defenseless.

Tudor always could exercise control, though, and predictably capitalized on the unimagined power of this new situation. At thirty-two, he could use age to bolster his authority—most dancers were at least ten years younger than that, with many still in their late teens.

Hardly anyone from England spoke of Tudor as downright cruel. That adjective came into use starting in 1940. Just as Rambert inflicted harsh criticism on her charges, so had he earned the right to abuse his dancers—with the difference being that her deprecations were random and not meant to hurt. His were the opposite. Rambert had learned her ways from none other than Enrico Cecchetti. She had seen the famous teacher and coach of Nijinsky stand in the wings and watch his protegé, waiting to hurl the most castigating remarks at the phenomenal dancer as he dashed offstage. "Imbecile," the Italian maestro would shout at the sweating, breath-gulping Nijinsky, who was Rambert's idol. "What a disgraceful performance."

Tudor got the point, all too aptly. But he was never one to mimic another's style. Nor did he when it came to mortifying dancer-underlings. With him it was usually an attack targeted to cause the most deeply personal humiliation. Generalizations would not do. He was a master surgeon capable of pinpointing the vulnerable spot with deadly aim. After all, he had much practice at this sort of thing with Hugh. Between the two of them the game was perfected to patent.

There were indeed vital issues in the relationship that many saw as pathologic. Hugh wanted his own importance. But how to get it? Although he was a magnetic presence onstage and devastatingly handsome and witty, on provocation, and the possessor of faultless taste—as his designs and drawings attested to —he could not forge a separate identity nor establish himself as a primary creator. Tudor wrote the ballets. Tudor was the revolutionary, the trailblazer. Hugh was a vehicle, and not even the featured vehicle. That category was reserved for such women protagonists as Caroline and later, Hagar. (Only three ballets— *Undertow*, *Shadowplay* and *Knight Errant*—featured a pivotal male.)

The nexus between Hugh and Tudor—often a desparate and destructive one, but also the source of creative energy—was not unlike that of an angry child to an abused parent. The child resents his dependence and behaves badly toward the parent. The parent is rendered impotent, sometimes by way of guilt. Not surprisingly, rehearsals were rife with conflict between this parent and child. The issue was authority. Starting with *Jardin* the dancers who were to buy into the tempest knew, however, that the rewards were worth the incidental damage.

"Maude did it this way," argued Tudor. "No, you don't remember anything," answered Hugh. "She did it this way." For Hugh these squalls had a high value. They called into question Tudor's sovereignty. After all, he was the choreographer. And they humiliated him as well. He had no desire to air his relationship with Hugh in a public arena, although the intensity was such that he temporarily lost awareness of the others. As private as Tudor was he had no choice but to be dragged before the world by his partner. Often as not, however, Hugh would become exasperated and go into a snit, while Tudor would sit quietly, even enjoying the explosion, for as long as it took to subside.

Hugh's shouting and pouting came as a shock to the unindoctrinated. When it was not a disagreement over how a dance phrase went, the problem usually involved a step he was having difficulty with—and his difficulties in the technique department were not inconsiderable. Sometimes Tudor would try, calmly and patiently, to ease the frustration. "Put the foot down in fifth position, yah?" And sometimes it worked.

Hugh's assaults on Tudor were unsettling. But with the two of them locked together, the dancers could retreat to their safety zone. Otherwise there was no haven in class. "Why are you doing this *battement tendu?*" he would ask some innocent. Or, before the whole cast: "Who are you supposed to be in this ballet?" The answers were not just for his ears. Intimidation was compounded by the embarrassment of a public hearing. And if the answer did not pinpoint the deeply personal one he wanted, the inquisitor kept up his interrogation until he got satisfaction, even stooping to personal attacks. Suffering Hugh's rage, he would often inflict pain on others—a kind of scapegoating.

But there were several varieties to his brand of rehearsal sport. Sometimes, for instance, he deliberately incited Hugh. Having become expert at sensing precisely the vulnerability of the moment, he would find the flaw and then brandish it on the tip of his rapier for all to witness. Doing this put him in control. It made Hugh a tantrum puppet.

"When this sort of thing happened," according to David Nillo, who joined Ballet Theatre two months before the opening, "Tudor would smile and smirk with pleasure. It was pretty hideous. He loved playing on people's weaknesses, even Hugh's. I came

to class, Tudor saw me and invited me to the *Jardin* rehearsal. I
had never seen anything like it. He was always picking his nails,
looking about and then tearing people apart. He gave me the
second lead after Hugh. He kept stressing how important this
ballet was and told us that we must not reveal anything about it
to outsiders. Yet there was none of that secrecy with the others—
Mordkin, de Mille, Fokine, Loring. Only with Tudor. He per-
petuated a cultlike atmosphere. And it seemed so strange to me.
Here were these two (Tudor and Laing) from a little *schmeierei*
theater in London. No one had even heard of them before."

Nillo—along with Hugh, Donald Saddler, Annabelle Lyon,
Miriam Golden and Nora Kaye (then still named Koreff)—took
class daily with Tudor and continued on contract following the
Centre Theatre three-week run, which ended in February. They
were considered "the Tudor dancers," the handpicked group he
would work with on future ballets. But Nillo did not last. One
of the ballets on the opening agenda was Fokine's delicate mood
work, *Carnaval,* originally danced by Karsavina and Nijinsky.
Now Fokine was restaging the famous ballet and awarded the
secondary but still precious role of Florestan to Hugh. He danced
the Ballet Theatre premiere. Then Fokine decided to try Nillo
out and Hugh flew into a rage.

From that moment, Tudor was finished with Nillo. *Jardin*
would remain his only assignment in a Tudor ballet. He was also
taken off as understudy in *Dark Elegies.* Apparently, no matter
the sadomasochistic nature of Hugh's and Tudor's relationship,
their loyalty to each other was unassailable. To cross Hugh was
to hopelessly alienate Tudor. "Your mother, drunk or sober,"
quoted Leo Kersley, characterizing their mutual allegiance.

On top of Hugh's resentment over losing the *Carnaval* role,
Nillo posed a threat for other reasons. He was almost handsome
enough to compete with Hugh. He was technically superior to
Hugh. And he did not take the apostle's vows. As much as he
valued Tudor—calling him "the playwright of ballet"—his skepticism and independent spirit kept him on the sidelines.

Not only that, Nillo recounted how he stayed at arm's length of Tudor, "who often asked me to dinner and up to the Windsor. We were always in a group after rehearsals. Once, on one of these evenings, he wanted me to stay overnight but I told him my sister was waiting up and expecting me. I think he felt rejected. No matter what the bond between Tudor and Hugh, they also had a very active sex life independent of each other. There was all the usual nighttime carousing—meeting in bars and partying—but never any hint of it at the studio." One of Tudor's passing fancies, photographer Dwight Godwin, inscribed on the back of his photo portrait of the choreographer: "Antony Tudor—also a lover, but just a one-night stand."

However, discretion was the byword. What Hugh flaunted—with his headlong entrances and exits, his rush of energy and high-pitched palaver—was a generalized sexuality, nothing that spelled out his preference. He reveled in stagey flirtations with women, although Nillo says the public display was only a ploy, one that contrasted with a more typically liberated, unapologetic attitude at Ballet Theatre. Dolin, for instance, never felt a need to be secretive. Just the opposite. He was entirely candid about his many affairs with men. "But Hugh and Tudor did keep it all under wraps," according to principal dancer Leon Danelian. "Their secrecy was surprising when you considered that they performed in England for members of the Bloomsbury circle and even rubbed shoulders with these intellectual libertarians."

For all their exposure to London's artistic elite, they were bound by a middle-class morality, which took its toll. Hugh, in addition to worrying lest anyone find out he was uneducated and a West Indian to boot, apparently needed to project a more or less heterosexual image. Tudor, who, it was said, could never forget that his father was a butcher, also seemed to absorb a certain guilt for seducing Hugh. This baggage proved backbreaking for both, often tying them together in less than wholesome ways.

14

●

Troop Buildup

BALLET THEATRE BEGAN with rapturous acclaim. *The New York Times*'s John Martin hailed the inaugural season as "the beginning of a new era." For three weeks the company played to sold-out houses, with hundreds of standees at each performance and delirious audiences clamoring for more. But because of their inexperience Orthwine, Pleasant and Chase had not anticipated a second move. They invested heavily in a season that could have run on and on but hardly lasted a month because of their limited theater contract. With the repertory in place and fully rehearsed there were no openings—anywhere in New York—beyond the dates reserved. On February 4, Walt Disney's *Pinocchio* moved into the Center Theatre.

For the same outlay of expense and preparation the company should have had the option to realize more value from its initial overhead. But contingency plans were simply overlooked and now with advance bookings eliminating the possibility of a tour—all appropriate theaters were already committed—there was nothing to do except hang on until the next season.

At this point Tudor could, with almost no backward glance, have returned to England. Harold Rubin, the would-be financier for London Ballet, was standing, checkbook in hand. The "phoney war," as Londoners had dubbed it, was in progress. In other words, normal activities had not yet come to an end. Maude Lloyd and Peggy van Praagh were carrying on without their leader, anticipating that he would be home soon.

All that Pleasant and company could promise until the fall was an occasional engagement at nearby summertime spas such as New York's Lewisohn Stadium and Philadelphia's Robin Hood Dell. These and a few others came to a scant dozen. Still, the desire to keep the troupe together was strong. A bright future beckoned. And Tudor, having sensed his new power and unblighted prospects, had little inclination to turn tail. Nor did Hugh need convincing that New York was a wonderful town.

So they stayed. Ballet Theatre set up headquarters in the A. C. Blumenthal mansion on Fifty-fourth Street at Sixth Avenue. The company would continue there for the next few months, taking class and rehearsing. By November, when Pleasant decided to reorder things so that there would be three different repertory wings, Tudor found that his hunch was correct: he would figure even more importantly in this providential enterprise than was originally planned. He was named regisseur, or director, of the New English division. Loring would head the Americana department, nurturing other works in his *Billy the Kid* mode, and Dolin would supervise the white tutu ballets lumped together under the heading "classical."

Prior to this next New York season, slated at the Majestic Theatre, the company took up residence with the Chicago Civic Opera, where Tudor again put his hand to choreographing opera ballets. By now he had become familiar with the dancers and invited a few more into his fold. It wasn't for nothing that he made wry observations about this one and that one in daily class.

He poked. He prodded. He wanted to know what lay hidden.

And he boasted a whole repertoire of sexual word games. One was the double entendre. When Miriam Golden asked him how "he thought up his ingenious lifts," he answered, "I always figure them out in bed." This reply intrigued her, for although it was *Elegies* in which he partnered her and performed those lifts, he wouldn't miss the chance to allude to sex. Tudor, the verbal, vicarious voyeur.

He sniffed out all manner of things. Fear, for instance, had a very strong scent for him. He knew who was bold or sensual, and by this acuity, found his Other Woman (or Episode in His Past) for *Jardin*. As a result, his casting experiments were, not surprisingly, astute. They yielded high rewards—beginning with the Cuban ballerina Alicia Alonso, who eagerly joined the circle, and Maria Karnilova, who would dance in *Judgment of Paris*.

He seemed to get as much sadistic satisfaction from initiating dancers into his mysterious and hieratic ways as legitimate pleasure from the moving performances they ultimately gave. Indeed, he savored his power. Look how alert the dancers became, sometimes just to avoid handing him an opening to one of his devastating remarks.

It was the essential intimacy of these encounters that he valued. When a dancer cried in hurt or humiliation Tudor took it to mean that he had gotten close to the person. And there was a certain pride in this accomplishment—the pride of having deepened for performance that one's understanding and conviction, but also the pride in his skill at manipulating the person. The little boy holding a fly by its wings and watching the thing try to squirm away.

Alonso remembered how, while rehearsing *Gala Performance,* which was to have its American premiere in February, he began mocking her. " 'Oh, this excitable, temperamental Cuban,' he said to me. 'Very savage, very primitive. You should try to be more educated.' He knew somehow that this attack would hurt me more than anything, that I was sensitive to not speaking

English well, and not having more schooling. I just looked and looked at him. Finally, he asked when I was going to start crying. I answered, never. And I kept my promise."

But that was hardly the essence of what Alonso learned from Tudor. At their first rehearsal, he walked over to her and asked, "How do you say hello to someone you like very much?" She made a movement with her upper torso and hands and then he told her to do the same thing in *demi-plié* and *arabesque,* turning her head to the side. "It was lovely," she recalled. "It was real. It meant something very special. It told the difference between Tudor and other choreographers. They think of steps as primary. He thinks of feelings as primary. His steps grow out of the feelings. Theirs just tack them on as decoration. Fokine was the only one besides him who could really get into character when showing a dancer her role."

Tudor loved Alonso's superb technique. He loved her spirit— that combination of vulnerability and defiance. He loved her depth and womanly passion. But he had to temper her natural expressiveness. She was accustomed to showing everything on her face. He believed that such grafted-on emoting was cheap and vulgar, that the most profound function in dance required that the movement itself characterize the affect. They compromised.

Later, she inherited the role of the Italian ballerina in *Gala Performance.* Back then the portrayals were straight, no mugging or exaggeration allowed. "Tudor was my cavalier and I remember, it was my first performance, he started teasing me onstage during our pas de deux. Exasperated, I slapped him on the spot. But with an absolutely calm exterior. All the burning stayed inside. Afterward he said, 'Oh, that was very good.' It stayed as part of the choreography."

It was easy for him to act out the roles in his ballets. He could get quite drawn into perfecting and deepening some point or other with the dancer rehearsing opposite him. But Hugh, high-strung and ambitious, always acted as a spur, trying to whip his mentor along more quickly. "Ant'ny, finish it, finish it," he would say. His involvement was nearly as intense as Tudor's, but he positioned himself as Guardian Angel at those times when Antony needed help—steering him forward or toward a break from a hopelessly blocked rehearsal.

As partners, they shared an equal stake in the creative result. And the truth is that Hugh's performances in ballets other than Tudor's hardly made a comparable impact. But throughout his two decades onstage and since, no one, according to consensus, has ever matched his theatrical splendor in the Tudor ballets. There are those like Leon Danelian, however, who said that "nothing attests to Tudor's brilliance more than his ability to choreograph around Hugh's deficiencies."

It was through these deficiencies, of course, that Hugh experienced his own vulnerability. Danelian said he "was shocked at the sight. . . . Here was someone touted as a premier dancer. Yet he had no elevation, no pirouettes, no *plié* and could rise only to half-pointe. He was brittle. But he was magnificent onstage. He understood the intent of every gesture and could magnify it so that audiences sitting high in the galleries got the full power. And he made a fuss about everything offstage, too. Star billing, dressing rooms. In whatever way he could call attention to himself."

When the Majestic season ended in March, Tudor knew that the best of his London ballets was being entrusted justifiably to a new order. These Americans were both plucky and sensitive. Despite the fear he invoked in them they delivered the goods. So far, though, he had created nothing of importance in his adopted country. And the next step Ballet Theatre would take —a change in administration—nearly dashed his prospects for doing so. In the spring of 1941, Richard Pleasant, finding fault with a budget that would not support the standards he insisted on, walked out. Inasmuch as those standards seemed fiscally impractical to Chase and Orthwine, no one stopped him. But his departure left the company without a strong artistic arbiter, a situation that would profoundly affect Tudor, in particular.

Into the breach came none other than Sol Hurok, for whom

ballet was synonymous with Russian—as in Ballets Russes, the original, or Ballet Russe de Monte Carlo, the successor. After all, he had sponsored both companies. A shrewd marketeer, he wasn't one to tamper with a product's identity. Hurok would do the booking and publicity for Ballet Theatre's third season in New York and its first tour. German Sevastianov, his aide-de-camp, would perform the duties of managing director.

In a way Lucia Chase was relieved to have such authoritative men take over. Now she could concentrate on dancing and leave office concerns to others. Furthermore, she always did choose to be a closet sponsor, preferring no one to know that she wrote the checks that sustained the company—over her lifetime she sank more than $40 million into its upkeep. She who controls the coffers, however, gets to make the important decisions. And Tudor, for one, could be grateful for this, since Hurok and especially Sevastianov were not exactly his allies. Hurok saw success as spectacle and ballet as a glitzy, aerial art that couldn't accommodate the relatively arcane explorations of dance drama, à la Tudor.

Sevastianov had an even more specific aversion to ballet as a twentieth-century phenomenon taking place outside Russia. He would put an end to the company's Anglo-Saxon stronghold, its English-American predominance. Besides, his wife was Irina Baronova, one of the baby ballerinas, and she had a natural predisposition to the quaint, decorative superficialities that characterized the Ballet Russe de Monte Carlo. Things would definitely be changing.

The posters advertised "The greatest in Russian Ballet by Ballet Theatre." A full-scale Russification had been accomplished by the time the company opened its 1941 fall engagement in Mexico City, followed by a month-long stand at the Forty-fourth Street Theatre in New York and then a tour of the Northeast, Middle West and Canada.

Tudor—ever astute to the atmosphere, if not inclined one bit to ingratiate himself with the new policy*meisters*—was not deterred from his major opus, a ballet set to *Verklärte Nacht*. He had completed half of it already. But after Sevastianov's arrival all his scheduled rehearsals were taken away. Knowing that in Pleasant he had a guardian of sorts, he proposed the work and secured a verbal promise that it would not go by the boards in the next regime.

Meanwhile personnel went through an upheaval. Sevastianov saw to it that dancers who were formerly principals would now be demoted to soloists. He cast a jaundiced eye on the likes of Miriam Golden, Nora Kaye, Muriel Bentley, David Nillo and more—most of them Jews—and brought in dancers, along with Baronova, from the Ballet Russe. It was said that he was anti-American, anti-Jewish, and anti-Tudor. Indeed, under his administration Tudor's salary, not to mention his status, went down by $50 a week—a sizable sum then.

Mutterings of discontent aside, the personnel had plenty to be occupied with. There was the three-month tour, for one thing. It established a modus operandi that would be synonymous with the company to its present day. Luckily this 1941 expedition, the first time out for Ballet Theatre, did not typify life on the road for its ballet gypsies.

The war was on and American troop buildup in full progress. So as the company made its way through roughly fifty one-night stands, trains commonly stopped to pick up soldiers en route to bases. When the cars overflowed, the armed troops took priority over the ballet troupes. Sometimes, that meant being rudely bumped from a train in the middle of nowhere. Even without the wartime expediency, though, this kind of fatiguing travel-performance schedule amounted to hardship.

But it did foster the kind of closeness Tudor thrived on. While he never freely talked about himself or revealed anything personal he loved the sense of community that came from being thrown together this way. What's more, he was used to the put-upon-artist identity. It was the great leveler. Everyone suffered equally. Commiseration became a bond. Often, with no time to remove stage makeup, the dancers would hightail it out of the theater with only minutes to spare before catching the train to the next tour city. Finally settled into seats, if they could be found, the not-so-glamorous ballet elite dined on meals of crackers, canned sardines and other pocket munchables.

Once at their destination what they called "the army game" continued. One person would check into a hotel room and at least two or three more would sneak in as nonpaying stow-aways—making for a company that not only danced together but literally camped together.

These were happy, hectic times. Despite Sevastianov, the choreographer from London saw himself as an important figure belonging to a major ballet company. He wasn't being called on to raise funds, to sew costumes or paint flats. He was an honest-to-god kingpin. His ballets were a staple of the repertory. He was ranked creatively along with Fokine and even in the vanguard of modern ballet. He couldn't complain. Yet.

15

●

A Doll's House

THERE WAS BOTH IRONY AND LOGIC in the wartime birth of American ballet. While the United States defended Europe against the Third Reich many refugees sought artistic haven on its shores. And as they incorporated themselves into Ballet Theatre it was the Russians who gained a foothold, reshaping in their image the company that was earlier a multinational enterprise. True, resources had to be conserved for the war effort, pinching the flow of goods and services, and many men of sign-up and call-up age disappeared from the civilian population. But America was not under siege. There were no threatening air raids, only token blackouts. Theaters stayed open. Antony Tudor could proceed with his career.

And he had at least one ballet biding its time in these two American years, one he would eventually name *Pillar of Fire*. His important works, thus far, had all been created in London; he lived on his English laurels. Ever since the spring of 1939, however, when he announced the London Ballet's second season, he had been preoccupied with *Verklärte Nacht*. This was the landmark score with which Arnold Schoenberg bade farewell to the hyperchromatic angst of postromanticism and nodded to the brave new twelve-tone music that lay ahead.

As ballet choreographers went Tudor was a connoisseur in musical matters. No astute observer could be surprised that the same person who set a ballet to Mahler's *Kindertotenlieder* would stand rooted to the spot where Schoenberg carried out his rite of harmonic passage. In *Verklärte Nacht* were the cries of a tonal universe splintering apart. The Expressionist result spoke to Tudor in a language of dramatic realism, a language that he had never explored quite this way before in ballet. Just as the composer got caught up in the poem that inspired his music—Richard Dehmel's *Weib und die Welt* (*Woman and the World*)—so did the choreographer connect to its theme. But for Tudor the *Transfigured Night* would have a potent theatricality that leaped beyond the text.

What he heard in the tension-fraught music, its chords twisted and tortured, bore just a passing resemblance to the story of two lovers who find their way to paradise after surviving a bleak winter's night. He elaborated on the details. He brought his own life into the picture. He set up the sociofamilial stresses that had dogged him from Central Street. No mere metaphysical reverie, the ballet would disclose every conflict and every attitude of its protagonist, Hagar. But not by way of generalized clichés, not by what Tudor called "ham-acting." Once again, but even more powerfully than in *Jardin,* the movements he devised would telegraph these inner states.

The story of a biblical Hagar is the story of an isolate, "an outcast wandering around in a no-man's land," Tudor would say years later. Indeed, the title *Pillar of Fire* derives from Exodus; it refers to the light guiding the people of Israel from Egypt at night. Choked by feelings of unworthiness, the heroine subverts her yearning for love. But love, according to the Victorian ethos, has a double edge. Sexual on one side, spiritual on the other.

Bad and good. Because Hagar does not think she qualifies for a mature, caring kind of love, she reaches in desperation for the love that will properly demean her, doled out by the merchant of eros next door. Everyone conspires against her. An older maiden sister, who looms as her own future reflection, scorns Hagar. A younger sister, this one a coquette, breezily ignores her and makes off with the kind, sensitive man Hagar longs to involve.

And then there is the larger social context—townspeople who hold their elbows close, who come and go and in twos and threes, engage in whispering campaigns while Hagar sits alone, friendless. Surely she is the object of their derision. And if not that, at the very least she is cut off from them.

But Tudor let himself be led by the serene resolution of Dehmel's poem, also mirrored in the music. The man Hagar loves ultimately returns her devotion both in the poem and the ballet. The pregnancy that comes from her liaison with the hypersexual stranger—a plot element not commonly known—is accepted by the husband-to-be. And if one goes along with the autobiographical clues of *Pillar of Fire,* then the transfiguration that takes place represents a kind of wish fulfillment on Tudor's part.

As he has said, there is something of himself in every role. Clearly, Hagar represents Tudor, although he danced the role of The Friend, the idealized man he would be in the best of all possible worlds—"normal," upstanding, principled, kind, wise. He even inherited the prospective role of fatherhood, without having to accomplish the procreation himself. He is seen as the antithesis of The Young Man from the House Opposite—an impulse-ridden, demanding, arrogant narcissist. But as Hagar, he cannot resist this Hugh Laing character, who wears his sexuality on his pant leg. At least in the ballet, Tudor moves beyond Hugh from the House Opposite, and all the self-indulgence he personifies. He passes through the phase and goes on to develop into a perfect prince, Hagar's sympathetic, noble protector.

These considerations, although lying beneath the surface, figured into the most acclaimed ballet Tudor would ever do for

Ballet Theatre. *Pillar* was seen as a work of genius, one that gets across complex issues by way of pure and stringent and powerful dance means, fusing natural movement with stylized accents in a brilliantly conceived ballet milieu. Despite being fixed in the Victorian period, its insights are universal and timeless.

He began with the score, one that Hugh tried, unsuccessfully, to lobby against. And what it forced him to do was choreograph without the obvious meter and rhythm grids that other dance-makers rely on as a structural basis. Schoenberg, even preserial Schoenberg, was hardly Tchaikovsky or even Stravinsky. Here Tudor would be left to whatever devices he could invent. The dance phrases would have to staple their own form onto the sweeping fabric of the music. The dancers would need help. Often he held listening sessions for them at the Windsor. Long before he started rehearsing or even selecting his cast he and Hugh would invite any of the likely prospects to their large room on Fifty-eighth Street and play the recording of *Verklärte Nacht*. It was compelling music, music of overripe passions, splintering conflict and extraordinary tenderness. By the time he began putting the ballet together it had become familiar to all.

Alicia Alonso remembered Tudor talking to her about the leading role in *Pillar*. But just before he was ready to start what would be many months of piecemeal rehearsals she developed a detached retina and had to leave Ballet Theatre. Meanwhile there was Nora Kaye. Karnilova had brought her to Tudor's class one day in the company's first season and the newcomer, determined to get the British choreographer's attention, planted herself in the front line. There she showed off a steely technique—multiple pirouettes, among other feats—to what she knew would be dazzling effect. But Tudor refused to notice her. He deliberately turned away. Afterward she stormed into the dressing room and announced to her friend: "I will never work with that Englishman, no matter what."

Of course, Tudor would not look at Kaye in class. That was clearly what she wanted him to do. But since he had perfected the art of ignoring such cues and ploys for attention there was no possibility of his accommodating her. In short order, though, an astute Kaye came to understand the ground rules. Tudor was just playing his usual game with her—a momentary one at that. The fact is, he posted her name on his rehearsal schedule for the very next day and she obediently attended. What he discovered at once was a lively personality, a wit and a dancer with the singular determination to have a big career.

According to David Nillo, Kaye began "mooching around" Tudor at the end of 1940, when the company took up residence at the Chicago Opera. By February she had wangled the role of the ballerina from Moscow in *Gala Performance,* which she danced at the Majestic Theatre in New York. Tudor never forgot her performance. He called it "marvelous," but was especially impressed with the fact that Nora rented a studio to practice the walk-on in the first scene. "All night she spent there and worked [by herself] to get the overturned-out walk" (being hampered by a naturally turned-in and inflexible hip). "That sort of thing doesn't happen very often." Not only did he have tremendous admiration for such a show of commitment, but he thrived on it as an avowal of her respect for his work.

Nora targeted a goal and went after it. As Donald Saddler observed, "The lady was driven." She had an uncanny knack for ingratiating herself and moved easily into the close sphere of Tudor and Laing. Over a period of a few months they had become the insular three, the trio that others regarded as "a closed unit."

"Nora isolated herself from everyone else," said Nillo. "It was as though she had made a conscious decision that her future lay with Tudor and Hugh. And she wasn't really wrong. After Baronova and Markova came into the company she had no chance to move up to the leading roles claimed by those two." What Tudor could offer Kaye, named after the heroine of Ibsen's *A Doll's House* by a father who had been Stanislavsky's student at the Moscow Art Theater, was a bona fide dramatic opportunity. She would have been a fool not to make him notice her.

It was a perfect match. Nora drank in everything Tudor expounded. Did he instruct her "to read all seven volumes of *Remembrance of Things Past*" in order to understand the Proustian subtleties of inference and interaction? She said so. She did so. Was there a ring of fire he wanted her to penetrate? A done deal. Before he was through with her, Nora Kaye would be America's dramatic ballerina *assoluta*. "I choreographed on Nora's defects," said Tudor in a lecture some years later. "She didn't have a beautiful line but possessed so powerful an armature that the character and her movements came out of that ability to project rigid strength."

The transformation was extremely gratifying for Tudor and Hugh; they even worked on such extracurriculars as Nora's dress and demeanor. Later they would introduce her to Vivien Leigh and Margot Fonteyn, hoping the British elegance and savoir faire would rub off, hoping to soften the speech, a nasal New York twang. At one point she was sent to a cult masseuse who would try to resculpt her body to look rounder and more feminine instead of so square and stubby compared to ideal balletic physiques.

If she gained, so did Tudor. Hardly anything was more stimulating to him than a dancer who performed heroic miracles to prove her fervent devotion—a Kaye specialty. Here was a gift to him. Nora Kaye turned herself over to Tudor carte blanche. She would be what he liked. He could reinvent this woman according to his wishes. But right now he wanted her to be Hagar. He wanted her to help him discover Hagar. When the rehearsals for *Pillar* began at Jacob's Pillow—a summer dance haven in the Massachusetts countryside founded by Ted Shawn—it was understood that those with Nora and Tudor would be private. In fact, the pas de deux between Hagar and The Friend (Tudor's role) would not be seen by anyone until final rehearsals, just prior to the Met premiere in April of 1942.

There was much to do before getting to the pas de deux. Tudor decided that he would have to sift not just Nora but the whole cast through the story's grainy details of truth. Everyone needed his indoctrination. It wouldn't be enough to arrange steps and movements. How did these small-town characters think? Whether in New England or London's suburbs, what was their lifestyle? Were the rooms wallpapered inside Hagar's house? And if so, what was the pattern? Did they have afternoon tea?

As P. W. Manchester said, "The audience could tell you what happened to these characters after the curtain came down. Where they went and what they did. That's how detailed and sure Tudor's concepts were." Indeed, he drummed into the cast the importance of this knowledge and how it would affect every moment onstage as well as offstage. Nora worked very hard. The Tudor mantra was no mystery to her. There were times when he would have her do a single step or phrase over and over, until he was convinced she understood what it meant. Nor was she immune to his harsh criticism or the near impossibility of pleasing him—she too came to teary grief. This was a technique he used in every conscientious rehearsal he ever supervised, so long as there was a hope of achieving his end.

Some of the sections came easily. Annabelle Lyon, The Youngest Sister, recalled how quickly Tudor choreographed her role and how detailed he was in the character delineation. "I remember his mentioning Simone Simon, the great French actress who was appearing then at Loew's State Theater. Nora and I went to see her and could understand from the performance that kittenish quality Tudor wanted me to convey. But it was his own comments that were the key to the role. That I was petted by the older sister and always looked at people from under my eyelashes, never making direct eye contact. Everything flowed from me with that clue."

So did Lucia Chase relish her role, that of The Eldest Sister. This was a bit of built-in typecasting, for the exchequer/de facto director of the company would make a natural matriarch. On the other hand Chase was by no means impervious to Tudor's hammering for perfectionism. In this and roles in his other ballets he reduced her to tears no less than any dancer.

Some tended to see him as caustic and needlessly cruel. But he was revered as well as reviled by those who clustered around him. Jerome Robbins—who, when he became a choreographer in his own right, also earned the reputation for being a harsh taskmaster—didn't let Tudor's manner deter him. If anything that manner became a model. But Donald Saddler, who, along with Robbins, danced in the corps of *Pillar* as Lovers-in-Experience, puts the matter in perspective: "The fact that Tudor chose us meant that he considered us worthy. Many people wanted desperately to get into the special classes he gave at the Gertrude Hoffman studio or into any small role in his ballets, but couldn't. So when he came down hard I took it as positive interest in me. He knew he couldn't destroy me but once in a while he would test me just to make sure. He was more like a teasing uncle, though, than an enemy."

Hugh, of course, came to *Pillar* with a great advantage over the others, and was already in his milieu. He did the "sex bomb" roles, observed Harry Mines, a Los Angeles friend of the Tudor dancers. And this one, The Young Man from the House Opposite, was the ultimate in erotic fireworks. Tudor himself spoke admiringly of Hugh as carrying the same persona on- and off-stage. There was no small amount of typecasting in placing the character as lower class—the stigma Hugh always tried to conceal but could glory in here.

Toward the end of The Young Man's sequence, Tudor gave Hugh the high compliment of letting him choreograph his own exit from the stage. He did this only when convinced that the dancer had genuinely become the character. And in that strut away from the fray, with his shoulders raised and his tight hips swiveling, Hugh said everything there was to say about this caricature of self-absorbed exhibitionism. He was the nefarious abuser of women who, flaunting his matinee-idol wares with the greatest vulgarity and Tudor loved it.

But he still had ahead of him a battle with the powers that were, namely Hurok and Sevastianov. Regardless of promises made by Richard Pleasant on behalf of *Pillar,* what landed onstage and what did not depended on decisions of the moment. Here Nora and her hidden agendas were invaluable—not by chance had she become friendly with Mae Frohman, Hurok's secretary. Hugh figured that Nora's inroad could now be helpful and he was right. At her request Frohman arranged for Hurok to see a finished excerpt of *Pillar*. He was so impressed that he called Sevastianov to his office commanding that Tudor be given first call on the company from that moment on.

As Tudor once observed, being a choreographer was not like being a painter or a composer or a novelist or a playwright. These others enjoy the option of solitary productivity. A choreographer must have dancers with whom to create and a company can either withhold or assign the necessary collaborators, the sine qua non of new ballets. In a fairer situation he would not have had to scheme for the award. But in the end his quiet euphoria over this triumph silenced any rancor on that score. The main thing was winning and he won.

6

Redemption

EARLY IN THE SUMMER OF 1941, Ballet Theatre was on a layoff period. But when a wealthy friend of Anton Dolin rented the farmhouse at Jacob's Pillow the dancers agreed to put $10 of their $15 weekly unemployment benefits toward room and board there. In fact, they were bursting for the chance. To spend two months with Tudor and Dolin, who would teach several daily classes, was no small enticement for these hardy enthusiasts. Money didn't matter. Nothing did really except the chance "to be at the beginning of something wonderful," said Karnilova, remembering those days. "We felt like we were the only company in the world. We were very proud. And so were the choreographers."

Now that there was a respite from performances and touring Tudor could give his full attention to *Pillar of Fire*. "Get up, get up," he would call softly every morning, poking his head through the sleeping dancers' windows. "Get your orange juice and come to rehearsal." Their cabins, scattered through the woods, were like small, primitive dormitories. Eight A.M. was not too early for Tudor to be shepherding his charges to their work arena, a gazebo up in the hills. First came rehearsals and after that he gave a class. Company class took place in the main building, which housed a large studio.

He already had chosen the cast. Even those who would dance in the ensembles—Lovers-in-Experience and Lovers-in-Innocence—were excited at the prospect. While there was considerable esprit de corps, everyone also put individual hopes on the project. Karnilova remembered that at first she was to understudy Nora. "But that lasted only three rehearsals," she said. Roles in Tudor ballets were possessions, fiercely guarded possessions. And Tudor gleefully fostered these rivalries. Ever the happy voyeur, he loved to watch the covert squabbles and simmering resentments between dancers—especially when his was the prize being contended for. Under the circumstances, there was slim chance that Karnilova or anyone would be allowed to learn the role of Hagar, should a need ever arise for a substitute. And until she retired from the stage no one but Nora would ever dance it.

Right from the start Tudor had already conceived the emblems for his *Pillar* characters. Still, he insisted on closed rehearsals for Hugh and Nora—the place was Mother Derby's Barn, a short distance from the main compound. It was here that they explored things in depth. Hagar's reflexive pulling at her collar, for instance, the first gesture she would employ—sort of an epithet— as the curtain opens and finds her sitting at the front-door stoop. The motion speaks volumes about the soon-to-be-ostracized woman. Around her neck is a locket containing a picture of her beloved father, now dead. As Hagar's fingers furtively tug at the collar, she telegraphs to the world, in a single move, what Victorian shame is all about and her deep need to conceal it.

Nor were the other rehearsals less investigative. The Youngest Sister, with a toss of her head, shows the abandon of omnipotence. The world is hers. She flirts confidently, secure in her power to manipulate. The Eldest Sister, as she pulls on her gloves, is all formality and New England self-righteousness. The Young Man presses the ball of his foot into the ground, lifts his heel, bends his knee and jackknifes his thigh out sharply before bringing it straight in an insolent climax. Everyone was defined in high relief. But because Tudor could frame his characterizations in choreographic episodes they never dissipated into static caricatures. They became, rather, a code to the dramatis personae.

The action of the ballet pivots on a triangle. Hagar stands poised between The Young Man, a neon sign of sex, and The Friend—he holds out the promise of a wholesome, complete relationship. This was the same Nora, Hugh and Tudor who were a troika on the train tours, an exclusive trio whispering and scheming—exactly what, no one knew. Nora giggled a lot. The two entertained her. They also controlled her. As she said, "I had no background. Tudor and Laing did so much for me. They told me what to read, what to wear, what to think. For years I was emotionally dependent on them."

After Jacob's Pillow they stayed together for a two-week company engagement in Mexico City. The three of them rented a house there, also inviting Annabelle Lyon, George Perper (Hurok's stepson) and Jeanette Lauret to occupy the other rooms. It was an enjoyable time—class in the morning, then rehearsal for the performances at the Palacio de Bellas Artes, then siesta, then a meal, then the theater.

But just before a four-day vacation at the end of this brief run, Nora took on yet another identity, courtesy of her mentor. At Tudor's goading she went off with Michael Van Buren, great grandson of the eighth president of the United States and married him some months later. Perhaps he could not resist this *liaison dangereuse* and its delectable implications—the linking to Hugh and Tudor through Nora. Her marriage to the tall, blond bespectacled Van Buren continued technically for a few years, but he was seldom on the scene. John Taras, at that time a dancer and already her close friend, said: "Tudor was always pushing people into bed with each other." The quasi–ménage à trois was consummated, symbolically, in *Pillar*. What Tudor may not have been able to accomplish offstage, he realized onstage—with great relish. Here was the voyeur as human engineer.

Nora also enjoyed little skits. Once, during an affair with playwright Arthur Laurents, she arranged a get-together with him and her husband, Van Buren. "We met for tea at the St. Regis," recalled Laurents. "Nora wore a glamorous black hat with a big brim and enacted this whole scenario—the husband was not to know about us. For her it was a delicious intrigue. She giggled a lot."

Tudor's sense of adventure didn't preclude more conventional pleasures, however. With the vacation beckoning and Nora otherwise engaged, he persuaded Annabelle to join him and Hugh. They could still be a trio, albeit a less conspiratorial, less intimate one. Annabelle remembered "going off to a jungle somewhere near Acapulco. We hiked through a very thick area that had no paths. It was hot. We were completely lost. But he was delighted by the challenge. The more difficult it became the better he liked it." This was one of those times when Tudor felt indomitable. In just a few months he would have a major work to unveil.

"We knew we had got a good ballet," he said, recalling the general elation over Hurok's approval of *Pillar.* And as soon as the word went out that Tudor was to have priority over the others for its rehearsals, an air of anticipation prevailed. After all, he was the great modern hope at Ballet Theatre, the only contemporary-minded choreographer who survived the Russian invasion. His *Jardin, Elegies* and *Judgment* ranked high among the repertory treasures. But behind Tudor's overly modest accounting was a sense of himself as the underdog, an attitude that hovered no less in his ballets than in his head. As evidence, most Tudor ballets dealt with characters destined for disappointment or worse.

But *Pillar* would be about redemption. Despite her self-demeaning act—the sexcapade with the unsavory Young Man— Hagar would move beyond sordidness and degradation to a state of bliss. The man she cherished would be sympathetic and wise.

And as they walked in the moonlight, he would illuminate her life with this love. He would be her salvation.

The ballet's poetically happy ending did not make the process of creation any easier for Tudor. Indeed, he brooded over the work for roughly a year—utterly engrossed with the character of Hagar. Nor did his victory over Sevastianov, who derisively dubbed the ballet *"Pills of Fire,"* preclude the torturous blocks he would suffer. Just the opposite. He went around the studio cracking his fingers, trying out a few steps, stopping, discarding, starting again, looking wild-eyed, biting his nails. Finally, just as complexities reached a breaking point and the whole rehearsal threatened to collapse, Hugh would throw a climactic tantrum, a curiously salutary tantrum that served to get Tudor off the hook. The gains from this seemingly spontaneous explosion were enormous. When the rehearsal resumed the slate would be clean, the accumulated frustrations cleared away.

Tudor's rehearsals were rituals in themselves. There was rarely an occasion when the spaniels, Barnaby and Jason, were not on the premises. And Hugh hardly went anywhere without his colorful parakeet perched on his shoulder. No matter how much strife or how intense the concentration, one could count, at least, on the ubiquitous dogs. Even on tours.

But such curiosities were of little notice while *Pillar* was being prepared. Sono Osato, one of the Lovers-in-Experience (the ensemble associated with The House Opposite and The Young Man), thought back to the spring of 1942 and said that it was "one of the most profound experiences of my life. I felt as though I had lost myself in a powerful novel and had become part of it and the music which swept me up. All of Tudor's love, anguish, hatred and passion are here. It was also fascinating in its structure. The choreography moved against the pulse, it was almost unrhythmic—just the opposite of Balanchine."

If that's how those in the minor roles felt, one can just imagine the kind of involvement Kaye had. She spoke of "living the character completely before Tudor set a single step, knowing exactly what kind of person I was. And then, when he began to choreograph, it seemed perfectly natural to move that way." So natural and subtle was the movement Tudor devised that the unsuspecting were not aware of its technical difficulty. "Fiendish difficulty," said Kaye. Since the object was to tell a story and give the full dimension of a character, in this case, Hagar, he would not simply provide a little dance, distinct from the mime— the traditional narrative format in ballet. Rather, he succeeded in integrating music, story, character and steps. They became inseparable. That was his genius.

When *Pillar* opened at the Metropolitan Opera House on April 8, 1942, the audience didn't think about these questions or analyze them. It simply reacted as though to the most wallopingly dramatic play—sitting breathless, throughout. For long moments after the curtain closed there was no sound—no clatter of applause, no whistling or cheering, just stunned silence. "They're not clapping," said Nora backstage to Tudor. "It's a disaster." But then came the thunderous swell of approbation, which Tudor, too shrewd to discount, had told her to anticipate.

So shrewd was he, in fact, that he controlled everything that happened next. As the cast assembled in the wings, ready to walk onstage, he shook his head. "Not yet," he said. The applause grew louder and louder. Finally he said, "Now." And they all marched onstage. Tudor described "a great burst of shouting from all over the theater." It went exactly as he had planned. He knew that there had to be a number of curtains to score a big success and, most important, to assuage his primary foe, Sevastianov. The Ballet Russe champion voted against *Pillar* and only over Chase's and Hurok's protests did he resentfully give in. After all, Tudor might be the most admired choreographer if one listened to the intelligentsia. But at the box office he could hardly count as a favorite.

In the end Tudor outsmarted Sevastianov. He knew what would happen at the premiere. But to properly "choreograph" the finale he told the dancers, in advance, "to ask everyone you know to send flowers and I'll do the same." Hundreds of bouquets filled the wing area. With so many flowers to be presented, the curtain calls could go on and on. And they did. Thirty times the great gold swag curtain opened for the cast to acknowledge its applause. Tudor was vindicated. But not self-righteous. "Conniving," he smilingly called himself years later. "That's my nasty nature."

As his own critic he knew where he stood in comparison to others. "I knew I was preeminent anyway," he said, sloughing off the importance of his level of public esteem. But Tudor could not acknowledge his vulnerability to the consensus or to company arbiters. At least for the moment, however, he didn't have to worry about that. Edwin Denby and John Martin, the two leading newspaper critics of the day, gave *Pillar* positively glowing notices.

Denby's analysis in the *New York Herald Tribune* singled out its structural marvels: "The work shows two different ballet styles: an improperly strained one that characterizes the anguished heroine, and a smooth, proper style for the nice untroubled neighboring boys and girls. In addition, both kinds of ballet are set against the non-ballet dancing of the exciting low-life crowd— they dance and whirl in a sort of wild rumba style, swivel-hipped, explosive and frenzied; while the calm hero, in contrast to everyone, comes on not as any kind of dancer but walking across the stage as modestly as a Fuller-brush man. Tudor fuses these heterogeneous elements brilliantly."

Expanding at a later date, he wrote that the choreography gave him "an intimate pleasure. That is, that the technical devices don't have the effect of tricks. . . . If Tudor uses a grand jeté, with high carriage and legs spread taut in the air, the carriage, the taut legs don't tickle you as a gadget would, they are a direct act. . . . At every moment you see the dancer as a person . . . not as an unhappily defective instrument of a choreographer's flights of fancy."

Martin, in *The New York Times,* gave no less an appraisal. He also wrote many essays on *Pillar,* each time unearthing new insights. "Consider Antony Tudor," he began one of them. "After *Pillar of Fire* it is impossible not to consider him, and seriously, for here is no glib talent but something very like a new force in the evolution of dance. . . . Tudor is one of the most important figures in the contemporary ballet. No, let's not quibble—*the* most important figure in the contemporary ballet."

One point that did not escape Denby's all-seeing eye was *Pillar*'s conclusion, which he thought "becomes so subdued, it turns static and the effect is indistinct. The heroine still seems strained and sad. . . . The long tortured and humiliated parts stay with you, not comforting, but very moving in their pathos."

The observation fits when applied to the ballet as autobiography. Tudor experienced no such happy ending in his life— that's why the finale didn't ring true. He and Hugh would stay locked in a kind of human bondage to the end, apart from a temporary hiatus. He would never go beyond his relationship with the infantile Laing. Although they shared what some regarded as "a love possibly greater than that between a man and a woman," it was a love in which each seemed to drag the other down with him, a symbiosis fraught with destructiveness, a *folie à deux*.

At least for the next five years Nora Kaye would be a significant part of that relationship. Nor could she escape the sadomasochism that Tudor and Laing invited her to share with them. So long as they decided that she needed to be fixed, reinvented and manufactured she stood to be regarded as defective. Paradoxically, she also rose from the lowly corps to become America's matchless dramatic ballerina.

Wherefore Art Thou?

FROM THE VERY FIRST American performances of his ballets Antony Tudor served notice of a major talent. Clearly, this was no *routinier* who cranked out choreographic patterns by the yard to high-stepping music, nor a merchant of dance as entertainment. But after *Pillar* he occupied a new realm, one that ranged far beyond the subtle appeal and sophisticated artistry of earlier works, one that proved compelling to all. Audiences flocked to see this amazing new ballet. They were dumbstruck by it. Even those who customarily turned up their noses at the hippety-hop aspect of standard ballet fare, preferring theater and other more thought-provoking enticements, caught the scent of drama here. No ballet created in this country had ever made such impact— either on the public or the press. It was a new day and a new art and Tudor epitomized both.

Naturally, his stock rose with the company's administrators. Like it or not, Sevastianov had to concede to Tudor the top choreographic rank. Maybe his nonglitzy view of the dance seemed an odd prospect to ballet hucksters like Sevastianov, but it was clear that the public did not want to limit its pleasure to spectacle anymore. When the suggestion for a ballet based on *Romeo and Juliet* was made, Tudor inherited the commission— by mandate. But unlike the situation with *Pillar,* wherein an exact premiere date was not set until very late, Hurok determined that *Romeo* would have its first performance at the end of a grueling six-month transcontinental tour. Rehearsals were catch-as-catch- can, but Tudor was to have a solid two weeks together with his dancers just prior to the opening. By this time they would all be back in New York and stabilized.

The tour was unforgettable. While the thrill of proselytizing invigorated everyone—it was a heady experience to perform for the clamoring crowds in Boston, Chicago, San Francisco, Los Angeles and Toronto, plus the roughly forty other towns and cities—it also proved exhausting. The company managed to rack up forty-eight one-night stands this time and gave a total of 143 performances in the six-month period. An exponential increase over what Tudor and Hugh were used to as English ballet gyp- sies. But the rigorous schedule didn't really faze them. And if they had to compare Ballet Theatre standards to Ballet Rambert or their own London Ballet, the balance would weigh in favor of this side of the Atlantic. The extravagant amounts spent on the productions here were mind-boggling compared to the threads-and-patches budgets they knew in England. The large- scale organization and bookings, courtesy of Hurok, were also a revelation.

But Charles Payne, chronicling the tactics of this tour, wrote that the dancers "fared only slightly better than cattle on the drive from Albuquerque to the Chicago stockyards." Typically they would perform and early the next morning get themselves and their luggage to the terminal only to find a long wait for a civilian train. Finally, they would pack into coaches—often unheated and lacking a dining car. The late arrival, after some six hours, would find them waiting in line for transport to a hotel where they would queue up again and wait for rooms to be cleaned. Then at last a restaurant line where, if they were lucky, would turn up something substantial among the war-rationed food.

Tudor loved the adventure and conquest of America, not to mention his hero status. Still, he did not preen. The fact is, he didn't really believe it. In the flush of success some other overnight celebrity might indulge his taste for pomp and importance, for material acquisitions, for special privileges. But Tudor was always a monk at heart. He never showed concern for money, nor a lifestyle that depended on having it. As Muriel Bentley observed, "He and Hugh lived in a single room, they cooked on a hot-plate and washed dishes in the bathroom sink. They had nothing." His adaptation both to adult life and the ballet world was that of an ascetic—even psychologically. He would not assume the pretensions of an arriviste, nor want to wear the symbols of his success like so many lapel pins.

He had none of the social climber's vanity, or at least he used none of those well-known ploys. His notion of eminence did not depend on a network of underlings and gofers whose very function would attest to that status. These were Americanisms that failed to rub off. Nor did he resort to decoy behavior to hide his homosexuality. Discretion and privacy, yes. But that was all. He lived openly with Hugh, made no attempt at heterosexual liaisons nor at profit from the illusion of same. One prominent choreographer, when going out to dinner with an entourage of males, would tag the event a "stag party," for the sake of propriety, telling waiters and other staff that one of the men was getting married. This type of subterfuge didn't interest Tudor. Nor, on the other hand, did he seek out such social clubs.

The only thing he would have appreciated was a ballet commission with exorbitant amounts of rehearsal time. And rather than widening his entourage he narrowed it. What struck most of the company dancers was the even tighter bond—post-*Pillar*—that grew among Nora, Hugh and Tudor. They were always in collusion, it seemed. On the trains they did a perpetual pas de trois and the others in the so-called "Tudor group" felt excluded more than ever.

There was good reason for Hugh's and Nora's wanting to be hermetically sealed off with Tudor. He had, according to consensus, "made" both of them. They had hung their career prospects on him. And in some respects they were very much alike—despite the fact that Hugh was a standard bearer of physical beauty and Nora hardly in that category, and that he lacked technical fluency while she was a gritty paragon of it. "Strong as a bull," she was said to be. While most dancers struggle through the thirty-two *fouettés* of *Swan Lake* Nora could make an all-night marathon of these whipping turns on pointe. But it was Hugh's and Nora's common quality, an overwhelmingly dramatic intensity, that powered Tudor's creativity.

Despite their extravagant gifts all three shared a deficit of self-esteem. "Nora seemed so strong to the world at large," observed Janet Reed, who shared an apartment on Fifty-second Street with Kaye and danced the Tudor-styled soubrette roles in his ballets. "But after Hugh and Tudor made her a star, she clung to them even more than before. They used her and she used them, professionally." Curiously, each had an Achilles' heel: Tudor, his excruciating slowness in creating ballets, a perfectionism that kept him locked for hours on a single small detail; Hugh, his sensitivity over being less of a technician than a stellar principal was expected to be; Nora, her physical flaws and poor line. These were the superficial elements, at least.

They also shared an unshakable fidelity and affection. But as is the case in any threesome, two often took after the third. Nora became the object of Tudor's and Hugh's mockery—good-natured though it was. They would mimic her nasal New Yorkese, her somewhat vulgar taste. And she was patently imitable. "Hey, babe. Ya wanna go tuh the antique staw?" she would ask Reed, or Muriel Bentley or Miriam Golden. But her social manner didn't match up with her intellectual profile. She was much better read and better informed than most dancers.

During the McCarthy era, Kaye was even identified politically by Red Channels, the directory of suspected Communist sympathizers. She had an abiding curiosity about world affairs and the arts. Her energy for these interests was inordinate. And she was divinely funny. Still, she made an incongruous picture. Sitting all those endless hours on the train sewing sequins on her scarves. And more sequins. And more sequins.

Of course, it was just idle handiwork. Something to pass the time. And when the three of them were not off in a corner by themselves, Tudor joined the fray. Often, he lent the dancers counsel—actually renaming Mildred Herman and Jimmy Hicks as the world now knows them: Melissa Hayden and Scott Douglas. He wandered from group to group, car to car, challenging this one and that one to word games—he was master of the quip and riposte. Janet Reed remembered stopping by once to chat with Nora, who was seated next to her constant mentors. Tudor turned to Nora and asked: "If you loved a girl who would it be?" "Janet," Nora replied. "I got embarrassed and walked away," said Reed. This was his typical confrontational tomfoolery, usually having to do with affairs of the heart and sex fantasies. Not only because sex was an innately provocative subject for him but because of the tremorous reaction it usually got.

And he liked tremorous reactions. They gave him an instant inroad to intimacy. He liked to see people inadvertently expose themselves. With great glee he told how, during an interview Nora had given to a newspaper, she said she never read press notices of her performances. "But then her purse fell open," he reported, "and out came a whole batch of clippings." As the inquisitor, Tudor had it both ways: keeping a distance and safeguarding his own privacy, while invading that of others. Continuous or casual conversation was not part of his repertoire. So whenever he approached, company members stood at alert. His gambits were well known. Those dancers confident of their skill at repartée simply girded up. Others skulked away or hoped they would not come to his attention.

All of this amusing play—what Kersley called "the swanning

around"—underscored Tudor's preeminent position at Ballet Theatre. He enjoyed using it. Both as a person and a dance-maker he was intimidating. He had yet to create *Dim Lustre, Undertow, Shadow of the Wind* or *Nimbus*. But his oeuvre was sufficient, starting in 1943, to warrant a "Tudor night"—a program devoted exclusively to his ballets, numerous and varied enough for an artistically feasible evening. More than any other choreographer, Tudor was concerned with originality. He did not recycle material over and over, developing certain trademark combinations of steps. Each ballet, ideally, grew out of a fresh impetus and had its own movement code. And this desire to avoid repeating himself would have to stand, at least, as the superficial reason for his relatively small output over the years.

When it came to *Romeo and Juliet* Tudor followed his iconoclastic game plan. Although he thought Prokofiev's famous score was "marvelous" when he heard an excerpt of it at a Queen's Hall concert, circa 1935, on seeing an actual performance of the whole ballet set to this music more than five years later, he deemed it useless for his purposes. "It was Prokofiev's *Romeo and Juliet,* not Shakespeare's," he said. What he wanted was something simpler and closer to the lyrical heart of the Bard's play. Prokofiev's sweeping, swollen rhetoric had little to do with the intimate ballet he envisioned. The same might have held for Tchaikovsky, but since he composed only twelve minutes of music on the theme, Tudor realized such a short ballet would not justify its production expense.

He finally settled on the composer Frederick Delius, a collection of whose works evoked the softly tender, bucolic mood Tudor saw as background for Shakespeare's play. He liked the rhythms Delius used because they reminded him of old Italian tunes that fit the quattrocento period. Just as he honored stylistic integrity for his first ballet, *Cross-Garter'd,* also Shakespeare in an Italian setting, so did Tudor go about this project with earnest fidelity.

The choice of Delius branded it an English ballet—playwright, choreographer and composer sharing a national heritage. More-over, it's likely that Tudor heard his friend Sir Thomas Beecham conduct some of the pieces at the same Queen's Hall where he listened to the Prokofiev. It was in October 1929 that Beecham championed Delius in a weeklong festival devoted to his compatriot.

Obtaining either full scores or instrumental parts during the war was difficult. But Antal Dorati, who would conduct the performance, sat with Tudor piecing a section from "A Village Romeo and Juliet" together with "Brigg Fair," "Eventyr" and "Over the Hills and Far Away." They listened to recordings over many hours and then Dorati painstakingly wrote out all the parts, note by note, also composing bridges between the pieces. Hurok was artistically astute enough to sign Beecham to conduct some of the performances and when the British conductor saw Dorati's work he pronounced it "Astounding! Perfectly astounding! It is precisely as written by my late friend."

And what Tudor devised as his balletic translation of the tale was a marvel of nuanced pantomime and pageantry, filtered through a veil of artful symbolism. The love scenes, all fragile interaction, were remarkable. But no stock swordplay here. In-stead, the Capulet and Montague men leaped at each other in a manner of stylized acrobatics, evoking a strangely powerful and mute violence.

As it happened, Tudor would have at his disposal Alicia Mar-kova, who came to Ballet Theatre in 1943 as guest artist. With her and Hugh in the title roles the ballet bore a final British stamp. Nora would have to sit this one out, not that she was exactly languishing for not being cast in *Romeo and Juliet*. But Markova was perfect as Juliet. Diana Gould, who saw her dance the role years later, wrote that the portrayal had such an "ef-fortless gossamer quality that it was as though she were thistle-down and propelled not by any apparent energy of her own but rather by the violence of those around her."

In her writing Gould caught the key to Tudor's concept. *Romeo and Juliet* would remain an island of starry idealism cut off from, if finally violated by, the seething familial furies in their midst. Lovers, as represented by Tudor, had to be impervious to society's dictates. His own experience led him to see them as fugitives of a code within which he (and they) could not live. Following decorum as he did—and not identifying as an outlaw, happy or otherwise—he created works that depict estrangement. Others might take comfort in playing the outlaw and redressing society's wrongs. Not Tudor.

But the character of Romeo reflects his changing perceptions of Hugh. In the beginning, Hugh was an innocent. From the Guardian Angel in *Adam and Eve,* to the open-armed, open-hearted Lover in *Jardin,* he was almost pure in his ardor. No matter how volatile as a personality, he had little power to flaunt in England—apart from terrorizing Rambert. Once in the United States, he exulted in his reputation, "a famous English dancer," and the bullying took on a nasty side. There was that occasion when he slapped the mild-mannered stage manager Alexis Tcherkassky for no apparent reason. He went the limit of what he could get away with and then some. Cruelty had become part and parcel of his behavior—which is not to say that Hugh no longer turned on the charm when so inclined. But Tudor knew the cruel streak and capitalized on it in *Pillar.* By the same token he took a different inspiration for Romeo in 1943 than he might have five years earlier.

According to Laing, as paraphrased by Selma Jeanne Cohen, "The key to the hero is in the prologue: a languid pose adapted from Rodin. The focus of the body is inward, self-caressing, for Romeo is full of self-love. Juliet is only the target of his emotional outbursts; in his tantrums he feels it is he who is making the great sacrifice. This is self-indulgence, not romantic love." Curiously, the description also applied to Tudor's persona.

If the minor roles suggested nothing quite so profoundly developed as Romeo, they were—as in all Tudor ballets—extremely important for their resonance of particular character, not stereotypes. Sono Osato, the sensuous dancer brilliantly cast as Rosaline, mentioned that Tudor was unique in distilling the essence of a situation. "He worked with Lucia [Chase] one after-noon," she wrote, "on a single instant of the Nurse's part, showing her how to evoke the sticky heat of the day by rising and gesturing with her arms as if to pluck her heavy skirt from her buttocks. He did not want her actually to move the costume away from her body, but to isolate the familiar act of doing so by combining the sensations of heat, clothing and damp skin in her gesture. Lucia eventually captured the moment but never looked quite so hot or sticky as Tudor did."

This was really the distinct difference between him and his peers. And he would always remain a stickler for these truths. He was a foe of the dramatic cliché, quite innocently a misfit in the dance world. His innovations, when noticed at all, were looked upon by some as the emperor's clothes. A few dancers, though, like Osato, had the sensibility to appreciate what he was doing.

She recalled being summoned to her first rehearsal of *Romeo*. He asked the cast, "What was the Renaissance all about? What were the key elements of that society? What was life like? How did they move?" If the assembled could respond only with an embarrassed silence, it didn't matter. Because by the end of the session they had discovered how "to move contrary to every position of classical ballet, keeping our knees slightly bent, our pelvises tilted forward, and our necks curved to suggest the pas-sive demeanor of women in Renaissance paintings. In contrast, the men stood very erect, strutted more than they walked, and imbued every gesture with the fierce masculine pride of fifteenth-century courtiers."

If substance was not a problem for him, time was. It seems that when artistic push came to financial shove he would not have his two unfettered weeks of rehearsal: Hurok picked up a last-minute engagement for the company in Canada and packed the dancers off—glad to fill the coffers with this much-needed revenue. But he held fast to the agreed-upon date of opening night. Tudor tried to fight it and what he called the ensuing "conflagration" was conducted all through intermediaries.

Hurok decreed that *Romeo* would have its premiere five days after the company began its spring engagement at the Met. He protested the ballet's incomplete state and Tudor, once again at loggerheads with management, said that, yes, if not postponed it most certainly would be presented in its unfinished state. Hurok did not budge. He would stick to the announced schedule, which listed the new work for April 6, 1943. Everything, including Eugene Berman's designs, was almost in order. But the fine-tuning of set placement on the stage and even the last sewing together of costumes were days away. The dress rehearsal was a contradiction in terms.

Besides all this, Hurok wanted a company spokesman to explain to the first-nighters an incomplete ballet based on "concessions to the war effort." Tudor wouldn't hear of such a lie. Not an apologist, he would do whatever speech-making had to be done. No matter what horror, he never showed a trace of it. In full makeup and costume of Tybalt, he came before the curtain—the same huge gold swag that opened and closed so many times for the unending ovations of *Pillar* one year ago—to apologize for the unfinished *Romeo and Juliet,* just ahead on the program. And then, as though he were merely announcing a cast change, he graciously invited everyone back four nights later for the final version. They were, as he explained, already ahead of the game, "since most ballets last less than a half hour and, incomplete, *Romeo* was forty-five minutes."

What Tudor could scarcely acknowledge, though, was the agony of trying to match the success of *Pillar.* Indeed, he had to compete with it. In the premiere season of *Romeo* his earlier ballet was being hailed as "the troupe's masterpiece, its raison d'être." Both critics and audience came expecting to be swept away again. Instead the choreographer of the moment reached for his most thoughtful, scholarly, poetic resources and gave the public a somewhat oblique permutation of literature's famous love story. As Diana Gould concluded: "The eye feasted, the senses surfeited, while the heart and the spirit had benefitted least of all."

John Martin's initial response was mildly negative. "The work is less a ballet by Antony Tudor than a pageant by Eugene Berman, whose beautiful but unyielding setting and sumptuous costumes quite swamp the stage. . . . [Tudor] has told a tale that must remain obscure to those who do not know it already."

But posterity has granted the highest rating to this ballet that shows ingenuity and insight far exceeding the spectacles choreographed by others to the Prokofiev score. Critic-historian David Vaughan counted Tudor's edition as "the finest of all on that overworked subject." And Deborah Jowitt called it "one of the most brilliant and interesting of recent ballets. . . . Tudor has set his version of this sad and lyrical equation in what might be compared to a continuous Botticelli frieze. There is an emphasis on elegant, agitated, fastidiously sensual flow rather than on volume. It is as if Tudor speeded up the heartbeat of the play, so tremulous is one's reaction to it."

Back in April of 1943, Edwin Denby took issue with John Martin. He regarded *Romeo and Juliet* as "a great success . . . fully deserved . . . a reverie that transmutes Shakespeare's fire into Tennysonian pathos . . . as carefully cut as an Eisenstein film . . . its rhythmic weight steeps the story deeper and deeper in a protracted and absorbing High Church gloom. . . . It has a few unconvincing moments, but it has a great many original and very fine ones. As a whole I found the piece fascinating. The plot of *Romeo* is that of Shakespeare's play. Tudor follows the action almost faithfully, but the individual thing about it is that the poetic message is not the same. The ballet's conception of mutual love is far less impetuous, far less straightforward, far less dazzlingly radiant. The difference is clearest in the character of Romeo, who in the ballet is never quite frank; he is like an object of love, rather than a lover."

What an intriguing assessment. How acute Denby's sensor. How transparent to him this highly personalized view of Romeo. And how powerful the autobiographical force in Tudor, for the description seems to belong to him.

Reveries and Nightmares

IT WAS IRONIC that Tudor enjoyed public adulation at the very time he had to fend off backstage insults. What he extracted in the way of commissions from his unfriendly arbiters came usually after vigorous lobbying. He knew with Sevastianov, and the same with Hurok, that his requests were met grudgingly, that he was not their man in any sense—least of all at the box office. *Swan Lake* and *Graduation Ball* and whatever fit into the category of circus spectacle pleased them infinitely more than another intellectual triumph by Tudor. Ditto, star vehicles and Russian ballets. Far be it for them to laud the choreographer who chased away their fanciful nyads and dryads. He also knew that Lucia, the silent exchequer, did not want to get caught in the line of administrative fire. True, she loved performing in his ballets and, according to her future codirector Oliver Smith, "she understood that Tudor was ballet history in the making." The depth of that understanding appeared somewhat lacking, however. She preferred to avoid him when possible—if for no other reason than that he menaced her verbally.

"From the time of *Pillar* Lucia and Tudor engaged in a love-hate relationship," recalled Smith. From then on he was a force to contend with. His methods, slow and time-consuming, required long rehearsal periods; his standards stood uncompromised. As he ascended in the hierarchy his entitlement grew, his threat to her grew. It would be difficult to refuse him with impunity. Considering all the choreographers beating at her door she felt beleaguered—by them and by the constant concerns that fund-raising was insufficient to ease the burden on her own personal fortune.

She owed them all a platform. There were still the Russians, Massine and David Lichine. And there was Agnes de Mille to take care of and Jerry Robbins, whose *Tally-Ho!* and *Fancy Free,* respectively, were coming up. The fists banged aggressively. De Mille and Robbins both drove a hard bargain. Tudor took a more civilized, haughtier and hence more intimidating approach. Still, Lucia's respect for him somehow never earned the pillar of controversy her wholehearted support. It seemed to Tudor that he'd been here before; the withholding of crucial patronage was not new.

But at least Sevastianov would be clearing out of the picture. Through a series of comical contretemps Tudor's foe ended up being drafted into the U.S. army. His replacement was John Alden Talbot, an old-money New Yorker whose direct manner differed refreshingly from that of the wheeler-dealer Slav who had just vacated the spot of managing director. An innocent on the ballet scene, he was stimulated by the company's leading personalities: de Mille, Tudor and Robbins. They taught him that wit, sophistication and bonhomie could be as much a part of this world as toe shoes and tutus.

Unfortunately, Talbot's trusting alliance with his elite charges did not last. Soon he was condemning those who had just recently enchanted him—getting down to serious business with them was nothing like being entertained by them. Not least of the disappointments was Tudor. The new director, in a complaint to Ballet Theatre's treasurer Harry Zuckert, wrote: "Tudor has been behaving so badly for the last month that I am now of the opinion that it is a very good thing to have Markova and Dolin within the company to counteract his influence. Tudor thinks he is a little dictator and gives every indication of behaving like a big one, if he had the power. It is really amazing the nonsense he can think up to cause trouble."

What Talbot, an inexperienced dilettante, regarded as "nonsense" would probably not stand up under scrutiny, however. Managers and directors from the private sector typically have trouble distinguishing between what it takes to run a real estate office and an arts organization. But when it came to choosing sides Talbot went along with Lucia, favoring the Anglo-American choreographers over the Russian ones preferred by Hurok. If Tudor indeed regarded Lucia as an antagonist, he must have also known that she was his strongest champion for now, with Talbot on board, he had the courage to contemplate another ballet, *Dim Lustre*.

Tudor worked on *Pillar* a whole year. *Romeo and Juliet* was a dribs-and-drabs affair that stretched out over a long touring period. Six months after its premiere he would produce his third ballet of the made-in-America series, *Dim Lustre*. Two in one year was a record and considering that he got this work together in something under sixteen days one could call the effort positively speedy.

Like most quickly completed challenges the ballet came as a last-minute assignment. He had spoken to Lucia about it—originally he had in mind something quite ambitious, a work based on Proust—but she sloughed off the request. As usual, time and money were not available. Surely it was her imperviousness to such pleas that caused him to speak of her as a "granitic personality." What bitterness he must have felt—always to be pleading, half the time to be denied. Worst of all was having to stifle his ideas for lack of a signal to go ahead.

One of these ideas, the Proust ballet based on *A la Recherche du Temps Perdu,* had been germinating for many years. But he knew that the whole complex project—one with a commissioned score and a scenario covering the multivolume epic—could not go forward at the present time. Hearing Richard Strauss's *Burleske,* however, made him reconsider. Maybe he could salvage just "the leftover ambitions." The score, written for piano and orchestra, brought to mind visions of softly glittering society soirées, shifting alliances and swooning ardor. Here were all the quirky humors and sudden eruptions of spirit that suggest Proustian strains. Even the ending, which casts a retrospective glance on what has preceded, turns ironic.

At the moment he was thinking of a one-act version, not the full-evening extravaganza that would call upon the company's massed resources. (In a way, he was still the same English madman who, against the sirens of war, had put together the London Ballet. Or an innocent.)

Meanwhile he spoke to Lucia about *Dim Lustre.* Impossible, she said. A few months later, however, madame impresaria called with the good news. "Antony," she said, "isn't it wonderful! We're going to let you do the ballet." The reason? Massine, then a specialist in popular ballets and a choreographer Chase apparently ranked over Tudor, had decided he could not do the work he promised her. That meant an opening for the pinch hitter. "But," she admonished, "it will be a bit of a hurry." Two weeks separated the telephone call from the premiere, that October of 1943. And possibly because *Dim Lustre* seemed a far less difficult thing than the Proust project he originally envisioned it flowed effortlessly. "I don't think of it as a major work," he said years later. "Something that pours out of me is not major, and I didn't have time to give it much consideration." Not about to look this gift horse in the mouth, though, he added, "If others consider it major I'll be perfectly happy."

It was Hugh who took charge following Lucia's phone call. "His faithful right hand and good sense came to the rescue and dealt with the logistics," Tudor recalled. Emboldened by Hugh, he gathered dancers he had worked with often—besides Hugh, himself and Nora, there was Rosella Hightower, John Kriza and Janet Reed. They virtually camped at the Goldfarb Studios, present site of the Ed Sullivan Theater. "Choreographers usually reach impasses," Hugh happily mused, generalizing his experience with Tudor to take in others as well. "[These are] the stiles you have to go over to get to the next meadow. But this just flowed."

The meadows they roamed may have given off mere essences of Proust's rueful trysts and deceptive visions, but as was the case throughout the Tudor oeuvre, *Dim Lustre* dug up the sod of dissolving relationships. The ballet was a discourse on love and illusion, the mind games people play with themselves. Distinctly Tudoresque, it turned out to be a fragile backward glimpse through the scrims of memory—the very opposite of what Hurok and company would applaud. The setting, an Edwardian ballroom, finds an elegant man and woman waltzing. A whiff of perfume, the touch of a hand, a stolen kiss transport the pair to another time, a remembrance of things past. Flashbacks. Sensual fragments. A blurring of then and now. A bittersweet realization that love, or at least flaming love, is transitory, that it is a fabulous trick the mind plays on its possessor, that it has the power to substitute illusion for reality and vice versa.

The symbols he used—a kiss on the shoulder, a dropped handkerchief, swirling couples that separate the two lovers, semidarkness that merges the past with the present, a suddenly brilliant light that dispels associations—prefigure outtakes from the 1962 film *Last Year at Marienbad.* What Tudor managed to do then, as he had with other ballets like *Jardin aux Lilas,* was summon his cinematic powers. A master of lighting, he suggested time lapses with blackouts and identity confusion with imaginary mirrors. Each principal had a reflection, another dancer to face who did identical, perfectly synchronized movements. The names of the characters, as in most of his ballets, were generic: A Reflection, Another Reflection, It Was Spring, Who

Was She? She Wore a Perfume, He Wore a White Tie. Only the female protagonists—Caroline and Hagar, from *Jardin* and *Pillar,* respectively—take on specificity.

Tudor often drew inspiration for his characters from great stage women. Besides Pavlova and Spessivtseva of the ballet world there were those actresses who mesmerized him. He had told Annabelle Lyon to see Simone Simon, that the experience would help her for *Pillar*. He tried to graft onto Nora the manner of Vivien Leigh, for whose 1937 play *The Happy Hypocrite* he had choreographed some dances. And then there was Madeleine Carroll, who had reduced him to "a lap dog." He worked with her, as choreographer, for a vehicle also in the 1930s called *The Toy Cart*. Before that his favorite heroine was Pearl White of silent films. And now, for *Dim Lustre* he had Luise Rainer in mind. Nora was sent to see this current incarnation of the feminine mystique—in the movie *Masquerade*.

Dreaming along with women who dream of ballrooms was something that started in Tudor's childhood. Young Will Cook sat at his mother's side as she would tell him about "her courting days and Mr. Burry's Ballroom" and show him "the dance card she saved as a souvenir." In a flight of fancy he soared from that proletarian dance floor to the grandeur of Proust and Strauss. Pretending, for him, was very much in order, as had been play-acting in his mother's clothes. These were the true origins of his impulse to make up dances—a child's imaginings of his parent's life. Whatever the repressed longings she felt, whatever the passivity that tied her to reveries, he became her attuned collaborator. Small wonder that he filled his psychic hierarchy with heroines or that his fantasies were so pungent.

In *Dim Lustre* Tudor danced He Wore a White Tie. But it was Hugh and Nora who took the central roles, both of them urbane people with a past. Theirs was a muted ardor, nothing cataclysmic like that in *Jardin*. Disenchantment and ennui figure importantly here. Toward the end The Gentleman with Her (Laing) and The Lady with Him (Kaye) pull apart gradually, the gulf between them filled by the more significant others they each recalled. So full of lambent drama was their interaction that "Nora and Hugh thought of themselves as the Lunts," observed Arthur Laurents.

Here was Tudor's first nonsatiric ballet to deal with disaffection in a primary relationship. And like the themes that formerly found their way into his scenarios this one could well have crept from the private quarry of his life; it told possibly of himself and Hugh—who were no longer the embodiment of absolute gratification for each other. Various fleeting love interests crisscrossed the picture, love interests that each pursued in his own style. *Dim Lustre* could stand as a virtual caption for the state of their engagement: always back to center but with loosened ties. What did not change lifelong, however, was Hugh's connection with Tudor's career.

The *Dim Lustre* reviews were somewhat mixed. John Martin wrote: "The choreography is copious and brilliant, the stage is constantly in motion and in form. If [the ballet] is perhaps on the mental side rather than emotional, that is in itself a novelty, and when it is done as brilliantly as this is done, a welcome one." But Edwin Denby found *Dim Lustre* to be "weaker both in the inventiveness of the dance detail and in the general over-all dramatic effect. . . . [It had] less conviction than manner, it was meant to look elegant but the effect was only a trivial one."

Nevertheless, Tudor's reputation remained undimmed. He was so buoyed, in fact, by the sense of his eminence that he shrewdly negotiated an important clause in his upcoming contract: to be named as one of the five to seven members of an artistic advisory committee to be formed. According to the terms outlined, the committee's duties would revolve around advising the board of directors on all matters of artistic policy—repertory, casting, rehearsal schedules. In short, Tudor was eager to democratize decision-making, knowing that equitable treatment meant taking these matters out of the hands of strictly business people.

But even if he had not established what was to prove a temporary control he could see his works becoming very much the foundation of Ballet Theatre. As their number grew—he now had eight ballets in the repertory—his importance solidified. He played his role of demigod to the hilt. Dancers danced around him, always looking for a nod of interest, always hoping to be discovered by him and with any luck cast in his ballets—but at the same time risking public humiliation should he single them out. Unfailingly, he rose to the occasion.

Years later, Tudor would sit in the audience watching a performance of *Undertow,* his 1945 ballet. He spoke of "being enthralled. I could never believe I had anything to do with its creation. The best things just came out of the blue. But not really. Rather out of your whole consciousness as a human being." And his consciousness—at least the part to do with the creative process—was infinite.

It took himself as well as Hugh to account, demons and all. And by the time he looked at a scenario suggestion by playwright John van Druten, he could put the personal pieces in place. The result was a ballet that seemed like a case study of all that he knew and came to believe.

By those terms, it depicted homosexuality, at least its superficial genesis, as the consequence of child molestation—a sordid encounter between an old man and a boy. It traced the life from a painful childbirth, to a rejecting mother, to distrust of all people, to a climactic love/murder redolent with pathological eroticism. Included in this panoramic tableau were the rough street characters who compelled and disgusted Tudor as a boy; a female Elmer Gantry with a mania for seducing her congregants; a nymphomaniac who incites gang rape. Nothing quite like this had ever taken place on a ballet stage before.

Ever the scholar, he researched the whole psychiatric literature—taking six months from November 1944 to *Undertow*'s April 10 premiere to read some thirty-four textbooks. And at the conclusion, with a scenario that rang true to his partner's near-paranoia, he was absolutely on the mark. Here Tudor would show in clinical terms Hugh's mangled perceptions, the imminent threat he sensed in the world. Here he would put him in a dramatic situation that arguably had a basis in reality.

Until now Tudor had not conceived a work with a male protagonist and naturally the lead would belong to Hugh. All the characters took names derived from mythology—again Tudor's universalizing tactic—except the hero, or antihero, called The Transgressor. But as he had done repeatedly in the past the choreographer used everyday people in his ballet, people who always appeared to be English more than anything else. If they had talked, in this case, the speech would have been cockney.

As before, Tudor's creative fantasies centered on women—and *Undertow* would boast a virtual parade of them, all aptly named as goddesses. Cybele, for instance, The Transgressor's birthmother, was the great goddess of nature. Tudor cast the beautiful Diana Adams in this role, and showed her recoiling from the son she had just given birth to after a difficult labor. In the ballet she casts him away, favoring Pollux, the immortal youth who is born anew each day. Not only is Hugh the Transgressor unwanted, he is succeeded by a superior being, opening even deeper wounds. And to whatever extent Hugh was repulsed by women, Tudor shared the reaction. For this ballet was not just about perversion and baseness, it was about women—save one innocent—as predators.

Brilliantly, Tudor revealed The Transgressor in naturalistic, nuanced terms, as a halting, fearful character. Those surrounding him were shown as the antihero would see them: half-formed or deformed. Tudor admitted as much when he said that "the main character had a perverted view of humanity, because of his birth and the type of childhood he had." For all we know he could have been describing himself.

Meanwhile there were other compelling attractions in store for Hugh on this odyssey to a warped adulthood. First, The Transgressor would attempt having a girlfriend, one who is pure and innocent. Next he would find himself in a slum—very much like Central Street—where he is distracted by a prostitute plying her trade, and then by a mangy group of young thugs advertising their own odd sexual allure. Before he was through, he would have encountered a gang rape, drunken bag ladies who urinate in the street and an assortment of society's hypocrites passing themselves off as upstanding citizens.

No one escaped Tudor's lens. The making of *Undertow* had the dancewright standing behind the protagonist and slipping glasses on the unseeing person. It was the view from Hugh's eyes as told by Tudor. And that view was an amalgam of the one's personal pathology and the other's childhood memories.

The moment of truth in this surreal documentary comes via The Transgressor's closeup encounter with Medusa: seductress non pareil, his mother in disguise. Commanded by her to perform the ultimate sex act, he becomes enraged and strangles her. The epilogue has him wandering alone, then hoping to escape the discovery of his deed. But that is not to be. Aganippe, the girlfriend and his social conscience, enters. She knows his guilt and points to him. He walks into oblivion. A revised finale has him curling into a fetal position. And that's the way the world ends: through climactic regression. The antihero wishes himself back to the womb.

Needless to say, *Undertow* was daring, controversial and avant garde back in 1945. Tudor had always been a man of his time and his time was that of Freudian enlightenment. Not enough to openly investigate his own psyche, however. He consulted a psychoanalyst once, "but sat in silence the whole time," he told Sono Osato. Later, he advised writer Arthur Laurents "not to be analyzed because it will interfere with your creativity." Nevertheless, he took the opportunity to dredge up the people of Central Street as they had appeared to little William Cook. "Dreadful," he called them. *Undertow,* with its title implying a potentially destructive force, caught Tudor in its wake as well as Hugh. Whatever the Cook family's emotional deficits, they might well have been compounded by the squalid surroundings he struggled to escape.

As it was, he had no trouble raising the awareness of those

who worked with him. And yet little of what he devised was ever spoken about. Not even composer William Schuman knew the story. Tudor merely asked him for music with various feeling states—four minutes of this and two minutes of that. Adams went through the semigraphic movements of childbirth without really knowing what they represented. There were many cinematic vignettes, telling little cameos that filled in the context of this contemporary tragedy, but the dancers had almost no idea how they fit. For a bride and groom pas de deux, Richard Beard knew only that he and Janet Reed "were a lascivious couple underneath our wedding costumes, barely able to wait for the bedroom where they would come off."

And to Alicia Alonso, who danced the nymphet Ate, Tudor gave a seminar on seduction—the subtext being that this rape victim also feels an erotic fascination. " 'Play with your hair and look at the boys,' he told me. 'Look at them as though you're a little eager and a little afraid at the same time. Feel as though you want to escape, but don't want to escape.' " He told her other things, also, "too dirty to repeat," Alonso said. Dancing as one of the boy-rapists in a subsequent cast, Zachary Solov remembered Tudor in rehearsal, whispering in his ear: "When you look in her direction notice the nearby boys and think how much you want to lick their dicks." To whatever degree he could crawl into his dancers' particular imaginations he brought out vibrant portrayals. Uncannily, he knew how to make exactly the remark that would stir the desired response.

But it took tremendous patience on their parts. Dancers are not attuned to long discussions on psychology and philosophy. Action is their modus operandi. Alonso complained about "the endless hours we would spend just sitting . . . and sometimes he would talk me into a mood or ask me what I thought about the art world, which I knew very little of. But he listened carefully to my naive comments. And then he would tell me to just move. 'This way, no that way.' And pretty soon he had created a dance.

He educated me for this too. By showing me pictures in books. I remember the Furies, with their tangled hair flying. 'This has something of your character,' he said."

Those who could adjust to Tudor's strange choreographic ways found great benefits. Not only did they recognize Tudor as a "genius"—the term is commonly used by dancers (and such critics as Denby and Martin)—but they pledged their loyalty unconditionally. And why not when convinced that he could make them great dancing actors? Alonso is remembered for her compellingly obscene vignette in *Undertow*—a moment unforgotten by those who saw it.

Each of the other small but choice female roles was meant to be an aspect of The Transgressor—and, ipso facto, an aspect of Tudor. Paula Tracy, another Medusa for a 1960s revival, also danced the Salvation Army lady (Polyhymnia) "and he told me all the filthy things she was really thinking as she proseltyzed on the street, especially her thoughts about a young man who grabbed her attention." Not surprisingly he cast Lucia Chase in the role—once more including her among his harem of perceived villainesses, the Ramberts and de Milles who, he thought, tried to dominate and disempower him.

Nora Kaye, for variously reported reasons, had no role in the original cast, although she danced Medusa subsequently. One source said that she was pregnant at the time, yet no one but Kaye danced *Pillar,* which was enjoying its fourth consecutive season in 1944–45; another suggested that Tudor preferred a dancer with long legs and beautiful feet—thus Nana Gollner. The legs were crucial to his symbolic image of Medusa; they stood as the equivalent of the goddess's serpent locks. With them she entwined The Transgressor in a love-death embrace, even conjuring a phallic image as one leg jutted in the air.

As could be expected, *Undertow* came as a shock to the ballet audience witnessing its Met premiere on April 10, 1945—six days after Tudor's thirty-seventh birthday. Nothing like it had ever been seen by the tutu-and-tiara crowd: an onstage birth, rape, seduction, a sex murder, surreal poetic allusions, like the finale, which has a balloon floating away from a little girl as she observes The Transgressor in his final throes of resignation. Raymond Breinin's decor, with its skyborne winged horses and spired houses, suggests an English Gothic fantasy. Here were the Four Horsemen of the Apocalypse, the avengers of everything. And the contemporary angst of William Schuman's commissioned score—the only such Tudor ever used—complemented the ballet.

Just as Tudor had predicted, audiences were somewhat bewildered. "If they are to gain the fullest enjoyment," he said, "they must be trained to do some of the work." The reviews were mixed. Edwin Denby applauded Tudor for managing "no vulgarity in his obscene images" and went on to write: "One keeps watching the movement all through for the intellectual meaning its pantomime conveys more than for its physical impetus as dancing. Its impetus is often tenuous. But its pantomime invention is frequently Tudor's most brilliant to date. The birth scene, an elderly man's advances to a prostitute, an hysterical wedding, drunken slum women, several provocative poses by the hero's victim, and quite particularly the suggested rape of a vicious little girl by four boys, these are all masterpieces of pantomime, and freer, more fluid, more plastic than Tudor's style has been. Brilliant too is his individualized use of the dancers. . . . *Undertow* suggests in many details that Tudor's style is more powerful at present than ever before."

Martin was apparently taken aback by the ballet. He likened it to "a kind of Greek tragedy in terms of the London slums or, perhaps more accurately, a sordid sex murder in terms of classic mythology. . . . Its form is far from immediately lucid." He did give *Undertow* credit for being "a courageous piece," however. Admirable, was the consensus. For many critics, and public as well, the ballet would remain unlikable.

No sooner had Tudor completed it than he plunged into Broadway. An offer to do the choreography for *Hollywood Pinafore,* using Arthur Sullivan's music, held out understandable appeal to him at this particular moment. And since he had no immediate plans for another ballet, it seemed both a practical and adventurous thing to do. After all, his friends de Mille and Robbins had turned musical comedy to their advantage, as choreographers for *Oklahoma* and *On the Town,* respectively. There was nothing to suggest he couldn't do the same. His experience with the lyric theater in London would surely stand him in good stead. What's more, a light entertainment might be just the sort of diversion from more serious challenges that he needed. Besides, the producer gave him carte blanche. The ballet he created for *Pinafore* was about a small-town girl who comes to Hollywood with the proverbial stars in her eyes—a subject he could well extrapolate on.

His choreography was just fine, according to all reports. But the show, which had its premiere in May of 1945, flopped. Nevertheless, he was committed to this Broadway fling for a year—having taken a sabbatical from Ballet Theatre. Hugh left with him and John Taras, who danced a number of smaller roles, agreed to look after Tudor's ballets in his absence. The company's slipshod rehearsal style hardly insured any kind of fidelity, though, to a choreographer's wishes. Typically, when Michael Kidd took over the role of The Transgressor "no one even showed me the steps," he recalled. "I was given an eight millimeter film of the performance, shot without a zoom from the back of the theater. All I could make out was a stick figure and his entrances and exits. What I did was improvise."

Six months after *Pinafore* came the Lerner and Loewe show, *The Day before Spring,* with a dancing role for Hugh. Unluckily, that one also earned poor notices, although the word here on Tudor's choreography, again, was good.

Hollywood

AT BALLET THEATRE guest artists came and went. From the time Hurok first became associated with the company, it ran according to what he considered the only box office mandate: international stars in classical works. So while Tudor and his largely American casts dominated the contemporary wing, luminaries such as Markova and Dolin, André Eglevsky and the two remaining "baby ballerinas"—Tatiana Riabouchinska and Tamara Toumanova—held forth in the standard nineteenth-century repertory.

By the end of the 1944–45 season Alden Talbot had resigned, a victim of the company's financial headaches. Oliver Smith succeeded him and, together with Lucia Chase, formed a codirectorship that was to last through three decades. At least they were in greater accord than Chase had been with Sevastianov, Hurok's puppet.

What's more, Smith proved to be the closest ally Tudor had

had lately—dubbing him "the greatest choreographer living" and naming him "the conscience of the company." When the new director stepped aboard that 1944–45 season, five of the twenty repertory ballets were Tudor's. Since the roster was always in flux—many dancers wearied of the arduous touring schedule and left—cast openings frequently came up. For the candidates hoping to fill them it was both a fearsome prospect and a dream opportunity. Tudor, who watched their approach with glinting pleasure, sat on his throne as demigod. He would send out one of his famously personal questions or appraisals and if the recipient was caught off balance he or she faced not just public shame but failed the master's audition as well. His reputation for evoking equal parts terror and awe was not unfounded.

Anyone who could face up to the challenge of working with him knew that mental jousting would be as important as performing steps. Self-defense was the first order of business—"all of it meticulously carried out by way of a facade," said Rosella Hightower, who joined Ballet Theatre in 1941, along with others from the Ballet Russe. "Tudor couldn't stand directness. He only felt comfortable knowing that the game rules were in place, that we would put up the proper maneuver for dealing with him. This facade, always built on humor, was his protection. He could control everything that way and at the same time keep people at a distance."

Hightower danced a second-cast Russian Ballerina in *Gala Performance,* which meant Tudor recognized her physical strength. She also originated the role, She Wore a Perfume, in *Dim Lustre.* But the former Ballet Russe dancer realized right from the beginning that she could never surrender herself unconditionally, as was necessary, in order to be his muse. "I always swiveled out of a clinch. I was too reserved to lay myself out the way Nora did." Several others professed to having the same potential as Kaye. What separated them from her, they said, was the singular, redoubtable, obsessive drive she claimed. No one among Karnilova, Bentley, Golden and others could sacrifice herself on the altar of Tudorian psychodrama like this.

Nor did any covet the role of muse so aggressively. As soon as Alicia Markova was out of the picture, Nora claimed what she regarded as *her* rightful role, Juliet—which had, of course, been made on the English guest artist.

This bit of miscasting aside, she knew one thing with certainty: her brilliance as a dramatic interpreter shone in the Tudor works as nowhere else. And as long as the likes of Toumanova dominated in that season's new ballets by Massine and Nijinska, as well as the classics, Nora could rely only on Tudor. Appearing in second casts, as she did in the Toumanova repertory, relegated her to second-ballerina status. Still, there were times when she could gain the upper hand. Annabelle Lyon, lauded by many as a superb Tudor dancer, had inherited Caroline (*Jardin*) from Viola Essen. Nora did not rest until she could claim that role also— despite the fact that she was felt to be less ideally cast than Lyon. The battle between Kaye and Alonso for Juliet, in the first *Romeo* at the Met (post-Markova), was the stuff of a major campaign and their rivalry, like something out of *Gala Performance,* went on for seasons to come. It was all Chase could do to keep peace between them.

There were two forces Tudor could seldom stand up to. One of them was the noisy, haranguing—and yes, even physically embattling—Hugh; the other, Nora, who worked in her own persuasive, less exhausting ways. Years later Tudor would admit that he found her "intimidating." Of course, she didn't have quite the psychosexual leverage Hugh did, nor quite the same dependency, nor would she resort to his ruthless tactics. But walking out of a rehearsal once because her mentor was insisting on an undoable step she hollered, "Fuck you, Tudor." That evening he called her, eager to patch things up and offer a compromise.

With Hugh, negotiations were on an altogether different plane. One night in New Orleans he and Tudor could be heard arguing in their hotel room until morning. It was a frazzling fight. It involved casting. "And what am *I* supposed to do if he dances that part?" Hugh railed over and over. His questions came like attacks. They weren't questions at all. They were clubs and ham-mers. "And what will that do for *me?*" he badgered nonstop, his voice high and strident, the rhythms staccato. In between came a few low, muffled answers from Tudor. He bore the pummeling like a just punishment being meted out. Abused and abuser seemed familiar with this well-worn script; years later, in *Who's Afraid of Virginia Woolf?* the playwright Edward Albee portrayed another such couple digging their teeth into each other's emo-tional flesh. In this case, release might have risked bleeding to death by both.

Battering, Albee showed, is the fallout of a *folie à deux* and a particular mode of intimacy. It resurrects feeling where there was only deadness. Pain as affirmation. But Tudor might have felt beholden to Hugh for a transgression. The guilt over original seduction? Or maybe a generalized need to expiate? "Even as they clung together, they destroyed each other," said Maria Kar-nilova. "They crawled out of the pits together. They were blood brothers." From somewhere there was damage, primary damage. And perhaps it had occurred in those mean streets of EC1 as well as in Barbados. In any case, ransom was being extracted.

Hugh hardly tempered his behavior in the more public arena of classes and rehearsals. The same basic script applied. And since his sponsor, Tudor, enjoyed high official status, he could rage without shame or retribution. When Michael Maule, a South African dancer, was rehearsing the "Rose" Adagio (a bravura excerpt from *Sleeping Beauty*) "Hugh screamed his criticisms of me in front of everyone," said Maule. "I thought Tudor had to be a coward to permit that kind of behavior. Finally, it took Nora to put him in his place. 'Oh, shut up, Hugh,' she said. 'Michael's the only one who didn't drop me.' "

These were manifestations of rage out of control. But they didn't go unrelieved by playfulness and conviviality on both their parts. After all, humor was fundamental to Tudor's social style. Those who could boast the wit to parry with him—like John Kriza and Jerome Robbins—simply geared up for the contest and enjoyed it.

Whenever Ballet Theatre was in New York, and especially during the summer, Tudor taught classes. Sometimes special sessions at Studio 61, above Carnegie Hall. Afterward he and Hugh took an entourage from the class down the street to the Russian Tea Room. Hugh would tell his jokes. Tudor would deliver his quips and everyone drank "lots and lots of gin," according to dancer Mary Burr, a very affectionate disciple.

As spontaneous as his jokes or tantrums seemed, Hugh rarely did anything without first plotting how to resolve a crisis and what the exact effect would be. Tudor, giving a series of *tendus* in class, would, by that choice, inadvertently point up Hugh's deficiencies. He, in turn, would go on the offensive, shouting his disapproval at Tudor. Then he would stalk out in a red heat, camouflaging with angry impatience the real reason for the walk-out: his own technical weakness. This way he saved face. No one had to see him struggle and fail. His timely and theatrical exit gave him the appearance of independence, of superiority.

Acting was his life, really. And in this he and Tudor were opposites. "Hugh was always performing," remembered Billy Chappell, "and trying to attract everyone's attention. Antony never performed—except at seeming unruffled. Of course he was often very disturbed. But didn't dare show it." Both of them found a haven in the theater. Tudor could vicariously live out situations in his ballets that he otherwise would not hazard and Hugh could bring glory to himself. "He struggled so over his homosexuality," said Hightower of Hugh, "that at least here, in the make-believe world, he could take control and gain respect. Maybe Tudor's hand on his shoulder was fatal. Maybe on his own, with a woman, he would have found a better outlet for his energy."

Naturally he loved the spotlight. And the formality of sets and costumes and makeup and roles. So adept was he at constructing his image that he had his back molars removed—to give him an even deeper hollow under his high sculptured cheekbones. "Giving up those teeth meant that he couldn't eat a steak," Hightower observed. "But it seemed a fair trade to him."

He didn't care whether the figures he portrayed were admirable or not, so long as they were important. Neither was the personality Hugh formulated in the studio necessarily appealing. The only thing that mattered was tactics and whether they worked. In the case of his hothead departures, Tudor generally paid no attention—he understood the ruse and it didn't interfere with what he was doing. But once in a while Hugh would stage his walkout during a crucial rehearsal, when he was desperately needed. Tudor would then become stony-silent, helpless in the face of his partner's intransigence. Ransom, again. Spitework.

And there were occasional signs that Tudor might not always want to bear the burden of Hugh. During an August 1945 stay in Los Angeles—the company had a series of engagements at Hollywood Bowl—they ended up, once, role-swapping. The hospitable movie folk were constantly throwing parties for Ballet Theatre at their fabulous homes and at one intimate, postperformance soirée Tudor drank " 'til he was feeling no pain," said Janet Reed. The night was warm. The pool at the host's hillside home was inviting. And in a rare moment of hedonist abandon, the pillar of restraint peeled off his clothes and ran across the lawn to the pool—hand in hand with Reed. "There we were, skinny-dipping," she recalled. "Neither of us had any sexual interest in the other. It was just lots of silly giggling. Tudor had a marvelous laugh. Everyone came to watch—they thought it was a hoot. But Hugh just looked on disapprovingly."

He was the exhibitionist, after all, not Tudor, and this reversal did not go down well. Hugh was more comfortable with Tudor the aesthete, Tudor the silent observer, Tudor the verbal provocateur—the one who *said* rather than *did* things.

Hugh adored the very image of Tinseltown. Stars. Glamour. Fame. He insisted that Harry Mines, a stagestruck journalist friend, take him on a tour of the studios. For Tudor, though, the celluloid trade per se failed to be as seductive. But they both loved getting together with Hollywood's British contingent— Greer Garson, Vivien Leigh, Clifton Webb, Constance Collier,

Vincent Price. And often, when the company played downtown at Philharmonic Auditorium, Tudor and Hugh could be seen after performances sitting in a secluded corner of the Biltmore bar with Oona Chaplin, the wife of the famous comedian so admired by the choreographer.

The dancers were all "good drinkers," according to Mines, who remembered the "stinger" parties at which "everyone turned a nice shade of green." At their rented bungalow near Hollywood Bowl, Hugh told stories and entertained while Tudor sat quietly—an established mode. "Hugh was like a train chugging," said Mines. "His words burst out like cannonballs."

But there were intense moments between them even in the company of others. Tudor might make an analytic quip about some aspect of Hugh's behavior. He'd then get a dissenting "I beg your pardon" from Hugh. And on they'd go—these great critics of each other who could become fiercely engaged in some bit of minutia as a battleground.

Meanwhile the long touring schedules kept the company in constant close quarters. On and off trains, in and out of hotels—intimacy was the order of the day. Lots of dancers became couples for a few months while many were happy to settle for an occasional amorous lark. Scrambling to and from train berths—not unlike the scenes in Billy Wilder's movie *Some Like It Hot*—kept them from being strangers in the night. One dancer remembered Tudor poking a head inside his upper berth. The uninvited guest twisted his head, smiled coyly and said "hello," but got no response from the occupant—who "was not attracted to Tudor and certainly didn't want to get into a situation of sexual politics. It could easily have backfired. And I wasn't the only one Tudor quietly had eyes for, but he would never resort to casting-couch tactics. He was too ethical for that sort of thing." After returning to New York the same dancer claimed also to have been "chased around a room" by Hugh, who frequently got himself in liaisons with women also. Muriel Bentley remembered a night of carousing in a berth with Hugh. "But we giggled and drank too much for our great expectations to come to anything." None of these shenanigans seemed to cause serious damage between Tudor and Hugh. In fact, they commonly alluded to their respective, freewheeling sexual adventures in the spirit of gamesmanship, without recriminations.

20

Hands across the Sea

NINETEEN HUNDRED AND FORTY-FIVE had been a tumultuous time. In April America's four-term president died: Franklin Delano Roosevelt did not live to see world peace restored. In May the allied forces finally declared victory in Europe. In August Japan surrendered. Americans were caught up in the euphoria of bringing their boys back from war—as heroes.

Tudor had spent the last five years traveling all over the land. New York was home now, but he had mingled, in a sense, with Kansans and Californians, New Englanders and Southerners. He understood what they were feeling. He also could project what had happened to those he left behind. Peggy van Praagh had written him many letters. Uncharacteristically, he answered none. The man who never failed to respond found himself unable to so much as acknowledge the many inquiries from his devoted dancer, the one who, with Maude Lloyd, had tried to safeguard and keep alive his London Ballet.

But Christmas 1945 brought an end to his silence, a silence that could conceivably be understood as guilt-ridden. A huge gift of foods and goods came to Therese Langfield from a William Cook. She didn't recognize the name at first, having known him only as Antony—which made the reason for using his given name all the more mysterious. Was it remorse over the years of abandonment? Legal difficulties tied to his failure to return to England? At any rate, the care package couldn't have been more appreciated, for she and the others had endured great hardship throughout the war. It wasn't difficult for Tudor to understand that—even without direct communication.

Nevertheless, at the time that he and Hugh had left his native city, Maude and the others had already begun to prepare for war. "We were busy making blackout curtains," she remembered. By September 1940, Hitler's *blitzkrieg* of London was well under way with nightly attacks lasting many months. The homeless filled shelters. Civilian casualties mounted to 30,000. Historic buildings were reduced to smoking ruins. Finally, came a respite. But when the German forces returned from Eastern Europe for "the little blitz" in 1944, it was to a people worn out by their prolonged deprivation, their anxiety. Sleepless nights and hunger—there was severe food rationing over a period of five years—had taken a heavy toll.

Surely Tudor imagined as much. And then there was his relationship with Hugh, which had lost whatever naive elements it might have once had. Struggle was still very much the mode both in Tudor's personal life and his work. He was revered and lauded. But not since *Pillar of Fire* had he won unmitigated praise, either popular or critical. The effort and anxiety of getting out a new piece began to fill him with dread, to say nothing of the persistence it took to get administrative consent for a new undertaking. What's more, his existing ballets needed the closest supervision, for they were highly perishable—depending on exact nuances for their very special aura.

· · · · ·

But the ending of World War II at least created a cushion of exhilaration. And when Chase and Smith received a wire inviting Ballet Theatre to Covent Garden—partly to celebrate the new peace—the two British subjects who had become de facto defectors from their war-torn country had much to contemplate. For these prodigal sons a London tour would necessarily be troubling. Much more for Tudor than for Hugh, since his responsibilities and impact were greater. Be that as it may, the company boarded the *Queen Mary* and set out on June 20, 1946. A spirited Ballet Theatre, off on its inaugural visit, was the first American troupe to go abroad after the war.

Tudor, returning to England with Hugh, had time to ponder his unfinished business during the trans-Atlantic trip. Not only would "the boys" face a reunion with Maude, Peggy and the rest, but there was the nervous-making prospect of introducing them to their American counterparts—the Yankee Caroline and Episode in His Past. Would it seem like a confrontation with former and current lovers? One could predict a certain unease, a not-so-covert curiosity, a challenge to rivalrous comparisons.

Looming beyond any of these concerns was the question of how Tudor might be seen. Would his countrymen—both strangers and friends—regard him as a traitor? A conquering hero? One who emigrated to the New World where he defined modern ballet for the Americans? One who became their guru? And surely he entertained a retribution fantasy. After all, he left as a pauper—begging on the steps of the ballet establishment. The United States had allowed him a latitude denied on his home soil. And now Ballet Theatre would play Covent Garden, the grandest forum in all London, the platform of the throne's choice, home of the Royal Opera and now the Sadler's Wells Ballet. He stood the chance to be vindicated of past failures. Ninette de Valois had once turned down the young choreographer who came pleading for a job. Now he could give her cause for regret. Now he could stand eye level with her favorite, Frederick Ashton.

But when the *Queen Mary* docked at Southampton that July morning his anticipation took a pensive, somber tone. At nine o'clock the ship dropped anchor and everyone waited on deck for the customs officials to process exit. The wait turned into four hours, during which Tudor and Hugh hardly spoke a word. Tudor clutched a briefcase, alternately standing and sitting on a wood-slatted deck chair. He and Hugh wore jackets and ties— the one looking somewhat like a prematurely balding poet professor, the other a Noel Coward type, his black hair sleeked back elegantly, his demeanor fashion-page perfect. What worlds they had nervously to contemplate. What torture to have so much time in which to do it.

When it finally came, the welcome saw nothing held back. The affection of Tudor's London group had not diminished. Nor was there any personalized blame for abandonment during the war. But in that crucial time span, nearly seven years, some things had changed. Antony and Hugh had left as a couple; on their return they verged on being a trio.

The added element in this reacquaintance picture was Diana Adams. The tall beauty whose shyness made her seem elusive to some and cold to others clearly transformed the program to a pas de trois. Nora, who befriended Diana in the same way she drew close to anyone with importance in the career circle, was still very much on the scene, although displaced at this point. The constellation had changed, not only in form but matter. While both men paid close attention to Diana, it was Hugh who singled her out on a one-to-one basis. Who would have guessed the outcome?

Backstage in her Covent Garden dressing room—early in Ballet Theatre's run—Diana sat on a couch. Hugh, stretched out with his head in her lap, gazed up at his *Undertow* nature goddess, his seductress-mother. He was oblivious to all else, his eyes signing singular devotion to her, his hopes fastened to the salvation she might bring him. None of it was lost on Tudor. He sat at a little distance, avidly observing the scene, "his eyes twinkling," according to Leo Kersley. "He reminded me of Shakespeare dreaming up *Hamlet*." Here was the Antony he knew, a voyeur taking in some private act, reveling in what his imagination would make of it and surely plotting how to use what he saw for a new ballet.

Curiosity about the American dancers ran high, especially for Diana. She had joined Ballet Theatre in 1944 at age eighteen—insecure, frightened and unworldly, with no awareness of her beauty or talent. Trained as a ballet dancer by her stepmother, and encouraged by her father, an English teacher, she came to the company not as a spirited or giddy girl who could relate easily to the others but as something of a loner. She was serious and thoughtful—prime material for Tudor—and in search of a family. Her parents had divorced and she no longer lived with either of them. Like her professorial father, Tudor held out vast intellectual appeal and happily embraced the ingenue. She hung on his every word, quietly absorbing what flowed from him to her. And as far as he was concerned she could not have come along at a more propitious time—this being a relative heyday for him, a period of strength in which he didn't depend, or didn't think he depended, on Hugh at all costs. He was ready to relinquish Hugh's support; in turn, Hugh would need to find someone else to control. Meanwhile Diana crossed their paths. Diana, eager for whatever role they would have her play. Diana, not suspecting, then, the pernicious nature of this ménage à trois.

What's more, she exemplified the textbook ideal of a ballet dancer. Too reticent to qualify as another Nora Kaye, she nevertheless lacked nothing in commitment to the dance, loyalty to Tudor and, not least, drive for a career.

Underlying this perfect dovetailing of psychodynamics was her self-deprecation. To wit: "It was wonderful to watch Tudor and to try to imitate him [demonstrating a role]," she said. "When he did it, it was marvelous. On me it was nothing." Her powers of observation had the sharpness of his best dancers. Witnessing him impersonating the Italian Ballerina she was quick to grasp that only the eyes moved, not the head, and that on that detail the crux of the character depended. In turn, Tudor saw her willingness to be any awful thing he desired. In *Undertow* she danced both the birth-mother and the seductress-mother, understanding that Medusa "had to be hideous [albeit with] a purely classical line." What perverse satisfaction he took in rendering the sublime grotesque—all in the name of realizing The Transgressor's warped view of women. Outwardly and offstage he could admire them. Up close, they posed an intolerable threat.

But, of course, it was impossible to draw the line between Hugh's and Tudor's perceptions in the ballets. Just as it was impossible for one to have this relationship with Diana exclusive of the other. The ground rules between them hinged on having no secrets with her and thus no secrets from each other.

Clearly, Diana's initial and primary interest was in Tudor. As he inspired others, he inspired her. She became an ardent disciple, but one who stood to alter his life. This time Hugh wanted to join the communion. Thus he became part of her avowal of the Tudor religion. She never understood why he had to have her, but acknowledged that the whole impetus for their relationship came from him.

Under normal circumstances Tudor might have been even more absorbed by the developing romance. But his odyssey to England, and to the Covent Garden of his opera ballet days with Sir Thomas Beecham, understandably distracted him. And there were other little encounters he was relishing enormously: introducing Nora to Maude, for instance. When these two Carolines met, Nora had the audacious humor to admit to Tudor's first muse, "How I've always hated you! At every rehearsal Tudor would say, 'But Maude did it this way,' as though no one else could match you, or that there was no reason to even try." All this came as a shock to Maude, who said, "Antony never complimented me directly—the last thing I would have believed is that he held me up as an example to the dancers at this big, wonderful company."

Everyone in London had heard about *Pillar of Fire* and its thrilling new star. While Nora was understandably the object of much curiosity, she had to keep a wary eye on Diana who, through her connection to Hugh, held Tudor's primary interest now. ("She felt that Diana was the key to Antony because she had Hugh," said Therese.) Nora was still dramatic *ballerina assoluta* as far as *Pillar of Fire* went and ranked far ahead of her new rival.

She was quite a hit in London, not just as Hagar, but as herself. Therese remembered "we were all so terribly shabby" that June in 1946. They had barely shrugged off five years of war before this reunion with Tudor took place in a pub near Covent Garden. And when Nora looked her up and down and said, "Oh, so yaw Therese," she didn't know whether to laugh or cry. "But when Nora started talking about 'Tooohduh' (in the land where his name is pronounced 'Tee-U-dah,' as in kewpie doll) it was frightfully funny," she recalled.

Ever the lavish gift-giver, Nora bequeathed Therese the black cocktail dress she was wearing. A few months later, Nora's next husband-to-be, Isaac Stern, met Therese and kept staring at the dress she wore. "I had no idea at the time that they even knew each other," she said of Stern and Kaye, "or I would've understood his confusion." On another gala evening Nora and several others had dinner with Ashton. She had just been on a shopping spree and happily bedecked herself in the whole collection of garnets she'd purchased that day. The shiny stones hung from her ears, her arms and her neck. "Nora," said Ashton, "if you don't take some of those off, I'm afraid you'll be mistaken for a transvestite."

At the very least these were happy times, illuminating times. On their first trip to the country house of Maude and her husband, critic Nigel Gosling, Tudor and Hugh came alone. As far as Maude could see, "they were the same as always." But the second time they brought Diana and "Hugh seemed positively in love with her, also possessive." Strange as it might have seemed, she remembered that "Hugh had some intense flirtations going with Aggie's [de Mille's] sister before he and Antony left for America." Therese also noticed "Antony's glee" over Hugh's involvement with Diana. "I had the distinct feeling," she said, "that he was thinking of his freedom to have other lovers now. But I can't forget what Aggie said, apropos of Hugh and his involvement with Diana: 'You can go to the outermost limits [of seduction] only if you know you won't be raped.' "

What cast the superficial glow around these events was Tudor's avuncular pose. Hugh was the child. The child chose a new toy. The parent had no trouble accommodating the excitement over it because he knew that the child depended on him over the long haul and this was but an infatuation—temporary by its very definition. But had things been reversed, had the parent adopted another child, there would have been raging jealousy. Hugh never matured. Tantrums were natural to him; they became his behavioral stock in trade. He negotiated deals by way of his ferocity and stamina. No one could withstand Hugh on the warpath. And, with the advent of Diana, nothing had changed. "Antony would roll his eyes at me whenever Hugh got exercised out of proportion," Maude recalled. "I never knew how he could put up with him."

So it came as no shock that Tudor had at least one other motive in sanctioning the Hugh-Diana affair: relief. Besides, he was enjoying a degree of authority right now—as artistic administrator he wielded considerable control, scheduling rehearsals, for instance. He still worried his ballets to death, "always seeming so desperate for [rehearsal] time," Richard Beard wrote in his diary. "It was pitiful to watch him steal moment after moment in hopes of completing an impossible task. But how great he is," wrote the worshipful dancer.

During one Covent Garden rehearsal for *Romeo and Juliet* he and Hugh argued over details of roles belonging to two absent dancers—each holding tenaciously to his position. Hugh insisted on his memory of how the steps went. Tudor, who refused to accept Hugh's word, threatened "to ring [the dancers] at the hotel" for verification. "He wanted to further goad his Romeo. But Hugh shot back: "I'll tell you what I mean later and don't go on being sarcastic." Temporarily, the snipers retreated. But on a break Tudor tried to cross behind the fire curtain and Hugh leaped out at him, violently locking his body in a chain of arms and legs and wrestling him to the ground. Another time, during an Italian holiday at Positano, an argument broke out between them. Tudor began walking away but Hugh ran up from behind and sank his teeth into the ultimate pacifist's neck. He would not fight back, whereas, for Hugh, physical combat was as spontaneous as verbal tirades. Apart from actual murder the two of them were seen as the Joe Orton and Kenneth Halliwell of ballet.

But the truth is they both had an anxious investment in victory at Covent Garden. It was one thing to be the mysterious prince over the waters and another to earn the crown on home soil.

Tudor, the realist, made accurate projections on the response he would get. He knew that *Pillar* would go over well but was concerned about *Romeo,* since it had fallen into a sloppy state over the past three years and was a particularly fragile ballet. *Undertow,* rarely offered as a tour vehicle over its few years in the repertory because of its controversial subject matter and general unmarketability to ballet audiences, was on the Covent Garden agenda; since the run lasted for two months Ballet Theatre could afford to present Tudor's risky docudrama. *Gala Performance,* the fourth of his ballets brought on the London tour, was of little concern; its high entertainment value made it a safe bet.

But what he could hardly have been prepared for was the massive snub at a preopening party. At the customary reception given Sadler's Wells's visitors in the crush bar at Covent Garden, Antony and Hugh found themselves being ignored by the resident company's administrators. Painfully ignored, spurned the way turncoats would be. "Neither Fred nor Ninette spoke to them," according to John Taras. There was satisfaction, though, in both the public and critical response to Tudor's work. The deepest compliment, by far, came from *The Dancing Times,* which praised him for "preserving his belief in the value of ballet as a serious contributor to the art of theatre in a country, where, as far as I can judge on the present showing, the vast majority consider it as a joke to be enjoyed lightly in revue-like fashion."

2

○

Dock Strike

TUDOR HARBORED NO ILLUSIONS about London's reception to *Undertow*, which came in for both negative notices and poor audience response. Critics were satisfied to label it as an outgrowth of Hollywood's fixation on the psychological case study, although John Percival considered the ballet "vivid and exciting." No one could accuse its maker of treating the ballet like a stepchild, however.

The overall impression his four works made was that of a serious, thoughtful contender—quite in contrast to the creative persona of his old chum Ashton, who himself fell short in that regard. "Oh, yes, they said I failed in 'the depth charge' department," confessed Sir Frederick, a year before his death in 1988. "And it stuck," he said laughingly. "For me, too. I used to say 'what is Antony doing now, another 'depth charge?' '" In 1946, with the war just over and the bombing still echoing, the expression "depth charge" took on a double meaning. Ashton, for all time, would be considered the lyricist, the master of poetic valentines and witty fripperies, while Tudor, who conjured up Chekhov and Joyce, would surpass his illustrious peer in matters of profundity.

Before the company took leave of London, Tudor had a reunion with Margaret Craske, just returned from an ashram in India where, throughout the war, she paid homage to her guru Meher Baba. Craske took her former student's invitation to join Ballet Theatre as its ballet mistress in the United States—just as she had done for his London Ballet.

At this point the disparate pieces of his life came together. All the B-Club friends had joined with his Ballet Theatre côterie. And his family—all the Summerses and Cooks, aunts, uncles and cousins—made their way to Covent Garden. The sight of Will as Antony Tudor, one of England's eminent sons and a member of this elite establishment, drew hushed awe from them. True, Alf caused a small stir with his singing over Chopin's *Sylphides,* and managed to make the others late to opening night. But his pleasure and attunement to the stage events were real, no less than that of the other relatives. Antony also caught up with Mim and Ashley. Seeing their daughter, Angela Dukes, grown up, he nudged her breast with his elbow and said, "Well, that turned out alright." She was only a little shocked and remembered that the now-famous choreographer who tried out ballet steps on her as a child dancer "had a collection of the dirtiest pictures imaginable."

When the season ended and the company reboarded the *Queen Mary,* he had accomplished his rapprochement with England. And even if London's ballet society had the false impression that "Antony was well taken care of in America," as Dame Ninette de Valois would later assert, amends had been made; his reputation glowed like a gem in the dark.

The voyage back was not without crises, however. A dock strike in New York forced the company to complete the trip by train—first from Halifax, Nova Scotia, where the ship docked, and then via another train from Montreal.

For the Tudor-Diana-Hugh troika it was a time of emotional maelstrom. Buoyed by the prospect of having a vital, possibly even complete, relationship with Diana, Hugh tried to pull away from Tudor. Maybe he would find his redemption through her. Maybe it was possible to assure his star status as a Tudor dancer and at the same time strike out independently—with a woman, with the identity he longed for. Certainly, Tudor had given his benediction and more. "Thank god you happened along," he had said to Diana some months earlier, referring to the burden Hugh had become for him. But at this moment—in gritty, rumbling coaches during a heat wave—he was testing the proposition. Prior to getting on the train, the three of them had had a major confrontation. Yes, Antony had formerly cheered this three-way game, one in which they would all be together. But now Hugh wanted to break the tie and stand as a duo with Diana. Would Antony let him go? Would he sanction the venture? Wasn't he, after all, a person of reason and understanding? Or would he now show the truth: his neediness, his pain over separation and his inability to relinquish control. Yes, that, and Antony seemed to prevail. No matter that their bond would temporarily go underground; it would not break.

Now it was just the two of them occupying adjacent seats, away from the others—Diana had gone to another coach somewhere. Over the next many hours to New York Antony talked and talked, calmly, a beatific expression on his face. "He looked like Saint Tudor," said an observing Richard Beard. Hugh listened. It was one of the few times he stayed silent. As he heard radiant descriptions of their experiences together, their accomplishments, their meaning to each other, tears streamed from his eyes. How could he turn away from the one person who affirmed his worth? Was there the slightest question of their mutual devotion? Could a Diana really come between them? Not likely. The train pulled into Grand Central Station at last. It was one A.M.

22

Drinking Tears

BALLET THEATRE HARDLY HAD TIME to collect itself following the London tour. Ten days after arriving back in New York the company opened a fall run at the Broadway Theatre, featuring the premiere of Ashton's *Les Patineurs*. But there was no quid pro quo. While a Tudor ballet would not enter the Sadler's Wells until 1967, Ashton was immediately courted by his American admirers. Chase and Smith arranged for him to rehearse his charming skater's sketch, a piece of trompe l'oeil bravura, while at Covent Garden. It was just the sort of thing to keep a box office lively—an advantage Ashton's works generally enjoyed over Tudor's. And now that Hurok no longer produced Ballet Theatre's seasons, the company welcomed any and all enlivening forces. "Trivial, but winning" was *New York Herald Tribune* critic Walter Terry's verdict on *Les Patineurs*. It became a bread-and-butter staple of the repertory.

As usual, Tudor was busy rehearsing his ballets—a record

number of seven appeared on the 1946–47 roster. With dancers coming and going there were always new additions to the cast and each time someone took over a role he not only saw to that person's indoctrination but he did some custom-tailoring. Even so, the atmosphere was too hectic for much good to come of the effort. A whole season's repertory had to be prepared in just two weeks. How he anguished over the insufficiency. Often, dancers for second casts had to learn roles by standing in the wings and watching. "We were lucky to get a run-through," recalled Enrique Martinez, then a soloist. "We all improvised. We all played follow the leader." Nonetheless there were gains. Following its New York engagement the company went back on the road for a grueling six months.

But few faulted the season. Ballet Theatre's reinstatement of its pre-Hurok ideal, to become "a permanent institution American in character and international in scope" pleased everyone, including those who fought for and won the policy of "building from within the ranks, thus rigidly eschewing the invidious guest-star system." It certainly pleased Tudor, who was happy not to have to compete with the Russians or their starry elite. And the company won critical kudos. According to critic-historian Anatole Chujoy, the 1946–47 season "will go down in the annals of ballet in America as amazing . . . the most successful it has ever had, artistically and financially." There was no indication here of disaster to come.

An inside view, however, took account of the fact that new ballets were not being produced. Tudor, for whom Chase and Smith had picked up the option on Bartok's new work, Concerto for Orchestra, also begged off. Antal Dorati, the company's music director through 1945, had shown Tudor the score. It positively delighted him, so much so that he asked Dorati to play a piano version of it over and over. Agreeing to do a new ballet, however, seemed impossible to him, given how occupied he was just taking care of those already in the repertory. Nor could he count on having the right casts when he needed them.

Years later, he would reveal to Leo Kersley that for the Bartok he had in mind an elaborate libretto based on the Tibetan Book of the Dead. "Perhaps I'll do it," Tudor said. "Sorry," Hugh answered. "Lucia stopped paying for the rights long ago." And even though he had made *Dim Lustre,* the desire to put his full-evening Proust epic onstage remained alive. While admitting "the impossibility of turning this magnum opus into a ballet," he nonetheless had written out a scenario based on the seven-part novel. During the London tour he had spoken to Benjamin Britten about a commissioned score, believing that the music should be largely vocal. Later, he came to an agreement with Gian Carlo Menotti, whom he considered "to be at the pinnacle of his powers then" as a composer of arias and songs. And he hurdled the last remaining obstacle, getting approval from Mme. Mante-Proust, the novelist's niece, to stage *À la Recherche du Temps Perdu.*

To do so he traveled to Paris, having been invited to a party at her house in Neuilly. Amid great formality and care as to seating arrangements he found himself "at the family table for the junior set, with Mme. Mante-Proust's two daughters, and to this day I cannot conceive of more perfection, more charm, more of everything it takes than had been accorded by le Bon Dieu to these ravishing young ladies. And so the party went its course, and my country oafish presence departed into the night dreaming of the Arabian Nights or some such nonsense. Mme. gave me her permission, providing only that I myself take over the role of Swann. And I had set my target as Le Baron de Charlus. This was an easy sacrifice and I sailed back to New York on wafts of happy accomplishment. But then . . ."

Menotti turned over the score and Tudor saw it did not suit his purposes. A year later the subject of the Proust ballet came up but by that time "many key figures were no longer with the company, people I'd worked with for quite a time and was at home with and they with me. They had gone to greener fields or less insecure futures, if such a thing can be envisaged. Both the Alicias, Markova and Alonso, were gone and even my Marcel, as a boy, Doria Avila, had disappeared. Muriel Bentley, who was to fill out the role of Mme. Verdurin, had flown the coop, and, needless to say, from the new batch of charmers taken in to fill up the required number for the *Swan Lake* corps and of the types needed for the Proustian chiaroscuro there would be none."

The unmistakably sardonic tone of his concluding statement and the implied populist priority of *Swan Lake* over something truly provocative that he might create summed up his view of things. He was supposed to be in a position of power, having every reason to thrive. When would he do a new ballet? There was a standing invitation, although conditions were far from ideal. But in 1947 he still had his favorite apostles and was recognized as the sine qua non of the company.

His preference to rehearse standing ballets, rather than make a new one, was both sound and understandable. The most significant works he would do in America—as well as those he brought from England—were all included in the 1946–47 repertory: *Jardin aux Lilas, Dark Elegies, Gala Performance, Judgment, Pillar, Romeo, Dim Lustre* and *Undertow*. But lacking the urgency to create and hating himself for being cowardly, he emptied his reservoir of disdain onto others.

So lost in details would he sometimes become, moreover, that the result "would lose its breadth and blood," he admitted. This is where Hugh came in. "Hugh, with his own enthusiasm and drive, would get the emotion back—everything I'd let slide." This was not so much an artistic alliance as it was a fundamental dependency. It became clear to astute observers on the scene that Tudor needed Hugh just in order to function. The loss of him, merely the idea of it, was incalculable. And the paradox that he himself had maneuvered the union with Diana must have caught him short.

Nevertheless, there was a marriage. It came—in 1947—as a great surprise to casual acquaintances and company members and even those across the Atlantic. "What could Diana possibly want from Hugh?" many asked.

The curiosity of Mim and Ashley, for instance, was a far-reaching case in point. The two gave a big party for the Royal Ballet people on their return in 1949 from a first U.S. tour. In the wee hours, when only Ashton and historians Richard Buckle and P. W. Manchester remained and the others had all bade their farewells, Ashley asked about Hugh and his two-year-old marriage to Diana Adams. "Oh, yes," said Ashton. "I saw them and they seemed quite happy." At that, recalled Manchester, "Mim exploded jubilantly. She slapped Fred hard on the knee and said, 'You see! You see! Hugh never really liked it.' The 'it,' of course was sex with another man, the idea of which repelled her. Only years later did she gain a little perspective and admit 'how important it was to love someone . . . it doesn't matter who.' "

But, in fact, bisexual liaisons were commonplace in ballet companies. "Most of the boys were gay," said Maria Karnilova, "while the girls had no other outlet. They all lived and worked and ate and drank and slept together. Marriage was not a much bigger step to take." Even today women in ballet have a difficult time establishing a healthy self-image. "The response they get from gay dancers is tepid," according to writer and former dancer Marian Horosko. "With so little feedback of their desirability they don't exactly shine. On the other hand, their male counterparts share a compassion and sensitivity that non-dancers simply don't have."

Still, everyone knew Tudor and Hugh to be a couple, even a talismanic one. Hugh's few flamboyant peccadilloes with women were considered just that—nothing serious. In real life, though, The Transgressor was ready to solve his dilemma. He would gladly opt for marriage over murder, although many question whether they were not the same thing under his ministrations. While it is conceded that Hugh had a deeply compassionate side, he also cultivated mayhem in his heart—often venting both on the same object.

Tudor took a separate apartment in the Fifty-second Street building, leaving to the couple the one he and Hugh had occupied. The three of them were seen together most of the time. Christmas cards often came addressed to all three. As Karnilova put it, "This marriage was not a twosome. It consisted of Diana, Hugh *and* Tudor." One must assume that the original plan—that of a trio—went into effect, that Hugh would have someone else to focus his not altogether happy attention on, someone he could easily control and manipulate, and that Diana could attach herself to the great god Tudor by way of Hugh. Both assumed a kind of guardianship over her.

But nothing was cut and dried. Sometimes Hugh stayed overnight or for a few days with Tudor. One weekend the three of them were invited to Samuel Barber's and Gian Carlo Menotti's Capricorn House in Mt. Kisco, New York, along with Gore Vidal. An entertainment mainstay for their famous get-togethers was a little mind game whereby everyone sat in a circle and a question was put up. The answer, calling upon the guests' powers of perception, required one to give not his own response but that of the adjacent person. Vidal recalled a question from that weekend: "Why are you here?"

The controversial author was sitting next to Diana and he was not about to let "the dicey moment" pass. "I answered, 'To advance my career.' After all, that *was* why she attached herself to Hugh and Tudor. The temperature in the room suddenly lowered." Not surprisingly, the game tickled Tudor. And it inspired him to make little puzzles of everything, especially in such appreciative company as Vidal's. "He mapped out the three-bedroom house for me," said the writer, showing which feet would travel where. With Tudor, the game was the thing. One could always count on lots of play-acting. He was the brains of the trio." And he knew how to accommodate.

There were advantages to bringing Diana into the closed, little unit—a respite, for instance, from Hugh's constant onslaught of nagging and demands. For Hugh it was deeper: as in a dream, reuniting with and winning over . . . who? The seductress-mother of *Undertow?* But also, "He was going through his near-psychotic period," according to Karnilova, "trying to make Tudor jealous and trying to punish him." Still, he longed for the "married-man" status as a way of fending off vulnerability.

Antony at about the time he joined Marie Rambert's Ballet
Club. The unbuttoned collar is an atypical bit of peekaboo
daring for the reticent young man. *(Connaught Palmer)*

Tudor as a young man with a mission: "to be that rara avis . . . a choreographer." *(Mollie Cook)*

Florence Cook in the hat made for her by her son Antony (né William Cook)— his theatrical flair already apparent. *(Gladys Scammell)*

Antony's parents: the live wire and his ungregarious other. *(Mollie Cook)*

Young Antony as Malvolio in Shakespeare's
Twelfth Night—he seemed the only professional
among the St. Pancras Players, a church group.
(Gladys Scammell)

The four Cook brothers,
circa 1930, all in perfect
fourth position.
Antony's father Alf
and his brothers
believed they were
descendants of the
explorer Captain
James Cook.
(Mollie Cook)

Antony, with his arm around Fred Ashton, was happy to be one of "Mim's geniuses" and a member of her plucky little Ballet Club—later to become Ballet Rambert. Mim herself appears sixth from left; others in the group include Alicia Markova (*standing fourth from left*) and Maude Lloyd (*standing third from right*). *(Reproduced by permission of Rambert Dance Company Archive)*

The sun
shines on London's
Mercury Theatre.
Being photographed
by his "guardian
angel," Hugh Laing,
Antony beams.
(Theresa Langfield Horner)

Gala Performance.
Nora Kaye (*left*)
and Alicia Alonso
(*center*) carrying
their famous rivalry
onto the stage,
courtesy of Tudor's
insightful portrait of
one-upping ballerinas.
Norma Vance appears
at right. *(Alicia Alonso)*

Unhappy partners
in *Jardin aux Lilas*—
with Tudor (as The
Man She Must Marry)
making all the decisions
about who pairs with
whom.
(*Above, left to right:*
Nora Kaye, Tudor,
Alicia Alonso, and
Hugh Laing; *below,*
Alonso and Tudor)
(*Alicia Alonso*)

His penetrating eyes could melt with kindness or cut through "to the soul of a person." *(Performing Arts Research Center, New York Public Library at Lincoln Center)*

Pillar of Fire. The original cast: A posed game plan with all
eyes on target and body language an X ray of intent. A yearning
Hagar (Nora Kaye, right) and her sisters—the Eldest,
a spinster, (Lucia Chase, *center*) and Youngest, a flirt,
(Annabelle Lyon). The upstanding Friend (Tudor) and the
Young Man (Hugh Laing, *far right*), a nefarious presence.
(Performing Arts Research Center, New York Public Library at Lincoln Center)

A Romeo (Laing) "full of self-love . . . Juliet (Alicia Markova)
only the target of his emotional outbursts."
(Performing Arts Research Center, New York Public Library at Lincoln Center)

Left: Dim Lustre. Illusion, ennui, and estrangement: Antony with Nora Kaye. *(Performing Arts Research Center, New York Public Library at Lincoln Center)*

Below: Undertow. The Transgressor (Hugh Laing) drawn to and repelled by the sexually ensnaring Medusa (Nana Gollner). *(Performing Arts Research Library, New York Public Library at Lincoln Center)*

A grueling four-hour wait: Tudor and Laing on board the *Queen Mary,* docked at Southampton, England, waiting for customs officials en route to London's Covent Garden in 1946. *(Richard Beard)*

Above: Pillar of Fire—
Hagar (Nora Kaye) in
clenched Victorian resis-
tance to the sexually
charged Young Man from
the House Opposite (Hugh
Laing). *(Performing Arts
Research Center, New York
Public Library at Lincoln Center)*

Camellias. Diana Adams
and Laing at New York
City Ballet, cast by Tudor
as the languishing heroine
and her abandoning lover.
*(Performing Arts Research
Center, New York Public
Library at Lincoln Center)*

In *Judgment of Paris* prostitutes almost have the upper hand
as they prey upon their man, the unseen Tudor. *(left to right:*
Maria Karnilova, Agnes de Mille, Lucia Chase) *(Performing Arts
Research Center, New York Public Library at Lincoln Center)*

Opposite: Shadowplay. A male
pas de deux—its inspiration
came to Tudor after wrongly
following "a blind alley."
*(Performing Arts Research Center,
New York Public Library at
Lincoln Center)*

Pillar of Fire. Tudor and
Sallie Wilson in one of their
infamous rehearsal confrontations. His regard for her,
ultimately, was great.
(Don Bradburn)

Jardin aux Lilas.
Gelsey Kirkland as
Caroline, with Erik
Bruhn *(above)* as The
Man She Must Marry
and John Prinz *(right)*
as Her Lover.
Kirkland translated
choreography into the
full dimension of
human experience,
winning the master's
supreme praise.
(Don Bradburn)

Right: Charles Ward and Gelsey Kirkland in *Leaves Are Fading.* Kirkland's all-out abandon drew Tudor from his twenty-five-year choreographic strike against American Ballet Theatre. *(Don Bradburn)*

Echoing of Trumpets. Inertia often gripped Tudor— as it did (*above*) in 1965, when setting his first ballet for a major company in nine years (Metropolitan Opera ballet, Maomi Marritt, Howard Fayette and Tudor standing (*left to right*)— but he also could be exuberant (*right*), caught up in the swirling momentum of a waltz. *(Performing Arts Research Center, New York Public Library at Lincoln Center/"El" Gabriel Israel)*

"Hugh was always under threat of discovery," she said. "In effect, he was saying: 'If you ever find out that I'm a lowly Caribbean or that I'm not educated or that I'm gay, I'll kill you.' "

But at least on the surface all seemed right for him now. He had Diana. He had Tudor as well. Nora also lived in the building—for another year and until her marriage to Isaac Stern at the end of 1948. She stayed friendly but was no longer part of the vital (or deadly) nucleus. Occasionally she would go to dinner with the "married three" but found those evenings disagreeable. "I couldn't wait to get away from them," she told Francisco Moncion, a principal dancer at New York City Ballet. "By the time we left the restaurant Hugh would be attacking Diana mercilessly. Once, on the way up the steps to their apartment, he was punching her hard on the arm. I couldn't stand it and just went home."

But in 1947, just after Diana and Hugh were married, Tudor broke out of his briefly fallow period. Now he would take up Mahler's *Das Lied von der Erde,* a labor of love and the most ambitious project of his career. This was the seventy-minute score he came upon in 1935, the one he proclaimed "the most marvelous music" he'd ever heard. This *Song of the Earth,* a symphonic setting for tenor and contralto of classical Chinese poems freely translated into German, would strain the resources of the company in every way. But prophetically, Tudor anticipated the bad times ahead for Ballet Theatre. He might never again have the chance to even contemplate *Das Lied,* with its Mahlerian dichotomies: loss and redemption, pain and bliss, cynicism and resignation. And if one considers the most striking image of *Shadow of the Wind,* the status of his personal life clearly emerges.

That image concerns a character called The Abandoned Wife —by any measure, a reflection of Tudor bereft of Hugh. Constrained from showing her sorrow to the husband who now prefers a young girl, she hides her tears—taking them one by one from her eyes, as though they were large, delicate globes, and then drinking them as, in a sense, Tudor had done. The very idea of drinking one's sorrow, of swallowing the pills of defeat, of taking back into oneself the secretions of sadness, is inspired—even if it also derives from oriental tradition. But the power of the gesture has not been forgotten by those cast members who, while describing the scene, invariably stop and just do the gesture.

Alonso danced the role of The Abandoned Wife, recalling that "Tudor was far ahead of his time. No one really understood what he was doing." A great deal could also be deduced from the music he chose. Mahler, whose own life when he composed the score was a monument of grief—his young daughter had suddenly died—came into the possession of Hans Bethge's anthology, *Die Chinesische Flöte*. It contained eighty poems, many of them by Li-Tai-Po, among the greatest of lyric poets. He sat down the next year to write this song cycle expressing a resigned awareness of the transience of life.

The themes of the ballet, not always based on the actual poems, presage the Zen Buddhist steps Tudor would take a few years later. The human experience, he affirmed, is cyclical; like the seasons it has neither a beginning nor an end. He already understood that one cannot seize or claim or possess life, that its very nature rendered it beyond grasp. As he explained to Therese Langfield, "You must be like a leaf floating on the water's surface. As the stream flows, it carries the leaf past the rocks." There were sequences that contrasted with the static quality of the opening—an intense one between the husband and wife (John Kriza and Alonso), a flirtatious one with a girl (Diana) and male ensemble of young soldiers, a solo for Hugh in which he portrays the poet-philosopher, drunk with wine and the earthly delights of hedonism, an old woman (Nana Gollner) remembering as a youth her parting from a lover gone to war, never to return.

Leave-takings, separations and the pain they cause—Tudor grappled with these in *Jardin* and *Dark Elegies*. They were old issues, crusty scabs that kept opening as he got jostled through one skirmish of the heart after the next. The straight spine, the ready wit, the wicked sarcasm—none of these really offered protection. His ballets were at once a source of anguish—getting them out was torturous—and a relief, for he used them to work through his unresolved liturgies. With *Shadow of the Wind* he counted more than ever on a reprieve. Perversely, the greater his need, the less likelihood of its being met.

Although "he detested the effort of making a ballet," said Oliver Smith, he hurtled into the task. Whereas Rambert would never have been able to consider such an undertaking—*Das Lied* required a full symphony orchestra, not the usual pit band of roughly forty players—Ballet Theatre could, with Lucia's consent, foot the bills. And Tudor logged many hours of rehearsal from January to the premiere on April 14, 1948.

During this same season Agnes de Mille was also preparing a ballet: *Fall River Legend,* based on the Lizzie Borden story. If Tudor and his old friend ever came close to despising each other, it was now. They had battled before over rehearsal hours—as had all other choreographers—but not like this. Both of them needed the time and what one gained the other necessarily lost. "I refuse to cry and slobber," he told dancer Glen Tetley. "Let her take off her panties and throw them at Lucia. I won't stoop to that."

So infuriated was he with de Mille that at one point he denounced her as a plagiarist to The Ballet Society. *Fall River,* said Tudor, derived much of its ambience and style and setting from *Pillar of Fire.* He was seconded by dance critic Ann Barzel, who called Agnes's new work "the best Tudor ballet she [de Mille] ever did!" Agnes was so stung by her friend Antony's public accusation that she refused to attend any performances of *Shadow of the Wind.*

Retreating

TUDOR'S MOMENTOUS BUT FORGOTTEN Mahler ballet had a grand total of three performances and the last of these played to a house that had dropped to 24 percent capacity. There was no word of mouth to spur attendance, nor any Hurok machinery to bolster public interest in this Met engagement, the first one Ballet Theatre would self-produce. In her summary of the season, dance historian Selma Jeanne Cohen did not even single out the ballet for comment—mentioning only *Fall River Legend* and Balanchine's *Theme and Variations* as the two significant premieres between November 1947 and April 1948. Indeed, it received scarcely a positive word. John Martin, according to the consensus, killed *Shadow of the Wind* with faint praise: "When Mr. Tudor goes all out, in certain sections, for Oriental ceremony coupled with delicate pantomime, the ballet takes on a pleasant decorative style and when he turns to the combination of ballet and modern dance action, an art in which he is supreme, his work conveys to the beholder emotional values of real dramatic impact, but for much of *Shadow of the Wind,* we do not find either the Orient or the West but we race from Mahler to Li-Po to Tudor and back again." Elsewhere he wrote, "To this combination of ancient Chinese classic hedonism already screened through a process of Germanic Weltschmerz, Tudor has deliberately added the academic formalism of the traditional ballet."

Martin's assessment does not account for the fact that a great deal was left undone at the time of the premiere. Some dancers had to improvise their parts toward the end of the ballet. The anguish that went into its birth proved as great as any Tudor had experienced, for in the three-year interval between it and *Undertow* he had managed to ratify the lingering doubts of his creative value. But no matter how strictly he maintained the separation of self-worth and newspaper reviews, there was spillage now from the written word of others onto his personal record. Nor could he forget the unfinished state of the ballet at its premiere.

Even worse, the company found itself in such dire straits that it could not support a work that lacked critical and popular approval. Seeing *Shadow of the Wind* dismissed, dropped from the repertory after a few performances, embittered Tudor more than any other career experience to date. Its fateful removal "not only devastated him," observed Oliver Smith, "but was a tragedy for the ballet world. After a year or so had passed, no one remembered it. Any chance of recovering the work has long been lost."

Part of the problem hinged on "Lucia's dislike of *Shadow,*" Smith conceded. Also it was costly and she had a reputation for being cheap. But a greater part had to do with Ballet Theatre's desperate finances and the debt incurred by hiring a full orchestra—not to mention the extra rehearsals so subtly complex a score required. But as things turned out there was little to argue about. The company now had to contend with a new tax status that disallowed more than 30 percent subsidy from any one source. The upshot: Chase would have had to exceed her donor's limit to meet the payroll and thus was forced to close down operations following the month-long Met season that ended on May 8, 1948. When she started up again the next spring Tudor's latest ballet was nowhere to be seen. "Lucia and I worked well together because we complemented each other," said Smith. "She liked to see to the day-to-day managing, to make sure that the next ballet would get on, while I took a long view of the company's course. Tudor was central to that view."

His appraisal of the choreographer didn't make a significant difference, however. Nothing short of full-fledged support—financial and philosophic—could have staved off the shadowy winds of Tudor's despair. What started as little gusts became gale storms. And in the aftermath of this fiasco he would sit in classes staring down at the floor, a picture of abject disinterest.

Tudor wasn't the only one to see himself at a loss. The marriage of Hugh and Diana and the company's decline—with no Hurok to keep the ship afloat—also spelled disaster for Nora. "The glass shattered for her when those two married," said Karnilova. "It meant that she no longer was in the inner circle. And she had behaved so badly, clawing her way to the top, only to discover there was no company left when she got there." Nora was originally chosen to dance the role Nana Gollner originated in *Shadow of the Wind*. At the same time de Mille had cast her as the crazed Lizzie Borden in *Fall River Legend*. But what Karnilova reported about Kaye was deeply true. Her world did shatter during rehearsals of those two ballets. She had what several described as a "nervous breakdown," which kept her out until the very end of the run. When she returned on May 5, it was for one performance only of the de Mille ballet.

"Nora was strong and fragile at the same time," according to writer Arthur Laurents, who kept up a close relationship with her from 1944 through 1950. "She had emotional problems, apart from Tudor. But that was true for most people who got so deeply connected to him." He remembered that Nora fainted during a rehearsal for *Fall River*. This was the beginning phase of her stress and afterward she told him what precipitated the fainting spell: "An image appeared to me. It was my father and Tudor as one person. I looked down at the man's feet and saw my father. When I looked up the face I saw was Tudor's." Karnilova, who had lived with Kaye's family for a few months, recalled that Mr. Koreff (Nora's father) "was a very severe and controlling person." Laurents also remembered that after Nora recovered "she realized that her psychic health depended on breaking with Tudor. But she revered him even during that time of lessened contact."

While stress was all around that spring of 1948, it seemed to fuel fiery performances from others besides Nora. She earned rave reviews for her portrait of Lizzie Borden. Diana, having graduated from Cybele to Medusa in *Undertow,* was called "compelling" by Walter Terry. And Hugh, in the title role of *Petrouchka,* came across "as a figure of essentially tragic dignity," according to John Martin, "giving a lift to the tone of the work as a whole and endowing the ending particularly with the significance of catastrophe."

Nevertheless, Ballet Theatre had come to an end for everyone. Perhaps not a final end, but one that left Tudor to wander free. With his fame spread worldwide it would not be unreasonable to expect offers from outpost companies. The one he took for seven months came from the Royal Swedish Ballet.

Unfortunately, it did not confer the kind of artistic pardon he needed. If he hoped to find his theatrical sophistication matched at this new haven he was bound to be disappointed. As it turned out he had far more to offer his welcomers than they him.

In the long view Tudor was a mismatch with the ballet world. But in 1948 the situation seemed particularly onerous. While he stood, arguably, as the most forward-thinking ballet choreographer of his time, he found no foothold in the places that could vouchsafe the high-skilled dancers required to perform his work. Neither London nor New York, those bastions of classical dance in which he spent a decade each, could embrace him wholeheartedly. To remain in these centers, where courage and confidence seemed to fail him, meant staging his existing ballets over and over. The alternatives were fledgling outposts like that in Sweden. For now, he would venture to the dance hinterlands—possibly risking self-exile.

The callback to Ballet Theatre came in early 1949. While the prospect may not have filled him with wild hope and exhilaration, at least he knew that returning to his fine-tuned collaborators would be a step up from the elementary level of dance as practiced in Sweden. There was little contest between the teeth-gnashing of big-business ballet in a free enterprise system and the calm nonadventure that the royal charter implied. Neither had everything; one invited creativity in a troubling setting and the other guaranteed stability without much chance for artistic satisfaction. Regardless, Tudor was still officially tied to Ballet Theatre and the thought of rehearsing five of his ballets with seasoned dancers was infinitely more compelling than teaching beginners, no matter how adoring and obedient they were. If nothing else, he now knew what each organization had to offer.

Most of the principal dancers in the Tudor group returned to Ballet Theatre, apart from Alonso and a contingent she took to Cuba. But chaos ruled the day—being on layoff for a year and integrating a virtually new corps saw to that. Maria Tallchief, now Mrs. George Balanchine, signed on as a guest for the three-week Met engagement in April. She replaced Alonso in her husband's *Theme and Variations* and Tudor also decided to cast her as The Other Woman (or An Episode in His Past) in *Jardin*. So ingrained was the Balanchine method of counting beats, though, that she admitted to having trouble learning the role. "It was very confusing to me," recalled Tallchief. "The steps were not defined in the music. That's why George bought me a record which I used to study at home—figuring the thing out there because it wasn't done at rehearsal."

Tudor, of course, had an entirely different approach to setting dance to music. "I always want the body to sing," he told writer John Gruen. "Therefore nearly all my phrases are as though they would be sung. That's why I'm against counting. No one can count if he's singing. Also a singer has a breath for a certain phrase. Now, we don't actually do this in dancing. But I do create my phrases with that sort of innate thing happening. And so, I devise in phrases of movement, not in a sequence of steps." This method, one that Ashton tended to use also, was foreign to most choreographers—even Balanchine.

Nevertheless, Tallchief acquitted herself respectably in this first and only foray into Tudor territory. But it was Nora, now fully recovered and apparently finding some stabilizing force in her marriage to Isaac Stern, who garnered some of the best reviews of her career. Martin, of *The New York Times,* wrote that in *Pillar* she had "even fuller command than before. Every movement is so inflamed by passion that it has lost the air of prescribed choreography altogether and become the externalization of intense personal emotion. When this kind of thing can be captured and held in form, we are really in the presence of profound art." And the same critic praised her in *Romeo and Juliet,* finding the characterization "a trifle lower than usual, with less of the airy childlikeness with which she has sometimes endowed it and more gentle melancholy. There was a lovely tone pervading it, and moments of singular poignance emerged.

"What a beautiful, richly colored performance [Laing's] is—passionate, impetuous, intense and utterly believable. He has never played with greater eloquence nor in closer rapport with Miss Kaye," wrote Martin, noting the value of ensemble work by inspired dancing actors.

All of this—not the printed word so much as the direct satisfaction—had to come as a bonus to Tudor after his sojourn to Sweden. But he still had a trial to get through. The company perched on a shaky foundation, its financial future uncertain. Contemplating a new ballet would be difficult enough given the stunning defeat he had suffered with *Shadow of the Wind.* And now that Ballet Theatre had been forced into a mode of scattershot preparation, he couldn't expect anything generous in the way of rehearsals.

His choice of *Nimbus,* a ballet about an ordinary young girl who fantasizes a more romantic life than her own, was the work of a choreographer who seemed overcome by disillusionment, trepidation, or both. Seeing that the public liked Americana themes, he tried to come up with one. The result was a mood piece. On a hot New York night the sleepless heroine leaves her tiny apartment and climbs to the rooftop of her building. There she dreams about an idealized love relationship. But nowhere in *Nimbus* did one see the depth or substance of the great Tudor ballets, according to critical consensus.

Rather, he went through the motions. Scott Douglas remembered "how distracted, disinterested and disheartened" Tudor was in rehearsals. "I felt he didn't want to do it at all, which made all his fiddling around hard to take. There was a whole extended corps passage we learned and then he made us reverse it."

He cast his côterie of dancers in the central roles—Hugh, Diana and Nora. And once again it was possible to read something of their personal constellation into the story. Nora played the anguished outsider, sitting on her bed and "screwing her legs in typically Tudoresque despair," observed Richard Beard, while Diana, by contrast, preened "and had a costume I remember for its feathers and fan." Of the Center Theatre premiere May 3, 1950, John Martin wrote: "Mr. Tudor, who has hitherto given us pictures of the insides of people's minds, in actions both realistic and symbolic, has turned away from all that and devoted his attention to a completely uninvolved, fairly sentimental little tale of lower-middle-class romance. Our heroine is a working girl who dreams of herself as an ethereal creature of infinite graces, who charms a 'dream-beau' without the least resistance."

The ballet may have satisfied Tudor's desire to work through his own dilemma; it certainly offered redemption, the kind Proust and other writers of autobiographic fiction obtain by reenacting a relationship close at hand. But it didn't bring him kudos of any kind, and one must wonder how cognizant he was of the general bewilderment that overtook him. From all appearances, his future with Ballet Theatre looked shaky. He and the company seemed to be declining hand in hand, in common dispiritedness. A fighter, a believer, an activist would have resisted sliding down the slippery slope. By this stage, however, the few rough threads of friction were worn slick. And he had willfully dropped a crucial piece of gear: his partner. Gone was the one person who brought passionate belief where ambivalence had encroached. At some level he did sense confusion and pain, for he tentatively sought out psychoanalysis. That too ended in defeat; this pillar of defenses was not a candidate to deal openly with his turmoil.

"I tried [a psychiatrist] just to see what it was like," Tudor told John Gruen, denying that he did so for any reason but curiosity. "It was a disaster. I went for an interview with a highly recommended analyst. He asked me why I came. I said, 'I thought you were supposed to tell *me* that.' I discontinued going." Later he read to dancer Bruce Marks a letter he had received from the analyst—who tried to point out that it was necessary for Tudor to free himself from self-thwarting attitudes if ever he were to realize his creative potential.

Instead he officially left Ballet Theatre, but not before coming to a showdown with Lucia. "He wanted to run the company," said Oliver Smith. "Like all geniuses do." But the idea was hardly farfetched—despite the tally for the last several ballets. Balanchine had been named artistic director of the New York City Ballet, established as such, ironically, during fall 1948, when Ballet Theatre slid into the ground. And Tudor was considered the equal if not the better of him then. He was, after all, not only its resident choreographer but his works were the company's hallmark. So his departure came as a great shock to the dance public.

One dancer described the atmosphere in those days as "high dudgeon." Madame Director treated her soon-to-be-ex-choreographer abysmally and he exerted pressure by boycotting rehearsals. Pandemonium reigned. There was an upcoming European tour sponsored by the State Department, but, for the Tudor ballets, no one to supervise them. Neither the creator nor his partner was available. "I had only one rehearsal for *Pillar,*" recalled James Mitchell, whom Lucia cast in Hugh's role. And I got no help learning the role. Nora tried. She'd say, 'Stand here. Exit there.' But it was like being thrown to the wolves." Under no circumstances would Hugh divide his loyalty between Tudor and the company. So when Lucia backed away from scheduling performances of *Undertow* on the tour because it was a risky ballet, one that frightened her, one that she neither understood nor had confidence in, Hugh took Diana by the hand and they left.

An era ended. Not on an up note as it did in 1937, when Tudor parted ways with that other impresaria, Marie Rambert. He was rising to the height of his powers then—having just done *Jardin aux Lilas* and *Dark Elegies,* those undisputed masterpieces. His strength had come from that knowledge. The last few years brought him no such affirmation. *Dim Lustre* in 1943 was too subtle to be a hit. *Undertow* in 1945 was admired but disliked. The profoundly poetic *Shadow of the Wind* from 1948 lay in shambles. *Nimbus,* for all its craft, was accused of being insubstantial. Had another choreographer created it, of course, no one would have argued that point. But Antony Tudor was supposed to be deep. He was the thinking man's dance-maker.

That same year he had made the first of his fugitive forays to Sweden. He would return there with some frequency in his new capacity: itinerant choreographer. As ballet minister with port-folio, he bore his treasures underarm from then, venturing to Japan, Canada, Australia, Israel and even back to London. He knew the value of his cargo. He distrusted his current creative skills. So he didn't fight the reluctance to make new works. But inevitably the fear of falling from the same high level at which he made his reputation caused him to withdraw from creating altogether. Looking at the practical side, though, he saw few possibilities of doing himself proud without a long residency at a fully subsidized company, one that had a cadre of high-skilled dancers sensitive to his aesthetic.

After closing the door to Ballet Theatre—almost for two dec-ades, as it developed—he traveled north again, this time to Denmark. There he found a superior organization: the Royal Danish Ballet, home of the nineteenth-century choreographer Auguste Bournonville. It had hosted the likes of Fokine, Ashton and Balanchine, who oversaw productions of their works in Copenhagen, and it was to spawn such dancers as Erik Bruhn and Peter Martins. Now the company invited Tudor to its stage. He mounted *Gala Performance* and *Jardin;* he even created a small ballet, *Arabesque.*

But the arrangement was time-limited. And besides, there remained untested waters in America—those of the still struggling New York City Ballet. Tudor returned to an invitation from that very stronghold of his rival, George Balanchine. Also ahead of him lay other courses off the beaten commercial path—as director of the Metropolitan Opera Ballet, an offer that came courtesy of his friend, Sir Rudolf Bing; as teacher-choreographer at Jacob's Pillow; as faculty member of the newly formed dance division at the Juilliard School, which would soon entice him to head its ballet department.

From this time on, however, he would never be permanently engaged with a major performing organization again—not the way Balanchine was with the New York City Ballet nor Ashton with the Royal. He was a man at odds with the workaday arts world. Functioning as a resident choreographer—namely, making ballets the way some make breakfast—did not come naturally to this *agonist.* He exited Ballet Theatre and the world witnessed the end of the most creative phase of Antony Tudor's career.

The House Guest

CHOREOGRAPHER-IMPORTS BOTH, Antony Tudor and George Balanchine were central to the development of modern ballet in America. But to think that they could have coexisted under the same roof is as preposterous as it is intriguing. Tudor himself once proposed that the two of them complemented each other perfectly. "George concerns himself with motion and I concern myself with emotion," he said. "Together we could make an ideally balanced company." In fact, the contrast between these utterly different paragons of twentieth-century ballet continues to be a heated subject.

One came from St. Petersburg, where he shone as an exponent of the Russian Imperial School, following Serge Diaghilev from there to the West and reordering ballet for his time. The other emerged in London with Marie Rambert, herself closely bound up with Diaghilev. They both ventured to the United States—Balanchine in 1933 and Tudor in 1939—and became the two most extraordinary influences on American ballet as it grew from infancy. But as Clive Barnes has written: "Tudor is the revolutionary and Balanchine the counter-revolutionary. Tudor expands upon the work of Michel Fokine, who looked at the ballet in Russia and decided it was time for a change. He saw its falseness and its artificiality. He saw the phoniness of ballerinas loaded down with jewels from their latest admirer prancing through indifferent choreography to the accompaniment of pallid music, while the dramatic structure of the ballet was a nothing, a mere excuse for ballet's bedizened amazons to shake their baubles at the audience."

Barnes argues that Tudor's genius was responsible for accomplishing all that Fokine outlined in theory. Tudor instinctively knew that human feeling and thought were part of his dance heritage. "Balanchine was the opposition," wrote Barnes, referring to his countervailing influence. But many go a step further, saying that Balanchine typically relied on a format provided by Petipa, which he ingeniously reworked and advanced as sublime variations on that model. His lean, speedy, streamlined and propulsive evocations of St. Petersburg, by way of that formalist Mozart and his renovator Stravinsky, evolved into a neoclassicism that defined ballet—spreading to regional companies around the United States as well as internationally.

Tudor, on the other hand, wanted nothing to do with formats. It was not part of his personal aesthetic to choose a piece of music, gather some dancers and proceed to set steps to the score. Rather, he relished situations, scenas, the joints of human connection and all that resonated from them. In other words, he refused—with the notable exception of the 1975 *The Leaves Are Fading*—to make purely abstract ballets, although even that one reveals a subtle narrative. Balanchine asked his dancers to function as marvelous physical beings, preferring them to rely on kinetic and musical instincts. He didn't demand character portraits or deep insights because there were few isolated emotions to perceive in his dances and because he generally viewed ballet in the same nonprogramatic mode typified by his chosen scores.

Nearly everything about the style and method of these two struck notes in opposition. They were the Mozart and Beethoven of dance. Balanchine composed in a calm, fluent script that exuded confidence. Tudor wrote and discarded, feverishly slashing his pen through the paper. Self-doubt paralyzed progress. Little that he did pleased his skeptical eye—partly because the creator himself was suspect, partly because the scenario, all-important, held within it the powers of redemption. Unsure of what his efforts would yield, he kept the doors closed. For Balanchine, on the other hand, nothing could have been more natural than open rehearsals; typically, lots of onlookers warmed the studio bench, watching or knitting. Whether a ballet was deemed a success or not did not consume him; there were plenty more where that came from. His assurance was monumental. Consequently, he had nothing to hide. But then he didn't risk self-revelation. "If I were feeling suicidal," he once told his biographer Bernard Taper, "I would never try to express this in a ballet. I would make as beautiful a variation as I could for a ballerina, and then—well, then I'd go and kill myself." Tudor, of course, would do just the opposite: pinpoint the elements that led to the character's demise.

While the two men rarely missed a chance to throw verbal darts at each other, they also had enormous mutual respect. "There's only one like nobody else," said Balanchine. "And that's Tudor." A compliment of any kind was rare from either of them. So with this unqualified praise, he doffed his hat. Tudor, likewise, always marveled at *Apollo* and *The Prodigal Son,* Balanchine ballets from the Diaghilev days. What came later he regarded as a different matter. True, Tudor was awed by his rival's ultimate success—Balanchine, with the inestimable support of New York City Ballet executive director Lincoln Kirstein, built the biggest ballet empire of a single choreographer in the United States. And Tudor was intimidated by how prolific and how fast Balanchine was. But his knee-jerk self-deprecation didn't keep him from understanding what accounted for those more than 200 ballets and why his own number was much smaller.

"George had only to go into his studio and put his step-step-steps together," he said. "Voila! A new ballet." Tudor knew he could do that, too. But he had different drives. Balanchine—in his way, an even more hidden personality than Tudor—was happy to forget about narrative for the most part and genuflect before the idol of lovely creations, before the grandeur and grace that the human body could personify. He sought to escape images of the drab and ordinary. Tudor wanted to penetrate them. In the mirrors of his life he searched them out. He wanted to say something about humankind and thus was not attuned to Balanchine's gift, which allowed audiences "to see the music and hear the dancing." Whereas the inventor of balletic neoclassicism saw himself as the agent of dance for its own sake, as the stationmaster in charge of connecting movement and music, Tudor needed to issue the grainy details of truth, the truth of his own and others' lives, the truth he could acknowledge in no way except as a stage creation.

Innocently, he tried to bring his bag of Everyman sensibilities into the imperial kingdom of ballet hauteur. By the end of 1951 the clash was already noticeable. All those reviewing *Jardin*—or, as Kirstein insisted on translating it, *Lilac Garden*—praised Horace Armstead's new decor and most sanctioned Karinska's costumes. But Tudor voiced disapproval. After concurring on the "divinely beautiful costumes," he went on to complain that "the people wearing them could not have had the thoughts my people had. The ambience of the family was wrong. It became a rich family. My ladies aren't rich. Caroline's family is falling on worse days, trying to keep up a respectable picture—otherwise, why is she going to marry that other man? And the scenery was a kind of eighteenth-century Watteau, very different from my slightly decayed garden; this was anything but decayed. I think really it's the difference between my middle-class, petit-bourgeois background, and Lincoln's."

And in 1964, when New York City Ballet staged an unsuccessful production of *Dim Lustre,* Balanchine, too, echoed across the chasm between himself and his petit-bourgeois peer: "I liked the ballet. But Tudor wanted it to be danced in simple dresses, middle-class English style. Here we wear beautiful, elegant gowns and tiaras—like kings and queens. So it's no use for us to dance it."

Both of them, however, abhorred the circus aspects of their art. They condemned bravura for its own sake. Balanchine kept his dancers light, fast and musical; as a result, technical virtuosity stayed neatly undercover—used in the process, never as an end in itself or a brazenly overt display of heroism. Tudor made even more stringent demands in his slow, economic movement style. Dancers were not permitted to take preparations for steps or show the slightest strain. From a standstill, one was expected to rise up on pointe. All physical difficulty had to be subverted to the dramatic message. Dance was not a mere collection of feats to be wildly applauded, rather a means of expression.

At this stage, though, the kings and queens at New York City Ballet had not yet been enthroned, Balanchine's cachet as neo-classicist still had not been carved out. The critics had—ahead of them—to reject modern realism in favor of this new abstract conceptualism. In 1950 the atmosphere was helter-skelter, catch-as-catch-can. Continuity simply didn't exist. There was nothing of the massive organization that the company would develop over the next decades. Neither the subsidies nor subscription audiences had evolved to their full potential. But eventually these two factors would raise the company's fortunes so high that it would play thirty-week New York seasons without any need to tour. The foundation was in place, however: namely, a permanent home at New York City Center, which also housed the New York City Opera. As the resident ballet company, NYCB enjoyed a great capacity for growth. But it was hardly Balanchine's private domain then. With respect to choreographers, a revolving-door policy prevailed. Everyone danced to a kind of laissez-faire tune—the goal being to assure a fresh stock of ballets and employ dancers as fully as possible.

Needless to say, dancers found City Ballet as attractive as choreographers did, notwithstanding the near-starvation salaries and limited amount of work. Staying with Ballet Theatre was no decent alternative; it meant endless touring. And after ten years the proselytizing thrill was gone. Not even the most committed nomad, among those with other options, would choose to continue on the dreaded, grueling, knockabout tours that precluded artistic satisfaction. Nothing could ever be fine-tuned what with slap-dash assembling of sets, floorboards and lighting untried, scratchy pit orchestras sight-reading the music, hungry and exhausted dancers defeated by long hours on trains and buses. This was not acceptable. Yet touring had to be the mainstay since the company had no New York home. Hurok still booked the Met, but his clients—Ballet Russe de Monte Carlo, among them—did not include Ballet Theatre.

In 1948 the Balanchine-Kirstein enterprise assumed its present incarnation, that of New York City Ballet, after accepting arts patron Morton Baum's invitation to make its base at the City Center. Ironically, the same offer to become New York's resident company first went to Lucia Chase, who wrongly figured that continued rentals of the big, glittery Met were a better bet than a home at the modest house on Fifty-fifth Street. The decision cost her beloved Ballet Theatre dearly: it seldom would have a decent New York showcase through the fifties and into the sixties. At the very point when Ballet Theatre hit a shortfall NYCB was born.

Balanchine's dancers, who had begun some ten years earlier, formed the nucleus. Long-limbed, swift colts trained at his School of American Ballet, they were a model of twentieth-century style. He inspired their loyalty. They tended to stay in this conventlike institution with a *paterfamilias* who took them from cradle to stage in one nonchalant leap. Touring was not a priority here. Not only did the company lack the means to attract the interest of presenters—the "pure" dance concept of neoclassicism had not yet caught on—but it did not seek them out. The shoestring budget didn't permit much in the way of sets and costumes, either, but already dancing and choreography had taken on a higher value at City Center than did stage trappings.

The aspect of overblown operatic spectacle that often dominates ballet would have little place here.

The atmosphere could hardly have been more different from Ballet Theatre's. Neither Balanchine nor Tudor approved of the star system. They vehemently opposed the cult of personality. To both of them it was a force inimical to High Art. But Ballet Theatre had cut its box office teeth on Hurokian galaxies. So when principals like Nora Kaye and Hugh Laing made their way to City Center there was inevitable consternation over how to treat them. Nevertheless, they were welcomed. In fact, a whole contingent opted for NYCB over touring with Ballet Theatre. Diana Adams and Janet Reed and Melissa Hayden, a rung lower than Kaye and Laing, were among those who defected, along with Tudor and Jerome Robbins who were looked upon as choreographers who could both round out and diversify the existing repertory.

Tudor had already cross-connected with Balanchine and Kirstein as long ago as 1941, when he'd been invited to create *Time Table* for American Ballet. The company needed new works for a South American tour, one of the few it made, so he obliged—with his very first ballet made in the United States. As was his wont, Tudor tinkered with it all the way up the gangplank of the ship that would take the troupe to Rio. Here was a wartime ballet predating Robbins's *Fancy Free,* one that also used sailors in a highly colorful, zany way.

But Tudor never could suggest such animated, showbiz exuberance as that. The high-spirited Americana of a Robbins and Leonard Bernstein, who had never seen battles fought on their own land, would necessarily be a remote idea for him. When City Ballet revived *Time Table* for its first season at City Center the critics duly noted Tudor's signature: nostalgia. The work was considered a bagatelle, though, a sketchy thing, apart from the sensitive pas de deux that "captured the poignance of youth and parting," wrote Robert Sabin of *Musical America*. John Martin called it "definitely minor, but charming and atmospheric and wonderfully made."

This was Tudor's first assignment at the new Balanchine-Kirstein citadel, to revive *Time Table* for the premiere season, January 1949. Not only was he an interloper of sorts, despite having been invited, but he had already taken on a somewhat tentative manner. After all, City Ballet was another's kingdom. He didn't reign here. Nor was this ballet a calling card he could present proudly. Principal Francisco Moncion, who danced in it, recalled how the rehearsals found Tudor at a loss, "scratching his head and trying to remember the different parts." At first he was patient, talking at length about the psychophilosophic milieu of the characters his cast would portray—to little avail. Gradually, he gave up. Nor did Hugh and Nora find a niche for themselves here. Only Diana did. And therein lay the hint of what was to come.

With Tudor coaching him, Hugh undertook Balanchine's *The Prodigal Son* and Anatole Chujoy reported that "Laing danced it with a simplicity and youthfulness that it had not possessed before. . . . His Prodigal was much more an erring boy than a deliberate squanderer, drunkard and debauchee." Diana, as The Siren, also inspired strong comment. Martin wrote, "She is well aware of the fact that she has an easy victim, and scarcely troubles to hide her contempt. One has never seen the role played this way and what it adds to the power of the work is inestimable."

Here was complete role reversal. In real life, of course, in the marriage, Hugh dominated. But when it was decided that these two should have their own vehicle, Tudor was recruited to do *Lady of the Camellias.* The Dumas fils story, rendered into one of Verdi's greatest operas, *La Traviata,* was utterly familiar to Tudor. A courtesan falls in love with a young man from a proper family and the disapproving father sunders the relationship. The libretto offered Tudor an ideal opportunity for typecasting: he would play Armand's father, the authoritarian role, and be identified in the program as John Earle. Once again, just as he did in the *Jardin* story, he would rob Hugh of the chance to have an involvement with a woman, this time, coincidentally and courtesy of Dumas. For the score his enlightened choice fell not on the overworked *Traviata* music itself but other Verdi pieces, obscure ones.

Typically, the commission came with constraints that proved uncongenial—already existent decors by Cecil Beaton that severely hampered the choreographic impulse, not to mention a limited rehearsal period.

"When you take a narrative like that," said Tudor, "you're bound to have something rather formless as a dancing structure. And then you're saddled with telling a whole story." He also found fault, justifiably, with the already existing costumes he was told to use—big crinoline skirts that impeded the dancing. He agreed with the critics that it lacked completeness and approved only of the central pas de deux. "I wasn't doing the ballet for myself; I was doing it for the costumes and scenery. I was doing it for Diana and Hugh. I was a short-order cook," he said, with barely disguised bitterness.

One hardly needed further evidence that New York City Ballet "could not find the proper frame for Tudor," as Kirstein would later write in a genteel defense for what happened. After all, Balanchine considered himself no more than a confectioner turning out enough pastries to keep hunger from the door of his dancers. Tudor was of another mold, although he, too, liked to minimize his ballets' importance. That way he lowered anticipation and the damage of a negative notice.

Nevertheless the critics found parts of *Camellias* transcendent. The premiere, in February 1951, drew from John Martin these remarks: "Echoes of the old romantic ballet style combine with free gesture to create an enchanting moment of rapturous young love. In effect, a choreographed novel of the late 19th century. . . . There could scarcely be a more inspired method of approaching the story of *Camille*. Tudor has caught the period and the conventions of the novel superbly and has translated them bodily in a new medium."

No doubt, Tudor reread the Dumas work—his first round had come in doing the Royal Opera's choreography for *La Traviata*—and pored over the Verdi scores by the hour, the late hour. It always showed. That was his way. He could not bypass narrative, anymore than could a great writer. Art, for him, was not an abstraction. It was the things he felt and that others felt. But there were many other reasons he became defensive in this association with City Ballet.

To begin with, he could not gear himself to Balanchine's breakneck pace. His best ballets took lengthy rehearsal periods. They evolved through a probing discourse with the dancers. He knew, however, that he would be expected to produce on the same schedule as Balanchine. He knew he had to fail that challenge, based on his demands—so alien to this company. Neither were Balanchine's dancers remotely in sync with Tudor's narrative subtexts. They were used to their busy baker who could pop ballets out of the oven with assembly-line speed. They responded to kinesthetics. They had little patience for Tudor's strange, Stanislavsky-like analyses, his seminars on characterological clues and subtleties. When he gave the *Camellias* corps a series of *bourrées*, with shoulders fluttering to suggest the flirtatious chatter at the courtesan's party, he got discouraged—seeing the movements done grossly, devoid of any meaning. And when Jacques d'Amboise was learning Hugh's role in *Jardin* for a second cast, he asked, "Where are the steps?"—uncomfortable with their sparse number and their pointedly dramatic implications, as opposed to the familiar Balanchinian abstraction. But Tudor had his defenses in place. "He stayed at a far distance from us," remembered Francisco Moncion. "We never entered the sanctum sanctorum. That was reserved for Hugh, Diana and Nora."

Creating in this atmosphere proved painful. So it was a relief that the next Tudor ballet to be staged at City Center would be an existing one: *Jardin aux Lilas,* or as the program listed it, *Lilac Garden*. The celebrated Nora Kaye had just arrived on the scene, prompting the need for a suitable showcase. And although Tudor took a dismal view of the production, as we recall, the critics raved. If the experiment to incorporate him and his dancers into the Balanchine aesthetic was going to work it would require a separation of the realm, it seemed. No actual merging was possible. The best that could be expected was an uneasy coalition. And Kirstein targeted the uneasiness, according to George Beiswanger, when he found *Jardin* to have "an unmistakable aura of tepid provincialism." He judged its success to be shallow, and "showing the very low stage of invention which served to set it in a fluttering frame that was not entirely earned." His pejorative words, somewhat unclear, nevertheless told where he stood; Tudor could hardly have much value for Kirstein's enterprise according to this attitude.

Meanwhile the press was busy cheering and heaped praise upon praise on *Jardin*. Philosophically, though, Tudor opposed the staging's overgentrification, courtesy of Kirstein. The four principals—with Tudor in his role as The Man She Must Marry and Tanaquil LeClercq as An Episode in His Past—all were considered excellent.

Tallchief, no longer Mrs. Balanchine, had not been asked to repeat this role she danced at Ballet Theatre in 1948. Instead, Tudor cast the new Mrs. Balanchine, LeClercq, who apparently had a better feeling for the character and in general proved more responsive to the idea of characterization. But insiders thought that Kaye and LeClercq looked mismatched. "Mother and daughter, not equals," was the peer consensus on the older dramatic ballerina and Balanchine's lovely new sylph—a long-legged, lanky blonde. Indeed, she exemplified the Balanchine ideal, coltish rather than womanly, while Kaye was never a dancer to his liking.

LeClercq first came to Tudor's attention when he was rehearsing *Time Table* at the company's old School of American Ballet on Fifty-ninth Street. But even as a distant admirer and one who had "a terrific time" with him in *Table,* she resisted his invitation to dance Caroline. "He was a marvelous partner, though. I remember running across stage and jumping onto him. He was rock-solid." The reason she turned down his offer for the leading role in *Jardin* had to do with his method. "Too hard," said LeClercq. "I always felt [in his choreography] that I had one leg shorter than the other. It would have taken too long to make his 'no preparation' style seem natural." Like a monk who refuses creature comforts, Tudor took the hard way. And he also imposed it on his dancers. But there was nothing arbitrary here: what he asked for yielded dramatic meaning.

Apart from the reviews, the iconoclastic choreographer heard little in the way of gratitude or approval for his work from Balanchine or Kirstein. The deceptively breezy atmosphere did not allow for such expressions. More significant, there was an unspoken acknowledgment here: City Ballet was the house of Balanchine. "Robbins felt that way, too, and still does," said LeClercq in 1989. But Tudor and his côterie kept on trying to carve a niche at the Fifty-fifth Street domain.

While Hugh found enough roles not requiring high virtuosity, and thus could sustain himself, Nora's situation was different. She could never hope to score as a Balanchine ballerina. Besides, her forte was dramatic dance. But she finally did hit her mark at City Ballet, thanks to Robbins, whose *Cage* brought stardom to them both. Here, too, was a misogynistic preoccupation similar to that in *Undertow*. Its treacherous protagonist, the leader of a "cult" of insect sisters, sets out to capture and destroy her male victim. The smell of his blood cancels any lingering affection or compassion that might come as a result of her mating with him and she launches the final, killing attack.

As usual, Kaye brought her unrelenting intensity to the role and won rave reviews—which emboldened her to paste a star on her dressing room door. The starless company's rule prevailed, however, and it was immediately removed. But the ballet remains a curious contradiction to the fact that Kaye and Robbins were then a twosome—"He was in love with her," recalled Janet Reed, acknowledging his attempt to form an enduring relationship with a woman. Kaye's allure for so many men—Michael Van Buren, violinist Isaac Stern, writer Arthur Laurents, choreographers Kenneth MacMillan, Robbins and finally Herbert Ross, whom she stayed married to—came, apparently, from her earth-mother appeal and vitality.

Still, *Cage* was not typical City Ballet fare. It flew in the face of Balanchine's dictum: "Ballet is Woman," which focused on idealization rather than denigration. And it hardly secured Kaye's place in the repertory. So Tudor was persuaded to do a work for her. At this point, the beginning of 1952, he knew with certainty that the company would not be more than a way station for him. The same held true for Nora.

But he tried to fulfill what came to be his last obligation at City Ballet. As was the case with *Lady of the Camellias,* Kirstein suggested the story line to him. *La Gloire* would be the backstage-onstage portrait of a reigning actress threatened by an ambitious ingenue. Much as Tudor resisted full-scale scenarios, this one would have seemed appealing to him. The intrigues were there, not to mention the yearning and the diva's ultimate downfall. In no small way, either, did the title character remind him of La Berma in Proust's novel. She, too, contended with a young rival. But the lines between the heroine's real life and those of her stage characters blurred in ambiguity; fragments from one side of the footlights reappeared on the other.

All About Eve, the film with Bette Davis as a Sarah Bernhardt and Anne Baxter as her devious protegée, became the model for Tudor's ballet. He already had his perfect cast—Nora as the great actress, desperately clinging to the top of her mountain and Diana, coolly waiting to usurp the pinnacle. How he loved watching such contests. The truth was Diana found favor with Balanchine; she met all his requirements and had every invitation to cross over to his camp from Tudor's. And, still married to Hugh, she occupied a coveted position as far as Nora was concerned. The ballet also put Nora in context of a whole corps of rivals, younger and more attractive than herself. This, of course, was a mirror of life for her at City Ballet.

But she was gregarious and that saved her. Whereas Diana exuded seriousness and clung dependently to primary relationships, Nora tended to gad about. Even her manner with Tudor was funny and affectionately offhanded. She called him "Toodie" or "Toodie-Froodie." She called Hugh "Huge Wang" and, in the wings before he went onstage, patted his genitals for good luck. She was "like one of the boys," said Harry Mines, and that made up some of her appeal to them. "Once, as she sat at her dressing table removing makeup and talking to a friend, the door opened and her then-husband Isaac Stern walked in. He had just flown in from Europe after a long tour, but Nora, without dropping a beat in her little monologue, saw him in the mirror, said 'Hiya hon' and went right on."

La Gloire gave her a plum role. She would portray Bernhardt in her best-known roles: Lucretia, Phaedra and Hamlet. Hugh, as Hippolytus and Laertes, would partner her. The decor, by Gaston Longchamps, was not foisted on Tudor as a prepackaged proposition à la *Camellias;* it came about in true collaborative spirit, cleverly convertible sets that could indicate both stage and wing area. The rehearsals, however, were not without their predictable agonies for Tudor. This time he gave himself an inexplicably perverse obstacle: three momentous Beethoven overtures—the grandiose *Coriolan,* the *Egmont* with its morse code drumroll and the *Leonore* no. 3, all blazing propulsion. Such a choice was dooming. No one could satisfactorily subordinate these Beethovenian fist shakers, least of all to do the bidding of a ballet. How he proceeded, given the handicap, is perplexing. But only after the fact did Tudor find fault with the music, mentioning that his choice had been "a terrible mistake."

A massive case of ambivalence might explain it. And, of course, here was a ready excuse for failure—one that any critic would, and did, accept. During rehearsals, though, Nora tried valiantly to perform magic tricks. "Come on, Tudor," she said, while he sat in a torpor listening to the music, unable to get into choreographic action. "Ride over it. They're only Beethoven overtures, for Chrissakes." She could hardly have been more wrong in her assessment. Other times she would roll her eyes and mutter under her breath: "Jesus, come on already." What finally materialized, apart from a few brilliantly devised sections, showed his creative gifts in disarray. Over the course of its five performances at City Center he fixed and tailored and tried to complete the choreography. But at the premiere Chujoy reported that "Kaye had only the embryo of a part and could only tear a meaningless passion to tatters. . . . Adams looked ravishing and fully capable of playing any role allotted to her."

Martin wrote: "Three Beethoven overtures played end to end would make any group of dancers look puny. We are supposed to see through to the personal tragedy of this declining trage-dienne. But even with a few offstage interludes to show her a bit more directly, this is an almost impossible assignment for a dancer, against the voice of the Titan roaring in the pit." Walter Terry found Kaye "at her most magnificent at the close when young heroines are denied her and Hamlet is her role." The implication: unable to crack the Balanchine gate of young fillies, Nora must play male roles and watch, with heartbreak, as others surpass her. Terry went on to say that "Tudor gave Kaye superb gestures, which speak of pride, arrogance, fear and dedication. But too much unfinished business, too many gaps, make the ballet seem like an outline and the corps members often merely wander, intrude, and provide remote support to the plays within the ballet." Curiously, the "pride, arrogance, fear and dedica-tion" also describe Tudor.

Still trying to capture a wider audience and establish itself for longer New York seasons, the company needed story ballets. In 1952 the public was not ready for whole evenings of abstract dance. So Kirstein, wanting to insure a supply of narrative works, commissioned a second ballet from Frederick Ashton (the first was *Illuminations* in 1950). Two days after the premiere of *La Gloire,* City Ballet presented its last novelty of the season, Ash-ton's *Picnic at Tintagel.* Martin called it "expertly planned, beau-tifully realized in stage terms, smart and stylish." The ballet proved just the ticket for a highly successful season. Thirteen years earlier Tudor had left London because the major patron, de Valois, belonged to Ashton. Now he had to step aside once again and hear the applause for his competitor, deemed more successful as a craftsman and more reliable as a creator. Now the place where he put his oh-so-tentative footprints seemed less likely than ever to become a haven. Without question he was an anomaly, this Stanislavsky of the ballet. Its world, so foreign to him, seemed to reward gorgeous utilitarianism, among other things, not theatrical depth. "When Tudor was replaced by a metronome," said Gore Vidal, the unjustly condemning metaphor referring to Balanchine, "I stopped going to the ballet."

As for Ashton's *Picnic,* few would remember it. But *La Gloire,* for all its problems, is still talked about. Positive responses came from Rambert, who said that no ballet she had ever seen has more tellingly conveyed backstage atmosphere. And John Percival regarded it as "a brilliant and engaging conception, even with the strange choice of music." Both saw *La Gloire* performed in London during New York City Ballet's tour that spring. Critic Doris Hering wrote that "the actress' whole existence was there— the tense dressing-room moments, the great scenes on stage, the flirtations with the leading men in the wings. And the whole was punctuated with Tudor's matchless ability to fuse dramatic gesture and dance impetus."

One can operate outside the pale of established practices only so long before being attacked. And when the guise of invulnerability doesn't work—everyone knew the dread and anguish Tudor went through facing a rehearsal room and a ballet to create— one becomes fair game. At Ballet Theatre there were Hurok and Sevastianov who enjoyed speaking of Tudor's "*Pills of Fire.*" It was hardly different at City Ballet, where Balanchine referred to his guest choreographer's last work for him as "*La Guardia.*" They weren't always sniping at each other, though. Once, as the two sat together in the theater watching a rehearsal, Balanchine acknowledged their common problem as choreographers—having always to come up with new steps for new ballets. "How many different positions for legs can there possibly be?" he moaned to Tudor.

25

Out of the Fray

NO MATTER WHERE they happened to be, both Tudor and Hugh collected motherly or sisterly types—guardians who would smooth the path and light the way. Betty Cage, an administrator at New York City Ballet, was one such.

It was she who appeared as witness when they became American citizens in the sixties. It was also she who used to entertain her friends with tarot cards. "One day Hugh got me to read the cards for him," Cage recalled. "When I predicted upheaval in his future, he became extremely agitated. 'Is something going to happen to my marriage?' he kept asking, nearly hysterical. The whole point of his interest in the cards that day fixed on this fear. And just a year later the marriage did come apart." It was at Jacob's Pillow in 1951 that Tudor created *Les Mains Gauches,* the ballet about palmistry; in a comic vein, it presaged the unhappy event while detailing the struggle of a wayward boy who seeks the attention of a beautiful woman.

By 1953 Diana Adams and Hugh Laing were divorced. They had lived together only three years, a period far from serene. The trouble, the inevitable trouble, began while the two were still with Ballet Theatre. According to dancer Mary Burr, Hugh "made Diana feel like a queen at first. He gushed over her, especially when we were doing *Undertow*. By 1948 and *Shadow of the Wind,* the picture was changed. She suffered so during those rehearsals. Her relationship with Hugh went sour. He was feeling inadequate to the ballet, while she had a major role and Tudor was letting her improvise a lot." If one simply read the accounts of their respective careers, starting at this point, the conclusion would seem logical.

Ballet Theatre had gone into decline. Tudor fell from his primary place in the heavens. Venus and Apollo, without their Zeus in the company and without the safeguarding of his ballets, without so much as an assurance that they could dance the roles he had created for them, saw their viability with Lucia Chase dwindle to nothing. When they defected to another's kingdom, they found a wholly reordered constellation. Diana's star was in the ascendancy. Still, Balanchine wanted to make the husband of Diana happy in order to keep her. He generously fed him many roles while Hugh "knocked himself out" to please the master. As it became clear that Diana no longer wanted to endure Hugh's domination of her life, she found other sheltering, adoptive arms—Balanchine's and LeClercq's. She always had a certain penchant for latching on to protectors, winning their sponsorship and making an agreeable *maîtresse d'honneur.*

In hindsight she would cynically question why Hugh had to have her and why he played out the fantasy of being in love. She rued the whole relationship, admitting that he wrecked her life, that he monopolized it by playing on her insecurities and isolating her from others. She could neither resist nor defy him. As a consequence, she was immobilized. Tudor may have thought he had escaped when Hugh married, but Diana insisted that, as a person and a choreographer, he was lost. She would not be lost, however. Hers was a forced and temporary alliance, for the moment that she sent out an SOS Balanchine threw her a life raft. This new captain wanted her aboard. So when she confessed that continuing with the company would be impossible because of Hugh, he told her not to worry: "I'll take care of Hugh. He won't be staying."

What precipitated the end of the marriage was the imbalance of their career fortunes. As Diana moved up the Balanchine ladder, Hugh lost his footing and slid down. Almost any male dancer would have found himself at a disadvantage at City Ballet, where nearly every pedestal had a woman on it. But in his case—being an apostle of Tudor and not an ideal porteur for neoclassical ballets—there was an even greater inhospitality. If one factored into that the loss of prestige he'd enjoyed at Ballet Theatre—not to mention the lid he now had to keep on his tantrums—the odds for unhappiness became great.

Predictably, Hugh did not accept with any degree of equanimity the dissolution of his marriage. For months he followed Diana around, trying to persuade her to stay with him. He stalked her apartment building and stood on the street under her window late at night—finally forcing Tanny LeClercq to keep Diana hidden from his sight. He sobbed to everyone who could be identified as a friend. After "crying and crying so hard" at the *Dance News* offices to P. W. Manchester, then an editor of the publication, he begged her not to write about the divorce or his misery over it.

Tudor and Hugh, each with a good reason to retreat from City Ballet, left. Diana went on to have an illustrious career there. Nora stayed for the upcoming European tour, having won a place for herself with *Cage* and, for the one season it stayed in the repertory, *La Gloire*. But whatever respite from embatlement Tudor enjoyed during the course of Hugh's marriage, he was in for major attack now that the wolf came running toward him—badly wounded. A near slaughter took place. And there was no escape, for the two, gamekeeper and wild animal, were locked in a clinch, merged with each other. Some called it love, some called it human bondage, some called it pathology.

Whatever the case, this mutual crippling became the most man-
ifest aspect.

"Hugh pilloried Tudor," said Moncion. "He bound, gagged
and imprisoned him. Whatever existed before now turned into
a mutual cage. I remember being around them with others. All
we could see was the whites of our eyes, because, out of embarrassment, everyone tried to look away."

The loss of Diana called up a rage that he would vent on the
one person who stood stoic, ready to be attacked. Guilty or not,
the accused took his punishment wordlessly—as he always had.
But there was a limit and, perhaps as self-protection from the
onslaught, Tudor drew the line at living with Hugh. The two
of them did not resume sharing an apartment when Diana left
the scene. Earlier, throughout the breakup, Tudor "had trod a
safe middle ground publicly," Moncion remembered. "Diana,
too, never hinted at what was thundering underneath. Once she
brought down that steely facade she became inscrutable. Whenever it was safe, but only then, Hugh became an enfant terrible
around Tudor—who would sanction or even savor the outrageous behavior."

Much later in his life Tudor would tell Gerd Andersson, the
Swedish dancer-turned-documentarian, that "without Hugh
Laing I wouldn't have had someone to tell me when I was doing
crap." So lost in the immediate process could he become that he
no longer saw the whole entity of his creation. But one must
wonder whether Hugh's judgments were always valid. In the
case of Diana, whose insecurities he played on, the effect was
deleterious; she hardly bloomed under his supervision. Perhaps
the same was somewhat true with Tudor. For all the value of
his support, Hugh, whose distrust bordered on paranoia, could
make an already wary Tudor even warier, could persuade him
of pitfalls that didn't necessarily exist.

He showed so strong a determination to succeed at first. The
fact that it withered over the years—years locked in this symbiosis—suggests that Hugh's was not always a salutary presence.
Predictably, Tudor would subscribe to scapegoating: to com-

pensate for being dominated himself, he sought to dominate others—through intimidation, through cruelty, through whatever means were at his disposal.

The end of his brief, ungratifying guest tenure at New York City Ballet left him free to pursue more concentratedly his options begun in 1950 at the Metropolitan Opera. As its choreographer and balletmaster—as well as director of the associated school which fed the ballet company—he would wield power, he would have every chance to cast off the interloper's raiments he wore at the House of Balanchine. But there was little hope of finding satisfaction here. By its very definition the Met troupe he headed was, creatively, a mere handmaiden to the opera enterprise it served.

Inevitably, it would not provide what he needed.

26

School Days

THE OLD METROPOLITAN OPERA HOUSE, which took up the whole block between Thirty-ninth and Fortieth streets at Broadway, was another haven for ballet dancers. A subsidiary of the mighty opera organization, the little company was held responsible for trotting out the nightly divertissements as specified in the various operas. It hardly represented an elite group, but its members at least drew regular salaries and could stay in New York—where everything that was anything happened. What's more, the Metropolitan Opera Ballet served as a potential springboard to both the New York City Ballet and Ballet Theatre, to which it had an initial association, starting in 1950. So the dancers always had hopes of advancement out of the company.

For Tudor it was a place to lick his wounds. Here he could find safety from the threat posed by fast-track competitors and judgmental critics. The new post brought him back in contact with a craft he had plied under Sir Thomas Beecham at the Royal

Opera. He was, after all, an old hand at arranging the little ornamental dances that served as filler-antidote to operatic *longueurs*. The Met would also be a place where he could lock tutorial horns with Margaret Craske. He'd brought the British ballet mistress to the United States, after they reunited during Ballet Theatre's 1946 tour to London. Now she was teaching her Cecchetti specialty at the Met school, just as she had taught it to him twenty years earlier. Her immense knowledge and great gifts as a teacher of classical ballet drew students from all over the city. So, too, was Tudor a magnet. From the time dancers jammed into his classes at Carnegie Hall's Studio 61, he was renowned as a teacher.

But shifting from Craske's student to her peer was a difficult negotiation. The two of them had a taste for sparring, and openly competed for idolatrous students. As she was wont to say, "Antony could acknowledge no other authority." In effect, they both sought dominion and were mesmerizing forces, though wholly different. She was propriety itself, a strict British schoolmistress with wispy gray hair pulled into a severe chignon and a plain, wrinkle-ridden face. She conducted classes of calm, numbered port de bras, a textbook of Cecchetti refinements. Often she carried the Bhagavad Gita with her, a reminder of her obeisance to Meher Baba. Indeed, she had tried to proselytize Tudor, but of course he declined—finding his own path later to another oriental philosophy, Zen Buddhism. She was as strong-willed, in her way, as he. And despite the contention between them he saw to her appointment both at the Met and Juilliard, as well as at the summer dance retreat, Jacob's Pillow.

Craske and Tudor engaged in brilliant repartée. Students did not relish getting caught in the crossfire, however. They overflowed the barre for classes alternately taught by the two masters—sometimes one would stay to watch the other; the incendiary remarks shot back and forth in salvos. The studio had a large gallery that drew many spectators, for the Craske-Tudor show was something to see and it extended through morning, afternoon and evening classes.

At the time he began this teaching phase of his career, Tudor was balding but not yet gray. He cut an unusual classroom figure in his street shoes, trousers and shirt and tie, which flew about as he whirled and turned. As the years went by he lost his hair—although he never coddled what remained. His pride was too great for such dishonesty. Instead he clipped the only hair he had, that at the sides, to a half inch. Sometimes he shaved his head. In this bald or nearly bald state he came to look like a falcon—his features sharpened, his demeanor threatening, his tongue acid, his swings from benign to menacing sudden. Gone was the softer poet-scholar. In his place was a penetratingly fearsome inquisitor.

In part, the effect was carefully manufactured. Tudor began to create a persona the moment he stepped onto U.S. soil. Because the young American dancers already found his British presence intimidating he consciously sought to capitalize on it. While he never took seriously the superiority attributed to him—there was a glint of mockery in his self-aggrandizing remarks—neither would he ignore such a custom-tailored advantage as had been thrust on him. He knew what to do: wrap himself in it. What better coat of armor could one wear against insecurity than preeminence? He did this notably at Ballet Theatre, but he perfected the role at the Met and at Juillard where, said his one-time student Muriel Topaz, "he was insular by design." If people fear you enough they'll stay their distance, they won't be able to glimpse your frailties.

Still, the disguise wasn't ironclad. A typically Tudorian contradiction came in his sudden blushing. It was involuntary, uncontrollable—this physiological reaction. So when he made a stridently sexual innuendo to a student, he often turned red. On the one hand, he shocked everyone in class with his personalized and specific remarks. But his own beet-bright embarrassment belied, in part, the Victorian sensibility.

"And what could *you* have been doing last night to have such a high leg extension this morning?" he would ask some poor humiliated boy or girl—both sexes were fair game. Apart from the harmlessly chiding remarks, though, were the ones he inflicted with what some say was malevolence. "What's that you're doing?" he would ask. "I thought I asked for an *attitude,* not an imitation of a dog lifting his leg over a fire hydrant." But the marvelous results he got, in spite of the sarcasm, made most students endure the dreaded hot spots in his classes. Those who could survive got a fair return. Still, they welcomed the occasional reprieve. Years later, at Juilliard, Sirpa Tepper remembered feeling "great relief when Eric Hampton [another student] came to class. Tudor was very attracted to him and the moment he appeared the heat was off the rest of us. We could relax. Eric would receive Tudor's undivided attention. A teasing attention, but very conscientious and never harsh."

What students learned from Tudor was not much different from what they would learn by creating a wonderful role with him. His classes were never rote exercises. Just because his charges wanted to improve their technique—to jump higher, to align themselves better, to articulate more clearly, to smooth their transitions into a buttery legato, to turn out from the hip, to become more flexible—did not mean that he would bypass the whole purpose of wanting to do those things. He always started from the beginning. What is this movement? What does it say? Why are you doing it? If, by some fluke, this questioning approach had been disallowed, he probably would not have opted to teach at all.

Quite naturally, he gave his students a rich experience—whether in the pure movement classes or the production classes, those to which he added a little scenario. Much thought went into the combinations he presented. Sometimes he devised them on the subway, riding from his apartment on Seventy-seventh Street, near the Hayden Planetarium. Now that he was sublimating his choreographic gifts he had every reason to transfer to the classroom what he formerly had saved for his ballets. Which is exactly what he did. Before, it was the company dancers at Ballet Theatre and City Ballet who profited. Now it would be those at the Met, Juilliard and Jacob's Pillow. Every combination he gave at the barre, every adagio in center work had originality, purpose and depth.

In the truest dramatic sense he succeeded in analyzing motivation for his students. Where did an impulse come from and why? Often he focused on the back, for that was the key to any character's feeling tone. The heart, according to Tudorian gospel, was not on the sleeve; it was in the back. The difference between Tudor and many other teachers lay in the fact that he did not train militia for maneuvers or conduct athletes' workouts. His unadorned idea was to form artists from dancers. Those who had the capacity for this grand design seized on the windfall.

"What impressed me so much was how he got us to use our minds to find solutions," said dance historian David Vaughan, who, in the fifties, attended three of Tudor's morning classes a week at the Met. "But what equally puzzled me was why he didn't make ballets with all the wonderfully imaginative things he made up for the classes. It was Mallarmé who said: 'It isn't with ideas you make sonnets, but with words.' The same is true of choreography. Tudor had the words, or the steps. Endless steps and movements and combinations. That's what ballets are. And he showed us everything. He did wonderful pirouettes."

He also coached musicians. Those pianists who played for his classes came in for no less strict standards than the dancers. When Betty Sawyer presented herself as an accompanist, one with very little repertory, she remembered that "he almost gave me an ulcer." But she was surprised that he even tolerated her. "If I couldn't find appropriate music he would silence me and sing 'Onward Christian Soldiers.' His cruelty was extraordinary. I remember a student who was very self-conscious about her chin, or rather her absence of a chin. In front of everyone he called her a 'chinless wonder.' " Sawyer gradually developed a large enough repertory to suit her taskmaster and she remained as his accompanist for the next two decades. During that time she saw another side to him besides cruelty, she saw that "he could look at both my quivering insecurity and my attributes and make a fair judgment. He did the same with dancers. He tipped the balance by his love of knowledge and his human understanding."

Contrary to what some thought, Tudor had not been hired to terrorize students. His main responsibility, as a matter of fact, still revolved around choreographing ballets for the opera. But for some reason those efforts were found lacking. Clearly he had no desire to pursue this type of choreography and it was John Martin's speculation that Tudor actually did contribute some superior dances for various operas but that he could not crank out hack work on a regular basis. But then neither could Balanchine, who also tided himself over at this opera establishment until Kirstein was able to finance a more suitable platform. Over the next dozen years Tudor would give up first his role as chief choreographer at the Met and then his directorship of the company, staying on only as head of the school.

Juilliard was another matter. The elite music school, which began its dance division in 1951, brought him together with such figures as Martha Graham and José Limón. If he chose to exile himself from brand-name ballet, at least he would find the intellectual environment of this alternative more in keeping with his standards. In fact, he was more attuned to modern dance, which, in its very genesis, dealt seriously—not commercially—with the subjects it addressed. Challenge, some would say a perverse challenge, characterized the Tudor career. He insisted, for example, on working within the frame of ballet, not modern dance, even though he found dancers of a sensibility closer to his own among the barefoot variety. Perhaps it was the traditionalist in him, or the disciplinarian, that accounted for the lure ballet exerted, for he always seemed to be at odds with its meretricious and artificial aspect of big business. "He was implacable," according to Sawyer. "He refused to give up the purity of ballet for the advantage of modern dance."

Were it not for the fact that the world saw him in retreat, rather than holding his own on international stages, this life might have satisfied him. But it didn't, because he had assimilated the very value system he strove to reject.

As a student at the old Juilliard on Claremont Avenue and

122nd Street, Bruce Marks remembered his first encounter with Tudor: "I saw this spine come walking into the class—an unforgettable entrance." One of the first things people noticed about Tudor was his carriage, it commanded attention. Marks, who, as a result of Tudor's influence, later joined Ballet Theatre, had no interest initially in ballet. He enrolled at Juilliard as a modern dancer. "But Tudor apparently saw I had another aptitude," he said. "And he challenged me to audition for the Metropolitan Opera Ballet. 'I'll bet you can't get in,' he would say. Of course I tried, after he dared me to. He knew I would. From then on I was a Tudorite, studying with him both at Juilliard and the Met, as well as dancing there in the company. We became very close friends. I saw how he operated. I understood his defenses. He would say: 'This isn't choreography, really, just a little thing I've thrown together.' "

And when Marks went to Tudor's apartment on Seventy-seventh Street to listen to recordings of Bohuslav Martinu's music (later chosen as the score for *Echoing of Trumpets*), the fugitive dance-maker would say, "Oh, I guess I have to do this." By affecting an absence of enthusiasm, he had a handy excuse if the ballet turned out to be a flop. The nineteen-year-old Marks, an eager audience for these admissions, positively adored his guru and was interested in all that the guru thought. Tudor's attraction to the new disciple was no less evident. But the young dancer, who would soon marry Ballet Theatre star Toni Lander, said that his idol "never made any explicit sexual advances because he was too repressed and too unsure of my reaction." When Tudor took him to a French restaurant for the first time, ordering fine wines, the guru's attitude was "nervous and tentative." Marks suspected that one object was "to get me drunk, but not at the sacrifice of our relationship." After that "I had dinner a lot with him, but Hugh usually came along and dominated the conversation. Then Tudor changed into this obedient docile person. 'Yes, Hugh,' he would say. Or 'Yes, Hugey,' with a little affection."

Clearly, Tudor enjoyed being with Marks and the other young

students whose adulation proved so irresistible. In their company he was full of spirit. Despite the fact that his activities now took place off the beaten ballet path he still exerted a powerful influence. He was the great Tudor and, if anything, enjoyed even more prestige among his starry-eyed disciples than as one among such rival choreographers as de Mille and Balanchine and Robbins.

The experiments he carried out in his classroom sometimes seem to us today like precursors of sensitivity training—every aspect of psychosocial drama was fair game. If Tudor spotted a dancer excelling in a certain combination and the one next to her making a poor showing he would get the two to confront each other competitively, not just as objective examples of right and wrong technique but as functioning egos. "Don't you want to tell her something?" he would ask the successful student, forcing peer criticism. The prodding would go on until a full public acknowledgment had been made and demonstrated.

In his first Tudor class, Tony Salatino remembered wanting to make a good impression on the much-feared teacher. "So I pulled up very strong and as he passed by me he poked my inflated chest and said 'too much ego.' " It was always the personal transactions that Tudor paid attention to, even though as Salatino recalled, "He was not too giving emotionally. But yes, he sought out intimacy. His desire to get close came through the work. The better a person understood what he wanted the closer his connection to that person. All of this was done through elaborate game-playing. In the end, his best students thought they had gotten close to him. It was an illusion. But the feelings are the same whether they're illusory or not."

Typically, Tudor would set up an environment and show some of the steps but not identify what ballet the segment came from. To simply tell his students that they would now be learning Rosaline's solo or a pas de deux from *Romeo and Juliet* did not satisfy his motivational requirements. He felt that early identification stifled the process of imagination, so he always played a carrot-and-stick game. If the contestants were supremely successful they might earn such a high compliment as: "That was rather good," or "Well, finally, you've come to your senses." Once, he found himself hopelessly engaged in teaching the grand pas de deux from *The Sleeping Beauty* to Salatino and his fiancée Sirpa Jorasmaa. Having spent a fruitless half hour just on the entrance, he finally asked the would-be *danseur noble:* "How much am I worth to you?" "A million dollars," answered Salatino. "Then bring me out like I'm worth it," commanded Tudor, taking the would-be ballerina's place. After that little verismo demonstration, the student next marched out with his proper partner, to Tudor's satisfaction.

Another time, while playing a recording of Tchaikovsky's *Sleeping Beauty,* the rhapsodic Adagio finale, he asked Salatino to get on the floor with Sirpa and "make love to her." Even if his subjects had been willing to go the limit there were all sorts of costume impediments to that end. But Salatino, being "very suggestible," took the cue almost seriously and "did get into the spirit of the thing." He was able to transfer the on-the-floor fervor to the formal upright steps. And on another occasion he remembered how Tudor put on the recording and made him and Sirpa conduct it while standing on tall chairs. "I cringed," he recalled. "But doing it wasn't objectionable."

Those who were reluctant could come in for painful experiences, though. Once he called on a very shy boy, asking him to yodel. The boy hesitated and Tudor reminded him, "I'm waiting." Another few minutes went by, everyone waited—and the student turned into a victim. The class was heartbeat quiet. The victim opened his mouth, but no sound came out. He repeated his silent scream several times and the atmosphere grew ominously tense. Hours seemed to pass. Finally, the victim cried. Still no words were spoken. The a cappella sobs came in huge choked shudders. Tudor continued to wait, saying nothing. Silence again. And finally a deep gutteral response from the sacrificial victim. Not a yodel, but some semblance of an attempt, one that finally satisfied the taskmaster.

"We were all very young and inexperienced," said Sirpa Jorasmaa Salatino Tepper, who had been a member of the Finnish Opera Ballet before immigrating to New York. "Tudor's ideas were too advanced for us, so he couldn't help feeling frustrated. Even so, I thought he was amazingly tolerant." Stuart Hodes, a student in the early fifties, found in Tudor a source of great encouragement. "I think he tolerated me well because my tack was self-deprecation. At any rate, he made me dance better than I could have with anyone else. His classes were not really geared for nonprofessionals. What made them difficult was the surprising juxtapositions of the steps." Tolerating underpar students was not something he did easily, though. Hodes remembered Tudor's remark to one such, who commonly took her place in the front: "I couldn't stand the sight of you there today." The girl dissolved into tears and withdrew to the rear. "But there was a glint of self-mockery in those words," Hodes observed. "And I think it took the sting off for her."

What put an even greater burden on the communication process was his distancing techniques. Tepper found herself "unable to respond to all those one-liners. . . . It was as though he were talking to himself. He made any dialogue impossible. The statements were really about himself and I suspect he wanted to be known, but couldn't find the means to elaborate or be direct." She and her husband invited Tudor to social gatherings where, with all the drinking, he let himself in for more than was comfortable. "He obviously enjoyed the adulation of Tony and the others, but he was very inhibited—especially when it came to relationships with men, which he tried to keep very private. I remember someone joking about the time he saw Tudor sitting on the beach in a lotus position, eyeing the beautiful young stallions. Hearing the story told, he went absolutely purple. And another time he was saying, 'Listen, honey' to Tony and I said, 'Don't honey him, he's mine.' Again he went purple."

Fortunately, his career at Juilliard had enough diversification to keep him from batting zero on the students' performance skills. As the compleat pedagogue, he knew his way around the stylistic differences between Ballets Russes and the Royal Ballet and New York City Ballet. Consequently, the students at Juilliard could learn, in his lecture-demonstrations, how a ballerina from each of those companies would dance *The Sleeping Beauty,* for example. But, when not instructing on these fine academic points he would often draw on personal information from the students as a stimulus for step combinations in the classroom. So absorbed in these little scenarios did he become that sometimes an entire ninety minutes would evolve as a single, coherent piece of choreography based on one of them. Because he encouraged students to report these personal incidents in class, they were left confused by his mixed signals. Did he invite them to approach or not? Salatino admits that he never knew when Tudor would welcome him at his table in the cafeteria and when he would not. Even though the two of them met for dinner frequently, prior to Salatino's marriage, there was always a chance that Tudor would decline an invitation for company. "When I spotted him having coffee before class and asked if he wanted me to join him he would sometimes say 'Of course' and other times say 'Not really.' But he took great glee in making cracks to Sirpa like: 'Tony really loves me.' "

In fact his twenty years at Juilliard, ending in 1971, were years filled with adoration. Whatever he did for the school was greatly appreciated, especially since his association there meant the sacrifice of working with a professional ballet company. For the school's student concerts he created a number of works in the early fifties: *Exercise Piece,* a technical display, and *Brittania Triumphans,* a group of Elizabethan dances. A decade later came *A Choreographer Comments,* a typically witty spoof on the whole arsenal of ballet feats from arabesques to entrechats, and *Dance Studies,* an exceptionally sensitive setting of a cerebral piece by Elliot Carter. And while he managed to create a number of little ballets that he further developed away from the school and titled, respectively, *Sunflowers, Cereus* and *Continuo,* his random comments about the Juilliard experience were rancorous. In the sixties when Stuart Hodes bumped into Tudor one day on the street he asked his former teacher what was new at Juilliard. "What could be new at Juilliard?" Tudor shot back. "It's just a place I go to teach." And yet his recrimination was directed more at himself and the fact that he was still there teaching than at the school itself.

But the associations he enjoyed were absorbing to him. Choreographer Paul Taylor recalled his student days and classes with "a twinkly, witty Tudor," although he himself veered more toward "the calm of Craske," whose containment he profited from greatly. "It was Tudor who taught me humility," said Taylor, "an antidote to my self-assurance." And then there was Martha Graham, who, in many ways, stood as Tudor's modern dance counterpart. They registered instant recognition of each other long before Juilliard. But staffing the same faculty they became familiar friends. Graham spoke of her "profound admiration" of him and fondly recalled letters he wrote her, "which he signed with little hearts." She, too, remembered his cryptic declarations to students. "Once, in the cafeteria, he summoned a girl to our table and said, 'You don't love yourself enough. . . . I see it in how badly you put your lipstick on.'"

Graham was the object of Agnes de Mille's adulation back in the early thirties. It was she Antony heard about from his friend Aggie just before he created *Dark Elegies*. And it was she they discussed in detail over tea at the Mermaid Tavern. Now Tudor and Graham not only shared an artistic conscience, but he became her peer critic—seeing everything she did and tugging at that artistic conscience without hesitation.

She made a prime target as a reluctant retiree, one who went on dancing long after her inevitable physical decline. By the sixties she was no longer performing her seminal works, but fashioning choreography that suited her present estate. One piece, for instance, *Voyage for a Dream,* was not prime Graham, by any means, but merely a vehicle to keep herself in the spotlight. With Tudor watching, however, there was no getting away with this self-deception. He came backstage after the premiere, having considered what he just had seen: Martha and three men drifting about on a boat—the centerpiece of a slick, elaborate set which suggested all-too-obvious bed metaphors for a ménage à quatre.

"So, you've finally compromised," he said to the diva of modern dance while a whole host of onlookers stood watching and listening in morbid fascination. She was stunned. But not too much for a hard kick in the shin that sent him hobbling away. "Antony smiled," she remembered. "He understood my crazy ways and idiosyncracies. I knew the work wasn't so good. I knew that he knew I knew. So the kick was justified."

It was during this period that he had many discussions with her about the options she chose. Few would have dared to do so, but it was already established that Tudor, as well as Graham, constituted a special oracular order. And besides, the debate of such issues was of vital importance to him—as long as the debate rested safely on someone else's shoulders. "What would you rather be remembered as," he asked the goddess Graham, "a dancer or a choreographer?" There could hardly be a more painful question. The whole inspiration for her landmark oeuvre came out of the rage to dance. How could she possibly separate one from the other?

"I would rather be remembered as a dancer," she told him. "What a pity," he answered. Thirty years later, at the remarkable age of ninety-four, she would dredge up that exchange. He had a way of getting to the cave of the heart. For others, if not for himself.

27

Disciples

ONE THING TUDOR could always count on during his years in exile was the adoration of his various hosts.

When he visited the fledgling National Ballet of Canada in 1952, to stage *Jardin aux Lilas,* he found, once again, a bunch of undeveloped dancers who were sketchily trained and woefully unsophisticated. But the company was not without promise, owing to the fact that its director, Celia Franca, had been coached by Tudor when, as a teenager, she took over An Episode in His Past, from *Jardin,* at the Ballet Rambert. First, she'd been his student and saw him as "extremely sarcastic and harsh, but not destructive, and so articulate that if you had any guts at all you would make use of his coaching. I just adored him, we all adored him. I suppose there is a bit of the masochist in all of us because we didn't even mind being beaten by him, verbally, I mean."

Just prior to a tour in 1936, some months after the premiere of *Jardin,* Peggy van Praagh had to bow out of all Ballet Club performances, so Tudor replaced her with Franca. "The learning experience was fantastic," she recalled. "He'd say, 'When you make this entrance, imagine that you have just arrived at the top of the crush bar staircase at Covent Garden. Its beautiful red carpeted foyer has a lovely balustrade leading from the dress circle down to the bar itself. And everyone's eyes are on you.' This remained in my memory when I made my first entrance across from downstage left down to downstage right. And he said, 'Use your arms as though you are using an enormous fan.' This kind of thing really really excited me, and although he could be very sarcastic, he could also be very encouraging. There was a pirouette *en dedans* at one place, an inside turn that must be done on pointe. Well, I never had a very strong technique, and out of the corner of his eye he saw me trying this pirouette, and I did three of them, on perfect balance. It probably never happened again. But anyway he said, 'Did I see a triple pirouette there?' Which was very sweet. He didn't have to say it but he did."

Responding to the call of his erstwhile protegée, just starting up a ballet company, he would see what good he could do. They were peers, technically—although he refused to acknowledge that she was, from this time, her own boss. He certainly ignored evidence that the young Canadians stood in awe of Franca, what with her stellar credentials from Sadler's Wells and a definable persona as well. According to Lois Smith, the dancer who would inherit leading roles in the Tudor ballets, "He simply squashed Celia. He never missed a chance to trample on her authority or to humiliate her in front of us all."

Some years later, however, she delighted in reversing positions with her tormentor. Holding the carrot in front of his face, she mentioned wanting to stage *The Planets* and *The Descent of Hebe,* early masterworks he had created for Rambert. They have never been seen outside of England, even though the originators are still capable of resurrecting them. "As I spoke of these ambitions," said Franca, "his eyes got bigger and bigger. He was so pleased, but wouldn't give me the satisfaction of saying so."

In 1952 the National Ballet of Canada was in its infancy, having everything to gain from Tudor's participation, regardless of what tradeoffs went into the bargain. Ordinarily, he would not have considered staging *Jardin* on an embryonic troupe like this. But Franca was astute artistically and had a wonderful memory. She had already learned several other roles in *Jardin* while still in London and Tudor knew he would have her excellent rehearsal assistance, as well as a seasoned Episode in His Past. What's more, she boasted a fine Caroline and Lover in Lois Smith and David Adams, respectively.

Perhaps just as significant, these two were married, and dancing married couples always comforted Tudor. The torturer's restraints came off in their presence and a somewhat mischievous but nevertheless avuncular, sympathetic person emerged. Throughout his life he would collect quite a number of them as close friends (Bruce Marks and Toni Lander, Tony Salatino and Sirpa Jorasmaa, David Wall and Alfreda Thorogood, Maude Lloyd and Nigel Gosling, Sally Brayley and Tony Bliss—of the last two only the wives danced).

Because of his commitments at Juilliard and the Met he could not remain long enough to complete rehearsals. But Toronto was close enough to New York for Franca and the dancers to travel to their Mohammed. Coincidentally, he was in the midst of staging *Jardin* just then for New York City Ballet, so the Canadians attended those rehearsals as well. This was just the first of several productions Tudor would mount for Franca's troupe, for he found gratification in their sensitive portrayals. Just as important as his sense of success was the feeling of family that developed. Shortly after the Canadian *Jardin,* Smith, Adams and some of the others came to Jacob's Pillow, still Tudor's summer stamping ground, a place where he gathered his flock. While he held forth in ballet, Pillow founder Ted Shawn and others of the barefoot ilk presided over modern dance.

At this point he had made a life for himself mostly without Hugh—although the divorce from Diana was only months away. While the Laings spent their last summer together—London, 1952—Tudor took charge of Hugh's dog. David Adams recalled that Tudor was keeping Hugh's "elderly dog there at the Pillow. . . . The poor thing's tongue was hanging out. Tudor said that the animal was 'my last link with Hugh' and looked teary-eyed when he made the comment. I had the feeling that Lois and I were a sort of replacement for Hugh to Tudor. He used to joke, wickedly, 'I love you both, but I can't decide which one more.' "

And there were others to take up the slack at this time. Sallie Wilson, for one, although her attachment would hardly console Tudor. Back in 1949 the seventeen-year-old Texan was among the many dancers who tried out for and won a place in Ballet Theatre's vastly vacated coryphée rank. The company had just scraped itself together after having been dismantled for a season. But it didn't take long for her to fall under the spell of Tudor. Once she did, ballet insiders were witness to an extraordinary episode of public sadomasochism. Over the next few years Wilson slavishly followed her god—to Canada, to Sweden, to Juilliard, to the Met, to the Pillow. It didn't matter that he gave her little benediction—just the opposite, he seemed to cast her out.

She lasted with Ballet Theatre only that one season but since Tudor also departed in 1950 she could feel a martyr's virtue upon being dismissed by Lucia Chase. She went directly into the Metropolitan Opera Ballet from there—with her savior—continuing to take classes from Craske and now from him as well. During this period he would indeed act as her agent when it suited him, although the consensus was that he found her unappealing. "Plain and peasantish," recalled Karnilova, who was a principal dancer then at the Met and saw Wilson "sitting in a corner always crying when I walked into rehearsal. Tudor would look at me, roll his eyes and say, 'She's completely mad.' " Some speculated that her hangdog devotion and teary wallowing provoked him into abuse. But he did work with her and even masterminded a new audition with Chase five years later.

"I was still a little on the plump side," said Wilson. "But Tudor told me to wear all black—tights, toe shoes and leotard—which would have a slimming effect and make me look more sophisticated. He coached me very carefully for this audition and went out to lunch with Lucia just prior to it. 'Don't duck your head down like you always do,' he said. 'Meet her glance straight on. Show confidence.' " But at the audition she complained that he didn't help her, that he set himself apart as though an impartial bystander. While such a posture would allow Chase to feel uncompromised in her judgment, Wilson only saw that Tudor refused to act wholly as a good agent would. Chase offered the newly attractive dancer a contract on the spot, knowing also that if she hoped to entice her wily choreographer back into the fold it would behoove her to take his cues—like hiring Sallie Wilson.

Not so surprisingly, Tudor still felt he had to hold his novice at bay. "Now you're going to have to fight me," he told her— just what she didn't want to hear. But he had a way of awarding dancers their most dreaded reality. While Wilson desperately wanted him to embrace her, to guide and teach her, he cast her out. Yes, she was assigned the roles he had in mind for her— Rosaline (*Romeo and Juliet*) and the sexy Lover in Experience (*Pillar of Fire*)—but was given brief and perfunctory rehearsals. Finally Sono Osato, who originated both of them, taught her Rosaline because, as Wilson said, Tudor "hated me" in it. "He was daddy," she explained, "but his approval always hinged on how strong or weak I was. Too strong and he pushed me away. Too weak and he did the same thing. When I got back into Ballet Theatre I think he wanted me to fail. Within a short time he went around saying: 'She's no performer.' That hurt me so much that I stopped going to his classes and ended up having almost no contact with him."

Gradually came a thaw, although the ice-to-warmth character of their relationship persisted over many years. When he let her, Wilson recited the Tudorian mantra with rapt, self-flagellating piety. "He was a very special man," she said. "You adored him; yet you hated him. He tinkered with people. He liked to get into their hearts and break them, thinking that's how to make a better person or a better dancer. With some people it doesn't work. I've seen some fall by the wayside, they couldn't survive. He could have told me to jump off a cliff and I would have done it.

He told me when it was time to lose my virginity. So I set about doing that. And I told him when I had done it. He gave a dinner party for me," acknowledging the rite of passage.

Her struggle to understand Tudor became perhaps the severest test of all. During that first summer at the Pillow, 1951, she learned *Dark Elegies*. Of the five performances the little company gave there was one in which she fell off pointe and felt she danced miserably all around. But afterward Tudor told her that it had been her very best attempt, perhaps seeing something she didn't. "That shattered everything," she said. "I had to sit back and figure out what he meant." To take an aggressive and direct path—asking for some explication—would not occur to her, for the seeds of their master/slave relationship had already been sown.

What kept her bound to him was the prospect of sharing in the creation of some marvelous role or the reinterpretation of an existing one—the same draw that Tudor exerted on all who volunteered for the chance. And in that summer of 1951 Sallie Wilson benefited hugely. The little works he put together at the Pillow during these years were marvelously witty, starting with *The Dear Departed* (1949), which he had done for Diana and Hugh. In addition to learning *Dark Elegies,* Wilson created a role in *Les Mains Gauches*. But the ballet she especially liked was *Ronde du Printemps,* a comment on seduction in all its guises, based on Schnitzler's play, *La Ronde.*

Tudor gave her the central role, that of the grand actress. She knew that he was deliberately casting against type in asking her to portray a marvelously confident creature, one whose worldliness and savoir faire contrasted with Wilson's own life experience and self-perception. But she also knew that he was bent on transforming her from that miserably masochistic head-ducker she persisted in being. "He was repelled by her nakedly nonexistent self-esteem," said Tudor's longtime piano accompanist, Betty Sawyer. "He didn't care much for her childish indiscretions either." When she confessed to knowing "nothing about men" and less about the feminine wiles used to seduce them, he simply had to require a correction. And it turned out to be trial by rehearsal fire for her. "All I could do was simper and dribble because I was in absolute awe of him and too shy to perform as he wanted me to," she remembered. "So he told me to sit down and just watch. He danced my part. And then I marked the steps from behind but wasn't at all reassured. And he kept making terrible remarks. Once he complained about my face and took me into the dressing room to apply makeup correctively. 'The only thing that will help is plastic surgery,' he said, laughing. It was funny to him, but not to me, of course. A few days later everyone went to the movies and I spent the whole night trying to put my role together."

Tudor's tough tactics paid off. Wilson was able to make the interpretive leap. But she insisted that "he didn't have to be so hard on me." Whether that was the case or not, he did seem severe. Often she would find herself cherishing a certain step but once he noticed her undue attachment to it he would change the step. She guessed that "he wanted to guard against pride and preciousness."

Creating new ballets was hardly the reason he came to Jacob's Pillow. But he did relish the chance to engage in friendly warfare with Craske. "Get up off your knees, sainted Mother Margaret," he would holler with playful affection while passing the meditating woman's cabin. She lived the strictly spartan life even there, having only a cot and a picture of her beloved Baba. And Tudor liked nothing better than teasing this selfless devotée. Many dancers learned her secret in dealing with the constant contestant: "Never be vulnerable to him." This was advice followed by Glen Tetley, who went on to become a well-known choreographer. But defenses commonly came down in this country ballet camp where Tudor had the chance to mix his barbs with pranks.

One morning Tetley remembered being awakened by an intruder. "I bolted upright," he said, "and found Tudor leaning on my chest. 'I just wanted to tell you about a rehearsal,' he said mischievously. But of course there was this wall around him personally. He played at familiarity, but never really let anyone in. Besides, he truly liked the careful image he'd constructed— that elegant, witty, controlled personage we all knew." Ted Shawn, on the other hand, was just the opposite of Tudor and came in for endless ridicule by the master of ridicule. Tetley recalled how Tudor would stare with smiling contempt at the modern dancer "doing his braggadoccio whirling revolutions. And when Shawn portrayed St. Francis in his famous Vision Scene, Tudor would stroll behind the stage wearing a tatty dressing gown and carrying his toothpaste and toothbrush. The floodlight would reveal him in detail to the audience. He plotted the timing perfectly. It was his way of showing hatred for everything Shawn stood for. But I think that the Peck's Bad Boy trappings covered the disappointment for his own career."

28

Contagious Discomfort

WHATEVER THE DISCREPANCIES between this ruler and those he governed, no adjustments would be made. Were his underlings inexperienced and provincial and shy and cowering? It didn't matter to him. He would make no concession, although the ones with a tongue and a mind and a spirit fared better. They came in innocence, as most young dancers do, with an invisible armor against personal invasions. But he violated the boundaries, he trespassed—and then took delight in his victims' discomfort. "Titty-to-titty," he hollered out to Earl Kraul and his partner, exhorting them to come close together for a *Jardin* segment they were learning in Toronto. "We didn't know how to brush up against each other," Kraul explained, "but Tudor took particular pleasure in embarrassing us this way. We were frozen with intimidation. And it never changed. Even a few years later, when he came to my dressing room after a New York performance and said: 'I don't even recognize your dancing.' I couldn't decipher the remark. Was it positive or negative? But I was too stricken to ask what he meant."

Often these Canadians were the very dancers Tudor would invite to teach his classes while he traveled to Stockholm or Tokyo or Munich. One of them, Grant Strate, guessed that "he asked me to replace him because he thought I would fail." While Tudor acted the part of booster, he frequently withdrew his support at the crucial moment—a tactic designed to force independence as well as raise adrenaline. In the case of Strate, whom he had encouraged to choreograph ballets for the Juilliard students, he showed avid interest and lots of encouragement—even skipping rehearsals of his own work in order to watch his protegé's. But after seeing the dress rehearsal of Strate's debut piece, Tudor yelled out a taunt: "I hear you're going to be a traveling salesman." Strate shot back: "They always told me you were a son of a bitch," recalling that this rejoinder and his bona fide anger tickled Tudor. "If you kneeled at his feet, he would step on your head. Some of us learned to stop kneeling. Maybe that's what he wanted us to do all along."

On the one hand he would speak disparagingly of his time spent teaching, on the other, he became visibly and excitedly engrossed in the course of a class. Sometimes he stood, legs apart, scratching his head to summon the next idea, so intent that no one could imagine those contradictory attitudes. Typically, he sat on his stool—one just high enough to raise him slightly above the dancers. There, with his back ramrod straight, he smoked and looked at the floor. Every once in a while his eyes flashed up, fixing on one person. When that happened there was great tension. Who would be the unlucky focus of his glance?

Despite the occasional socializing, Tudor no longer had the sense of community that marked his years at Ballet Rambert and Ballet Theatre. He frequented such bôites as the Baci Ball in Greenwich Village where Tudor disciples understood Hugh to be part of the domestic picture. But as Strate said, "There was a loneliness one sensed about Tudor." And his few attempts at reaching out for another relationship were usually aborted. Strate recalled being invited to dinner. "It was just the two of us. The air was charged, but neither he nor I took any initiative." The apartment on Seventy-seventh Street, tastefully appointed with heavy dark Victorian furniture, had walls of bookcases and records. To the occasional visitor, he would wave his hand past these collected treasures and confess: "From all this I can't find a single idea for a ballet."

His reprieve from academia and such perfunctory efforts as the 1954 *Offenbach in the Underworld,* which he created for the Philadelphia Ballet, came with a call from Ballet Theatre. The company would be celebrating its fifteenth anniversary that first month of 1955 and a gala season at the Met was being planned. All the dancers turned up and the occasion proved to be one of those happy reunions that look back to better times.

However, Ballet Theatre was still and would remain in artistic doldrums. Not even with the coaxing of Lucia Chase and Oliver Smith would Tudor consider returning to the fold, except on occasion to rehearse his ballets. But in the next season he would set his *Offenbach* on the company and again dance his roles, as would Hugh and Nora—in New York and on the South American tour that followed.

There were some changes and surprises during the gala, one of them involving Lucia's son, Alex Ewing. Because he had just graduated from college at the time and was temporarily at loose ends he decided to give his mother a hand at running the company. "It was about to go under," he explained, "and I thought maybe I could help. One day Tudor passed by the office and poked his head in. He had always been warm to me and as I grew older he seemed even sheepish, a bit diffident. 'Do you suppose I could be paid my royalties?' he asked politely. He'd never received any for all that time and I'm sure my mother knew that he hadn't." Ewing began to right the situation. So impressed was Tudor that twenty years later he asked him to act as executor of his estate—an offer Ewing declined but which he "found touching."

Things had not changed much between Chase and Tudor.

There were still times when the two of them did not speak, even while attending the same party. Ewing likened the recalcitrant choreographer to "a bird—rapacious, bright-eyed, alert—that would flit away in an instant." So much for the mode. But he also saw the mind at work. "Whatever else he felt, Tudor enjoyed those wars with my mother. He was a person viewing the scene from afar. He saw the whole thing as a spontaneous comedy."

So it was business as usual. Rehearsals were run in a shabby manner and Tudor had little patience for them. He took out his discontent on the dancers, further provoked by Hugh, who was back in his familiar role as tormentor. From the time Laing left City Ballet his stage career had become spotty and desperate. He no longer could depend on being part of a Tudor package, since his helpmate was no longer attached to a major company. In 1954 he ventured out to Hollywood, contract in hand for the screen version of *Brigadoon*. He would play the role of Harry Beaton. But whatever the reason, his hopes never materialized. Not only did he fail to make the necessary connection for a film future but his scene in the picture was reduced to roughly a minute. "He was just miserable the whole time," observed David Nillo, who by then had established himself as a movie dancer with Valerie Bettis. "He lived in a dump off Hollywood Boulevard and came to me frightened, lonely, weeping. He just couldn't crack the scene and cried and cried about how the big stars pushed him around and how he had no more importance."

Back in New York Hugh worked for a while as a photographer's assistant. The beckoning of Ballet Theatre's anniversary gala could not have come at a better time. It offered him an escape, albeit temporary, from the shadows. But the disparity between his and Tudor's situations—one sustaining a relatively prestigious role in the dance world, the other having none—had to leave an angry residue somewhere. And most agree that when Laing was on hand Tudor's moods turned darker. Enrique Martinez, who danced Mercutio in the gala season, likened Tudor in rehearsals "to an angel one moment and a devil the next. He slashed people to pieces. Once he called someone a half-wit, but the following day he apologized, saying, 'I was wrong. You have no brain at all.' People were always hysterical crying. Sometimes they could leap from there and make progress. Other times it just destroyed them."

Little could these near-strangers at Ballet Theatre imagine the other side of their seemingly mean-spirited taskmaster, a side reserved for close friends and, literally, distant relatives.

29

Found but Still Lost

As far back as the 1930s Tudor had been a student of theology. Curious about how religious thought functioned and what needs it met for its believers, he found himself exploring the whole range of salvation systems. Not for spiritual, mystic values so much as a method that could help him disengage from fear and self-doubt. His friend Therese Langfield once tried to explain "the spiritual comfort" he offered her at a time of crisis, but then took back the word "spiritual." "He would hate it," she said. And she was right. He mocked people, like Ted Shawn, who used the term to attain some kind of theatric holiness. It was always the humanistic tracts, the Eastern philosophies, that enticed him, rather than those with rigid moral codes dependent on anthropomorphic authority. Tudor was born, one might say, with a Zen koan in his mouth. Deliberately cryptic and perplexing to those who would know him, he epitomized a Zen master's spartan mode of communication—long before formally encountering it. He was already an ascetic and would, in a matter of time, embrace the body of transcendental knowledge called Zen Buddhism.

It was in 1957 that he phoned Mary Farkas at her home/headquarters in Greenwich Village. He wanted information about the First Zen Institute of America, which she led. Would it be all right for him to drop by and pick up whatever pamphlets there were? And to talk to her? Of course. But Mary Farkas, a tiny muffin of a woman with short brown dyed hair and a face that broke into the same squinting smile no matter what the statement or question confronting her, did not know that the voice on the line belonged to Antony Tudor. She was an admitted Anglophile—a great fan of Claude Rains. And so convinced of the voice's identity that she did not ask for the movie actor's name, but wrote it down in her appointment calendar. What a windfall! Claude Rains as a prospective member of the Zen Institute. Instead, another British gentleman appeared. Surprise proved greater than disappointment, though, and much later in their relationship she would confess to Tudor her girlish fantasy that the celebrated actor had called for information.

But just then she said nothing. Nor could she know that this transplanted Londoner had, some three decades ago, presented himself to another woman, one not so docile and adoring as she would be, one in charge of another type of enterprise. In contrast, here he would seek a palliative—not the wonderment that made his head reel at chez Rambert or the unbidden frustration that would prove so corrosive. Here, it was Farkas who stood to be enhanced. For his part, Tudor always welcomed admirers outside of the ballet world and he was warmed by her embrace. He thrived in these equitable engagements because they were free of the awe and exaltation that dancers heaped on him, because his contaminating reputation did not follow him here and because he would not be met with fear. Propriety would act as a safety valve on his ready abuse of power. He could relax.

Finally, he would make his peace with a matriarch—a kindly, unthreatening and passive woman, one he held dear. To enter her home, one checked one's weapons at the door. There would be no need nor basis for them, since she asked nothing of him. Neither would depend on the other for worldly success or material gain, thus permitting no chance for disappointment. At last Tudor might find the so-called emotionally corrective experience. He would even enjoy a marriage of sorts, eventually, as he and Mary Farkas held forth in the roles of president and general secretary, respectively. Mr. and Mrs. First Zen Institute of America. Whatever the past acrimony with Rambert, de Valois, Craske, Chase, de Mille and Franca, this liaison could prove an antidote. But even here he enjoyed playing some of his more harmless games. Farkas was, after all, a fan. And once settled into their prescribed roles, which turned out to be no different in this supposedly rarefied realm than anywhere else, she became vulnerable, showing him a framed triptych of photos of herself. The poses were artfully theatrical and could have been identified as dance stills. She knew he would offer a comment on them. He knew she waited to hear it. "Pure poetry," he said with his deliberately enigmatic tone and a mischievous glint in his eye. Was the remark mocking or a genuine appraisal? He immediately looked to see her response. "I laughed," she admitted, "in order not to show any further interest in his words."

Despite her initial air of equanimity and her smile that shouted silences, Farkas displayed strange lapses into vanity. She cared about what Tudor thought. She certainly did not empty her ego of the need for validation. Not in the purest sense. Nor did her institute function according to classic hierarchical rules. "We are not a monastery," she asserted. There are and were no Zen masters, for instance, except for dignitaries from Japan who made occasional visits. Nor did the residents float about in black robes. Farkas practiced a more democratic method. This suited Tudor: it imposed no restrictions on his personal life. It did not ban material possessions. In short, it was civil and nonradical. He would not have fit otherwise.

At first he attended the Wednesday night meetings. These were public. And they established an antiauthoritarian atmosphere by way of silent meditation. Then, he started dropping in for one-on-one visits at her Waverly Place residence, as did most of those who ultimately became members. She decried certain forms of Buddhism as antifeminist. With that in mind she had chosen to do without masters or teachers, urging instead the pursuit of individual, self-motivated enlightenment.

Tudor became a bodhi sattva, a being on the way to wisdom. Like all the other candidates, he took as his guiding principle "to do the best that is possible under the circumstances, to proceed with clear thoughts, using meditation as a facilitator." He certainly found himself in the right place. Here was a director who dedicated herself to "dealing with relationships," who saw life's biggest struggle as solving the problems that people have with each other. "We hold to an unwritten and unregulated code of behavior but those who come here had better find out what it is." In other words, Farkas offered a practicum free of personal probing, free of the requirement to take oneself to task for self-inflicted wounds. The teachings of founder Sokei-an Sasaki Roshi were simply that. They differed in mode from psychotherapy, which is invasive and locks in place such identifications as "doctor" and "patient." That kind of well/sick dichotomy was off-putting to Tudor. He wasn't ready to turn himself over to another supposedly wiser being for anything, much less an overhaul. But Zen Buddhism, with its generalized laissez faire system, was certainly benign enough. By contrast with a clinical approach, it could not cause further pain. Its immediate end would not involve discovery of emotional deficits but rather a transcendence from vulnerable fronts in his ongoing battles and disappointments. Not surprisingly, he had found this path appealing as long ago as 1937, the year he made *Dark Elegies,* which de Mille later described as "full of the Zen communal spirit." Its main thrust is the sharing of unspeakable grief.

And this was another significant advantage to incorporating Zen Buddhism into his life: it provided him a family. At Juilliard and the Met he was a kind of *paterfamilias,* but only for the duration of classes and rehearsals. Those associations, moreover, were fraught with intense expectations; one could even think of them as "transference" modes—the assigning of the same potent feelings for a parent to a substitute. It was wearying to wield so much power, especially for one who felt powerless over his own creative paralysis and thus frighteningly powerless in the greater ballet world.

But now that he no longer had a company to tour with and belong to he lived with a certain isolation. So when, in 1962, the First Zen Institute bought a building on Thirtieth Street off Lexington Avenue, he left his large uptown apartment and became one of the ten cooperative resident-owners of the stately four-story brownstone. Farkas and associates transformed it appropriately into a "blackstone." Little touches, like the paint job and large potted pine set next to the door of the lower entrance, gave the structure a slightly exotic look compared to others on the street.

Tudor disposed of the furnishings from Seventy-seventh Street. To his new apartment, with its clean expanse of white walls and light streaming in the windows, he brought only a few pieces. "The place suited him better," said Grant Strate, comparing it to the old dark digs, where "loneliness wafted from the walls." He invited selected friends to his hospice, showing them the public room where he "prayed," cooking dinner for them. On those occasions Hugh was invariably present. But although the two of them had daily contact when Tudor was not out of the city, their lives took on separate aspects now.

There were the students, for instance, always seeking Tudor's attention. There were all those "flighty little boys fawning over him, those flighty little boys who were not too talented and half Tudor's age," said Ballet Theatre dancer Leon Danelian. "He was like a Buddha to them. They were swayed to Zen Buddhism in the hope of becoming dancer-protegés." Tudor accepted the situation for what it was and devilishly confessed to making heavy demands on his naive acolytes. "I left a boy meditating for two and a half hours the other day," he told Stuart Hodes, chuckling with satisfaction over the sensory deprivation he had inflicted. It was one of those games: "How much do you love me? Enough to make a fool of yourself? Enough to pass through any of my trials by fire?" But the formality of these Zen meetings had a certain dramatic appeal. They began and ended with chanting in Japanese. Next came the main order of business, silent meditation, with congregants sitting in a lotus position, followed by a reading of a Sokei-an lecture. After the final chanting came tea and informal discussion and socializing. Tudor was the official timekeeper, the one who determined when to end the meditation period. And he relished this one vestige of the all-powerful being. He also performed the ritual with great physical dexterity and savoir faire, having first studied yoga before coming to Zen Buddhism. Bruce Marks mentioned that Tudor "also slept in a yoga position—the fetal one. He would block himself lengthwise between two chairs so that he could not stretch out." Shades of *Undertow*.

Not only did he invite friends often, he actually turned the place over once to Maude Lloyd and her husband Nigel Gosling. They had come to New York to complete work on a biography of Rudolf Nureyev. "I need to be closer to Ballet Theatre," he explained to them, citing a period of heavy rehearsals. "No one will be using the apartment so please stay in it," he implored. "But I knew better," said Maude. "He was aware of our limited finances and wanted to save us two weeks of hotel bills. It was the kind of thing Antony would do." On another trip, when he was busy with his classes and couldn't spend the evening with them, he cooked "a feast" and left it at their hotel.

What Tudor still managed to do during this period in the late fifties was maintain his alliances. Now and then he did drop in at Ballet Theatre to see that those of his ballets still in the repertory were kept somewhat up to par. He refused all invitations to create new ballets, however. These invitations came from the world over, for the Tudor reputation continued to grow—despite the fact that he had virtually withdrawn from the business. But now Nora was coming close to retirement. So when pressed to contribute a new work for the Met's Ballet Night—an annual showcase for the ballet company as a separate entity from the opera—he reluctantly agreed.

The result was *Hail and Farewell,* the first part being an obligatory exposition of academic maneuvers with the pièce de résistance consisting of four solos, one of which was Nora's. For the music he chose Richard Strauss's sublime *Four Last Songs.* Yet the same distance that he confessed to experiencing sometimes in the studio apparently dogged him in this effort. Years earlier he had Hugh to bridge the chasm between conviction and creative thought. It was Hugh who would jostle the dancers out of a dispiritedness that came from Tudor himself. Hugh, who "would move into the rehearsal, and manage, with his own enthusiasm and drive, to get the emotion back—everything I'd let slide," said Tudor. Now he was left to his own devices and apparently could not find the ignition key. Whatever it was that sparked the connection between him and what he created had died, at least for the present. It could not have been entirely coincidental that the *Four Last Songs* came when he was learning, through Zen, to disengage from worldly concerns. But for him disengagement had always been a drawback, not an advantage. When he practiced it in life, it took a certain toll, forcing him to stay outside. When he allowed it to permeate his creative impulses, he lost even the means for vicarious involvement with a life; he could no longer live through the scenarios of his ballets.

Hail and Farewell—with the only important part being the Strauss songs—had its first and last performance on March 22, 1959. Tudor could take little encouragement from the notices or general response, despite Walter Terry's favorable words about "glowing choreographic images, haunting and exquisitely lyrical." Thereafter he ended his association with the Metropolitan Opera Ballet Company, except for *Fandango* and *Concerning Oracles* (an expansion of *Les Mains Gauches*), which he did in 1963 and 1966, respectively. Shortly after *Hail and Farewell,* however, he made a lively showing in a television documentary series titled *A Time to Dance.* Here was a Tudor who belied any hesitancy or ambivalence. Whatever disconnection or disinclination he suffered creatively it did not show in his semiscripted talk with Martha Myers, head of the dance department at Smith College and the series's host. He looked casually dapper, with a handkerchief in the pocket of his double-breasted jacket and white peach fuzz growing along the sides of his head. He spoke in lilting British tones and sounded like an earnestly forthright, even animated, college professor, folding his arms picturesquely. What came across was an eminently appealing personality with a touch of the poet in his language. In answer to Myers's question about what distinguishes modern ballet from nineteenth-century ballet he talked about how the picture had been enlarged. "Instead of always having princes and enchanted princesses, gypsies, forlorn little dryads and sylphs, we've come to grips with people/types that are familiar to us in everyday life." He identified Hagar in *Pillar of Fire* as being "subject to all the inner disturbances man is heir to." Yes, he knew them firsthand, but gave no hint in his manner, of direct experience.

With him in the documentary—for what would turn out to be their last performance venture together—were Hugh and Nora, demonstrating excerpts of his and others' ballets. The Transgressor in *Undertow* danced the strangely halting steps, while biting the nail of his thumb and sliding it from one side of his mouth to the other. This, which conveyed the antihero's panicky defenselessness, and Hagar's hand to the temple were Tudor's interior symbols. In the course of the documentary he would also hark back to *Swan Lake* and point out how choreographers of a hundred years ago "placed the woman on a pedestal and had the cavalier stop dancing while he was showing her." Although he didn't say so, this was a tack Balanchine often used. *Jardin,* on the other hand, "shows the woman and man both dancing at the same time."

In the *Dim Lustre* excerpt, Tudor supplied a caption to the segment that Nora and Hugh danced: "Estrangement." It was the word he used to characterize their pas de deux. They were no longer in love, he explained. Indeed, the 1943 ballet coincided with the time when he and Hugh saw the "in love" aspect of their relationship slip away. But he ended the demonstration by dancing his own role with Nora in *Pillar,* the famous pas de deux for Hagar and The Friend and one of the most ecstatic episodes he ever created. Here were his swirling, ineffably tender love feelings. In the easiest of all possible worlds, he might have expressed them openly, to someone trusting and wholesome.

After these segments were shot, Hugh retired completely from the stage, although it was clear that time had not taken a toll on his dancing. Nor on Nora's. But one year later she had a change of heart and foreswore performing again. Ballet Theatre was at the end of its tether, having barely scraped by over the past decade. In 1960, however, came the chance for a tour to Russia. Here and in the Met season that just preceded the tour she marked her last appearances.

30

●

A Trumpet's Mean Echoes

LUCIA CHASE WENT INTO PRODUCTION OVERDRIVE for this twentieth anniversary season. As was the case for the preceding celebration, five years earlier, she now saw a chance to pull the company together, bring back the celebrity troops and make a rallying stand. But without much organizational or economic stability she could hardly promise a reasonable standard to those dancers and choreographers she beckoned. To make matters worse, a European tour was in the offing, one that would include a debut in the Soviet Union. The season began in Cuba, where Ballet Theatre represented the United States in a Festival of Dance. It then continued for a two-week run at the Met, which was a de facto rehearsal period for the all-important visit to Moscow.

But Tudor and Chase ended up in one of their stalemates. The choreographer found the impresaria's means and methods deplorable. With a ragtag company that had just returned from a layoff and saw very few familiar faces among its ranks she was going to tough out the upcoming season. Half flibbertigibbet, half expedient monarch, Lucia would call on her Yankee determination to pull this one off. She had a singular goal: to get the show onstage, no matter what. Meanwhile her adversary had a reputation to protect, which put them at distinct odds with each other. Once again they clashed, and both lost. No votes of confidence were exchanged. Chase wasn't even certain about whether to choose *Pillar of Fire* as one of her tour offerings. Would the Russians like it? Did they want it? Tudor's response to her lack of support and shoddy preparations came in the form of a boycott. He attended only one rehearsal of *Pillar,* seeming like an alien to the scene, merely observing unfamiliar rituals.

"He just sat there," recalled Tommy Rall, who had been cast in Hugh's role. "There were all these new dancers and an impossible number of ballets being rehearsed, for lack of a better word. Nora told me that Tudor probably wouldn't help me, since he and Lucia had had a terrible fight. He spoke only once and that was to Nora: 'You've gotten fat,' he told her," unable to condone her participation in an affair he discredited. Rall had known Tudor from 1944 to 1947 when as a fifteen-year-old he'd been taught—by this pillar of silence—The Green Skater in Ashton's *Les Patineurs.* He recalled that period as "a wonderful time." But Tudor had not been consulted about the casting for this present revival. Since he would not cooperate with Lucia she did the job herself. And now the cast would pay the penalty. "The only coaching I got came in John Martin's notice," said Rall. "It would have made all the difference to hear those words while I was rehearsing. He wrote that I came nowhere near capturing 'the elegant distillation of evil.' That little description was the key information that I never got."

There was a certain irony here. The dancers, not least of them Rall, were terribly honored to be given roles in these landmark ballets. *Pillar* and *Jardin* and so on were the glory of Ballet Theatre. Nor were all these cast members unfamiliar to Tudor. He had trained some of them over the years. With just a little guidance, even partial cooperation, the results might have been respectable. As things stood, Rall and the others felt understandably hopeless.

Tudor's stoicism was remarkable. The fact that he could sit through a rehearsal of *Pillar* and stay mute, not lifting a finger to save the ballet synonymous with his name, required utmost disengagement from what he held precious—that, or utmost defiance of his nemesis, Lucia. Was this a war of wills? Would he have the last word at the sacrifice of his most valued work? Was he proving something to himself or to her? Perhaps he looked on the whole episode as a Zen exercise: "Want nothing, accept everything." His observers remained unconvinced, however, for he had not yet arrived at a state of tranquil beatitude. The nerve endings still transmitted static. Quite a different picture from the assured, upbeat, fluent figure in the Martha Myers film. How unconflicted he seemed there, his explanations spilling in a forthright, articulate stream. How imperturbable. That was the Tudor he bargained for, not this one.

If indeed Mary Farkas and company were helping to smooth away the trouble their power didn't travel far enough to cancel Lucia Chase's negative feedback. Before this 1960 nadir and afterwards "her presence always raised Tudor's hackles," recalled Bruce Marks. "He would always refer to her as 'that woman.' He could not abide Lucia. She worked on the basis of expediency, not fine artistic judgment. And she was always going back on her word—first agreeing to something, then canceling it. But it was fear of her thoughtless decisions that made him strike out at her. Most important, though, I think Hugh poisoned him against her."

By the end of the season Nora had retired from Ballet Theatre. *Pillar,* lacking a dancer who could take over the role of Hagar, was dropped from the repertory. Tudor's reputation grew shakier from this point, for now it was not just a matter of a retired choreographer, one who no longer created new ballets, but one whose acknowledged masterpieces were coming into question. The occasional supervision, which often yielded as much con-

sternation for the dancers as help, wasn't enough to keep the
ballets up to par. And as they became more endangered the
rehearsal tensions grew. Marks remembered when, in 1962,
the company relocated to Washington, D.C., and was preparing
a big revival of *Jardin*. To this point he had been a Tudor favorite.
"But when he lashed out at me—I was dancing The Lover—and
said, in front of everyone, that I had no idea what the ballet was
about, I knew that fear was operating. Two days later he sent
me a couple of bottles of very expensive wine. A peace offering.
But I understood what was at risk. He was afraid of hearing the
critics say that *Jardin* is old-fashioned, not the brilliant thing they
originally proclaimed it to be and that maybe they were wrong
in the first assessment."

But no matter what kind of notices his ballets received Tudor
could hardly see himself as flourishing. What he needed was a
shelter far away. So off he went to Stockholm for the second
time, as guest choreographer of the Royal Swedish Ballet and
then the next season, in 1962, as artistic advisor. That same year
he detoured to Germany. At the invitation of his former Juilliard
student Pina Bausch—who would later set the dance world on
its ear with her own choreographic avant gardism—he did the
honor of staging *Jardin* for her Folkwang Ballet in Essen, with
Bausch herself as Caroline. But he did not want to uproot himself
altogether from New York where Juilliard and the Met were still
his anchor. Consequently, he did not stay away for long periods;
the teacher-replacements he arranged in his absence were never
meant to be anything but temporary.

Meanwhile the Swedes offered him the directorship. Since that
first visit, in 1949, they had let Tudor know that the post was
his to take. The company was put at his disposal and these dancers
were every bit as adoring as their New York counterparts, but
less temperamental.

He realized from the first that it was important to encourage
the young troupe. Gerd Andersson remembered the pride he
imparted to her, a schoolgirl then. Fifteen years later, this sister
of Bibi Andersson (Ingmar Bergman's leading actress), would

become his Swedish Nora Kaye. She found him to be "a mixture of kindness, sarcasm and seriousness. . . . You had to make a personal choice whether to take a joke positively or negatively. Whatever the difficulties, we all knew that what we got back far exceeded them. But we could not get him to stay in Sweden because he wanted only to live in New York, which he considered home." True enough. His magnetic field was New York—with Hugh and the hub of dance activity, even though he consigned himself to its fringes.

Whatever the case in Stockholm, he roused himself finally to make a major new ballet, but only after much pleading on the part of his hosts. The pressure was off here. He need not feel like a choreographer in a fishbowl. The critics were less prominent and wielded less power. There was no Lucia Chase to quibble with him over deadlines and rehearsal limits. He had carte blanche, but also a grinding fear that showed in his "angry resistance," said Andersson. "I had to shut my ears to it. In the beginning it was very bad. He kept looking for excuses not to come to the studio. His assistant had to collect him every morning or he would not have appeared at all. And when we did the big pas de deux he said, 'You finish it' and went down to the bar. He didn't complete the last few steps until a pause in our dress rehearsal."

None of his consternation showed by the premiere of *Echoing of Trumpets*. What's more, it was a ballet entirely different in mode and theme from anything he had previously done. It was a war ballet, one that depicted actual horrific events—murder, rape, pillaging. It took into account the influence of Kurt Jooss, the great German Expressionist whose most enduring and famous ballet, *The Green Table*, dealt with the same subject. Tudor had seen the work in London, shortly after its 1932 premiere, and never forgotten it. But an even more striking departure was the abandonment of his stream-of-consciousness sensibility in favor of straightforward narrative.

Until now his major ballets had reflected a Proustian-Bergsonian ideal. Apart from *Undertow,* with its case history montage as seen by the protagonist, they dealt with resonances of events, not the events themselves. *Dark Elegies,* for instance, showed the fallout of tragedy, the shades and interplay of grief and how it resolves. *Pillar* depicted the shame of eroticism, not so much the sexual act itself. Even a minor classic like *Sunflowers* focused on changes in relationships following experiences, rather than the experiences per se.

But *Echoing of Trumpets,* titled *Ekon av Trumpeter* in Swedish, did not take this approach. And Tudor admitted that some of the things he envisioned for his war ballet, a barbed wire enclosure, for instance, "symbolize that there's no way out. I didn't realize until I actually started staging the work that the setting I had conceived closed me in as a choreographer." Clearly, these words go beyond a description of mere physical detail. He did begin in the usual way, though, by searching for music.

The score he found turned out to be one by Bohuslav Martinu, the remarkable Czech composer of this century who, like Leoš Janáček (*Sunflowers*), followed in the footsteps of Antonín Dvořák (*The Leaves Are Fading* and *Tiller in the Fields*). Tudor remembered hearing Martinu's Symphony no. 6, subtitled "Fantaisies symphoniques," and likened "one passage to gunshots, another to a plague of locusts." It served as a catalyst, for at some level he knew that he was expected to deliver a ballet. There were no further excuses for shrinking back from the obligation.

For now he was satisfied to focus on a vignette that had been told to him by a dancer in Athens, one with a particularly harrowing image of helplessness and brutalization. It involved a victim and a sadist, a starving child reaching for a piece of bread and a Nazi soldier grinding the child's hand into the ground with the heel of his boot. The theme fully engaged Tudor. And it hardly required an actual war to be of interest. But in the course of his musical research he discovered the story of Lidice, the Czechoslovakian town that the Nazis destroyed in 1942 as punishment for the murder of a leading Occupation official. Martinu dedicated a short work to the martyred townspeople. But Tudor favored the symphony, so he simply combined the heroic tale with his preferred Martinu score. The result was a ballet of high craftsmanship and powerful narrative, one that he completed in two months.

He needed to caution against seeing it as time/place specific, for then his universal themes would be obscured. In revealing statements he told *The New York Times* critic Jack Anderson that his attempt in *Echoing of Trumpets* was to show "how people always seem to want to dominate each other. Everyone knows that's a stupid thing to do. Yet they keep on doing it. They never stop torturing each other with a kind of mild viciousness."

As if this remark did not quite tell enough the conversation went on.

Anderson: "Is there a *mild* viciousness?"

Tudor: "Oh, yes. It exists. I've known some specialists in it . . . even in ballet studios." (And here the reporter noted "a wicked glint" in his subject's eyes). Finally, an admission from Tudor: he was well aware that he brutalized dancers. Turning to the ballet under discussion he continued, but clearly he was speaking as much about his own motives as applied to human nature as about the war mentality: "Take the soldiers," he said. "They don't really rape the women in the village. They just torment them until they make the women feel degraded and, in so doing, they degrade themselves. It's this mutual degradation which, I think, prevails when people are under the conqueror's heel."

To what extent Tudor could consciously apply this weighty truism to himself is unknown. But the way he stated its psychodynamics shows the most astute perception. At last he was able to answer a question that countless disciples, adoring fans and friends had asked him: what makes Tudor so mean?

But for *Echoing of Trumpets,* he once again divulged nothing to his cast. He knew the events would be clear enough through the dance gesture. And when a particular image struck him as helpful he would share it. In a newspaper he had seen a photo of a woman who refused to give over the body of her dead child. If Gerd Andersson, who danced the role of the bereaved fiancée, wanted to draw on it for the death pas de deux with her betrothed the image was there for the taking. But Tudor didn't help her understand why, in this climactic duet, the enraged woman kicks his limp body. No verbal explanation would illuminate the reaction. Only instinct would bring her to the knowledge that a loved one's dying can translate as abandonment and thus incite the anger. In a typically flippant answer to why he preferred to say little, Tudor mentioned that he didn't "like to communicate anything to a dancer through the mind, especially considering what some dancers' minds are like!" What made him so formidable was this very gift for talking out of both sides of his mouth. No matter how stinging one of his clever remarks could be some dancers rightly knew, as Michael Smuin did, that "Tudor was always laughing up his sleeve at us." In other words, not really intending to be vicious, but not able to keep from taking advantage of his thin-skinned victims or, for that matter, of his own ready wit. Those who were superior enough to feel immune to the barbs relished the mischief.

In most of Tudor's ballets, this one included, he put the emphasis on the process rather than the result. And that explains his use of the participle, "echoing"; it denotes a live, ongoing situation rather than something inert, final and past; in that sense the title of the ballet falls into line with the fundamentals of Zen Buddhism. He used another participial title in 1975, when he created *The Leaves Are Fading.* But at that time he made a point of using the word fading, rather than the more common falling. The latter, he said, suggested a dead state. Leaves are still attached and still alive while they fade, not so by the time they fall. Nor did he trust to naming feelings for the dancers because he did not want a glib response to a true emotion for which he had gone to the considerable trouble of devising a choreographic symbol. And yet it was not unusual for him to change steps, custom-tailoring to the cast, as he went from company to company teaching his ballets. "When he could not remember certain parts of a ballet," said Juilliard teacher Muriel Topaz, "it was because he had given so many different versions to different dancers—not because his memory was uncommonly poor."

Apparently the Swedes were ecstatic with *Echoing of Trumpets,* even though Tudor left some details unfinished before rushing back to New York. But over the years and after many return trips to Stockholm he would polish the ballet and even supervise the filming of it. Upon its premiere on September 28, 1963, local critic Anna Greta Stahle wrote: "It has been 20 years since Lidice and nearly 20 years since *Undertow.* But with *Trumpets,* Tudor seems to have rediscovered the great wellspring of his master-works—compassion. May it be, indeed, the beginning of a new, great creativity."

Three years later the ballet had its American premiere under the auspices of the Metropolitan Opera Ballet. In the past it was Ballet Theatre that occupied the great, glamorous house and presented the works of Antony Tudor—as a major attraction. Now, in these fallow times, the choreographer without a home opted for *Ballet Night* as the relatively lowly platform for his first full-scale effort at the chandeliered emporium in sixteen years. Here were the only professional New York dancers he felt suf-ficiently familiar with any longer. It would not be a grand event, for *Ballet Night* was the single evening per season devoted to the little poor-cousin company. But, ironically, it was his mystified New York audience that felt the absence over all these years most acutely. And Clive Barnes's review in *The New York Times* re-flected the event's importance. Describing Tudor's appearance—before the same gold curtain where wild eruptions for the 1942 *Pillar of Fire* had broken out—the critic wrote:

"He stood there with diffident pride, while the audience cheered. It was not one of those lightweight, bleating ovations either, but the full-throated cheers of an audience profoundly moved and wishing to express its feeling in some corporate ritual. . . . After years in a wilderness of half-hits, near-misses and flops, here was Tudor, one of the great choreographers of the century, back delivering the goods." Barnes went on to delineate between the realism of *Trumpets* as an antiwar ballet and "the purposely detached world of perfume advertisements" of *Jardin* as well as "the desire-under-the-elms town setting" of *Pillar.*

But he defined Tudor's realism as "a picture of contemporary violence with no romantic shadowing, a picture that rings completely true. . . . It is a bleak, clear-eyed work. The soldiers, their buddy-boy togetherness reflected in their roistering chaindances through the inert village, and the raped, humiliated yet defiant women are real peasants, not artistic symbols for peasants. And the work has a detail of focus most unusual for ballet. There is no mime whatsoever in the work and hardly any acting in any conventionally histrionic sense.

"Interestingly, to reach this grimly factual idiom, Tudor has mingled classical ballet (for these new-style Trojan women dance on full pointe) and bluntly stylized folk-dance for the soldiers. Yet the spectator is not aware of any stylistic discrepancy, for even while we watch the starkly impressive choreographic outlines we glimpse through these to the character of violence, just as, say, we glimpse through Shakespeare's poetry to the character of Hamlet." Barnes ended by suggesting that *Trumpets* could be "a fresh beginning." This was a leitmotif generally found in commentary on Tudor; everyone seemed to wish he would make a comeback and eagerly took each sign of that possibility as a cue to writing open love letters. Indeed, he didn't lack for cheerleaders.

Fortified by his success, Tudor was open to suggestions. Now Oliver Smith, who recognized a potentially formidable Hagar in Sallie Wilson, persuaded the stolid conscience of the company to revive *Pillar of Fire* for her.

What lay ahead of Wilson, as a result, was both a major coup and unimaginable trauma. But Tudor faced a different reality: the more important the work the greater the stakes over its reception and the more severe the trial. No one had ever danced Hagar but Nora Kaye, so it had lapsed from the repertory during the five years since she'd retired. Keenly aware of this, Smith wanted to see it reinstated. The king's gold should be on view. What's more, Wilson had developed into a remarkable dramatic ballerina. She was thought by many to be the rightful heir to

Kaye, having assumed many of her roles, but not this one, not Hagar.

It took just a little pressure for Tudor to agree. Although Wilson sensed his reluctance and felt that without Smith as ombudsman she would not have inspired the choreographer's confidence, the time was right. Tudor certainly did not want an important ballet like *Pillar* to languish in the corner of audience memory. The risks, however, were great. A poor performance and he could see the squandering of his hard-won reputation.

And yet Wilson was well prepared. After fifteen years of worship she knew that there would be good days and bad days. On the good days he would gleefully say things like: "Nora will be furious." No one, not even a favorite like Kaye, escaped his "mild viciousness." But by the time they approached the last rehearsals, she saw a complete breakdown in communication. Tudor took the offensive, scorning everything, and she imagined herself to be the object of his contempt. "When he walked around snorting, surely it was me," she thought. "But no, the lights were the problem. And then he told his friends to skip the first performance because 'It would not be good.'" Nothing compared, though, to the final dress rehearsal when, in front of the whole cast and orchestra, he flew to her side and whispered with quiet rage in his voice: "You're a dancer who has no sense of dynamics." With that, he grabbed his hat and coat and ran out the door. All activity came to a shuddering halt. "I stood rooted to the spot," Wilson recalled, "deeply humiliated, unable to speak or move." "Everyone knew he had just torn me to shreds, even without hearing the actual words. And then they left, silently, trying to slip away unnoticed so that I would not be further mortified. I stayed.

"Mostly I sat on the empty stage and meditated . . . having the whole weekend to try to digest what happened, put myself back together again and figure out where to go next. Then came the performance, my debut, the revival of *Pillar* after a five-year absence. Nora was out front. Everybody had come. I went through it without remembering a thing. But suddenly it was over and I went walking in the basement. At least for a half hour. When I got to my dressing room there was Tudor—and Hugh—waiting. The door had been locked and I opened it, we all went in. No one said a thing. They both sat down and Tudor picked up a newspaper, which he started to read. I was flustered and didn't want to ask him what he thought. So I tried a silly question. 'Was my braid the right color?' 'I have no complaints,' he answered. "It was two years and many *Pillars* later that he came running backstage after a performance and kissed me. 'That was your first *Pillar*,' he said. 'How strange he should pick this one,' I thought. I had been very distracted throughout. But that didn't stop me from spending the next twenty years trying to figure out what he saw."

Curiously, Nora Kaye had no part in coaching Wilson in the role of Hagar. It had been so incontrovertibly her trademark that anything a successor might copy would have been regarded as theft. Nevertheless, Tudor couldn't resist making his invidious comparisons of Kaye and Wilson. "Nora always did eight pirouettes here," he would tell Sallie, who could manage only three each time she came to the section. But then the new Hagar happened to see a film of *Pillar* and observed Nora doing only one and a half pirouettes. The more desperately Wilson needed Tudor's approval, the more scarce she found it. He even jokingly tried to pawn her off on Hugh, after the marriage to Diana Adams ended. Gradually, however, she became an asset to him—dancing many roles in his ballets as well as serving as his treasured emissary.

But in 1966 the company's preeminent choreographer was on tenterhooks; any candidate for a major role in his ballets had the power, via her reviewed performances, to crown or dethrone him. And there weren't many contenders at that—after 1950 no "Tudor group" existed. With Ballet Theatre still failing to regain the glory of its halcyon beginning two decades ago and the Tudor works not receiving the ecstatic notices of yore, everything became a trial all over again; Sallie Wilson proved no exception to the rule. Tudor's reputation was on the line with her ascent to

Hagar. If he were to plot an ideal time for a major commission it would not be now, not when he was hard put just to sustain the high rank of his ballets. On the other hand, his disillusionment with all that occupied him in America was such that an invitation to the Royal Ballet, soon to arrive, could hardly have caused greater excitement—or terror.

3

Royal Redemption

THAT TUDOR WAS UNIVERSALLY RECOGNIZED as one of the few great ballet innovators of the century seemed to serve only as cause for his further intimidation, for he shrank from most opportunities that came his way; a fear of failure found him subject to an ever-narrowing tolerance for risk. Of the many ballet companies that extended invitations to him only the rare one was deemed worthy of consideration and those he thought about he seldom accepted. Instead there would be feigned disinterest, or flimsy excuses belied by the facts, or such quasi-sardonic misstatements as: "There are plenty of younger choreographers more talented than I, so please ask them. Besides, I haven't anything more to say." The truth is there was only one Tudor and each company begging his presence knew this. Therefore it was prepared to go on bended knee promising the extensive rehearsals and acquaintance periods he needed. That didn't change his mind.

Nothing seemed to. Not since he had become a solo act. Not since he'd lost Hugh Laing and his nerve.

According to Leo Kersley, the longtime Tudor observer: "He was a very cagey bird to get. You could write letters, send telegrams and ring him up and get only evasions, very tricky. But I figured out a game plan for [artistic director] Beryl Grey, who wanted him to come to the London Festival Ballet and put on *Trumpets*. Simple, I told her. Send a wire saying 'I am so delighted you can come. I've booked seats on such and such a flight and have announced the first night for such and such a date and so will meet you at Heathrow.' I was right. She did it. He came."

Taking the decision out of his hands was what worked, of course. But a whole different climate prevailed when the Royal Ballet delivered its momentous invitation in June of 1966. Tudor's customary reluctance, his wariness and excuse-making, did not surface this time. Instead it was clear that the crown had finally acknowledged him, that the prodigal son had just been awarded the most prestigious prize of his career—and the severest challenge. This was the invitation, albeit belated, that he vaguely imagined over many years of mailbox-checking. This was the bid from the company that mattered, the one that appealed to his pride—forgetting Zen Buddhism, and its egoless states.

The Royal, no longer the struggling Sadler's Wells that ran about a length ahead of Ballet Rambert in the London dancing sweepstakes, now literally reigned supreme. It was England's national company, complete with the crown's charter. Mim and her troupe had been left in the dust. But the times had changed, too. Before the war, local audiences were comprised of the intelligentsia; ideas and innovation had been the essence. Afterwards the hunger was for escape entertainment, for the spectacle of the classics and a genre known as "legs-up ballets." Whatever Antony Tudor's value, it was no longer in vogue. Mass taste, with its box office power, determined the aesthetic.

Nevertheless, his moment came precisely when resident choreographer Kenneth MacMillan took an offer from the Deutsche Oper Ballet in West Berlin to be its chief dance-maker. That was

1965. At the same time an even more telling event occurred: the Royal Swedish Ballet traveled to Paris with its proud calling card, *Echoing of Trumpets*. Until then London's critics had neither seen nor passed judgment on it.

Incontestable proof came with those notices. Sir Frederick Ashton, knighted in 1962 and now the Royal Ballet's director, needed no second thoughts on the subject of his friend Antony's creative vitality. Of course he must come. With the last doubt cleared from the path it was time to return.

Over the postwar years he had stayed in touch with London ballet society. On family visits he not only called on Rambert whose troupe performed the Tudor works but he stopped by to chat with friends, many of whom had gone over to the Royal and Ashton, his erstwhile competitor. And in the early fifties when the company toured New York he and Hugh would have Fred and Ninette and leading dancers Margot Fonteyn and Michael Somes over for dinner. "We had great times together," recalled P. W. Manchester. "Everyone got along so well. There was such warmth and friendliness." But nothing ever came of the bonhomie or the open lines of communication. Until now. The same de Valois (newly titled Dame Ninette) who had turned Antony Tudor down in 1935 for lack of "professional" qualities, and who referred to him all these years as "that Englishman abroad," saw herself succeeded in 1963 by Ashton. The new director would redeem his old colleague whose ballets raised "the depth charge" against his own oeuvre. He did not want to bear the same burden of guilt as de Valois. Let the record be clear: his tenure would be free of this blemish.

After all these years as persona non grata the émigré choreographer was being summoned to the England of his birth, his youth, his dreams. Retribution at last—possibly. Or defeat. Did he dare? Could this Prufrockian outsider risk breaking his neck before *tout* London? Did the equipment still work?

Whatever, there would be no resolution through cajoling, through tomfoolery, through evasions. With the enormous hierarchy of the Royal Ballet everything had to come down through official channels. The company functioned "like the Bank of England," said Kersley. "There is one person who tells the secretary to write the invitation, and another who posts the letters and another who opens them." Tudor knew there was little margin for vacillating. Yes or no. Those were the choices he had. The answer—the only one he could live with—was yes. But he advertised everywhere his tremulous heart. By the time he left New York for London in early fall of 1966, he had already sent out fliers, as it were, personal admissions that this decision might be his undoing. "What have I let myself in for?" he asked Betty Sawyer while having coffee with her one day in the Juilliard cafeteria—his lips twisting in a wry smile, his fingers twiddling nervously.

"He talked about it obsessively," according to Sawyer. "I never saw him go through such anguish. There were other times when he questioned his ability, but never to this degree. I remember a big, messy manuscript that he slapped down on the table once. It was *Offenbach in the Underworld,* written in faded pencil. 'This is what my mind looks like,' he said, disgusted. But the Royal Ballet summons was different. It was a thing that brought out awful fear." Even worse, he had no means of escaping it. At this relatively late stage of his career Ashton dangled England's seal of approval. It could be the ultimate reward, in many ways, not least the redemption of his earlier lockout from Establishment ballet. Therefore he could not reject it. He would have to face the terror, no matter that it came, unwittingly, from himself.

For the time being he dealt as best he could with the panic by means of a kind of broadcast therapy. In letters he wrote to Rambert—which unfailingly acknowledged only his fondness for and gratitude to her—and to Maude Lloyd, he invented witty jokes describing his dread. "Just nauseated with nerves," he wrote. "I sent a note to Mr. Tooley [general director at Covent Garden] telling him to get one of those pretty little boxes ready . . . the ones they have in the Egyptian rooms at the British Museum. It would be so nice to be with you all, but I'm going to have to have my nervous breakdown in seclusion." At first he turned down Maude's invitation to stay with her and Nigel at their home in Victoria Road, West Kensington. Shortly afterward he relented. There was comforting humor among close friends. Better to laugh out loud at his misery, than sit on the bed of his "pretty little box," bent over in pain. It was a generally happy reunion he had with the Goslings, but they were quite aware of their friend's Sisyphean labor. He would leave in the morning and return at the end of a workday. One evening after rehearsal he began to giggle while confessing to them that "in five hours I only wrote one step!" Yes, he giggled because self-mockery eased the wretchedness. It was the best he could do.

Meanwhile there was the ballet to worry about. Tudor knew the company both from his occasional sojourns to London and from its tours to New York. But not intimately, of course. Not the way he had to know dancers in order to work with them. His approach was to watch company class, to sit silently on a bench and pick out his best prospects. Everyone was alert to his presence. Everyone knew its purpose. Everyone took an appropriately wary position, given Tudor's reputation which, inevitably, preceded him. By the time he'd made his choices the ballet was, for all intents and purposes, still a mystery. Again, the man who practiced the art of enigma stayed true to his calling. He did not tell his cast what the ballet was about or what it would ideally convey. "How dotty," said Dame Ninette, "to keep the story a mystery to his dancers. I never could understand what Antony gained by doing this."

But he did arrive with a few sketches already drawn up. He'd been ruminating for some time on *Les Bandar-Log,* a short piece by the twentieth-century composer Charles Koechlin. His music, which abounded in harmonic subtleties and all sorts of delicate tonal ambiguities, appealed strongly to Tudor. Because the score was too short, however, for what turned out to be a twenty-five-minute ballet, he borrowed fragments from *La Course de Printemps,* a symphonic poem also by Koechlin. Tudor's selections were made with extraordinary sensitivity, according to John

Lanchbery, who arranged them. The music took as its inspiration Kipling's *The Jungle Book* and Tudor had used his classes at Juilliard to develop dances depicting its characters—primarily the monkeys. He wasn't interested much in Kipling from a literal point of view, but the situation had inherent possibilities for him. What he had in mind was an allegory, using the jungle as a symbol for civilization and identifying the protagonist as an innocent enduring his rite of passage, his journey to wisdom. Even then, however, he kept the ideas to himself. As a result the observers couldn't make head or tail, so to speak, of what they saw. "We didn't know whether these monkeys were supposed to be funny or not," said P. W. Manchester, recalling Tudor's *Dance Studies: Less Orthodox,* the piece she saw at Juilliard in 1962 and one that served as a sketch for this ballet. "If not, we were embarrassed for him."

Four years later, in London, he was casting the new work— in his wonted style: with sensitive nobodies. Tudor preferred people who were unformed and as yet undiscovered. He liked their malleability, but more than that the fact that they had still not become enchanted with their best features or begun to capitalize on them. Awareness of one's celebrity status was dangerous. It became an obstacle to his artistic goals. He needed complete surrender and dedication on the dancers' parts, not a predetermined idea of what persona must be preserved. So when he found Anthony Dowell for the central role, plucking him from the corps, it was with a joyous stroke of luck. For here was a dancer who epitomized the naif, an unworldly creature oblivious to the forces that swirled about his head and sought to dominate him. Here was a person not unlike Kipling's boy-hero, Mowgli. In this, his only ballet besides *Undertow* to feature a male lead, Tudor settled on Dowell, a young man with a strikingly polished technique but practically no sense of himself as a stage personality. He was unduly quiet and reserved. In a word, he was the exact opposite of Hugh Laing.

The Transgressor, too, had been an innocent. But he encountered the world through a haze of sickness and distortion. The Boy with Matted Hair, his healthy counterpart, harbored no such delusions. Consequently, the ballet Tudor would call *Shadowplay* had a humane point of reference. There would be no demons to exorcize, no Medusa-monster mothers to throttle, none of society's confusing hypocrites to placate. To be sure, the young hero would discover the jungle's temptations and menaces but because he did not suffer The Transgressor's emotional disturbance he had the wherewithal to pass unharmed through its thickets of peril and intrigue. He would endure trials of character and integrity and inner strength, trials that would come in the form of domination attempts.

First his peace is disrupted by The Arboreals (monkeys) who scramble and swing along creepers and branches. Then he confronts a genus called Aerials, partly birds of bright plumage and partly Cambodian temple dancers. But his ultimate test involves The Terrestrial, a powerful deitylike figure whose object is to possess the boy, and The Celestial, a seductive goddess with only a small resemblance to other predatory females.

The leap from the dramatis personae in Tudor's life to characters transformed by the Zen Buddhist universe is obvious. A prime example is The Terrestrial, who represents the auteur and illustrates his power over the inexperienced boy-hero. The important point of *Shadowplay,* the name itself a reference to the popular entertainments given in Far Eastern countries, is its remarkably simplified and lucid system of understanding the human jungle. Looked at aesthetically, the ballet differs from other Tudor works in its poetically surreal ambience. He abandons "real" people and now deals with symbolic figures. Curiously, this step away from close personal contact is the step that Zen provided him. In a sense, *Shadowplay* can be regarded as his staged koan. Just as the words for this riddlelike poetry are ambiguous, so are the images he created intentionally enigmatic. The result of Tudor's play with shadows—like those of an Oriental puppeteer who uses a screen and lights to suggest characters—was an ingenious ploy. He particularly prized the letter a woman wrote saying: "I didn't understand the ballet but couldn't get it out of my mind."

For Dowell, the experience was similar to that of the letter-writer who didn't understand but was captivated regardless. He became a tool of Tudor's. Still, no matter how elated he was at being chosen, the extremely reticent dancer also knew that guarding himself would be more essential than ever. "Because Tudor kept us in the dark, we never knew what we might stumble over," he said. "I think he saw me as raw material and therefore liked me, but it was a very uneasy situation." The making of *Shadowplay,* then, was like a ballet within a ballet. The very act Tudor took, that of possessing Dowell, had its basis in the story line. As for the other leads, Merle Park as The Celestial and Derek Rencher as The Terrestrial, their personalities neutralized somewhat the tensions between the choreographer and his chosen protagonist. While the Celestial conjured up the old and new Tudor goddesses—Pavlova, Spessivtseva and now Shiva—her importance was relatively muted. She exerted a potentially de-structive power over The Boy but not as the Medusa had, for Tudor had taken a certain distance from the woman as nemesis. Before, she was either the personification of his own vulnerability (Caroline, Hagar) or the ultimate antagonist, a virago for all seasons—possibly even a symbol of Hugh. Here, however, The Boy's primary connection was to The Terrestrial.

This seems to have had some bearing on Tudor's break-through: finally, a male pas de deux. After all these years of hiding behind a woman's skirts, as it were, he put aside disguises of what he considered the verboten relationship—that between two men, that between The Boy and The Terrestrial. What he did here, although it had no erotic overtones, was far more open and direct; he left the solace of self-obfuscation—as in Robbins's *Facsimile*—to others. The idea for his new-age pas de deux came as a sudden inspiration:

"Most of the ballet was shaping up," he said, "all but one segment. "I had called a rehearsal with Dowell and Merle Park.

Leaving the subway for the studio, I said to myself: 'Tudor, you're out of your mind. It's not a pas de deux for Tony and Merle. You need Derek. This must be a scene for the two boys.' I sent Merle home, began working on the trouble spot with Dowell and Rencher, and everything fell into place. But this didn't emerge from conditioned thinking. It was like a thought out of the blue. I'd been up a blind alley."

In other words, he'd simply taken too much for granted prior to this epiphany. The ballet's central focus reflected the influence of the man-deity on the boy-hero. Tudor's blindness had been to that fact, because of his misplaced loyalty to the male-female ideal. Without any glimmer of consciousness over this sudden "attainment of wisdom," he ended up amending an aesthetic conceit by being truthful to his instincts.

This is where he tried to direct Dowell, too. Later there would be a production of *Jardin aux Lilas* for the Royal Ballet and the elegant British dancer, still somewhat immature and not yet a starry eminence, would inherit Hugh's role, The Lover. He would remember how meticulous Tudor was "in getting every finger position just so." He would remember being asked to demonstrate a step for a senior person—how doing this went against his grain of discretion, how he felt as ashamed in carrying out the command as did the humiliated dancer who needed the demonstration. He would remember the perverse pleasure Tudor took in instigating such intrigues and manipulating these situations of oneupsmanship. But he also learned things that no one else could have taught him, "how to think and be imaginative . . . or how to find an awareness of the lighting onstage, how to put myself in the light and feel it sculpting and shading me." Later he would visit Tudor in New York, where at the Zen abode, there would be a cooked dinner and Dowell would find his master to be "weird and wonderful and wicked." Over the years he would also receive the occasional postcard. But the one thing that remained was the dancer's guardedness around his dangerous mentor. "Something told me to be wary. Even after I got over being tongue-tied with him."

Meanwhile, Merle Park helped to ease the atmosphere during *Shadowplay* rehearsals. By being able to quip back and forth with Tudor, she took some of the heat off Dowell. Still, Tudor's penchant for vagueness hardly helped the young initiate to relax. "What did I do here?" the fey choreographer would ask, the day after showing a sequence of steps for the first time. And then Park or Rencher or Dowell would have to repeat what they had seen him demonstrate only once. If their memories failed slightly, he would reply: "Oh, is that what I did?" not "That's wrong, here it is." He kept them constantly guessing. He tried to put his dangling dancers through the same blind terrors that he experienced. In passing off the anguish to them, he likely found relief.

But Dowell's intense shyness would require Tudor to go the extra step. He loved working with a dancer of such classical purity and musicality—especially one unsullied by a celebrity ego. He knew, however, that he must break down the master/disciple barrier to get what he wanted. The following scenario, which Tudor acknowledged as a departure from his usual rule with dancers, took place during the first rehearsals:

TUDOR: Where do you think we should start? Do you prefer to enter stage left or stage right?

DOWELL: It doesn't matter to me.

TUDOR: Oh, you must have a preference.

DOWELL: Oh no, it doesn't really matter.

TUDOR: Oh. Do you prefer to enter middlestage, or upstage, or downstage?

DOWELL: It doesn't really matter.

TUDOR: Perhaps you prefer to start onstage?

DOWELL: It really doesn't matter to me.

TUDOR: Well, let's suppose we start onstage. Would you prefer to start in the middle, or over in one of the corners?

"By then," said Tudor, "he knew I was a nut and he was nervous." The diabolical choreographer simply couldn't resist. Although his conscious goal was to set Dowell sufficiently at ease to work well, he found himself so delectably drawn to the game of intimidation, one evoking the subtlest, Nabokovian kind of mockery, that he achieved just the opposite by surrendering to it. As it was, Dowell had all he could do to make sense of the choreography. "I knew Tudor had clear ideas about the ballet, its shape and the pattern of its steps. But for me they were something intangible, something he had just grabbed from the air." The path, as Tudor steered him on it, was full of flora he had never experienced before and that was just what the dancer needed for inspiration: a sense of true astonishment at what he beheld.

In the moment when The Boy with Matted Hair discovers the Bodhi tree Tudor came up with a fanciful means of enlightenment. But this only after a few rough starts. Dowell remembered being prodded with many questions which he could not answer, questions that left him drawing a blank. He'd never been *asked* to think about a ballet before. Dancers are told to do, not to think. And now this madman wanted him to describe the *kind* of tree he was gazing at. The madman remembered the rehearsal well. He had given the boy clues: "Tell me by your body. I want to know if it's a little tree or a big tree or a spreading shady tree. We haven't got it. We'll deal with it tomorrow."

The next morning, Tudor remembered, "I was on the way to rehearsal and at Earl's Court there was a fruiterer and by some absolute miracle I saw a beautiful mango in the window. The first I had ever seen in London. And I went and bought it. I took it to the studio and concealed it, and then I said, 'Now let's get down to this tree. And Dowell looked up and said, 'It's not there.' I told him to put his hands behind his back. I put the mango in them and said, 'That's the kind of tree.' Then he looked at the fruit and asked what it was. He'd never seen a mango before. And his eyes opened with wonderment, and he looked up at the tree, and it was perfect."

And it was Zen.

Another instance of revelation for Dowell came with Tudor's metaphysical hint of how to feel while sitting under the tree: "The sun is coming out of you—it's radiating from your back."

What the master drew from his charge so astutely—or perhaps intuitively—was that magical evanescence. The less in control and the more ingenuous his performance, the better Tudor liked it. A witness to similar testimony was Sallie Wilson, who, when distracted, could please her mentor greatly. Of Nora Kaye, too, he found less to be more. "She would come offstage sometimes and say, 'I was good tonight.' Actually, she was terrible—she'd just been enjoying herself onstage." He liked Dowell's egoless state and especially that it could exist in one so high-skilled technically. Often the dancer who has attained a staggering virtuosity consciously knows and admires it; The Boy with Matted Hair didn't. As Tudor said: "I can't stand dancers who love to dance. Ninety-nine out of a hundred think the theater was created for them. That's wicked, really wicked. Only one in a hundred realizes it is for the audience." Spoken like a true bodhi sattva, that being who sacrifices his own nirvana for another's enlightenment.

It was toward the end of the rehearsal period that he asked Ashton—his peer and benefactor—if he would like to stop in to see for himself how things were progressing. "Oh, no," said Sir Frederick. "I don't like to interfere." But Tudor was eager to sense the goodwill of Ashton's sponsorship. He disliked feeling like an interloper or an isolate. He actually needed to belong, imperfect as such incorporation might be at the Royal.

As Dame Ninette explained, in terms that mark Tudor as a distinct outsider: "We had all of our own to worry about—besides [Kenneth] MacMillan, John Cranko and others who were clamoring to do ballets. It was still hard for us to include Tudor."

The ballet, given its premiere on January 25, 1967, was received with ecstatic notices. "A work to be savoured at first sight," wrote dance critic Mary Clarke. "Tudor shows us all in passages of extraordinarily beautiful, easy dancing. . . . The ballet recognizes ugliness, in men as well as in animals, but it is, itself, a thing of beauty." Four months later the Royal Ballet would tour New York with Shadowplay and Clive Barnes would write that it "has as many meanings as an onion has layers, but basically it seems to be about the realms of experience and the attainment of grace. . . . Tudor has produced a strange and engrossing work that, even at first glance, has the look and feel of a major work."

Despite the milestone that *Shadowplay* represented, Tudor saw—on opening night—an unmistakable sign of his benefactors' ambivalence. As he left Nigel and Maude for Covent Garden, they wished him luck. "Where are they taking you to supper afterward?" she asked, referring to Ashton and other high-placed associates. "Nowhere," he said, explaining that no fête had been planned, that no one from the company was honoring the occasion of his first ballet for the Royal. "We were shocked," Maude recalled. "To think that there would be no postpremiere celebration for Antony, who was certainly a special guest, was beyond words. We were aghast at the lapse in courtesy, that Fred and the powers that be would overlook their obligation as host. So we quickly set about having our own party for him."

At six o'clock she rushed out to buy cold chicken. This, after calling those she could count on at the last minute: Rudolf Nureyev and Margot Fonteyn, who were dancing that night in another work on the bill; the French choreographer Roland Petit, who happened to be doing a commissioned work for the Royal that same season; and the Blisses, Sally and Tony—they had flown from New York to be with Tudor on his big night. Not a bad guest list for such an impromptu celebration and the honoree was ecstatic at this show of devotion. Rudi and Margot were stars, of course—a category of dancer Tudor really didn't work with. He, the dashing Tartar whose defection from Leningrad to London had made international ballet history, and she, the Royal's darling, its prima ballerina, comprised the most glamorous partnership of the day—anywhere. As it turned out, they were close to Maude, who put them close to Tudor. Not only was he supremely happy with his little supper party—he always preferred intimate gatherings—but Rudi sat and talked with him most of the night trying to coax agreement for a ballet from the reluctant, ever-evasive choreographer.

There would be many evenings hence that the Goslings and their Antony would spend together with "adopted son" Rudi.

Often in New York. And on those occasions Hugh would inevitably be included. He wasn't jealous, according to Maude—because the onetime dancer, now completely out of the limelight and stripped of the allure he once possessed, had nothing to contest. "Rudi doesn't think about me at all," Hugh cried petulantly. "I don't count." But he did everything he could to get the charismatic star's attention. Whenever they were all together Nureyev remembered Laing "delivering his exalted opinions right away and with grand passion."

Meanwhile Tudor had a genuine admiration for Nureyev. Not just his daring, his star power and magnetism, "but the truthfulness of his dancing." Over the years the Russian would continue asking for his own ballet by Tudor. "Well, when's it going to be?" was the perpetual question. But nothing, from all the affectionate badinage, ever came of the request. Just jaunty evasions. Tudor certainly didn't project himself as the forbidding maestro to the likes of a Nureyev. This man, after all, was a hero in his own right, a fearless adventurer, the first in a line of Soviet defectors to the West. But even he succumbed to Tudor's "aura of great intellect and delightfully acid remarks." Like most other dancers, Nureyev felt himself "being totally perceived [by Tudor] in a single, stunning glance." Toward the end of rehearsals for *Knight Errant,* the next ballet Tudor would do for the Royal, David Wall, the lead dancer, became injured. "Antony wanted me to step into the part," said Nureyev. But that didn't happen, either, owing to the company's reluctance to award the Russian new roles. After all, its recumbent male principals were already smarting over Nureyev's presence and his usurping the spotlight. The administrators did not want to add further insults—so Tudor's request was denied.

Some fifteen years later, when Nureyev took over as director of the Paris Opera Ballet and instituted an all-Tudor bill, he wanted the choreographer to come and supervise. But one excuse after another was offered: "There's a problem with the dog" or "Hugh is sick now and wouldn't be able to make the trip." Clearly, these were just polite refusals; on the rare occasions

Tudor chose to accept, neither Hugh nor the dog accompanied him—not anymore. But he did finally approve a program, selecting, after careful consideration, several works for Nureyev to present.

Throughout Nureyev's future acts of derring-do, Tudor made a point of being in attendance for those that occurred in New York. One of the Russian's first attempts at original choreography was a ballet based on Henry James's *Washington Square*. It turned out to be one that Oliver Smith dearly wanted Tudor to do for Cynthia Gregory and Nureyev. But the timing, in the late seventies, was not ideal and, as Tudor would tell Smith, he'd been over that terrain in *Pillar of Fire*. So the impresario brought his idea to Nureyev, who at first would not touch it because the script was so perfectly Tudorian. He reconsidered, though, and produced an elaborate ballet version of the story for his Paris Opera Ballet.

Of course, Tudor attended the New York premiere. But backstage at the Met he told Nureyev that he was reserving judgment for the time being. "In three days I'll call you to say whether it is a rave or a disaster." True to his word, the judge from the high court rang on the appointed day. "It's a rave," he said. Of course, Nureyev could never be sure, with Tudor, where good humor and seriousness parted company. It didn't matter, though, because their fondness for each other was never in doubt. Twenty years later, when Tudor won his most prestigious award, the Kennedy Center Honor, he chose Nureyev to give the personalized ceremonial salute—but a schedule conflict ended in Margot Fonteyn's doing the duties.

32

The Subject Was Roses

AFTER THE SUCCESSFUL *Shadowplay* a return engagement to England was inevitable. Only the time and terms remained for negotiation; even before his first Royal Ballet commission was a fait accompli plans were already under way for a second work—to be produced in November 1968 by the company's touring wing, still called Sadler's Wells. Something of a Cinderella, it was the long-suffering troupe sent off to the industrial hinterlands. Tudor was well acquainted with the lifestyle, both in his native and adopted lands. Naturally, he had happy memories of those vagabond days, for they were days that had brought him a sense of family and belonging.

He felt relief now at having passed the Covent Garden initiation and as a reward, of sorts, he could look forward to trudging along on the tour itinerary. It did offer certain compensations—not least among them David Wall, who was Dowell's counterpart then at Sadler's Wells. He had already developed as an artist, however, and in due time would join the Royal proper. He, too, would end up in England's balletic hall of fame, retiring to a high administrative office.

"The first time Tudor came into my life," Wall remembered, "was by way of a rose. It was 1965 and I had just arrived in New York to dance *Sleeping Beauty* with the Royal Ballet. I was staying with a close friend and unpacking my things when I noticed, above the bed, a single, lovely rose in a vase. Chris saw me admiring it and said:

'Oh, I forgot to tell you. I saw Antony Tudor today and mentioned that you would be arriving in a few hours. At that moment when you came up in the discussion we were walking past a florist's. Tudor insisted on stopping in to buy a rose for you. "Put it near his bed," he said, handing it to me.' " A wreath for Spessivtseva and a rose for Wall. Floral tributes were a specialty of the house. Gestures instead of words—how like this man to opt for symbols and run from declarations or offer only the most cryptic, contradictory utterances when a direct and personal comment might be in order.

It is possible that Tudor noticed the strikingly dramatic dancer before and/or during the New York engagement—and liked what he saw. But at their first encounter, a year later in London, Wall said he was "too intimidated" by the famous choreographer to even strike up a passing conversation. "I was taking class at the Baron's Court studio and had slipped into the seniors' dressing room. There he was, changing, to get ready for his *Shadowplay* rehearsal. I said 'hello' but completely lost my nerve at the sight of him—he was so austere—so I shot out as quickly as possible." Not long afterward he would see *Shadowplay* and be struck with the same wonderment his contemporary Anthony Dowell experienced. It was the only Tudor work Wall knew; it "dazzled and confused" him. More than that, he "saw Dowell in a way he never was, before or since."

Two years later, in 1968, the little company's prize dancer and the intimidating choreographer were formally introduced. The place was Coventry, one of the itinerary stops, and director John

Field, who couldn't have been happier winning Tudor's consent to join the tour, officiated at the meeting. Then he discreetly left the two and they sat over tea for several hours. "Nothing explicit was discussed," said Wall. "We talked in generalities. My feeling is he just wanted to know me." Tudor had come aboard to begin rehearsals for *Knight Errant,* his new ballet and Wall, star of the Sadler's Wells, would have the central role. The Knight whose errant ways Tudor would document was worldly and exuded nothing but confidence onstage. No matter that he might have been secretly cowed by the guest dancemaker; his profile fit the role perfectly.

Meanwhile the company was thrilled to have him, quite apart from the prestige. Having a master choreographer to create a ballet constituted a windfall anywhere, let alone on the stage of a subsidiary troupe. Shortly after arriving he looked over the dancers, chose his supporting cast for the work that had Wall as its raison d'être and began immediately. The subject: a choreographic translation of the eighteenth-century literary classic, *Les Liaisons Dangereuses.*

He was positively delighted with his prospects—the pressure of a serious work did not apply here, for *Liaisons* would belong to what Wall called Tudor's "wicked-giggle" genre. What's more, the touring company atmosphere put him at ease, not least because these ballet gypsies functioned like a family, not the Bank of England. Before the company left Coventry for Glasgow, Tudor checked out of the three-star Leo Frick Hotel and put himself "on a par with us," remembered Wall. "So he booked into the homely little bed-and-breakfast place my wife and I had reserved and did the same in each town. We ate together after performances and then stayed up all hours of the night talking."

A close relationship developed between them and Tudor actually liked certain aspects of the drudgery milieu, the constant touring/performing schedule that let him catch the dancers with their guard down. Luckily there were no one-night stands; the company could remain in a single city for at least two-week periods, thus it was the best of all possible tour situations. And because he had not done this sort of thing for so long it caused him no particular exhaustion. Over the three-month rehearsal period they danced eight performances a week, "trying to get through each bloody day," said Wall. "As a result, we were putty in his hands. Our distractedness made it easier for him to move in. We had no defenses, since the main goal was to keep the troupe from disbanding."

How like Tudor to choose the 1782 epistolary novel of Choderlos de Laclos and imagine it as a cunning variation on the Restoration comedy of manners. And how like him to tread where balletic others knew not or feared. Apparently he'd seen Roger Vadim's 1960 film starring Gerard Phillippe. No doubt he'd also found the perennially shocking tale lively night-table stock.

It has since been made into both a long-running play and two high-profile Hollywood movies, but then it was less known. His trailblazing didn't begin with de Laclos, however. When he stumbled onto Pachelbel's *Canon in D,* the Baroque ditty that has become part of our universal pop culture, it was the same; few knew it even existed before he set his Juilliard ballet, *Continuo,* to the captivating little fugue. And the idea of an ineffably sorrowful song cycle—*Kindertotenlieder*—as appropriate for choreography originated with him.

What marks Tudor, in fact, as a rarity in the often middlebrow, acrobatic genre of ballet is his attunement to the fine arts. No rinky-dink music by Minkus and Pugni for him—nor, for that matter, any of the circus bravura, strutting exhibitionism or smiling, *en face* revelries. His was and is a different realm altogether. The de Laclos scenario, for instance, with its focus on *les jeux d'amour* as a paradigm of perversity, could hardly be further from the ballet stage's hippety-hop rituals. Beyond its appeal as a work of cleverness and sophistication, though, the subject was immensely attractive to Tudor. An intrigue of the heart, a game plan for the manipulation of emotions—almost nothing could pique his bad-boy curiosity more. Such, in fact, is the connective tissue running through so many of his ballets—especially the black Brechtian comedies: *Gallant Assembly, Judgment of Paris, Ronde du Printemps, Les Mains Gauches*. He was described as a man who laughed up his sleeve at bumbling innocents, as one who looked at human behavior—his own included—with bemused curiosity. Likewise, the arena where sexual diversions and emotional armlocks played themselves out—through domination, deceit, degradation—captivated him. So it was entirely natural that, in his literary wanderings, he and de Laclos would meet. Indeed they had already done so in *Gallant Assembly* and *Judgment of Paris*.

Tudor reveled in the novelist's campaign strategies. Here he was plotting conquests with the precision of a chess game—using people as pawns and sex as a gambit. In the end, however, morality rears its implacable head and wins. In choosing the seventy-ninth letter as the episode's basis, Tudor got to focus on The Chevalier. Once again it is the man who wields control: The Chevalier seduces three women in a single evening—amid carefully crafted comings and goings—and then betrays them to their respective husbands. But in a typically no-one-is-safe ploy the eponymous Casanova gets his comeuppance when the female antagonist, in turn, betrays him. The contrast between *Shadowplay* and *Knight Errant* could hardly be more striking as regards the central character. Purity versus iniquity. Adam versus the Serpent. All of which places Tudor pretty much in a moralistic, biblical bind. The closest he ever got to a nonjudgmental state was Zen Buddhism, which, indeed, neutralized his Calvinist background. Nor did he turn a deaf ear to society's drumroll and the coming Revolution signaled by de Laclos, but instead aptly named his characters: A Gentleman of Parts, Ladies of Position and Lady of Consequence. These, too, were couched in double entendre.

Meanwhile the two months that went into the making of this ballet were about as happily antic as any he'd known. Little notes to Maude, Nigel and their friend Muriel "Tiny" Monkhouse were addressed "Dear Trio of Sugarplums." Another time it was "Poor lambs, . . ." Once, to confirm a weekend visit to London, he wrote: "Lovelies, J'arriverai toutes suites chez vous. Oh, joy! Love, Antony." The ballet afforded all kinds of playful challenges—not least thinking up a pun for the title. He finally settled on *Knight Errant* only after the Royal Ballet's board of governors nixed as too risqué his first inspiration: *Chevalier d'Amour,* which refers both to the titled hero and a certain parasitic condition that accrues to such promiscuously oriented gadabouts. And then there were the Richard Strauss scores he chose: the softly glittering incidental music to *Le Bourgeois Gentilhomme* and the deceptively seraphic prelude to *Ariadne auf Naxos.* Together, and for the purposes he put them to, these represented a model of musical enlightenment. Strauss, too, knew how to mock highblown schemes and unrealistic ideals.

Not least of all was Tudor's involvement with his cast, including the delicious little confidences Wall brought to him throughout the rehearsal period. It seemed the dancer had been having an extramarital affair and sought out Tudor as counsel. As was his wont, the master gamesman reveled in the role of witness. He could savor the vicarious experience without risking disaster. Again, he was having his ballet within a ballet, he was analyzing for Wall the tortuous intricacies of forbidden alliances and the illusions each partner creates. To make matters even more complicated there was much playing on jealousy, just as the scenario suggested. Freda Wall, for instance, believed then "that Tudor was mad just for David . . . because the part he gave me, which he described as Red Riding Hood, was that of a boring character—I thought Tudor found me boring, too. Only later did I find out that he really liked me."

He also loved the psycho-sex dramas that became the essence of *Knight Errant*—and, as usual, his veristic casting heightened the adventure. For the virginal character he chose nineteen-year-old Margaret Barbieri, a devout Catholic with nothing but pure thoughts, and inexperienced as well. In the pas de deux with Wall he had her kneeling, at one point, while her partner stood legs astride, hips thrust forward within inches of her face. "What are you looking at?" Tudor asked her. "What is that?" he kept on, until, at last, he got her to utter some clinically polite term for the part of Wall's anatomy she was confronting. "He was dead serious," Wall remembered. "But Maggie wasn't the only flustered person. We all waited to see who could not tolerate the horrible embarrassment. It was mental disrobing time. By the end of those rehearsals he put us through, nobody had any emotional modesty left." What he wanted from Barbieri was the shocking revelation that would come to the character. No more. But that's not to say he didn't delight in the method he employed. "He knew how timid I was," said Barbieri. "So he didn't explode at me the way he did with the others. But very painstakingly he made me do all those things with David . . . until I actually got hot under the collar. We had one rehearsal, just the three of us, that lasted two hours and had only five steps to show for it. The steps weren't important, though, only what transpired between us was."

Yet for all the shared intimacies Tudor could not easily allow physical contact. Freda remembered that when David hugged him he didn't reciprocate—maybe for fear of betraying more than casual affection; he was always beset with a certain strangeness. But he came to dinner many times and, on one of those occasions, Mrs. Thorogood, a cockney, joined them. "They were hilariously, outrageously crude together," Freda said, describing her mother and Tudor who went off to another part of the garden for their tête-a-tête. "In an instant they sniffed each other out and he was speaking cockney and they were cracking the filthiest jokes."

Meanwhile, all of Wall's delight in being chosen for the lead role came to nothing. Just prior to the Manchester premiere, which took place on November 25, 1968, he injured himself and had to be replaced by Hendrik Davel. Only later, in the spring, would he impersonate The Chevalier on the stage of the Royal Opera House. But the ballet was intended for a small theater where its subtleties could be gleaned. For Tudor, one of its happier aspects was the very intimacy that only a little house could accommodate. He lamented that Royal performance as "a miserable, flawed charade" because of the Garden's unsuitability to the ballet.

There were rave notices in Manchester. But some of the press traveling there for the premiere faulted *Knight Errant* for Davel's ineffectual performance. And Craig Dodd took Tudor to task for the ballet itself, naming the choreographer "a Dr. Jekyll and Mr. Hyde"—with this latest work belonging to the latter. "The irony of the whole business," he wrote in *The Dancing Times,* "is surely that in the source material Tudor came so near to the sort of ballet on which his reputation rests and at which he is unsurpassed. If anyone is capable of distilling the essence of the novel, the amorality and irony, he is surely that person. Instead he chose to ignore the whole canvas and present us with an over-enlarged brushstroke."

At the same time that *Knight Errant* was playing, the Royal Ballet had also committed Tudor to staging his *Jardin aux Lilas.* But this early masterpiece was no stranger to London audiences. Ballet Rambert had kept it in the repertory, even without the benefit of Tudor's on-location coaching. He never disputed with Rambert her rights to it or to *Dark Elegies,* which brought the two of them their place in the theatrical sun. Although he raged against her during his decade at the Mercury Theatre he never stopped feeling gratitude for the creative foundation she laid for him. Taking these ballets away from his first patron was unthinkable; he could not have such a confrontation with her. His alternative was to give only lip-service approval to her custody of them. He certainly felt no desire to supervise Rambert's productions of *Jardin* and *Elegies.* But now he would step forward and claim what was his in an aggressive way—putting an authoritative stamp on a brand-new staging of *Jardin* at the major ballet establishment. For the occasion there would be original costumes and decor that paid homage to the famous Hugh Stevenson designs.

All was not as it looked from a distance, though. Tudor was supposed to be rehearsing two ballets—*Jardin* and *Knight Errant*— at the same time but in different cities. The reason he agreed to such a plan might have had to do with confidence, not misjudged, as it turned out, for—*mirabile dictu*—he actually wrapped up *Knight* several weeks ahead of schedule. Still, he would need more than this time allotment to set *Jardin* on a virgin company, even when that company was the illustrious Royal Ballet. The fact that he took on such an impossible task says more, perhaps, about his lingering self-destructiveness than possible inflexibility on the part of his Covent Garden hosts. At any rate, the person he left in charge of *Jardin,* Michael Somes, was not sympathetic to the challenge. The former partner of Margot Fonteyn and one-time *danseur noble par excellence* had now become assistant director to Ashton.

What Tudor imagined Somes might be able to do for the ballet is unclear. But when he saw the results the full realization of his mistake came crashing down. And when he was informed that Somes had overseen rehearsals by counting beats of music for the dancers, he all but tore his eyebrows out. Counting beats, as we recall, was not for Tudor, not for movements that need to be grasped and assimilated in terms of a whole thought rather than a discrete measure, not for choreography whose thrust is emotive rather than rhythmic. "He was appalled at the dress rehearsal," according to Glen Tetley, who sat watching that November 11, 1968. "It seemed to be his first glimpse of the production. I saw him leap out of his seat and race back and stop the thing. Next, he was onstage with the cast, his face purple. Poor [Svetlana] Beriosova. He really screamed at her. 'You could have done this in a telephone box with your stiff spine,' he said." The woebegone Caroline never recovered from the battering she took. Nor did her portrayal improve. While the Royal's prima ballerina earned kudos for most of the roles she danced, this one apparently eluded her. Fernau Hall, the dance critic, said that Beriosova "was, in her life then, already too downtrodden and abused to portray so exploited a character."

Whatever the reason she and Tudor could not work together, the rest of the cast, except for Georgina Parkinson, came in for similar problems and earned equally low critical grades. But John

Percival, writing for *The Dancing Times,* pointed out that "There is nothing in the Royal Ballet style that prevents people from dancing *Jardin,*" and went on to name those among them who had performed the ballet so well while they were still members of Rambert's company. Obviously, Tudor had trusted to this umbrella protection and took comfort in the general familiarity *Jardin* enjoyed in London. But he was so beset with the dismal prospects that he boycotted the premiere and told his friends Maude and Nigel to stay home. Letting others rehearse his cherished masterpiece came down to a decision that was inexplicable. Could it have been his wishful dependency? Did he believe that being at home in England meant being able to loosen his artistic control—without sacrificing good results? At any rate, he agreed to a pro forma policy and let the company's senior principals assume the leading roles. It wasn't at all like him. Tetley thought that Tudor "had something like a death wish, otherwise he would not have left Somes in charge. He's too shrewd. He knew better."

But there was still a chance to salvage *Jardin,* he thought. A second cast, one of his own choosing, was being put together and, as if to prove an object lesson, he gave these dancers—especially Anthony Dowell and Antoinette Sibley—his undivided attention. They redeemed the Tudor reputation, so much so that Percival reported that "the vastness of Covent Garden need not invalidate the nuances of Tudor's choreography. . . . Sibley and Dowell both have by nature the reticence, the sense of strangled emotion, which suits the ballet so well, and they danced as though they really believed in it."

Sibley gloried in her experience with Tudor and his ballet. "Other choreographers might encourage you to explore," she said, "but only in a superficial way, only in terms of how to make the steps look good or the dancer look pretty. MacMillan's *Manon* is a case in point." Ashton, on the other hand, recalled "how embarrassed many of the dancers were with the underlying motives in *Jardin*. They just didn't understand those sentiments in the sixties."

Not surprisingly Tudor would stay in the category of émigré

choreographer. What began as the possible flickerings of an eternal flame ended as a two-year fireworks display for his mother country. It was just a fling. True, he proved with *Shadowplay* and even *Knight Errant* that the embers of creativity could heat up sufficiently to produce major ballets again. But, as his career repeatedly showed, he stayed aloof from the organizations to which he would have to bond for any chance of self-fulfillment. Here was a man who, in the themes of his ballets, paid homage to the community. He could not mingle in its personal politics, however; he could not work within the frame of interdependence. Just as The Boy with Matted Hair made his peace as a sort of enlightened isolate, so did Tudor. It meant that he could neither belong nor resolve his ambivalence, which was, perhaps, at the very heart of this hurtful disengagement.

As de Valois concluded, albeit defensively, "I think he would have ended with us the same way regardless of everything. If there had been no war to turn his back on, if there had been no recriminations, it would have been the same. I think Fred was better, period, and I never could figure out what the press fell for. His scenarios always left one with a big question mark. But I'll give him this compliment: I don't believe he really belonged to the theater in the sense of choreographing for the masses. He was too sincere—and so intelligent, such fine taste. Poor Antony. I think he was sad. He didn't know where he was in the world."

True enough. Back in New York, which might have seemed a haven after his dismal conclusion with the Royal Ballet, he wrote to Maude from "miserable, filthy, steamy, torrid Fun City.

"Out of my mind to return here. Nothing but horrible little impedimenta—no peace and quiet, no meditation possibilities."

33

Togetherness

ONE SIGNIFICANT DETOUR, however, stood between London and New York. It was Australia. Before Tudor could bid final farewell to the United Kingdom he had to travel to this far part of the commonwealth, for one of his faithful—Peggy van Praagh—had planted her pioneer self on its untried stretch of land and held out her hand to him. Named as director of the Australian Ballet in 1963, she did what his other English disciples had done when administrative challenge beckoned: she called on her erstwhile mentor. Would he visit and perhaps stage one of his ballets, even deign to create a new work for her fledgling company? But of course.

Actually, he had already returned to New York following his stint with the Royal Ballet. What he faced back at Juilliard was without compelling enticement; the dancers were, by definition, less than professional and after his indulgence with the Walls and Dowells and Sibleys, he had little taste for his old stamping grounds. Nor did Ballet Theatre's constant queries draw much response; he continued to slough off these bids to rejoin the company for lack of simpatico. It was his way to keep distance; inertia guaranteed a touch-me-not attitude. And then there was Lucia Chase. His dealings with her, remembered with bitterness, stood as a caveat against returning. So why not visit Peggy? Australia. Down under in the outback. Why, it was even the birthplace of his mother, whose migrant parents were Scottish and English. The idea reincited his wanderlust.

This sojourn, like the important one that preceded it—in fact, like every working side trip out of New York—amounted to but a brief encounter. One could hear the curious tone of aloofness in his ordinary little exchanges with people. He once said to Met dancer Edith Jerell, "Jerrell, you don't have ballerina legs." "How do I get them?" she asked, in pained agreement. "I haven't got the foggiest," he answered. "You'll have to find out for yourself." None of the affectionate conspiracy here of a Balanchine, who would knock out a solution to his dancer's dilemma. Tudor didn't join his coworkers in the ordinary problems they confronted. He set them on a lonely course, one as lonely as his own. To wit: his little junkets were usually one-shot affairs wherein he would come and stage a ballet for some modest troupe that would appropriately kiss his feet and brave his excoriations. Then out again, once more an isolate.

Now he was about to embark on another mercy mission— except for the Royal Ballet's summons, he was always the visiting nurse, flying in to minister to the latest ballet infant. But this time he would be accompanied by Hugh. Maybe, just maybe, restoring his partner to active collaboration would be profitable. He knew, as an old hand would, what to expect from solo expeditions and no longer valued such freedom. Besides, Hugh had nothing to do. His little photography sideline was short-lived and taking a trip like this would nudge him from the reclusive existence he had fallen into. What's more, Peggy would be delighted to have the both of them.

The Australian public understood nothing of Tudor's sophistication. He staged *Pillar of Fire* in July of 1969, after a two-month rehearsal period. And, together with Hugh, who did the designs and assisted at rehearsals, he created a new ballet, *The Divine Horsemen*. Its subject was voodoo and its setting the Caribbean. Hugh's influence, based on his familiarity with island rituals and magic, didn't seem to help. Whatever effect he may have had on Tudor's creativity years ago would stay buried. After all, the incentive was gone: when Hugh had his career as a dancer he was empowered to rub the golden lamp and drag brilliant ballets from the Tudor genie; now, it really didn't matter. They were far more fascinated by the country, its scenery, food and climate. The trip was a travel adventure for them. Hugh loved mimicking the Aussie accent. And Tudor would constantly point out similarities to Hugh's native island. "These fruits are just like those in Barbados, aren't they, Hugh?"

The two had made a trip back to the British West Indies once, but the flamboyant island boy shrugged off subsequent appeals to return. "He was afraid of something there, of being ostracized," according to a close friend, Marja Odell, who once asked him to accompany her to the Bahamas. "I think he feared being branded homosexual."

At any rate, *The Divine Horsemen* came in for neither critical nor popular acclaim. Within a short time, both it and *Pillar,* which the audience did not like either, disappeared from the repertory.

The bounty from this export was not artistic, obviously. It was personal. A new era had begun for Tudor and Hugh, an era of appreciative companionship. Being together for day and night on end brought a comfort that had been absent over the past two decades. At ages sixty-two and fifty-nine, respectively, all the wild oats, so to speak, had been sown. These were different life stages. And if the dynamic between them had not really changed—"in rehearsals it still looked like the mouse [Tudor] watching the rattlesnake [Hugh]," according to Scott Douglas—at least they could now be philosophers. Hugh had weathered illness: emphysema and lung surgery. He'd been through a wrenching divorce. He had failed to find any enterprise to take the place of his stage career, which ended while he was still in his forties. He'd been severely reduced in both fortune and fame. Tudor, in fact, had been sending him a monthly stipend to cover expenses—from his first moment of need. There had never been a question that he would do otherwise.

Their bond had hardly dissolved; it only lapsed somewhat. Clearly, Tudor felt responsible for Hugh. And he was a loyal, vastly generous friend. Even when Tudor had constructed a busy life for himself—teaching day and night classes, polishing the occasional production at Ballet Theatre, flying off on a junket— he spent most of his leisure time with Hugh. And tried, somewhat unsuccessfully, to merge the two phases of his life socially. They lived apart but always phoned each other first thing in the morning. Sometimes Hugh would come along to a party thrown by the Juilliard kids and grab his chance to perform. What role would he play? Raconteur? Outrageous flirt? Joke-teller? Sallie Wilson also attended these parties, still in her trail-Tudor mode. But of the two, Tudor had greater tolerance for Hugh. Sallie's mordant attention to her mentor was seen by him as burdensome and cloying, while Hugh always let go—to revel in his solo act.

34

●

Cocktails on the Sand

IN 1971, WHEN TUDOR HAD COMPLETED twenty years at Juilliard, he retired and went on pension, with never a backward glance. "I lead a marvelously indolent life," he would say two years later. "I think it's gorgeous. I get up in the morning. I look for my glasses . . . where did I put my glasses? I look for them for two hours. Finally, I find them. I sit down with the paper. I make the coffee. Roughly that. A gorgeous wasting of time." As a retiree, he was close to being on a par with Hugh. Meanwhile he had the satisfaction of knowing that his years of teaching had served him well. Notably as a palliative against the awfulness of doing high-pressure choreography. But also as a neutral ground for pursuing his life's work.

Teaching had been a passport of sorts. And when a call came from sunny Southern California—would Tudor consider a three-month residency for the months of January through March at the lovely University of California at Irvine?—it didn't take much persuasion. Such a move would enable him and Hugh to escape the dreary New York winters. No less than oceanfront accommodations in nearby Laguna Beach came with the offer. The weather would be mild and the sea and sand, literally at their feet. How gorgeous! The first expedition, in what would become an annual retreat from the Atlantic Seaboard's most merciless season, took place in 1973.

Apart from the hectic summers when it is deluged with tourists, Laguna is a sleepy little town whose main street is Pacific Coast Highway. It looks almost like an afterthought to the sloping green hills and picturesquely craggy shoreline—a length of village that just sort of grew up along the surf and main road. Wood frame houses line the beach and a few rectangular motels, exemplars of Southern California nonarchitecture, do a brisk business on weekends. The area boasts its share of retired folks, some of whom are responsible for the touristy art that shopkeepers take on consignment. During the days of Jack Kerouac it attracted a hippie contingent and following that it became a gay haven. Although the locals tend to come from the Midwest the atmosphere is tolerant to most lifestyles. The town constitutes a tiny oasis of liberalism, cut off from the right-wing rigidity that marks the rest of Orange County. It lies in a lovely cove that attracts lean and leathery beachophiles and rubber-suited towheads—who cluster on their surfboards waiting for the perfect wave; until it comes they look like a covey of blackbirds bobbing on the water. Local sport. But nothing about Laguna Beach is contrived. Even unsightly telephone poles are allowed to mar the vistas. And maybe that was part of its charm for the two decidedly English gentlemen who, annually, joined the winter population.

Home became the ultra modest Vacation Village. Its name wrongly conjures up visions of a manicured Disneyland, which happens to be just minutes down the freeway. "VV"—as Tudor referred to it—boasts a main building that is a three-story stucco affair, as simple as a rectangular box; it faces the highway on one side and the ocean on the other. In the beginning years, Tudor and Hugh luxuriated in adjoining rooms with a common kitchenette and bath. Thereafter, when University of California at Irvine was no longer part of the picture and didn't pick up the tab, they shared the unit as a single—the same one every year. It faced the ocean, but with a view partially blocked by other buildings right on the sand, their flat roofs sprung with television antennas. Frugality prompted the doubling up; all their lives they made do with the most meager ménage. Friends noted that they behaved like paupers, without any need to.

In fact, Tudor took great pride in his spartan ways. He awarded himself a kind of merit badge for his independence from wealth and vanity. He did not have it in his heart to walk among the privileged. He could not playact grandeur, although for the press he often made pronouncements on the godlike status a choreographer must live up to. In a letter to his niece in New Zealand, he wrote about Anthony Bliss, "who is now the director of the Metropolitan Opera, married to Sally Brayley, a Canadian girl whom I first met when I put on something in pre-historic time for the Canadian National Ballet. Then she came and joined the Met Ballet. At any rate, the Blisses are very well connected and move among the 'beautiful' people and the rich ones. I've been accepted as an equal—to a degree—by lots of rich people who know from nothing. I have my little one-room flat [in New York], do all the shopping, cleaning, washing myself, never eat out but cook for myself and am as frugal as my father."

Tudor came from an era whose bourgeoisie regarded thrift as a virtue. "Look how good a poor person can be," he seemed to say. "And how much better informed, to boot. Conspicuous consumption, the very symbol of pretense, is beneath me." Indeed, he had to stand by those values because the assignment he had taken on at University of California at Irvine would not bring gratification to a renowned but vainglorious choreographer. The fine arts department at UCI was hardly a paragon of enlightenment. Many years after Tudor had joined the dance faculty as special spring trimester guest, a professor from an allied field asked about the all-Tudor program that was being prepared. "Is this something to do with English architecture?" he wanted to know. Nor had the dance students ever heard of Antony Tudor. Their world was inestimably limited. But their ignorance turned out to be a plus: they could approach him fearlessly. They could behold this strange bald falcon with the sometimes cutting quip and the frequently bizarre question—"Why are you doing that *plié?*"—and be amused rather than quake in fright. He liked being liked. He blossomed in the openness. He enjoyed traveling without the baggage of a reputation; here he was just another guest teacher. But as it turned out he did not get the welcome one would expect, for Eugene Loring, an old peer from the early days of Ballet Theatre and now chairman of the UCI dance department, resisted the idea of having to contend again with the English choreographer. Now the stakes were low, however, and Tudor could tolerate the mild political dissension between himself and Loring.

At this point he was not seeking creative fulfillment, just a surcease from the harrowing pace of New York. UCI, with its acres and acres of rolling green meadows, was inland, and only a fifteen-minute drive from the coast. Life here was immensely appealing.

It all began that January day in 1973, at Los Angeles International Airport. Marja Odell, a Dutch-born graduate of the dance department, had been dispatched to the airport to pick up Antony Tudor and Hugh Laing. Her mission was to collect them and their little dog Chenpo and deliver them to Vacation Village, a one-hour trip from terminal to door. True, the beautiful dancer was a stranger. But as had been the case for other felicitous meetings, the chemistry was right: Tudor and Hugh instantly saw Marja as an ombudswoman to their Southern California mirage. On the appointed day, over the next five years, she would be waiting as their plane touched down. And for each of the upcoming eleven arrivals when she found herself in Paris or London or some other far-flung place she would, unfailingly, send flowers in lieu of greeting them personally. That was the least. Once again, there would be a happy pas de trois.

She was twenty-one and warmly ebullient, not burdened by

fear or veneration. And she was a perfect guide to their new digs, the town and university politics. The best times they ever had usually included a Marja, a wonderfully neutralizing force; otherwise Hugh could tip the balance. She moved into their lives with smooth, laughing ease. Each weekday morning Marja would pick up Tudor and drive him to his class or rehearsal, whichever was scheduled for that day. He usually taught class three mornings and rehearsed the other two. And then she drove him home. Occasionally, he took the bus, but mostly she taxied him both ways. When they arrived back in Laguna, shortly after noon, it was cocktail time: the three of them would have their vodka martinis and then Hugh would serve the superb lunch he'd prepared—chicken livers were a *specialité de la maison.* Following that there would be several hands of gin rummy. And close to sunset, which came early in winter, the three of them, with Chenpo, the little Lhasa apso dog, would set out for their long walk on the beach, just some twenty yards from Vacation Village. With or without her, the walk was *de rigueur.*

"Hugh was definitely the boss," according to Marja, "but Tudor was the strength." Just like some marriages in which the wife makes all decisions but the husband is the provider and source of strength. Often, an exasperated Hugh would holler from the kitchen, "Come in here Tudor and help me. How do you expect me to do this all myself?" "Yes, Hugh," he would answer, and dutifully lend a hand. But he managed to get back at his taskmaster with wryly affectionate criticisms of the cuisine. While Tudor was off at UCI, Hugh kept house; he did the shopping and cleaning. He was happy. They both were happy. One was noisy and never stopped stirring up negative attention; the other was quiet and contented and pensive and peaceably watchful of everything, except for a witty punctuation here and there. He loved nothing better than sitting on the large patio of the Laguna Beach Hotel and observing people—their antics, their timidities, their attentions to or boredom with each other. He loved going to the movies—there was one theater, which changed its bill every week. They caught the early show, for reveille was

at six A.M. The morning beach walk, well after an hour's meditation, usually turned up familiar faces. Tudor gloried in his
anonymity and the freedom of exchange he had with his fellow
beachniks. Ballet was totally foreign here. And the pleasure-
seeking all of them had in common was as much as they ever
needed or wanted to know about.

Marja provided more personalized entertainment—via tales of
her amorous escapades. Tudor and Hugh were a positively avid
audience. They took vicarious delight in the adventures she regaled them with, and they always prodded her for the details.
The whole thing was very playful—the old experts got to dole
out advice and then hear how the next episode of the saga would
turn out. When their favorite tall, outdoors girl was offered a
pizzazzy job as a Las Vegas showdancer, they went with her to
a local branch of the May Company, a department store, and
bought makeup, which Hugh taught her to apply. Israel "El"
Gabriel, a faculty member and former dancer from Israel's Bat-
Dor Company, took over her guardianship of Tudor and Hugh
when Marja left. Until then she and "El," or "St. Gabriel," as
Tudor called him, were the closest friends of the sojourners. Their
closeness came through informality and they had special dispen-
sation to enter where others were barred because their affection
was genuine—not based on celebrity-mongering or a desire for
upward artistic mobility. Tudor could discern instantly the difference between Marja and "El" and those who might place an
extrinsic value on his friendship. He was no recluse. The only
world he needed to shut out was the dance world.

Dear Marja,
    We had thought you were still gracing the Étoile, and cock-
tailing at the Ritz, and shopping on the Faubourg St. Honore
and having supper at the Tour d'Argent. But here you're back
and swinging all your talents in Vegas again. I guess you didn't
get to make the white slave bit to S. America. We are going
to miss you terribly in Laguna but it is reassuring that you are
comparatively close by.
                                                Old Baldy

35

Starry-Eyed

"Have Ballet Will Travel." That was the unspoken motto Tudor adhered to while visiting professional companies. But he also had a functional portfolio—*Sunflowers, Fandango, Little Improvisations, Continuo* and so on—for university-mongering. And although he always took great pains in rehearsal, the years at UCI being no exception, he felt the freedom to remain aloof from the rest of the faculty. Marja recalled that "he was interested in doing what he needed to do at school and then returning as quickly as possible to the beach"—the real point of his westward trips.

But Laguna turned out not to be an isolating experience, for it brought about a reunion with the retired originators of Ballet Theatre, who now made their homes in Los Angeles. People like Muriel Bentley, Miriam Golden and David Nillo came on happy pilgrimages to Vacation Village. Just as before, Hugh would hold forth—eager for his audience of old friends—and Tudor would pepper the conversations with his spare but well-chosen witticisms. He took deep pleasure in these Sunday afternoons, these drafts of nostalgia and continuity, and a gently affectionate tone replaced the fervor of high-strung and hectic performing days. Above all, he welcomed his reunion with Nora Kaye. She had helped her husband Herbert Ross become a pillar of Hollywood and together they enjoyed his successful film career as producer/director. They tried to entice Tudor into their celluloid world of the rich and famous, but he passed on everything except the friendship. Once again, he found his Hagar irresistible. He was special to her and she never failed to treat him accordingly. He loved her for it.

Eventually, both of them would rejoin Ballet Theatre, now called American Ballet Theatre (ABT)—she in a quasi-advisory position, he as an elder statesman. After all the years of resistance he finally acquiesced. This was his only artistic home. No matter that he squabbled with Lucia and walked away from it and her. In the end, he belonged here.

By the early seventies, the company had begun a new era of stability, one that coincided with a ballet boom such as the country had never seen. Audiences thronged the box office, not just this one but the New York City Ballet and others as well. Ever since Rudolf Nureyev made his famous leap to the West—first to the Royal Ballet and then, in an overachieving conquest, to other major companies—an alert public stood ready to storm the gates. It had glimpsed a new kind of ballet hero. His defection from Leningrad was followed by that of Natalia Makarova and then Mikhail Baryshnikov, both of whom landed at Ballet Theatre. A Russian invasion all over again. Despite the unhappiness it caused within the ranks—American dancers felt cheated once more—the Soviet presence had a salutary effect. It led the way to a galaxy of international guest stars, for whom a diversified repertory was strengthened. More efficient boards of directors were recruited to complete the success cycle. Ballet Theatre now enjoyed better organization and played New York seasons that were not an insult. There were two of them a year, at Lincoln and City centers. Washington, D.C., also hosted the company twice annually at the Kennedy Center.

Most significant, Tudor now taught only during the three winter months (UCI). The rest of the time he was free and that explains the option he finally took: to resume what the world regarded as his rightful work. For two decades he had blocked such a possibility. But with the peak of his creativity now presumably passed, it was safe to come back. Perhaps no one would expect him to do new ballets. It was conceivable, at sixty-six, for him to cry "too old" without being disbelieved. And that's just what he did when pressed. Meanwhile the scene was set for a rapprochement with his patron/nemesis, Lucia Chase.

But he resisted—verbally, at least—the first efforts to bring him back. "They've just come to me with the offer of a permanent job, co-director or something," he said to *The Washington Post*. "I don't know exactly what they have in mind but I'm sure I'm not interested. I told them, 'That would mean Lucia could phone me any hour of the day or night and it would be legal.' So the answer is no—it's as simple as that." When asked what the basis was for his disaffection he pointed to Lucia's casting policy vis-à-vis his ballets. After all, she chose the casts, and that amounted to a kind of castration. "She puts people in my ballets I don't approve of but I don't care. I'm past it. Someone called me an old master the other day, which I thought was the kiss of death." Before the interview ended, though, he took one last mischievous poke at himself. "Of course, it would hurt me if they didn't think so," he said. But Tudor was nothing if not crafty when it came to disingenuous excuses for his refusals. Practically in the same breath as criticizing Lucia's supervision of his ballets he lauded ABT. "Why should I go . . . [to various other companies], especially when they probably won't dance my work as well as Ballet Theatre does? I went to the National Ballet of Canada to stage *Dark Elegies* and I couldn't find one girl with the capacity to do the first solo."

In the summer of 1974, several months before the season officially got under way, Chase and her reluctant choreographer came to an agreement. Tudor would have a title, associate artistic director. The program book heralded its new associate with his full-page portrait.

It was a new scene he discovered and one that tested his powers of adaptation. For one thing, there were all these illustrious dancing actresses—the Kirov's Natalia Makarova, the beloved Italian ballerina Carla Fracci and the Royal Ballet's startlingly expressive Lynn Seymour; they were looking for Ballet Theatre's grazing pastures and his were considered prime. He could hardly ignore these exceptional artists, nor did he want to. His boycott of stars did not have to be carried to unreasonable lengths. He would give the system a try. Not a little of his desire hinged on a new possibility: that these luminaries could lend his ballets a certain cachet; the effect would be beneficial. Fracci, for one, seemed to encompass for him all the positives of the star personality: "She is terribly valuable," he explained, "because she knows her theater so well. She has that sales pitch of hers. What she does with my works is not really quite my concept, but it's valid. She gives my movements an intonation that, to me, is slightly operatic. I never felt I was doing what might be called operatic movements. But she is a star and she knows her business."

Clearly, Tudor was pleased to have such a salesperson. In the best of all possible worlds, however, he would not need one. Like Balanchine, he would eschew the star system, preferring dancers who grow toward the work, rather than adapt and distort it to their specifications.

Fracci had come to Ballet Theatre strictly on a designated basis, one that named which ballets and which performances the guest star would do. Makarova's situation was somewhat different. First of all, her desire to dance Tudor ballets and other important choreography came at the expense of defection from the USSR. Hers was a sacrifice of love. And Tudor held the Kirov dancer in highest regard—"a great, great ballerina," he said—particularly after seeing her portrayal of The Swan Queen. He talked about her being "so completely and totally of the moment—of *it*—that it was a totality of being, one of the greatest performances

I'd ever seen." He also found her to be a fascinating personality. Their battles in rehearsal, with Makarova at a distinct verbal disadvantage owing to her fumbling English, provided the company with constant comment. Few dancers ever stood up to the fearsome and mighty Tudor. And although she put her customary intensity to the task of learning his ballets, the two of them were usually at loggerheads.

This dancing actress ultimately rejected the whole Tudor aesthetic because she thought his characters lacked heroism. "They are provincials, little people in small towns tortured by their passions. I did not sense in them the main thing that makes a Chekhovian figure (which Tudor's are supposed to resemble) unique: the longing for a new life in which there will be a spiritual center, a high goal. I felt nothing of the kind in Hagar, an embittered old maid, desperate from her inability to find a man. It seemed to me that this exhausted her character, so dissimilar to mine. I was quite unable to get into the skin of this ill-fated spinster."

Touché. Of course, she and Tudor passed like strangers in the night. He was perhaps the first existential man in modern ballet, one who was conversant with Freud and Camus, Joyce, Proust and Stanislavsky. Makarova came from a world that subjugated the individual and thus could hardly give credence to ordinary people, the ones who led lives of quiet desperation. His kind of repression—the self-inflicted kind—was inconceivable to her. Once, in a rehearsal of *Pillar,* he was heard telling her that Gayle Young (The Friend) "is not the one you're supposed to be afraid of"—thus indicating the chasm between his intentions and her understanding. But finally he found a common ground with her in the Russian film, *Lady with the Dog,* one of his favorites. "It was the sublime expression that the woman conveyed with her clear eyes," wrote Makarova. "Longing for love while disbelieving in it. Everything then fell into place." After the next performance Tudor told her: "Now you're doing what you have to."

Often, however, any observer could see that he had focused

his Zen sights on leaving bad enough alone. His self-styled en-
actment of the guideline "want nothing/accept everything" had
a way of looking downright perverse. Makarova described how
he enjoyed her helplessness, tossing her like a puppy into the
flow of his ballets, then observing whether she could swim or
not. At rehearsals he was not so much sparing, she thought, as
stingy with his commentary. In *Dark Elegies,* for instance, "I
forgot I was dancing a village girl, just overlooked it." He refused
to bring this salient fact to her attention, even though nothing
could more thoroughly destroy the ballet than this misconception. He stayed silent, testing her. Fortunately, one of the cast
members pointed it out to her and she made the necessary ad-
justment in time. He had been perfectly willing, though, to permit a disaster, to lift no finger to save his ballet or her. Rather,
he let his energy turn to anger and then he vented it indirectly.
Watching Makarova from the wings he would mutter such nasty
comments as: "And whose bed did she just get out of?"

"Ballet is Woman" was, in many ways, as axiomatic for Tudor
as it was for Balanchine—although their definitions were worlds
apart. One heroine stood on a pedestal, ennobled; the other was
the very vehicle for despair. But both choreographers created
ballets for men, also. And Tudor made some predictable choices
when it came to casting Hugh's roles. No matter what he decided,
though, it would not go down well with Hugh; he suffered an
unparalleled case of ownership. When *Undertow* was revived with
a young but gifted unknown, Steven-Jan Hoff, Tudor found his
new Transgressor to be more than he could have hoped for. He
took great pains in coaching him, much to Hugh's discomfort.
For it was not easy to watch someone usurping this prized role—
especially now. Phillipe de Conville, Lucia's aide-de-camp in the
sixties and seventies, remembered the opening night of the revival. "Hugh spent most of the time yelling in the lobby, the
State Theatre's Grand Hall. He ranted irrationally. It was impossible for him to stay in his seat and watch the performance
more than a minute or so at a time. He was so nervous, hysterical
actually. He hated Steven. It killed him that this was happening.

Afterward I saw him and Tudor walking away together. One was silent and the other was gesticulating wildly and still ranting."

Some things—Tudor's dealings with Lucia, for instance—just didn't change, not at this point anyway. Nevertheless, he was the feather in her impresaria's cap. He brought glory to ABT and she accepted his artistic eminence—even though she may have lacked the deepest appreciation for what he meant to the history of dance. "Lucia finally got to be queen for a day when she mounted the company's first full-length *Swan Lake* in 1967," said de Conville. "She considered that to be the highlight of her career." He also remembered sitting next to her at the Kennedy Center when Tudor's *Romeo and Juliet* was being performed. "She slept through the whole thing and woke to the applause forty-five minutes later, saying, 'I love this ballet.' "

36

Not Fading

Tout New York came out for the event. It was an important local debut: Gelsey Kirkland and Mikhail Baryshnikov dancing *Giselle*. In fact, there wasn't an empty seat at Lincoln Center's State Theatre. In fact, ABT could count on sellouts whenever the program listed Baryshnikov. With this stunning virtuoso in its deck—his depth and versatility were as extravagant as his gift for devouring space and sculpting designs in the air—the company held the trump card. He could dance the classics with a veristic ardor that made old-fashioned mime seem like today's vernacular. He could impersonate American pop heroes like Jimmy Cagney, courtesy of Twyla Tharp's *Push Comes to Shove*, with dead accuracy, never mind the culture gap. Which troupe he would choose to join in the West was as carefully considered as which partner he would invite to dance with him. Unhesitatingly, he invited Kirkland, from the ranks of Balanchine's New York City Ballet; a neo–baby ballerina, she was *peau de soie* waft-

ing on the breeze. Kirov taste, which Baryshnikov and Balanchine were steeped in, seemed to cross generational lines. Both
exponents were properly dazzled by her purity and speed and
powers of articulation—which earned her principal status at age
seventeen. She was part flint, part flower, but neither of them
had any idea that the doll exterior belied a questing, sensitive
soul, much less an extraordinary capacity for torment. That
would come later. And it *would,* unquestionably, be picked up
by Tudor. He shared much with her. The two of them were
deeply drawn to self-mortification.

But for now, Kirkland let herself be carried along on a dream
journey. She had first laid eyes on Baryshnikov when New York
City Ballet had toured the Soviet Union several years before—
which is when he first saw her. In 1974 she giddily received and
accepted his invitation, opting for Baryshnikov and the hectic
but colorful American Ballet Theatre over her alma mater and
its often chaste neoclassicism. She was hardly prepared, though,
for the rigors of sharing the spotlight with an instant idol. But
it didn't matter at the moment. Nothing did.

She was Giselle, the fey peasant girl with one foot already in
the netherworld of Wilidom. And he was Albrecht, the aristocrat
whose tragic fervor dominates her utterly. His pathos and passion
joined to her ethereal ecstasy. It was gripping. The audience burst
into rapturous applause, having just witnessed a *Giselle* to store
in a time capsule.

Tudor was there. The curtain calls went on and on. Ten minutes after everyone else had gone from the theater he still sat in
his seat, Hugh next to him. It was only the rarest performance
that pinned him to the spot and this was one such. The totality
of it enthralled him. But Kirkland, in particular, captured his
attention. Her simplicity—in place of the high drama so many
ballerinas opted for—positively stunned him. In fact, he found
everything about her extraordinary. It was much before this *Giselle,* however, that he had taken note of Gelsey Kirkland. She
came to Ballet Theatre in 1974, the same year he reunited with
the company. Right away Lucia was after Tudor to do a new

ballet. She badgered and badgered. He kept resisting. Finally, success; consent was dragged from him. But one of the givens involved Kirkland. Yes, he would submit to the torturous ordeal and this young dancer who had moved him unlike anyone in many years would be central to it. And yes, he would also stage his latest full-scale ballet, *Shadowplay*—for Baryshnikov. Kirkland would have the female lead in that, too. There were compensations for plunging into stressful waters all over again. This fiercely gifted artist was one of them, the prime one.

The process of mounting ballets had undergone some changes over the years. As a consequence Tudor now had the help of a choreologist, someone who could teach a cast the rudiments of an existing work from an elaborate, though still relatively primitive, system of notation. He was happy for the assistance, especially because his memory proved unreliable, and called upon Christopher Newton, the Royal Ballet's chief choreologist, to take charge of the *Shadowplay* rehearsals. If he had not been working on a new ballet he would have given closer personal supervision to it. As it was, he only attended the last few sessions and offered Baryshnikov and Kirkland his typically idiosyncratic clues. When certain steps seemed to baffle the Russian turned Boy with Matted Hair and he admitted to doing them simply because that's what he was taught, Tudor became perceptibly defensive. "How could you possibly know how to do it," he said to Baryshnikov, "[since] you never asked me what [the steps] were all about?" There was a tone of hurt here. Compared to the artistic revelations that marked the creation of the ballet, particularly the way in which he completely possessed Anthony Dowell, this was a letdown. It had to be.

At the last minute he gave Baryshnikov books on Zen Buddhism and Kirkland one on female deities in Eastern religions. She understood that it came too late to be of use. But Tudor sensed her disquietude over not knowing everything there was to know. He also might have grasped how terrified she was of asking him questions. Meanwhile they were all engaged in a whirlwind—with many roles being rehearsed simultaneously.

Ballet Theatre was at a peak of excitement: Baryshnikov-Kirkland. Twyla Tharp. And for the cognoscenti, the return of Antony Tudor. The public was agog.

For sheer anticipation value, though, nothing came near *The Leaves Are Fading*. This would be Tudor's first ballet for the company in twenty-five years. He knew that the critics and Ballet Theatre, its present and past members, would all be waiting to see what he finally produced. "People are mad to expect anything at all," he told *The New York Times,* going on to explain that, at sixty-seven, "I can't move and when I choreograph I like to show every movement that everyone does." But information to the contrary slipped out, despite his absolute rule on closed rehearsals and despite his heated laments. One thing had changed over the past fifteen years, perhaps owing to Zen Buddhism or a consciously learned technique—silence was unnecessary. Protests, he discovered, were of value. By announcing his anxiety, instead of hiding it, he could lessen expectations and divest himself, to some extent, of an almost paralytic fear. "I'm foolhardy to have attempted the ballet at all," he continued. "I didn't want to open it in New York [but] in some little town in Oregon. The whole thing is madness. Why put myself at the mercy of the great American public in order to commit suicide—in order to hear people say, 'Tudor isn't what we thought he was.' Last year Ballet Theatre had an all-Tudor evening. As I left the theater, I overheard someone saying, 'Three ballets in one evening. That's a bit much, isn't it?' I agreed wholeheartedly."

Clearly, he suffered a fraud complex. Believing in part that his successes were a fluke and that his lack of talent would be found out, he turned to confession and disclaimer. It worked wonders. How lucky to find a remedy.

By this time the dance world counted a long list of luminaries with bids in for a Tudor ballet. Now, at last, the master was back at work—without satisfying any of them, however. None of the Russians—not Nureyev, Baryshnikov, nor Makarova—would ever have an original Tudor. That gift went to Cinderella Kirkland. It was she who served as muse in his return to choreography. Although he felt positively trapped into committing to a ballet, the prospect of collaborating with a kindred soul took some of the pain away. That and the idea of appropriating sections from works done at Juilliard—*Sunflowers* and *Continuo*—reduced the burden. The tone of the ballet, however, would come from the Romantic poets he was reading at the time. The text would focus on seasons as metaphor, thus the title: *The Leaves Are Fading*. He wanted its mood to span summer, winter, fall and spring and he needed music redolent with bucolic lyricism. In Dvořák's long-neglected *The Cypresses* he found the perfect complement to his vision of Proustian remembrance.

What he would finally present was altogether different from his previous ballets. *Leaves* would be an abstract work, whereas everything else had been theme-oriented. Actually, he'd been experimenting along these lines ever since he began teaching at Juilliard. And even *Shadowplay,* which also drew from classroom sketches, bordered on the abstract. At least it was a far cry from *Jardin* and *Pillar,* with their very specific household conflicts. Even *Nimbus,* his last work for Ballet Theatre, and *La Gloire,* his City Ballet valedictory, dealt with a particular scenario. But only the unimaginative create in the absolute abstract, for some remote theme can usually be discerned in substantive works, no matter how seemingly abstract. And Tudor, while conceding that *Leaves* falls into the nonnarrative category, preferred to think of the choreography as "empty" rather than "abstract." Indeed, the ideal state of Zen Buddhism involves emptiness, having no agendas or expectations or needs. For him, no dancer was just a body. He or she was a person who suggests an emotional entity—ideally empty of goals or mannerisms. *Leaves,* predictably, would involve a hidden psychodrama.

Just as predictably, the rehearsals were revelatory and excruciating. For all the artistic satisfaction she gave him, Kirkland also "drove Tudor crazy," according to cast member Richard Schafer. "She drove everyone crazy. But she was the full reason for *Leaves* and that left him dependent on her." He conducted his affairs in an orderly way. He was used to following plans and schedules—she was used to struggling against them. Her late arrivals would have him sputtering with fury. Once, after waiting for forty-five minutes, he stormed into Lucia's office and screamed at her: "Your dancers have no discipline." But everything changed the moment Kirkland tiptoed in, Phillipe de Conville recalled. "Gelsey would quietly put on her slippers and dance three steps and Tudor would melt." There was nothing manipulative in her behavior—rather, anxiety ruled the day. "She would be late to her own funeral," said Schafer. Tudor, of course, would attend his own in a punctilious fashion. Different modes, similar motives. Apart from the new confession therapy, as a way of diffusing the press, he hid his vulnerability; she laid hers out for all to see. But penetrating analysis was the sine qua non for both of them. So he tolerated her questions. "They came in a flurry, often at the beginning of rehearsals," said Schafer, "and they went on for about fifteen minutes. Tudor would grin and give her an epigram for an answer. It would have a calming effect. It satisfied her."

Over the two-month rehearsal period, Tudor was visibly nervous. But, as usual, he delivered his risqué comments unendingly, appearing jovial much of the time. Hugh made the occasional visit toward the end but stayed quietly watchful. In a rare moment of candor Tudor whispered to Schafer: "What's an old man like me doing a lyric ballet like this?"

On July 17, 1975, at New York's Lincoln Center, the answers came in. Clive Barnes, describing the premiere, wrote: "At the end, Ballet Theatre's two directors, Lucia Chase and Oliver Smith, rose in their seats (together with most of the audience) and applauded their hands off. It could have simply been relief after so long a wait. But such relief must have been heightened with the surprise of recognizing that this reluctant choreographer had come through with a major ballet, all the more welcome because it stands outside the body of his existing work. . . . Mr. Tudor's ballet could have been so awful. And had it been, respect to genius would have demanded the suggestion that it was not all that bad, even though awful."

No one needed to wait for the reviews, however. No matter what his chosen form, Tudor was back. He had made a ballet that turned away from angst and found an idealized reverie—a dappled remembrance of romantic things past, an ephemeral vision of all that is tender and delicate, loving and lovely in feelings. But, crucially, it bore the clear imprint of his signature, allowing that inviolable space between the partners, a space crowded with unspoken words. And the downcast eyes and the shoulders that reach out gently, tell of quiet sorrows mingled with joys. The performance, not surprisingly, was marvelous. Girls in body-skimming silk, their sleek heads exposing demure napes, had a new eloquence in the upper back. The whole fifteen-member cast danced with fresh inspiration. And Kirkland, for whom Tudor supplied phrases within phrases within phrases, rendered each one as a gorgeously subtle variation on the other. The central duet for her and Jonas Kage was awesome. Barnes wrote that Kirkland's "knowing youthfulness has never been more tellingly used and Kage's ardent gaucherie completed a picture of young love remembered." Perhaps it was this quality, this "ardent gaucherie" possessed by the chosen male dancer, that Tudor knew he could not get from a Baryshnikov or a Nureyev. Besides, it is not a leading role in the standard sense of the word, and asking a celebrity-dancer—other than a Kirkland—to perform in such an ensemble piece could be seen as an affront.

By curtain call time, there wasn't a dry eye onstage. Kirkland wept openly as she took her bows, so did the others—"for the sheer beauty of the ballet and the experience of performing it," said Schafer, who spoke of "the trembling emotion that swept over the whole house." Finally, the evening's hero came from the wings, led out by the heroine. He made his way unceremoniously to centerstage. The theater shook and roared. He just stood still, beaming, and then pressed his palms together in Buddhist fashion to acknowledge the deafening ovation that engulfed him. At that point he turned beet-red—a Tudor specialty.

The victorious blush lingered but briefly.

37

Best Friends

No triumph ever outlasted its welcome for Tudor. That he
was a man at odds with the world he worked in is an under-
statement. In fact, bewilderment continued to catch him up, even
at seventy years of age.

Gelsey Kirkland did not desert him. True, her life would become a nightmare of high-speed drugs and her career a house of
cards, ready to topple at the merest gust. But when he consented
to another ballet, she managed to climb over the as yet small pile
of personal debris and cut a path to him. Toward the end of
1978, they started back to work again—on *Tiller in the Fields;* it
was not a masterpiece. Whether the growing maelstrom of her
life interfered with the creative process and sent out disturbing
signals or whether he, too, could not find his way to a satisfying
artistic resolution is not known. There are clues everywhere that
he was not immune to her feckless downward spiral. He stood
and watched it happening. Another theory is that he finally lost

his nerve and could not risk a wholly new venture—thus he put less imagination to the task. But the most logical explanation is that he simply had to answer constant badgering from the company for a new ballet. And here was Kirkland, whose luminous talent brought him to *Leaves*—in his opinion, it stood the litmus test of whether he actually had another major work in him. Having proved it, he saw no further serious obligations. Perhaps he could trust to serendipity this time.

The music for his new ballet would again be Dvořák, the set designer Ming Cho Lee, the tone folkish—as in *Dark Elegies,* as in Mahler, who shared a Bohemian heritage with Dvořák. As though Kirkland was inextricably linked to the wistful lyricism of this pastoral composer, and as though she could materialize only as a neoromantic image, he tried to make the ballet a sequel for her. But this time he permitted a stronger narrative, one with a startling denouement: the final scene of *Tiller in the Fields* reveals a pregnant heroine. The gypsy sylph stands quietly onstage, drops the coat she's wrapped herself in, and voilà—a watermelon! Not only was this a bizarre turn, but the dancer in question hardly looked pubescent, let alone womanly.

To underscore Kirkland's diminutiveness, Tudor cast the hugely magnificent Patrick Bissell as her partner—this after Baryshnikov temporarily left the company. "What are we going to do now that your friend Misha has gone off?" Tudor asked her half cynically. But the choreographer did not stint on gorgeous sequences for principals and corps—most of it in the mode of a peasant frolic. Perhaps what he intended for his enigma variation was another danced koan, but the thudding physical reality of a swollen body somehow seemed preposterous on a ballet stage. Stylized murder, erotic love—any number of things works in the theater. This, however, did little but create social distance in critics and audience alike. Still, Tudor did not waste his opportunity—he never did. He let Kirkland materialize in all her strange, knowing willfulness. He contrasted it with Bissell's innocence, with his actions so unpremeditated and trusting. He characterized their relationship as a seduction, reversing the traditional roles, and he gave them myriad swirling lifts made all the more striking by the dancers' size difference. Kirkland's small-ness simply pointed up her silken fluency as she moved through Bissell's arms in lightning swift direction changes. Despite the puzzling scenario, no one watching could fail to understand how she inspired Tudor, how, through a profound understanding of his movement ethos, she found its single impetus and organic wholeness.

New Yorker critic Arlene Croce allowed that the ballet "has Tudor's eye and ear, but what," she wrote, "could be on his mind?" One must remember how awestruck he was at Kirkland's performance in *Giselle*. Implicit in that fey presence was a magical power. And this is what he apparently saw in her real life. Willful, yes. But not self-possessed, rather, impelled by external forces. In every sense Kirkland, the person, was an outsider—different, like him, from others. Her disharmony with the dance com-munity was no less strident than his own—perhaps less in control, but no less strident. Not only did her extravagant gifts attract him, but the two of them shared a kinship. Working together again, then, was satisfaction enough. Whether *Tiller* would be a masterpiece mattered less than the precious process. "The whole rehearsal period was a lively experience," said Richard Schafer, whom Tudor had appointed as his ad hoc assistant. "He had this joke up his sleeve and kept it from all of us until the very end. We knew nothing about the oddball twist the plot would take. Doing the ballet was a lark for him—nothing like *Leaves*. He was very nervous about that. Here, too, Gelsey was the whole focus of his interest."

Indeed, he had seen her become anorectic as a ploy for with-drawing from the production of *The Turning Point,* a semiau-tobiographical ballet movie being made then by Herbert Ross and Nora Kaye. The plot, which drew on Kaye's choice of a dancing career over motherhood, examines the conflict of giving up one for the other. In *Tiller,* Tudor lets Kirkland have both. He confers poetic justice. He provides succor for the wounds from her on-again, off-again relationship with Baryshnikov. And the work suggests a certain irony for Tudor—for all his cries of being too old to show the movement and therefore too old to choreograph, these final entries to his log, *Leaves* and *Tiller,* would stand as ballets of nonstop dancing; they left his detractors with their mouths hanging open. As for the ending, he had always been fascinated by the symbolism of pregnancy. It figured into *Pillar of Fire*—The Young Man from the House Opposite impregnates Hagar—and *Undertow,* which begins with the onstage birth of The Transgressor.

Tudor was not ready to discharge Kirkland after *Tiller,* even though he had closed the book on any further choreography. But the sight of her struggling against the tides of dissolution didn't bode well for the future. In an effort to keep her from being pulled into deeper waters he held out his hand. Would she like to dance *Jardin?* It would be perfect for her, he thought, and for him. So he broached it one day while they were standing in a deserted hall at the Met's rehearsal studios. Yes, she would love to dance Caroline—but not the way she had in the past, not helter-skelter, not superficially, not by way of a choreologist. Tudor realized that if Gelsey and such a technician were left to their own devices "only one of them would walk out alive from the rehearsals."

No, he would have to agree to studying the role with her so that she could understand every moment of it. During their sessions he would have to stand in for all the other characters in the ballet, because the company dancers who knew the steps didn't understand them. This was certainly a reversal of standards. All his life Tudor had been the taskmaster. Now Gelsey Kirkland would hold him to the very principles he instituted. Talk about being caught on one's own petard.

A few weeks later they had a two-hour rehearsal. In that time they explored only one gesture, a very subtle one at the beginning when Caroline is first seen onstage. Her lover has not yet entered—when he does, she rushes forward and rises on pointe. The gesture they rehearsed precedes that dramatic moment, but it tells everything about Caroline's state. To know the state and the gesture, Kirkland needed an answer. Who is the lover? "He's your best friend," Tudor told her.

How Tudoresque. Some other coach might reel off a litany of clichés like: "The lover makes you tremble with passion, or melt with desire. Your heart leaps at his appearance." But to hear that he's your best friend? That's a curve ball. It conjures up a surprise, original and undiscovered, one that can introduce a whole new associative current. It also is a barometer of Tudor's own mindset. Hugh created the role, nearly half a century ago. He was the best friend and he was the lover. Now, more than ever, he was the best friend. Tudor always worked from the present, in other words, from truth, from its immediacy. And when he evoked the past or youth, as in *Leaves,* it was a past remembered through consciously nostalgic eyes, not an attempt to put himself back into the moment as he was then.

Kirkland never got what she wanted. Nor did Tudor. His outreached hand could not stave off the tide. She left the company a few weeks later and he never saw her again. Nor did he really understand what happened—neither the drug culture nor its deadly force was within his ken. He came from another era, another world. By the time she rescued herself, it was too late. Luckily, for a brief interlude, their paths met. Posterity benefits still.

●

38

On the Home Screen

"I'M MATURE NOW," Tudor told television talk-show host Dick Cavett. "I don't do things like that anymore." Abusing dancers, that is. The celebrity interviewer, who typically invited leading arts figures onto his Public Broadcasting program in the late 1970s, tried to ask the choreographer with the forbidding reputation a few questions. He had some faint idea that it wouldn't be easy, but when he came face to face with Tudor—just prior to the premiere of *Tiller in the Fields*—the gently ingratiating Cavett could not exactly claim another conquest.

His guest, authoritatively bald, big-boned and robust, strode from the wings on cue. Television audiences who did not recognize this Svengali of the ballet saw a self-possessed falcon of a man in his early seventies, a vital and virile specimen. Dressed in a pinstriped suit and rep tie but showing no undue interest in his appearance, Tudor met his host head on. A steady, direct gaze, a glinting smile—these intimidated Cavett somewhat, but not as much as the issues he wanted to broach. Did he dare? He should have, for Tudor answered everything with utter direct-ness, if not to the interviewer's satisfaction. He was funny and forthright at the same time and Cavett, in his more successful moments, actually jumped into step. He probably would have been happier if the show's researchers had not brought him such touchy material, though.

The less controversial the better the going in this case. For instance: had Tudor always preferred making dances to dancing himself? Of course. "In order to punish other people and to punish myself." The answer came without the drop of a beat. Grinning. This was instinctive wit and devilish truth—be careful, Cavett. And what about those unlikely beginnings in London's tough East End and at Smithfield Market? Well, yes. It was there that he "learned all the right language to use when things go wrong in rehearsal. And shifting all those sides of beef and veal halves during a strike—why, that provided muscle for lifting girls in the air." A perfect practice ground for ballet. Tudor took a well-coached Cavett through the music halls he attended with his family as a tot, "and where I think my father liked the chorus girls." With that, the guest put his hand behind his head, mock-seductively, and started to sing "Follow the footsteps in the snow," a devouring smile on his face. Yes, and then he told about seeing the legendary dancer, Loie Fuller, "waving gauze through the lights." This and the music hall treats "made me love the theater, made me want to be part of it."

The guest was putting on quite a show. Mr. Gregarious him-self. His manner, neither self-conscious nor self-important, sug-gested total involvement. Animatedly, his hands sprang into the air for fuller expression. Seated, he would cross an ankle high up on his leg and hoist himself in the chair, punctuating some avowal or other. All the while Cavett looked for openings—and courage. But this was not the arrogant, cutting personality he had been warned of. This was a good sport, one who lovingly launched into his old cockney. Cavett, provoked to compete, tried out a studied imitation only to be told that it sounded inauthentic. He rallied by issuing an appraisal of Tudor's presently evolved speech: "a combination of Claude Rains and Alfred Hitchcock, I would say." What else from those early days? Well, there was Agnes de Mille, "who had an absolutely wonderful solo recital program—something like a geographic and historical magazine. . . . She was a great, great talent," said the ultraobjective judge, even while admitting that his friendship with her was "an off-and-on thing." No false blandishments here.

Back to the monstrous reputation: abusing dancers. Tudor took no offense. If anything he asserted himself with a kind of bemused bravado. "Breaking people down is not very hard," he said, still smiling, "but you cannot do it unless you pick up the ashes right away and turn them into a phoenix. Of course I've been terribly tempted to lay the dancers on the floor and walk on them. You can't, though. The unions won't permit physical violence." This whole humorous escapade was light years from the earnest performance he gave in the 1959 film, *A Time to Dance: Modern Ballet*. In two decades Tudor went from being a proper poetic professor reciting perfect prose to an irreverent quipster whose insights get turned on himself. He was giving Cavett the assimilated version of Antony Tudor and relishing it, the version softened by Americanisms like "yeah," the version which let go of those muscularly British enunciations that others from the U.K. hang onto for gain.

The interviewer could have thrown out any question but he chose to be cautious. Knighthood, for instance. He apparently wanted to ask Tudor whether he smarted over not being knighted. Instead, he feebly wondered aloud whether many British dance people received such recognition and why some did while others didn't. This path dwindled nowhere. Next came a favorite Cavett ploy: presenting himself as an amateur practitioner of the specialty performed by his guest. It drew laughing derision from Tudor. "If I were one of your dancers and you told me to put my arms up like this," Cavett proposed, "wouldn't I be justified in asking what the feeling of the movement should be?" The steel trap snapped shut. "Ah, but what you're doing is just reaching for parallel bars. And, besides, it's hypothetical what you're saying. You're not going to come to me and I'm not going to accept you," said Tudor, positively beaming. Cavett, still trying to grapple with the choreographer's mystique— cold personality but melting vulnerability in the ballets—mentioned a comment often made, "that Tudor has no feelings. Do you buy that?" Answer: "I'm rather a hermit, not a social being who goes to parties. I have good conversations with my characters and when I want them to stop I just put on another record."

Getting the master gamesman to talk about Zen Buddhism was equally hopeless. As Tudor did even with those he had known all his life he professed to "not knowing what it is, really, other than a nice way of passing time. . . . It's restful, you don't have to talk, it keeps your back straight." The answer seemed like a deliberate trivialization. But it was at once Tudor's way of staving off self-aggrandizement and shielding himself. He was not about to share his innermost thoughts on the subject. Often he did the same thing discussing his ballets. Of *Dark Elegies* he once said: "It could look very nice as a design for a tablecloth if you considered it from above." Nor was his answer to the Zen Buddhism question a lie. The kind of knowledge he was being asked to deliver is antithetic to the principles of Zen. But he did succeed in frustrating Cavett, just as he had Agnes de Mille and others.

Normally intrepid, the interviewer decided to tiptoe around the subject of Hugh Laing. The name never came up, except by implication. "Artistic relationships are closer than a marriage, aren't they?" Cavett asked rhetorically, hoping for a bite. What he got was: "You tell me"—the kind that merely snaps the line. Tudor instantly sensed the gingerly approach and dropped the bait back in Cavett's lap. But when it came to open subjects, Nora Kaye, for instance, no one took distance. Tudor praised his muse to the skies: "She had a total theater presence. We don't have many like that. She *was* dramatic, with nothing artificial added on. Whatever she did it turned out right."

Just as easily he disputed her apocryphal tale, which Cavett

338 · S H A D O W P L A Y

passed along here—the one about Tudor forcing Proust on her.
"No, I didn't make her read Proust at all. She thought I was
doing a Proust ballet and wanted to get the lead, so she told that
story to everyone." With this, Cavett confessed to Tudor: "I
find you intimidating." And Tudor confessed, too, of Nora: "I
found *her* intimidating." Smiles and chuckles. But his affection
for Kaye, foibles and all, went undiminished. "I remember the
first time I saw her, at a long narrow studio on Madison Avenue
where I was giving class. There was this girl who stood right in
front of me. She wore a short white tunic and a big bow in her
hair. She looked like that funny lady . . . yes, Fanny Brice. She
kept wanting me to look at her, so I looked away, spying out
of the corner of my eye that she did seven pirouettes! Furious
that I would not admire her accomplishment, she stormed out
and told the kids in the dressing room that she'd never dance for
that Englishman. The next morning we started our work
together."

Throughout this little narrative Tudor gave every imaginable
embellishment. He shifted in his seat to indicate each turn of the
tale. He twisted his neck around and moved his eyes like a
Kathakali dancer to show how stealthily he glimpsed her performance. No doubt Cavett enjoyed it, even though he was not
part of the fun.

39

"Love, Antony"

Shortly after *Tiller* Tudor talked a great deal about his age. The subject came close to being an idée fixe. So when he decided to make out a will, it was his friends, the Blisses, who obliged him. He put a great deal of trust in them, even agreeing to be the godfather of their baby son. Indeed there were constant favors being exchanged. Tony, who was a member of the Metropolitan Opera's directorial troika in the seventies, filled Tudor's ticket requests. Whenever the company put on an unusual twentieth-century work like Britten's *Peter Grimes* or *Billy Budd* or Berg's *Lulu* or Weill's *Mahagonny,* he was sure to see it. For the will, Tony referred Tudor to a colleague. The document was drawn up and signed immediately. Whatever it stipulated, Hugh disapproved. For one thing, it did not name him as trustee of the ballets—that post went to Sally Brayley Bliss. So Hugh instigated the drafting of another one, but despite his daily nudging, Tudor never signed it.

Meanwhile the annual winter trip to Laguna was upon them. Besides his teaching obligations at the university, there was ABT, which always toured this time of year and regularly landed in Los Angeles during the month of January. Consequently the no-longer-recumbent choreographer felt obliged to make his way at least once a week from Laguna to rehearsals at the Music Center in downtown Los Angeles. Sometimes "El" drove him, but just as often he took the bus, which he adored. It gave him quiet time. And on the way back he would stop at Central Market and browse among the rich variety of tropical fruits and farm-fresh vegetables.

But on the morning of January 12, 1979, while getting ready for a cast-change rehearsal of *Tiller* first, to be followed by a trip to Central Market, he felt ill. By chance, Hugh stopped in to see him, knowing he would be on his way within minutes. When he discovered Tudor lying in bed fully dressed he knew something critical had happened—the complaints were of nausea, coldness and some pain in the left arm. The desk clerk summoned help, which arrived virtually within minutes. The attending doctor made an immediate diagnosis—heart attack—and administered emergency treatment. Nevertheless, by the time the seventy-one-year-old Tudor entered the hospital's intensive care unit twenty-five minutes later, he went into fibrillation. The worst had happened. An expert cardiac team kept him from further disaster, though, and he passed the crisis.

Ever-inquisitive after recovery, Tudor took this latest clue to his advancing death in stride. For him, it was merely another step along nature's path—one that he obsessively commented on, one for which he'd been taking his philosophic pulse over some time already. But for Hugh, an alarm had been sounded. Now he would have to contemplate the idea of life without Tudor, an unthinkable proposition. Throughout their remaining years his chief concern seemed to be whether he would be unlucky enough to outlast Tudor. Actually, neither of them wanted longevity at the sacrifice of togetherness. Fate would smile on him who died first. Yes, Caroline, the lover is your best friend. No matter that he had been an albatross around your neck, an uncontrollable abuser, a dependent hellion, a jealous fishwife. Without him, there was nothing.

And vice versa. To preserve Tudor's life, Hugh took the initiative a step beyond doctor's orders. He designed a diet that not only cast out the offending fats and salt, but consisted exclusively of grains, fruits and vegetables. He put both himself and Tudor on this macrobiotic plan and observed it with strictest vigilance. The remaining eight weeks in Laguna became a convalescent period and a time when the two of them adjusted to a considerably simpler lifestyle. There would be no jumping back into rehearsals, even the teaching at UCI came to a halt, never to resume again. By the end of the calamitous winter retreat they were both many pounds slimmer; eventually Tudor would lose his robust demeanor and come to look ever more like the ascetic who rose at six to meditate, who pored over his prayer notes, who indulged no dietary vices. From that point on he spent more time corresponding with friends. Invariably those letters would reflect a good-natured mockery—of his infirmities or poor memory.

Over the next few years he would write to Marja from Laguna, referring to "the health diet that makes Hugh and me look like withered sylphs." He enjoyed his now-industrious correspondence. His need to feel connected to people had always been strong, despite the opposite impression he gave to many. But in these postcardiac days he actively drew relatives and friends close. Even Rambert mellowed for him in retrospect. When her former disciple wrote he did so entirely without rancor. Indeed, he could now properly idealize Madame. At the half-century mark of her Ballet Rambert came this message to the nonagenarian:

Dearest Mim,

Fifty years a company—That is truly magnificent—and I suppose record shattering. How about that!

Isn't it lucky that you can take all the adulation in stride— or else you would be puffed up with pride and vanity and such like miserable deadly sins. But meantime all of us humble disciples, being immature, can indulge them for any little parts we were favored by the gods to play in this beautiful saga.

Love, Antony

Earlier, on a greeting card, he scribbled: "Isn't it time we made your position as my fairy godmother legitimate—together with all your other blessed godchildren?"

And then there were the relatives. Tudor's late brother Robert, who had lived his whole adult life in New Zealand as a forest ranger, had given him a sister-in-law and nephews and nieces, all of whom he embraced through the mails. If anything were to happen to Hugh his immediate plan was to book a flight to New Zealand and "be with my family." Once, before his brother died, Tudor made a momentous visit there. But it was the letters, and visits from the nieces, that bound this family to him. These letters, a mix of candor and charm, were characterized by a graceful prose that flowed in streams of varied cadences. Just like his dance phrases. He could interject just the right lyric touch of philosophic musing, never anything too somber. He was a model correspondent—engaging, personable—and he always managed to remember and comment on details of the other's life.

Even while his brother Robert Cook was still alive, Tudor's chief correspondent in the family was his niece, Connaught Palmer. But the information he sought out—details of their childhood—required the cooperation of Robert, as in this letter fragment:

A propos the cows on the farm, I would like you to get Bob's reaction to the name Obenum. I think it was a place we reached by horse tram when we were taken as tiny tots to visit my father's Aunt Cass . . . maybe 1914? or thereabouts. Also, the other day I had the radio on and heard a piece for cello by Brahms being announced. Two minutes later, after a piano introduction, Rostropovich entered with the cello and I jumped because I saw my grandfather Cook sitting and playing in a house at Forest-Gate. The house I had absolutely forgotten.

But I think there was a greenhouse and it lay about 5 minutes' walk beyond the butcher shop. Does your father remember this house and did our grandfather play the cello or am I totally insane? He, happily, does not dwell on the past as much as I do, for he has a lot to occupy his mind. The weather here is still stinky and cold and after a winter of chills in Laguna we are getting fed up with it. . . . Love to you all, including your husband's relatives. AT [surrounded with little handdrawn hearts.]

He may not have been a climate poet like Wallace Stevens but Tudor typically elaborated on weather moods before getting to his text. "21st March—the first day of Spring and at last the sun has come out after weeks of typical rainy North Sea weather—*trés Anglais*—" The only thing, in fact, that he complained about without qualification was the weather. His other clear-voiced musings came couched in irony.

But letter writing hardly supplanted Tudor's career—even though he had given up the position of associate artistic director in favor of the titular Choreographer Emeritus. True, the relative constancy of his attention to Ballet Theatre between 1974 and 1978 was a thing of the past. Now, when he and the company both happened to be in Southern California at the same time he would not budge from Laguna or even consider attending a performance in Los Angeles. "I loathe Shrine Auditorium," he said of the mammoth barnlike theater where ABT played. His presence on the scene, though, could not be discounted. If anything, his artistic stock continued to rise on the world market.

The days when he felt something in common with the dancers, however, were gone. "I used to know people who happened to be dancers," he told Maria Karnilova. "Now I have dancers who are not even people." He was referring to the phenomenon of facelessness that marked the current crop of splendid technicians confronting him. They were stronger and more physically perfect specimens than their predecessors, but they also suffered a certain vapidity. Even Baryshnikov, who succeeded Lucia Chase and

Oliver Smith as director of the company in 1980, complained about the fact that his dancers "had not acquired the cultural baggage that goes into making an interesting artist." Yet Tudor had to entrust his fragile ballets to them. As always, but now with greater vigilance, he had to scavenge for his prime recruits—dancers who might show him the intelligence, the seriousness of purpose and the commitment he needed. Meeting those demands had never been a simple matter in the past, nor would it be now.

As the fortieth anniversary of *Pillar of Fire* approached Cynthia Gregory prepared to dance Hagar. It was 1982, some years after Sallie Wilson had vacated the role, and no one else had really claimed it. Gregory, who had danced in *Undertow* and other Tudor ballets, stood as Ballet Theatre's most regal American. The year in which she was promoted to principal status Tudor asked her if she would take a minor role in *Echoing of Trumpets*—"or do you have an *étoile* complex?" he wanted to know. He loved few things better than decrowning royalty. Still, *Pillar* was an appropriate acquisition for Gregory and she rehearsed it privately with him. "He always let me go early, though," recalled the dramatic ballerina. "The steps came easily, but I had the feeling I bored him." Then she suffered an injury which kept her on the sidelines for several months. They came together again at the dress rehearsal. "He told me that I would be fine—that was the last thing he ever said to me. After my debut, he didn't come backstage. A few days later Charles France [Baryshnikov's aide-de-camp] told me that 'they' said I must never do *Pillar* again. Meanwhile everyone was avoiding me. I felt like a leper. After hearing this judgment I decided there was nothing to do but quit. I resigned from the company right away."

Eventually Gregory would rejoin ABT. She was a highly valuable dancer and a star with a considerable following. "Whenever Tudor saw me, he would look away and I did the same. Years later there was a partial thaw. We would say hello and goodbye, nothing more. But I always regret not being direct, not telling him I was sorry, not asking him what he found so detestable. As things turned out I never got the chance."

At that fatal performance "Tudor turned the color of purple," recalled Lise Houlton, then an unknown dancer who replaced Gregory as Hagar. "I was backstage the night Cynthia danced *Pillar* and he brushed past me, asking what I thought of the performance. I said it was a beautiful ballet and he just grunted. I don't know exactly why he favored me over her. I know I had a harder time with the steps than she did. In rehearsals he took great delight in how I struggled with those steps. This was his way of getting close to people. He was captivated by their different agonies and went beyond the street level sense of the word."

Hugh didn't attend rehearsals much. And Tudor seemed to be of two minds regarding them: happy, involved and energetic—as he was with the dancers, especially Lise Houlton—or despondent and fatigued, as in his descriptions to Maude Lloyd and Therese Langfield. Houlton remembered a particular *Jardin* rehearsal. A great feeling of frustration came over him and as he began to lecture the dancers on how they lacked the force of imagination, how they failed miserably at conveying a nocturnal garden with people waltzing, "he got up and swept across the studio with such ardor and elegance that my mouth hung open. Elaine Kudo and I looked at each other as though to say, 'This is one of those marvelous moments we'll never forget.' " Such a demonstration was rare, though, for Tudor. He refrained from telling dancers to "do it this way, not that way." His preference was for verbal images. For *Jardin* he would tell the cast "to start the ballet with a sigh and end it with a sigh." Often those who did the best were the ones who came from modern dance and who, like Houlton, weren't good "with the knitted brow." Tudor's name for that brand of interpretation was "ham-acting"; he couldn't stomach it and later suggested that Gregory was guilty of just that.

He probably wouldn't have pinpointed the defect, though, had she the temerity to ask. It was his inclination to dodge questions—earnest or otherwise—from those he'd cast out of heaven. Prejudices died hard, if at all. Typically, his remarks were intended to throw people off guard. He built a lifelong reputation for saying things he didn't really mean and vice versa. At a board meeting in 1977, Lucia Chase introduced Joyce Moffatt as the company's new general manager. "I'm so delighted Joyce is here," Chase began, "even though I hate women ma—" Tudor cut her off midword to interject, "So do I." A flustered Chase added the qualifying part of her statement: "women managers." Everyone laughed at Tudor's little confessional joke. But it illustrated how he used ambivalence as a social ploy. Yes, he hated women, especially some of them. But he said so jokingly. People then assumed the opposite to be true. He had them coming and going.

His Peck's Bad Boy image was more enjoyable now that it took on a relatively benign character. And as the eighties saw him grow progressively frail, even his bitterness subsided somewhat. There were kind remembrances for Chase, who, he recalled, showed her heroism decades ago by sitting up all night in a coach along with the dancers. Since hers and Smith's retirements there was no one to encourage him to do much for ABT. Jane Hermann, who "adored Tudor," would not take over until 1989. In 1983, though, he told the new director Baryshnikov that he would be agreeable to reviving *Dim Lustre*. His last confrontation with the work, New York City Ballet's 1964 production, left him feeling dissatisfied, to say the least. By mounting it now he could get the bad taste out of his mouth. But when he looked over his casting prospects and the company's estate he became disheartened. Who would dance it? He called a meeting with the four who most interested him—Gelsey Kirkland, Lise Houlton, Magali Messac and Leslie Browne. Everyone thought the preliminaries had already been discussed and fully expected rehearsals to begin. "Instead Mr. Tudor sat us down for a talk," said Houlton. "He told us how disillusioned he was with Ballet Theatre, implying that its direction by Misha and Charles left much to be desired. But he spoke in a very dignified way—no petty backbiting. In fact, it sounded more like a swan song than an explanation for why we would not be doing *Dim*

Lustre. And then he addressed each one of us, lovingly, without harshness, giving a little caption to our problems."

He ended the session with Kirkland. "And only Gelsey can tell us what she's after, why she's trying to destroy herself." His withdrawal of the ballet left everyone stunned. Was Tudor resigning, thumbing his nose at the administration? Baryshnikov, who tried to wear two hats—that of the company's most celebrated dancer and that of chief—was already beset with criticism. He wanted the wagons to circle, not roll away. But he needn't have worried. Tudor was hardly deserting. He would cast and rehearse those of his works that were already in repertory; he just didn't find the present a propitious time for a difficult revival.

Even when, in 1985, he finally agreed to go ahead with *Dim Lustre* the outcome fell far below the hoped-for standard. The decor, replicated from 1943, was dowdy and ineffectual, the lighting a disaster. In a long letter to the designer, Tudor explained how intricately cinematic the blackouts were. They had to signal flashbacks, they had to denote a change from past to present, one facilitated by memory and mirror images. Like a voice in the wind, he saw none of his warnings heeded. The blackouts were handled clumsily, to the ballet's detriment.

Throughout the rehearsals Hugh was always at Tudor's side. By this point he had taken on a stronger persona, that of protector. While Tudor had his physical strength Hugh functioned as a necessary adjunct, often an emotional one. But now he clearly was Tudor's legs. What Hugh always needed, in fact, was to be needed—as he hoped Diana Adams would. And had he become a father that role too might have enhanced his desire to lead and control. Happily, Tudor had to rely on Hugh—to get him to rehearsals, to accompany him everywhere. As one became weaker the other grew only stronger. Tudor deferred to Hugh except on the very fewest issues. During the *Dim Lustre* rehearsals, for instance, there was debate over whether to grant an interview for advance publicity to *The New York Times*. First there was consent, then it was withdrawn—each time Hugh seemed to have the upper hand. Jennifer Dunning finally got the go-ahead to attend rehearsals, speak to Tudor and write the article. "Tudor confused me with another reporter," recalled Dunning, "and asked if I still took classes with Martha Graham. Not wanting to challenge his memory, I just said no, rather than explain that I had never studied modern dance. But then I became afraid that he would sneer wickedly at me and accuse me of not being the person he thought I was." Even at a feeble seventy-seven, Tudor remained fearsome.

But not to his peers, of course. Once, converting his serious concerns to humor, he reported to Maude on an illness of Hugh's: "He promised he wouldn't last past the fourteenth and here it is the twenty-eighth. He lied and I'll never believe him again!" Another time he wrote about an opening of *Jardin* at ABT. "Neither Hugh nor I attended. The rehearsals were awful—quel fatigue!" To Therese he wrote:

> . . . having to discard the gorgeous and never-to-return joys of the past, we'll return to the present and the antiques of New York—Tudor 76 Laing 73 and Chenpo (the oldest and frailest and most to be pitied at 13 years). We have become home bodies, don't like entertaining, but will with a little pressure— easily applied—because we have little resistance to blandishment. So, this is a note, mid-year, to tell you that you have been a treasured part of our lives.
>
> Love, Antony.

And five months later:

> . . . Some things get bigger, some smaller. I know I'm gently shrinking—shorter, skinnier, balder, more toothless, etc. You name it! But life is still to be cherished and it is great to have Hugh around. We try to look after each other but with memories that bring great strange, momentary lapses, it becomes a touch & go situation—as ever! So I am cheerful anyway but not enough to join in the rollicksome game of Xmas cards. A barbaric custom, I've decided. So I'm just mailing loving

thoughts to my best and longest friends and Therese is right at the top of the list. Take care of each other.

Antony

But to Maude came a doleful confession:

I've become too forgetful, too old, too lacking in energy, too prone to cantankerous irascibility and superciliousness. What an ugly thing to arrive at! Was I always like that? How is it that even your best friends won't tell you?

The Sound of His Voice

THE TELEPHONE RANG. It was Roger Stevens on the line from Washington, D.C. "Mr. Tudor? I am so pleased to say you've been nominated to receive this year's Kennedy Center Honor. Congratulations." The official greeting arrived in the mail several days later. It was the award previously given Balanchine, Graham, de Mille, Robbins—the most prestigious one this nation can confer on figures in the performing and popular arts. So. Antony Tudor had not been forgotten by the highest jury in the land, after all. To whatever degree his self-doubt had been fed by being passed over formerly, the score, in 1986, was now settled.

And other juries had pinned notable merit badges to his lapel as well. Recognition had come in 1985 from London's Royal Academy of Dancing, where he finally received the Queen Elizabeth Coronation Award, in 1976 from Brandeis University—the Creative Arts Medal—and in 1974 from *Dance Magazine*. But

New York's Handel Medallion, the Capezio Award and one he shared with Martha Graham, the first Dance/USA National Honors, all fell to him in the bonanza year, 1986. In what he liked to call his dotage he would be fêted—despite the interference Hugh ran, for the "best friend" did not relish these fêtes. They took Antony away from him. And Antony was his exclusive property. Years earlier, Capezio, the dance wear mogul, wanted to name Tudor as its award recipient. But Hugh, in a typically possessive and suspicious protest, persuaded him that the offer was an insult—too little, too late. By the second time around, however, Capezio got an acceptance. No matter how controlling Hugh needed to be, Tudor would make the crucial decisions—especially now, with time running out.

Better than anyone, Hugh understood what the Kennedy Center Honor meant to Tudor. Yet he would deny the man he hovered over and guided and protected the pleasure of his company at this moment of ultimate ceremonial splendor. It was America's version of a royal party, with the president of the United States on hand and the whole country watching via telecast. Long ago the implacable choreographer had forfeited his chance to become Sir Antony Tudor—by emigrating from England. But he was not above accepting the next best thing. And Hugh behaved predictably—depriving Tudor of the final satisfaction by refusing to attend. Out of pathological spitefulness, some say, and despite Tudor's begging. "Why didn't you go to the Honors ceremony?" Joyce Moffatt asked Hugh, a few weeks later. "I didn't have a white tie," he told the former ABT manager. "C'mon Hugh," she replied, letting him know his flimsy excuse was transparent.

By the time Tudor reconciled himself to Hugh's holdout tactic, he had already determined to thumb his nose at the spoiler and enjoy the event fully. He let no disappointment linger. He had lived a lifetime with this strangely vulnerable, willful child and now was no time to question the behavior. Besides, a côterie of stylish admirers (former students) had gathered—one of them with a Park Avenue address; these women knew exactly how to assist their favorite wizened imp for his journey to Washington, D.C., and his "palace" appearance in the capital. There was lots of fussing over, even without Hugh, who, in fact, would not have gotten into the proper indulgent spirit. And in these days of dietary restrictions Tudor reveled in his few, furtive slides back to pleasure.

Shortly after he received the official White House notice he wrote to Therese:

> This has been my summer of being fêted & honored with odds & ends & now when I thought it was all over, now arrives this last one & Hugh says I've got to send you a copy of the announcement. So it is herewith; all our old friends like Martha Graham, Agnes de Mille, Jerome Robbins have already had it, so I should be better informed. All I can think is that my dinner jacket would qualify as an antique, not having been worn for about thirty five years. It is obviously a fairly impressive irritation & again, all I think of is that when Fred got his knighthood he spoke frequently of its troubles. Being a "Sir" was very expensive because he had to travel as "SOMEONE," which meant more expensive hotel rooms, bigger tips & such pains in the rear-end. I'll get through it, I hope & still be able to spend most of my waking hours on the subway system. How are we doing. Slowing down, down, but going down fighting—doing our morning stretching exercises religiously. It now takes me about five minutes to struggle out of bed every day; the knees are not as flexible and my adrenaline seems never to be available, and with all our humid 90 degree weather, it has been like breathing in soup or milk, which is much worse with Hugh & his emphysema. Isn't this a jolly note. Better stop now or else. Embraces to you and Charles.
>
> Antony.

The awards ceremony took place December 7, 1986, and it turned out to be a reunion of sorts. Among the other honorees was violinist Yehudi Menuhin, married to Diana Gould from the Ballet Club. As they all convened—the award recipients, their escorts and friends—Diana, estranged from her former choreographer for half a century, walked over to him. "Antony, it's Diana, old Diana," said the now gray-haired, gaunt woman, who had been a statuesque beauty when they both trod the boards of Rambert's Mercury Theatre. "It's high time for Tudor to receive this award," she went on. "I'm thrilled for your success. You know, I loved working with you all those years ago." He smiled—"with disdain," she said—and replied: "Yes, I suppose you did. Even when you altered the steps."

Just following the Kennedy Center Honors Tudor and Hugh set off on their annual migration to Laguna Beach. This time— this last time they would make the journey together—a painful prospect loomed: Nora Kaye's death. Diagnosed with an inoperable brain tumor, she was installed at her palatial Brentwood home in a hospital bed. Her loyal Laguna Beach contingent made its sorrow-weary way to Los Angeles a couple of times over the next months. And every afternoon Herbert Ross telephoned with a report on her condition. Once, when Nora bravely set up a little footprint ceremony for the Dance Gallery collection of California choreographer Bella Lewitzky, Tudor and Hugh agreed to come and cast their famous feet in cement for posterity. At this point Nora was gravely ill, but rallied for the occasion and played host from her wheelchair. She and Herbert treated them to a hearty lox-and-bagels brunch on the patio. The sun shone. They sipped champagne and Tudor saw his muse smiling. "I feel better today," she said. "I think I'm going to make it."

She didn't. On February 28, 1987, Tudor's Fanny Brice died. The one who called him "Toodie-Froodie" and defused any lingering superciliousness, the one who attached her great dramatic talent to his inspiration, the one who commanded his unending love. To her funeral, where bank upon bank of mauve-to-pink flowers blanketed the whole front of the nonsectarian chapel, came the ranking hordes of Hollywood royalty—notably, Jane Fonda, Barbra Streisand, Shirley Maclaine, Bette Midler, Anne Bancroft. Few would recognize the two elderly men sitting alone in the front row, one of them alarmingly frail and skeletal, the other with a deeply creviced face and shock of steely gray hair. Who would ever know that they were the survivors of Nora Kaye's most important pas de trois? As first one person then another eulogized her these two sat impassively. And then, in a crashing, heaving, convulsive eruption, Tudor began to sob and sob and sob. It was a stupefying sight. His whole body shook and trembled. The British stoic turned Zen Buddhist who, all his life, had prided himself on transcending pain and masking vulnerability, surrendered to it now. Muriel Bentley, who could not help but notice and be moved by this unimaginable spectacle, reached out. Still shaking, he clutched her to him.

He and Hugh returned to New York a few weeks later. In the copious correspondence he kept up these last few months there was no mention to those who knew her fairly well of Nora's death. Nor had he written to anyone of his mother's or father's death, decades ago. Certain sorrows stayed hermetically sealed. After his mother became a widow she lived an exceedingly lonely life, sometimes complaining that whole days would pass without her hearing the sound of her own voice. But Florence Cook's son would be spared that degree of solitude.

There were rehearsals to attend, for one thing. And even though it was only with great effort that he got himself to the Ballet Theatre studio at Broadway and Twentieth Street, once there he made a difference. He was the Grand Old Man of the company, but not in name only. A stranger might hear his strained, weak voice and notice his gait—small, shuffling steps—and disbelieve that he could help anyone do anything. And while he was aware of his diminished power, he bore it in silence. Once roused he could still be an enlightening force and one day Baryshnikov spotted him sitting alone on a bench in a long corridor, his hands poised on his lap. He didn't know what impelled him to do it, perhaps it was the still-powerful image Tudor cut—an ancient Chinese philosopher, maybe, or a venerable seer transported beyond the mundane activities of mere ballet dancers.

Whatever, Baryshnikov came over, kneeled before him and kissed his hand. Without breaking his repose, the master uttered "I like that," with a purity and directness that asked for no reply.

Curiously, Baryshnikov had been smarting the past year over a remark made by the Grand Old Man: "I suppose the Russian director likes my ballets, but for all I know Lucia may have stipulated at her retirement that they stay in the repertory." No great vote of confidence in that remark—but then Tudor was known for withholding endorsements. He didn't play politics. Never had. Baryshnikov, in at least one speech, made reference to the remark, vigorously denying any lack of regard for the Tudor works. Apparently, he sensed Tudor's disapproval. It was no secret that the Grand Old Man looked askance at the ballet heartthrob's commercial exploits, which would later include manufacturing his own perfume, "Misha," and a line of dance wear. "Tudor said there was something shameful in wasting time and talent on Hollywood soap operas and Broadway star turns with Liza Minelli," recalled Marja Odell.

Meanwhile there were those whose loyalty did not come into question. Sallie Wilson, for instance. She was assisting him with the *Pillar of Fire* rehearsals on Saturday, April 18. "He was already in the studio when I arrived. My students had given me a birthday party, which I was coming from, and I remember floating through the door, in a cloud of balloons. Tudor kept on with what he was doing, glanced at me as though I always appeared this way, and asked no questions."

It was an important rehearsal. Ballet Theatre would be opening its Met season in two days with *Pillar*. Forty-five years had passed since the ballet's momentous premiere and its maker had been through countless rehearsals for countless opening nights. But history has a way of dissipating, so that the present takes on its full importance, so that the moment is all that matters. Perhaps it is prescience that lends specialness to a given event and perhaps that's why this rehearsal was inspired. Tudor spotted "three critical points that had not been right for a long time and fixed them," recalled Wilson—smudged details that somehow got carried from one performance to the next. Now, he was clear-eyed, vital and engaged in a way that she had not seen in a long time.

The next day was Easter Sunday. Hugh came over to the Zen Institute. Of the two of them he was certainly hardier and could make the subway trip without much exertion. Antony cooked dinner in the evening but instead of Hugh's going home, as usual, he decided to spend the night. The trains weren't too safe after dark. Both of them had already confronted muggers. And perhaps he had a premonition. Antony complained of fatigue and went to bed early. Some hours later, after both had been asleep, Hugh heard muffled cries from the kitchen. He came running. There was Antony on the cold floor in the dark. Hugh scolded him for not having turned on the light. He helped him up, took him to the bathroom, gave him "his heart pills," and settled him back in bed. The quiet lasted only a few minutes. Then came those awful rasping sounds. Hugh quickly moved onto Antony's bed and held him in his arms. The two of them could hear nothing but those final gasps of breath before a life ends and the survivor is left alone. It was over in a minute.

Tuesday Ballet Theatre opened at the Met. The man synonymous with its history—the man who struggled heroically to survive its vicissitudes, as well as his own—was gone. What words would be expressed to convey his passing into oblivion? The rightful spokesman was the company's director. Certainly, his title obliged him to make a curtain speech prior to the performance. But "when Baryshnikov was told it was his duty to act as chief mourner . . . he balked. He said he wouldn't do it, and that was that. Someone else could go out and pay tribute to Tudor. Some people at ABT thought he was acting from pure pique, the bad temper of a spoiled brat who was being forced to remember that there was a world beyond the one he knew, a history beyond the one he was so single-mindedly trying to create." The staff finally prevailed on him, however, and he made a brief, rather perfunctory statement: "Tonight we want to honor

[Tudor's] memory. His whole life was dancing, and he was truly loved by this company. We remember him with great affection and gratitude."

No one who knew Hugh believed that he would stay alive long. Chenpo, to whom he had transferred all his love, had died the year before. Now Antony. "No one needs me anymore," he wailed. "I have no one to take care of." Those who tried to console him and visit him and offer their friendship were met with hysterically angry rages on the phone. He never really believed they cared for him, rather that their bond with Antony brought these people to his door. After hurling a string of intolerable abuses at Annabelle Lyon and Muriel Bentley and Sono Osato, and later—long distance—even Maude Lloyd, he slammed the receiver down. Except for one or two caretakers he cut himself off and became a wretched recluse. "He was alone, bitter, sick, miserable, and full of hatred," said Bentley. "Inevitably he would will himself to die."

His wounds—the original wounds to do with various stigmas—never healed. They were only exacerbated by his partner's death. On the day after Antony died in his arms Hugh cried out in the lawyer's offices not at being bereft, but at being scorned by Alf and Florence Cook. Wrongly, he would not let go of the idea that they rued his relationship with their son. It wasn't true. Florence's letters to Antony invariably acknowledged Hugh. "Love to Hugh," she often added in her sign-off. In fact, he brooded over the will. Although Tudor left him well provided for—having dispersed a sizable estate into accounts all over the world—Hugh was neither named executor nor trustee of the ballets.

For all intents and purposes, he shut himself off. A few custodial types saw to his needs and heard out all his ranting tirades. He emerged in public for Tudor's June memorial, which was held in the Juilliard Theater and drew the entire New York dance community. The last to speak on a program that included Agnes de Mille, Jerome Robbins, Clive Barnes, Sallie Wilson, Baryshnikov and others, he walked to the microphone in a dignified manner. "Tudor gave so much, more than he ever took," said Laing of his soulmate. "He asked for very little. Just perfection. He was a very simple person. A very complicated simple person." The words were choice. They hardly reflected his state of emotional disarray. Several months later Ballet Theatre exhorted him to help with a revival of *Gala Performance*. Everyone agreed that it would be beneficial for him to have an involvement in something. He agreed to assist Sallie Wilson in the staging and to design new sets and costumes. But it took little to incur his ferocious wrath previously—and now even less.

Sallie bore the brunt of his rampages. He struck her once at a rehearsal. Another time, when she visited him at his apartment, he knocked her down and bodily threw her out of the place. "He was on the edge of madness," said Glen Tetley, in relaying these incidents, "and she was quite scared." But Hugh's contact with Ballet Theatre proved helpful. The *Gala Performance* premiere was to take place at the new Orange County Performing Arts Center. Everyone encouraged him to be there and to return to Laguna, which he did.

The staff at Vacation Village reserved the same room, 307, the one he had always shared with Antony. And Hildegarde Huestis, a former journalist and ballet fan who had befriended the two of them in the last couple of years, tended to his every need and wish. But he was quite alone, quite miserable. He often stood outside his door leaning on the rail and looking out at the ocean. Or he lingered in the small lobby, sometimes finding a staffer to talk to. "I have three doctors," he told an indifferent desk clerk who didn't know him. "It's very important for me to stay physically fit because of my work," he said, embellishing the truth. To those he wanted to hold at bay he reeled off his ills, his low weight, his physical discomfort. He wore his infirmities like a hero's decoration. But when Marja visited him the true story came out. He confessed a lifetime's burdens to her. "My marriage to Diana was the saddest mistake of all," he said. "I ruined her life and caused her pain. Antony, too. I hurt him terribly." It all gushed in a projectile stream, like a purge of guilt. "I know I'm going to die soon," he cried, "and I can't wait."

The next day, while crossing Pacific Coast Highway, the driver of an approaching car did not see him in the crosswalk until it was too late. He suffered broken ribs and bruises from the accident, nothing life threatening. But the doctors knew he would get his wish: they discovered bone cancer. Hugh returned to New York. One year and three weeks after his Antony died, so did he.

Epilogue

"I'M ENOUGH OF A MEGALOMANIAC to want a hundred books written about me," Antony Tudor told the British dance critic Fernau Hall. But none ever came to pass, despite attempts by various writers to gain his cooperation on a biography.

"Want nothing, accept everything" was clearly one Zen Buddhist dictum that Tudor had trouble living by. With all his creative and intellectual accomplishment—a record, in fact, that put him on an exalted plane in the dance world—he never achieved the internal freedom of wanting nothing and accepting everything, regardless of his adherence to this body of Eastern teachings.

But one afternoon in Laguna Beach, California, he and I sat across a table from each other. It was February 1986—a typically mild day, cleansed by a recent shower, with the sun softly lighting a few billowy white clouds as they bounded high across the sky. I had arrived at the winter haven where he and Hugh Laing regularly escaped the harsh months of New York's climate. Our scheduled interview was to result in a profile of Tudor, one that would serve the *Los Angeles Times* with a feature article publicizing American Ballet Theatre's upcoming season in Los Angeles.

He met me in the lobby and during those first moments I tried to suppress my shock at his appearance. Here was just a shadow of the man. Frail and underweight, painfully neat in his nondescript, ill-fitting clothes, he no longer projected an image of authority. Not that his authority ever rode on a puffed-up chest or any other trait of self-importance. Still, I expected some hint of the austere manner evidenced in photos and descriptions of his behavior. There was none.

After the meeting and greeting amenities he said, in his cloudy voice, that the restaurant where he held a lunch reservation was several blocks away. He shuffled effortfully toward the lobby door, with me at his side. I checked my instinct to open it, sensing that he would claim the duty; he did. Tudor was not about to discard a lifetime of chivalry for the sake of some pesky physical weakness. As we made our way along the narrow street, he allowed me to entertain him with a surreal freeway story—a near-accident I encountered on the way, with two cars in a slow-motion spin but no collision. As he became involved his voice grew somewhat stronger. He also asked questions, the kindly conversational type, about my family.

By the time we arrived at the oceanfront restaurant, a spacious pink-hued room in the Laguna Beach Hotel, Tudor was wondering aloud what kind of relationship I had with my husband and college-age sons. "Are they afraid of you?" he inquired, in keeping with his sensor for intrepid women. "To the contrary," I laughed. "I'm afraid of *them*." He seemed satisfied with the humorous exchange. But more than that, he took satisfaction in my agreeing to tell him whatever he wanted to know.

The tone for the next two hours was set. This would not be a hardcore interview properly focusing on Ballet Theatre's revival of *Dim Lustre* and limited to matters detailing this ballet or that production. Rather it became a freeflowing, open-ended dialogue, touching on movies and concert singers and the attitudes of winter residents at Vacation Village. "I don't much like them," he proudly asserted. "Neither do they like me. We tolerate each other." These were the days when Tudor made such pronouncements of misanthropy. Indeed, he wore them like a banner. So long as he was being accused of ill will, he might as well own up to it in the most forthright manner. During our discussion the originator of the so-called psychological ballet was still a refreshing exemplar of crypticspeak. And a guileless, candid one. He leaped nearly with glee to answer the notorious charges and ad hominem condemnations. "Dancers used to find you fearsome and aloof," I said, with a conspiratorial smile. "There's no mystery about that," he answered mischievously. "I was icy and distant." What irony. Here was the dance-maker who plotted the intricacies of contemporary human yearning in his landmark ballets. Yet he talked about being "solitary and not crazy about people."

At no point, however, was he retiring. Another seventy-eight-year-old with such moribund signs might have withdrawn his interests from the world, shriveling into his immediate web of physical difficulties. But the kind of creativity that was Tudor's suggests a fundamental connection with his sources of inspiration: music, theater, literature—all things that speak of the human sensibility. He would not likely give them up.

Once we were seated, my initial perception of him as feeble fell away. His blue-green eyes penetrated dead target across the table. They glowed with a benign intensity, though not necessarily looking for a response, just contact. An imposing presence, he was lean, linear, like a Giacometti sculpture—or a hairless monk sitting tall.

Apparently he felt both comfortable and stimulated. His talk became more vigorous, his smile beatific. He seemed to enjoy the alert dialogue. I delighted in his candor, the absence of platitudes; he performed. The food arrived and the aroma of his omelet with scallops—verboten to macrobiotic dieters such as Tudor and Laing—evoked memories.

"My father was a butcher," said the man who almost never divulged anything personal. "I remember the fragrance of fresh prosciutto in his shop." But perhaps because my manner was more conversational than formal, or because my questions were broad, rather than pinpointed to his ballets, or for whatever reason, Tudor suggested something wholly improbable: "Next time, a book," he said, almost as a non sequitur.

I let the offer drop. At the time, writing a biography had no place in an already crowded picture. Quite possibly, he sensed that I was disinclined to assume so major a project—even with a figure I admired extravagantly—and therefore he felt free to make the offer. Also, because others had badgered him for authorization to do his biography, he may have thought that just by giving me the nod it was a done deal.

Halfway through the service, a young waiter approached the table. He apologized for interrupting and then blurted out that he had to ask "who you are because I can see this must be an important discussion. I'd just love to know what great things are being planned. A movie or something?"

I introduced Tudor grandly, but not too grandly. The waiter beamed. Tudor beamed. How simple and direct his gratification. How unspoiled was this closet megalomaniac. On the one hand he would never apprise strangers of his specialized celebrity. On the other, he carried no presumptions. Yet it was hard for me to reconcile what I saw with what I knew—that at least earlier in his life Tudor harbored crippling self-doubts and nagging disappointment. It didn't matter that dancers the world over venerated him or that he single-handedly illuminated ballet as a serious, probing art form. Tudor could never become a genuine, full-blown megalomaniac. There was too much self-abnegation for that.

The profile I wrote ran in the *Los Angeles Times* on Sunday, March 16. That same day, "El" Gabriel stopped by Vacation

Village to have brunch with Tudor and Hugh. They all commented on the article and then Tudor announced to "El," "And isn't it nice, we're doing a book together. So I won't be one of those dead people who have books written about them." They stayed in Laguna until early April, with Tudor apparently noting my frequent byline. Meanwhile I knew nothing of his expectation that a book would proceed and therefore never called him. In fact, I'd put his comment completely out of mind. A month later I received the following letter:

> Ever since "that" appeared I have been meaning to write this "thankyou" note, because everyone has praised your article, and I sense what a busy woman you are, contributing, contributing & getting around, getting around. So very, very busy and I'm glad you took time off for the interview with me.
> Now we are back in the wet, racy springtime of New York— dank.
> But you get around so much, even for *Dance Magazine*.
> I'm very happy that you are so in demand, & with good reason.
> Thank you again, I am,
> Yours truly
> Antony Tudor

Only after rereading it much later, did I notice the emphasis on my being "busy" and the possibly sarcastic implication that I had squeezed Antony Tudor into a packed schedule. If so, how sadly mistaken that notion. Were his words conveying hurt or defensiveness? After all, he had made the supreme invitation— to write his biography—and I had never even acknowledged it.

In a subsequent letter, following my proposition to him a year later to do the very thing he suggested, he referred to "the book you say you wished to write about me." Somehow he never trusted the sincerity of interest in him—mine or anyone else's.

It was the end of December 1986, when I rang him again in Laguna. First, congratulations on the Kennedy Center Honor. And then:

"Mr. Tudor, I want to propose something, but you need not respond right away. A book. Maybe the same one you mentioned last February. The one that's been incubating in my head lately."

"Oh, dear, oh, dear," he said, which I took to mean: "I want to, but I don't want to."

"Think it over," I said. "I'm leaving for winter vacation with my family. I'll call you when we return, around the middle of January. We can meet in person, perhaps, and discuss it."

He seemed to like the prospect, eagerly mentioning lunch again at the same restaurant and adding: "We were gorgeous there." When I next called to set a date he expressed more interest in lunch at the Laguna Beach Hotel than the informal visit I had in mind. But at least we made an appointment. A week later, however, he called to postpone it. "Unexpected dental work," he said.

I told him that meanwhile I was trying to get a proposal together, just a rough outline highlighting his career. Could he or Hugh recall an anecdote—something characteristic, something that a prospective publisher might find engaging? He told me to call back in a few days. They would put their minds to the task. His tone was extremely friendly and approving then; it remained so throughout several other calls, in which I reported that a high-placed editor—whom he turned out to know—was already interested in the project, if it ever came to pass. Finally, he apologized for not having an anecdote at hand.

But next up was our meeting. "Be sure to ring before you leave Los Angeles," he said.

The appointed day, February 23, finally arrived. And I put through a call to Vacation Village. The operator rang his room. There was no answer. I left word that I would arrive sometime after half past twelve that afternoon.

One year nearly to the day from my previous trip to Tudor I set out on this new mission. It was a rainy, blustery day—the kind that blew my tin can of a compact car all over the freeway. Precisely at half past twelve I arrived. The clerk rang Room 307 and within a few minutes he appeared in the lobby.

His expression was stony, his mouth drawn into a narrow line, his color gray. I was flabbergasted at the sight. "Why didn't you call?" he asked reproachfully. "I did. You weren't here."

He went on to say that he positively wouldn't be doing a book with me or anyone. Instead, he was writing his memoirs ("every word about my life")—to be published posthumously. I was not about to get up and leave at this revelation. Nor did I try to dissuade him. It seemed important, nonetheless, to spend as much time as he would spare with me. For no clear reason, just an instinct.

I found myself bridging the chasm. There was no need, I told him, to make a decision one way or the other, regarding a book. I picked up the threads of previous conversations and he began to soften. We talked about his Kennedy Center Honor. It had taken place two months ago and I had watched the delayed telecast. Margot Fonteyn was touching, I said. He agreed, explaining that "Rudolf [Nureyev] was originally supposed to speak but found himself in a schedule conflict."

"You looked especially elegant in your tuxedo," I said, because he did and because I could understand that a small vestige of vanity remained even for Tudor. "That's because I'm gorgeous," he quipped. Somehow we got to the subject of *A Room with a View,* the movie based on E. M. Forster's novel. He considered it marvelous, not just on its own merit, but—as I suspected— because of his identity as an Englishman.

"Even more marvelous the second time I saw it," he said, "than the first. I could feel the tears rolling down my face when the credits ran up the screen against the background music . . . that beautiful voice and Puccini . . ."

Tudor crying. Everyone who has ever seen his ballets could vouch for his depth of feeling. But, crying? An unimaginable sight. He loved every detail of the film, including the choice of Kiri Te Kanawa who sang "O Mio Babbino Caro" from *Gianni Schicchi.* He agreed that her British-styled Italian fit the material perfectly. How understandable that Forster's Edwardian love story, with its English characters conflicted over propriety and passion, would capture him.

We talked a little about Nora Kaye, who now lay dying. ("She caught up with me—traveling from protegée to equal over half a lifetime. Time turns relationships around.") We talked about *Shadow of the Wind,* his forgotten 1948 ballet, one that dancer Muriel Bentley had described to me. When I relayed to him the gesture that will be remembered by all who saw it—The Abandoned Wife picking up tears from her lap and one by one swallowing them—he stopped me.

"Not like that," he said, slightly altering the gesture, "like this." I believed then that he could appreciate concretely why his assistance with a book about his life and his ballets would be invaluable. Forty-five minutes after our meeting began he got up and said he had to be in his room for Herbert's phone call, a report on Nora.

"You're resolute about this project, aren't you?" he said. "Yes," I admitted, feeling a tinge of optimism because it was he who brought the subject up.

"Well, would you promise to tell me everything, even the most intimate details of your life, if I were to agree?" he teased, smiling a serious smile and locking his eyes with mine.

"I have nothing to hide," I joked. "Neither do you, really."

It was left that I would send him a proposal, outlining the scope of the book. Five days later Nora died. Better to postpone this business. I certainly didn't want to impose on him now. Shortly afterward he and Hugh returned to New York. Six weeks later he was dead.

BIBLIOGRAPHY

Andersson, Gerd & Aberle, Viola, *Antony Tudor* 1985 film documentary.

Baryshnikov, Mikhail. *Baryshnikov at Work*. Edited by Charles France. New York: Knopf, 1976.

Balanchine, George. *Balanchine's New Complete Stories of the Great Ballets*. Edited by Francis Mason. Garden City, New York: Doubleday, 1968.

Barnes, Clive. *Inside American Ballet Theatre*. New York: Hawthorn Books, 1977.

Briggs, Asa. *A Social History of England*. New York: Viking, 1984.

Buckle, Richard. *In the Wake of Diaghilev*. New York: Holt, Rinehart and Winston, 1983.

————. *George Balanchine, Ballet Master*. In collaboration with John Taras. New York: Random House, 1988.

Cohen, Selma Jeanne. *Antony Tudor Part Two: The Years in America*. Brooklyn: Dance Perspectives, 1963.

————, and Pischl, A. J.. *The American Ballet Theatre: 1940–1960*. Brooklyn: Dance Perspectives #6, 1960.

Chujoy, Anatole. *The New York City Ballet*. New York: Knopf, 1953.

————, and Manchester, P. W. (compilers and editors) *The Dance Encyclopedia*. New York: Simon and Schuster, 1967.

Clarke, Mary. *Dancers of Mercury*. London: Adam and Charles Black, 1962.

Coton, A. V. *Writings on Dance 1938–68*. London: Dance Books, 1975.

Croce, Arlene. *Going to the Dance*. New York: Knopf, 1982.

De Mille, Agnes. *Dance to the Piper*. Boston: Little, Brown, 1952.

————. *Lizzie Borden: A Dance of Death*. Boston: Little Brown, 1968.

————. *Speak to Me, Dance with Me*. Boston: Little, Brown, 1973.

Denby, Edwin. *Looking at the Dance*. New York: Horizon Press, 1949.

Fraser, John. *Private View*. New York: Bantam, 1988.

Gruen, John. *The Private World of Ballet*. New York: Viking, 1975.

Hall, Fernau. *An Anatomy of Ballet*. London: Andrew Melrose, 1953.

Haskell, Arnold. *Balletomania Then & Now*. New York: Knopf, 1977.

Kirkland, Gelsey, and Lawrence, Greg. *Dancing on My Grave*. New York: Doubleday, 1987.

Kirstein, Lincoln. *Thirty Years: The New York City Ballet*. New York: Knopf, 1978.

Koegler, Horst. *The Concise Oxford Dictionary of Ballet*. Oxford: Oxford University Press, 1972.

Makarova, Natalia. *A Dance Autobiography*. Edited by Gennady Smakov. New York: Knopf, 1979.

Newman, Barbara. *Striking a Balance*. Boston: Houghton Mifflin, 1982.

Noble, Peter (editor). *British Ballet*. London: Skelton Robinson, 1949.

Osato, Sono. *Distant Dances*. New York: Knopf, 1980.

Payne, Charles. *American Ballet Theatre*. New York: Knopf, 1978.

Percival, John. *Antony Tudor Part One: The Years in England*. Brooklyn: Dance Perspectives, 1963.

Rambert, Marie. *Quicksilver*. London: Macmillan, 1972.

Reynolds, Nancy. *Repertory in Review*. New York: Dial Press, 1977.

Sexton, Christopher. *Peggy van Praagh: A Life of Dance*. Melbourne: Macmillan, 1985.

Stansky, Peter, and Abrahams, William. *Journey to the Frontier*. London: Constable & Co., 1966.

Taper, Bernard. *Balanchine*. New York: Times Books. Revised edition, 1984.

Taylor, Paul. *Private Domain*. New York: Knopf, 1987.

Van Praagh, Peggy. *How I Became a Ballet Dancer*. London: T. Nelson & Sons, 1959.

Vaughan, David. *Frederick Ashton and His Ballets*. New York: Knopf, 1977.

Weightman, Gavin, and Humphries, Steve. *Making of Modern London*. London: Sidgwick & Jackson, 1983.

Weymouth, Antony [Cobb, Ivo Geikie]. *Of London and Londoners*. London: Williams & Norgate, 1951.

Wood, Neal. *Communism and British Intellectuals*. London: V. Gollancz, 1959.

SOURCE NOTES

INTRODUCTION

page
3 *"a butcher's clerk . . ."*: Walter Cronkite, Kennedy Center Honors Ceremony.
4 *"Now, especially this . . ."*: Tudor letter to Therese Langfield Horner.
4 *"Antony was probably . . ."*: Therese Langfield Horner to DP.
4 *"Young, bonnie and . . ."*: Agnes de Mille, Kennedy Center Honors Ceremony.
4 *"one of the . . . "*: Ibid.
5 *"Dear Antony . . ."*: Ibid. Margot Fonteyn, Ibid.

CHAPTER 1

8 *"less of a . . ."*: Asa Briggs, *A Social History of England.*
8 *"My father could . . ."*: Tudor, quoted in Hilary Ostlere, "The Tudor Spirit," *Ballet News,* April 1982.
8 *"of a vague . . ."*: Tudor, quoted in Cyril W. Beaumont, "Antony Tudor: Choreographer," *British Ballet,* 1949, editor, Peter Noble.
9 *"my son and . . ."*: Mollie Cook to DP.
10 *"Everyone in the . . ."*: Gladys Scammell to DP.
10 *"And whenever we . . ."*: Ibid.
11 *"Uncle was such . . ."*: Ibid.
11 *"They liked to . . ."*: Ibid.
11 *"fancy needlework when . . ."*: Ibid.
12 *"We went to . . ."*: Ibid.
14 *"wait three hours . . ."*: Marilyn Hunt, oral history, at Dance Collection, p. 19.
14 *"in those days . . ."*: Tudor lecture, UC Irvine.
14 *"people in a . . ."*: Tudor lecture, UC Irvine.
15 *"The dentist around . . ."*: Ibid.
15 *"they'd sing their . . ."*: Ibid.
17 *"poet's eyes"*: Marie Rambert, quoted in Helen Dzermolinska, "The Days of a Choreographer's Years," *American Dancer,* June 1941.

18 "fantastically dynamic . . .": Marilyn Hunt, oral history, Dance Collection.

19 "There was enough . . .": Tudor lecture, UC Irvine.

20 "Will told me . . .": Gladys Scammell to DP.

20 "I did cut . . .": Tudor lecture, UC Irvine.

21 "Antony was the . . .": Leo Kersley to DP.

21 "a young, friendly . . .": Agnes de Mille, *Dance to the Piper.*

21 "a hovel, a . . .": Angela Dukes Ellis to DP.

CHAPTER 2

24 "We were all . . .": Billy Chappell to DP.

25 "she could not . . .": Maude Lloyd to DP.

25 "They never stopped . . .": Dame Ninette de Valois to DP.

26 "and then, in . . .": John Percival to DP.

28 "The enjoyment of . . .": Peter Stansky and William Abrahams, *Journey to the Frontier.*

28 "watched everything with . . .": Agnes de Mille, *Dance to the Piper.*

CHAPTER 3

29 "all the new . . .": Antony Tudor, "Rambert Remembered," *Ballet Review,* Spring 1983.

29 "the world's greatest . . .": David Vaughan, *Frederick Ashton and His Ballets.*

30 "had conceived the . . .": Cyril W. Beaumont, "Antony Tudor: Choreographer," *British Ballet,* 1949, editor, Peter Noble.

30 "a slight reserve . . .": Marilyn Hunt, oral history, Dance Collection p. 1.

30 "Mim's little geniuses . . .": P. W. Manchester to DP.

30 "wanting to play . . .": Tudor lecture, UC Irvine.

31 "absorbed the northern . . .": Ibid.

31 "I got my . . .": Ibid.

31 "I've got it . . .": Ibid.

32 "I never had . . .": Sir Frederick Ashton to DP.

32 "We shuddered into . . .": Diana Gould to DP.

33 "A monkish man . . .": Ibid.

33 "and I spied . . .": Maude Lloyd to DP.

34 "This boy has . . .": Tudor lecture, UC Irvine.

34 "not a good . . .": Marie Rambert, *Quicksilver.*

34 "had obviously tried . . .": Cyril W. Beaumont, *British Ballet,* p. 169.

35 "apart from the . . .": Therese Langfield Horner to DP.

35 "I was used . . .": Maude Lloyd to DP.

35 "Mr. Tudor has . . .": *Observer,* May 3, 1936.

35 "Antony always wanted . . .": Margaret Craske to DP.

35 "locking out all . . .": Observer, March 27, 1932.

36 "they were as . . .": Leo Kersley to DP.

36 "he had a . . .": Richard Buckle, *In the Wake of Diaghilev,* New York, 1983.

36 "Antony was serious . . .": Sir Frederick Ashton to DP.

37 "stand about and . . .": Mary Clarke, *Dancers of Mercury.*

CHAPTER 4

39 Hugh Skinner's (Laing's) arrival, described by Leo Kersley to DP.

40 "Have you ever . . .": Marilyn Hunt, oral history, Dance Collection.

40 "climbing trees and . . .": Ibid.

40 "I was as . . .": Ibid.

41 "would kill for . . .": Ibid.

43 "a resounding flop . . .": John Percival, "Antony Tudor," *Dance Perspectives.*

44 "a striking example . . .": Arnold Haskell, *Balletomania Then and Now.*

CHAPTER 5

46 "trying it on . . .": Leo Kersley to DP.

46 "the Mortal's conflict . . .": David Vaughan, "Antony Tudor's Early Ballets."

49 "pompous, aloof and . . .": Agnes de Mille, *Speak to Me, Dance with Me.*

51 "something altogether ravishing . . .": Mary Clarke, *Dancers of Mercury.*

CHAPTER 6

53 "nostalgie de coterie . . .": Ibid.

57 "Never accept the . . .": Mary Clarke, *Dancers of Mercury.*

57 "Hardly a day . . .": Peggy van Praagh, *How I Became a Ballet Dancer.*

58 "contrite and on . . .": Mary Clarke, *Dancers of Mercury.*

58 "It would be . . .": Marilyn Hunt, *Ballet Review,* Fall 1983.

59 "If you ever . . .": Agnes de Mille, *Speak to Me, Dance with Me.*

59 "My God, Hugh's . . .": Ibid.

CHAPTER 7

63 "For the first . . .": Fernau Hall, *An Anatomy of Ballet.*

64 "a bossy sort . . .": Marilyn Hunt, oral history, Kennedy Center.

64 "Desperately in love . . .": Ibid.

65 "She always holds . . .": Tudor lecture, UC Irvine.
66 "At the height . . .": Marie Rambert, *Quicksilver.*
66 "Embraces and filigrees . . .": Agnes de Mille, *Speak to Me, Dance with Me.*
66 "Oh, Antony . . .": Therese Langfield Horner to DP.
66 "I will not . . .": Leo Kersley to DP.

CHAPTER 8

72 "a specialist on . . .": Marilyn Hunt, oral history, Kennedy Center.
74 "I say, where . . .": Agnes de Mille, *Speak to Me, Dance with Me.*
74 "Again and again . . .": Ibid.
76 "Hugh was the . . .": Ibid.
76 "the way one . . .": Ibid.

CHAPTER 9

80 "would insist on . . .": Peggy van Praagh, *How I Became a Ballet Dancer.*
80 "I never thought . . .": Richard Buckle and John Taras, *George Balanchine: Ballet Master.*
82 "It came out . . .": Marilyn Hunt, oral history, Dance Collection.
83 "I wasn't secure . . .": Tudor lecture at UC Irvine.
83 "I made for . . .": Marilyn Hunt, oral history, Kennedy Center.
85 "I thought it . . .": Ibid.

CHAPTER 10

88 "his native land . . .": Agnes de Mille, *Dance to the Piper.*
89 "We went down . . .": Marilyn Hunt, *Ballet Review,* Fall 1983.
89 "the last five . . .": Agnes de Mille, *Dance to the Piper.*
90 "became demented . . .": Marilyn Hunt, oral history, Kennedy Center.
92 "They were very . . .": Maude Lloyd, quoted in Marilyn Hunt, *Ballet Review,* Fall 1983.
94 "a very wasteful . . .": Agnes de Mille, *Dance to the Piper.*
94 "not to dismiss . . .": Laurence Gowing, *The Dancing Times,* July 1937.
94 "what those long . . .": Ibid.

CHAPTER 11

96 "growing up within . . .": Gavin Weightman and Steve Humphries, *Making of Modern London.*
97 "I used to . . .": Tudor lecture, UC Irvine.

98 "all but beating . . .": Agnes de Mille, *Dance to the Piper.*
98 "whereas nobody foretold . . .": Ibid.
99 "Even when the . . .": A. V. Coton, *Writings on Dance, 1938–68.*
102 "a funeral service . . .": Marilyn Hunt, oral history, Kennedy Center.
102 "the towers of . . .": Ibid.
103 "with performances every . . .": The Dancing Times, June 1939.

CHAPTER 12

110 "The greatest collaboration . . .": Selma Jeanne Cohen, *ABT: 1940–60.*
111 "the best that . . .": Ibid.
113 "With sure and . . .": John Martin, *The New York Times,* Jan. 21, 1940.
113 "The man, and . . .": Clive Barnes, *The New York Times,* Jan. 23, 1966.

CHAPTER 13

115 "I get drunker . . .": Marilyn Hunt, oral history, Kennedy Center.
115 "We were watching . . .": Selma Jeanne Cohen, "Antony Tudor: Part II," *Dance Perspectives,* 1963.
115 "hanging around on . . .": Jerome Robbins, Tudor memorial, Juilliard, June 9, 1987.
117 "Imbecile": Leo Kersley to DP.
118 "Put the foot . . .": Marilyn Hunt, oral history, Kennedy Center.
120 "Antony Tudor—also a lover," Dance Collection, New York Public Library.

CHAPTER 14

121 "the beginning of . . .": John Martin, *The New York Times,* Jan. 21, 1940.
124 "Ant'ny, finish it": Janet Reed to DP.

CHAPTER 15

130 "an outcast wandering . . .": Marilyn Hunt, *Dance Magazine,* May 1987.
132 "I will never . . .": "Dick Cavett Show," PBS, 1979.
133 "marvelous": Marilyn Hunt, oral history, Kennedy Center.
133 "All night she . . .": Ibid.
134 "to read all . . .": Nora Kaye to Muriel Bentley.
134 "I choreographed on . . .": Tudor lecture, UC Irvine.

CHAPTER 16

138 "get up, get . . .": Maria Karnilova to DP.

140 "I had no . . .": Selma Jeanne Cohen, *Dance Perspectives.*

141 "We knew we . . .": Marilyn Hunt, oral history, Kennedy Center.

142 "living the character . . .": Selma Jeanne Cohen, *Dance Perspectives.*

143 "They're not clapping": Marilyn Hunt, oral history, Kennedy Center.

143 "Not yet": Ibid.

144 "Conniving": Ibid.

144 "I knew I . . .": Ibid.

144 "The work shows . . .": Edwin Denby, *Looking at the Dance.*

144 "an intimate pleasure . . .": Ibid.

144 "Consider Antony Tudor": John Martin, *The New York Times,* April 22, 1942.

145 "becomes so subdued . . .": Edwin Denby, *Looking at the Dance.*

CHAPTER 17

147 "fared only slightly . . .": Charles Payne, *American Ballet Theatre.*

148 "stag party": Janet Reed to DP.

150 "But then her . . .": Tudor, quoted in *Dance Gazette,* June 1986.

151 "It was Prokofiev's": Marilyn Hunt, oral history, Kennedy Center.

152 "Astounding, perfectly astounding": Sono Osato, *Distant Dances.*

152 "effortless gossamer quality . . .": Diana Gould, *Dance and Dancers,* July 1955.

153 "The key to . . .": Selma Jeanne Cohen, *Dance Perspectives.*

154 "He worked with . . .": Sono Osato, *Distant Dances.*

154 "What was the . . .": Ibid.

155 "the troupe masterpiece": Selma Jeanne Cohen, *Dance Perspectives ABT—1940–60.*

155 "The eye feasted . . .": Ibid.

155 "The work is . . .": John Martin, *The New York Times,* April 10, 1943.

156 "the finest of . . .": David Vaughan, *Antony Tudor's Early Ballets,* paper presented at the University of New Mexico, 1985.

156 "one of the . . .": Deborah Jowitt, *Village Voice,* July 1971.

156 "a great success . . .": Edwin Denby, *Looking at the Dance.*

CHAPTER 18

159 "Tudor has been . . .": Charles Payne, *American Ballet Theatre.*

159 "granitic personality": Tudor lecture, UC Irvine.

160 "the leftover ambitions": Tudor letter, archives, Dance Collection at New York Public Library, Lincoln Center.

160 "isn't it wonderful": Ibid.

160 "I don't think . . .": Jennifer Dunning, *The New York Times,* May 9, 1985.

160 "His faithful right . . .": Tudor letter, Dance Collection Archives.

161 "Choreographers usually reach . . .": Ibid.

162 "her courting days . . .": Tudor letter, Dance Collection Archives.

163 "The choreography is . . .": John Martin, *The New York Times,* Oct. 21, 1943.

163 "weaker both . . .": Edwin Denby, *Looking at the Dance.*

164 "being enthralled . . .": Tudor lecture, UC Irvine.

165 "the main character . . .": Ibid.

166 "Dreadful": Marilyn Hunt, oral history, Dance Collection.

169 "If they are . . .": Tudor lecture, UC Irvine.

169 "no vulgarity in . . .": Edwin Denby, *Looking at the Dance.*

169 "a kind of . . .": John Martin, *The New York Times,* April 15, 1945.

CHAPTER 19

172 "the greatest choreographer . . .": Oliver Smith, quoted in Hilary Ostlere, "The Spirit of Tudor," *Ballet News,* April 1982.

173 "And what am . . .": Richard Beard to DP.

176 " 'til he was . . .": Janet Reed to DP.

CHAPTER 20

183 "It was wonderful . . .": Selma Jeanne Cohen, *Dance Perspectives 18.*

184 "How I've always . . .": Maude Lloyd to DP.

185 "Nora, if you . . .": Richard Beard to DP.

186 "to ring at . . .": Richard Beard diary.

187 "preserving his belief . . .": *The Dancing Times,* August 1946.

CHAPTER 22

191 "Trivial, but winning": Walter Terry, *New York Herald Tribune,* Oct. 3, 1946.

192 "we were lucky": Enrique Martinez to DP.

192 "a permanent institution . . .": Selma Jeanne Cohen, *Dance Perspectives 6, ABT: 1940–60.*

192 "will go down . . .": Anatole Chujoy, *Dance News,* June 1947.

193 "Perhaps I'll do . . .": Leo Kersley to DP.

193 "the impossibility of . . .": Tudor letter, archives, Dance Collection.

193 "*to be at . . .*": Ibid.

193 "*at the family . . .*": Ibid.

193 "*many key figures . . .*": Ibid.

194 "*would lose its . . .*": John Gruen, *The Private World of Ballet*.

195 "*Oh, yes . . .*": P. W. Manchester to DP.

197 "*the most marvelous . . .*": Marilyn Hunt, oral history, Dance Collection.

199 "*the best Tudor . . .*": Agnes de Mille, *Lizzie Borden*.

CHAPTER 23

200 "*When Mr. Tudor . . .*": John Martin, *The New York Times*, April 15, 1948.

203 "*compelling*": *The New York Times*, April 17, 1948.

203 "*giving a lift . . .*": *New York Herald Tribune*, April 17, 1948.

204 "*I always want . . .*": John Gruen, *The Private World of Ballet*.

205 "*even fuller command . . .*": John Martin, *The New York Times*, April 28, 1949.

205 "*a trifle lower . . .*": Ibid. April 22, 1949.

205 "*What a beautiful . . .*": Ibid.

206 "*Mr. Tudor, who . . .*": John Martin, *The New York Times*, May 4, 1950.

207 "*tried [a psychiatrist]*": John Gruen, *The Private World of Ballet*.

CHAPTER 24

210 "*George concerns himself . . .*": Betty Cage to DP.

211 "*Tudor is the . . .*": Clive Barnes, *The New York Times*, March 27, 1966.

212 "*If I were . . .*": Bernard Taper, *Balanchine*.

212 "*There's only one . . .*": John Taras to DP.

213 "*divinely beautiful costumes*": Nancy Reynolds, *Repertory in Review*.

213 "*I liked the . . .*": George Balanchine, quoted in Anna Kisselgoff, *The New York Times*, May 1, 1983.

216 "*captured the poignance . . .*": Robert Sabin, *Musical America*, February 1949.

216 "*definitely minor, but . . .*": John Martin, *The New York Times*, Jan. 15, 1949.

217 "*Laing danced it . . .*": Anatole Chujoy, *New York City Ballet*.

218 "*When you take . . .*": Nancy Reynolds, *Repertory in Review*.

218 "*could not find . . .*": Lincoln Kirstein, *Thirty Years: The New York City Ballet*.

218 "*Echoes of the . . .*": John Martin, *The New York Times*, March 1, 1951.

220 "an unmistakable aura . . .": George Beiswanger, "Short Story Ballet," *Dance Magazine,* June 1942.

223 "Come on, Tudor": Francisco Moncion to DP.

224 "Kaye had only . . .": Anatole Chujoy, *New York City Ballet.*

224 "Three Beethoven overtures . . .": John Martin, *The New York Times,* Feb. 28, 1952.

224 "at her most . . .": Walter Terry, *New York Herald Tribune,* Feb. 28, 1952.

224 "expertly planned, beautifully . . .": John Martin, *The New York Times,* March 2, 1952.

225 "the actress's whole . . .": Doris Hering, *Dance Magazine,* May 1952.

225 "How many different . . .": Tudor lecture, UC Irvine.

CHAPTER 25

227 "knocked himself out": Betty Cage to DP.

229 "without Hugh Laing . . .": Gerd Andersson and Viola Aberle, *Antony Tudor.* Documentary, 1985.

CHAPTER 26

243 "What would you . . .": Nan Robertson, *The New York Times,* Oct. 2, 1988.

CHAPTER 27

244 "extremely sarcastic and . . .": John Gruen, oral history, Dance Collection at New York Public Library, Lincoln Center.

245 "The learning experience . . .": Ibid.

248 "Now you're going . . .": John Gruen, *The Private World of Ballet.*

248 "He was a . . .": Ibid.

250 "Get up off . . .": Glen Tetley to DP.

CHAPTER 29

260 "full of the Zen . . .": Agnes de Mille, Tudor memorial, Juilliard, June 9, 1987.

263 "would move into . . .": Tudor lecture, UC Irvine.

263 "glowing choreographic images . . .": Walter Terry, *New York Herald Tribune,* March 24, 1959.

264 "Instead of always . . .": *A Time to Dance,* documentary, 1959.

CHAPTER 30

271 "symbolize that there's . . .": Tudor, quoted in Jack Anderson, *Dance Magazine,* May 1966.
272 "how people always . . .": Ibid.
274 "It has been . . .": Selma Jeanne Cohen, *Dance Perspectives,* Part II.
274 "He stood there . . .": Clive Barnes, *The New York Times,* April 3, 1966.

CHAPTER 31

286 "I didn't understand . . .": Selma Jeanne Cohen, *Saturday Review,* May 13, 1967.
286 "Most of the . . .": Tudor, quoted in Lillie F. Rosen, *Dance Scope,* Fall/Winter 1974.
288 "Where do you . . .": BBC documentary of *Shadowplay,* 1967.
289 "Tell me by . . .": Ibid.
290 "She would come . . .": Jean Battey Lewis, *The Washington Post,* Dec. 23, 1973.
290 "A work to . . .": Mary Clarke, *Dancing Times,* March 1967.
290 "has as many . . .": Clive Barnes, *The New York Times,* June 18, 1967.
292 "Rudi doesn't think . . .": Maude Lloyd to DP.
292 "but the truthfulness . . .": Ibid.
292 "there's a problem . . .": Rudolf Nureyev to DP.

CHAPTER 32

301 "a Dr. Jekyll . . .": Craig Dodd, *Dancing Times,* January 1969.
303 "There is nothing . . .": John Percival, *Dancing Times,* January 1969.
303 "the vastness of . . .": Ibid.

CHAPTER 33

307 "These fruits are . . .": Marja Odell to DP.

CHAPTER 34

309 "I lead a . . .": John Gruen, *The Private World of Ballet.*
311 "who is now . . .": Tudor letter to Connaught Palmer.

CHAPTER 35

317 "They've just come . . .": Jean Battey Lewis, *The Washington Post,* Dec. 23, 1973.
318 "She is terribly . . .": John Gruen, *The Private World of Ballet.*
318 "a great, great . . .": Ibid.
319 "They are provincials...": Natalia Makarova, *A Dance Autobiography.*
319 "It was the sublime . . .": Ibid.
319 "is not the . . .": Sallie Wilson to DP.
320 "and whose bed . . .": Enrique Martinez to DP.

CHAPTER 36

324 "How could you . . .": Mikhail Baryshnikov, *Baryshnikov at Work.*
325 "People are mad . . .": John Gruen, *The New York Times,* July 13, 1975.
327 "At the end . . .": Clive Barnes, *The New York Times,* July 19, 1975.

CHAPTER 37

330 "What are we . . .": Gelsey Kirkland to DP.
331 "has Tudor's eye . . .": Arlene Croce, *Going to the Dance.*
332 "only one of . . .": Gelsey Kirkland to DP.

CHAPTER 38

334 "I'm mature now . . .": "Dick Cavett Show," PBS, 1979.
337 "It could look . . .": Jean Battey Lewis, *The Washington Post,* Dec. 23, 1973.

CHAPTER 39

341 "Dearest Mim": Tudor letter to Rambert.
342 "be with my . . .": Sally Brayley Bliss to DP.
342 "A propos the cows . . .": Tudor letter to Connaught Palmer.
344 "had not acquired . . .": Mikhail Baryshnikov to DP.
349 "I've become too . . .": John Percival interview with Maude Lloyd, Sadler's Wells Theater Project.

CHAPTER 40

350 "Mr. Tudor . . .": Roger Stevens to DP.

351 "Why didn't you . . .": Joyce Moffatt to DP.

352 "This has been . . .": Tudor letter to Therese Langfield.

355 "I like that . . .": Mikhail Baryshnikov, Tudor memorial, Juilliard, June 9, 1987.

356 Tudor's death described by Hugh Laing to Muriel Bentley.

356 "when Baryshnikov was . . .": John Fraser, *Private View*.

357 "No one needs . . .": Muriel Bentley to DP.

358 "Tudor gave so . . .": Hugh Laing, Tudor memorial, Juilliard, June 9, 1987.

EPILOGUE

365 "Ever since . . .": Tudor letter to DP.

A CHOREOGRAPHIC
CHRONOLOGY

BALLETS

Cross-Garter'd: November 12, 1931; Ballet Club, Mercury Theatre, London.
Scenario: After a scene in Shakespeare's play *Twelfth Night*
Music: Arranged from organ works by Girolamo Frescobaldi
Decor: Pamela Boquet
Costumes: After Burnacini
Cast: Olivia: Maude Lloyd; Maria: Prudence Hyman; Malvolio: Antony Tudor; Sir Toby: Walter Gore; Sir Andrew: Rollo Gamble; Fabian: William Chappell; Attendants: Elisabeth Schooling, Betty Cuff.

Mr. Roll's Quadrilles: February 4 or 11, 1932; Ballet Club, Mercury Theatre, London.
Music: Old music
Costumes: Susan Saloman
Cast: The Leaders: Prudence Hyman, Antony Tudor; Pas de Trois: Maude Lloyd, Elisabeth Schooling, Betty Cuff.

Constanza's Lament: February 1932; Ballet Club, Mercury Theatre, London.
Music: Domenico Scarlatti: *The Good-Humored Ladies*
Cast: Diana Gould.

Lysistrata: March 20, 1932; Ballet Club, Mercury Theatre, London.
Scenario: After play by Aristophanes
Music: Serge Prokofiev: piano pieces from opp. 2, 3, 13 and 22, and from 2nd and 4th piano sonatas
Decor and costumes: William Chappell

Cast: Myrrhina: Alicia Markova; Cinesias: Walter Gore; Lysis-trata: Diana Gould; Her Husband: Antony Tudor; Lampito: Andrée Howard; Calonice: Prudence Hyman; Her Husband: William Chappell; Other Athenian Women: Elisabeth Schooling, Betty Cuff; Handmaid to Myrrhina: Susette Morfield.

Adam and Eve: December 4, 1932; Camargo Society, Adelphi Theatre, London.
Scenario and music: Constant Lambert
Decor and costumes: John Banting
Cast: Adam: Anton Dolin; Eve: Prudence Hyman; Serpent: Antony Tudor.

Pavane pour une Infante Defunte: January 1, 1933; Ballet Club, Mercury Theatre, London.
Music: Maurice Ravel
Decor and costumes: Hugh Stevenson
Cast: Infanta: Diana Gould; Buffoon: Walter Gore.

Atalanta of the East: May 7, 1933; Ballet Club, Mercury Theatre, London.
Music: Eastern music arranged by Theodore Szanto and Paul Seeligg
Decor and costumes: William Chappell
Cast: Sita: Pearl Argyle; Vikram: Hugh Laing; Goddess: Diana Gould; King: Antony Tudor.

Paramour: February 20, 1934; danced scene in Oxford University Dramatic Society production of Marlowe's *Doctor Faustus,* Town Hall, Oxford.
Music: William Boyce
Arrangement: Constant Lambert
Costumes: John Lear
Cast: Alexander: Walter Gore; Thaïs (His Paramour): Diana Gould; Darius: Hugh Laing.

The Legend of Dick Whittington: May 28, 1934; danced interlude in *The Rock* by T. S. Eliot, Sadler's Wells Theatre, London.
Music: Martin Shaw
Decor: Eric Newton

Costumes: Stella Mary Pearce

Cast: The Cat: Patricia Mary Page; Dick: Joan Birdwood-Taylor; The Cook: Joan Birdwood-Seton; A Sailor: Gladys Scott; The King of Barbary: Eileen Harris, Phyllis Bull; Alice: Betty Percheron.

The Planets: October 28, 1934; Ballet Club, Mercury Theatre, London.

Music: Gustav Holst

Decor and costumes: Hugh Stevenson

Cast: "Venus": Mortals Born under Venus (The Lovers): Pearl Argyle, William Chappell; The Planet Venus: Maude Lloyd (with Tamara Svetlova, Nan Hopkins, Joan Lendrum, Margot Hawkins); "Mars": Mortal Born under Mars (The Fighter): Hugh Laing; The Planet Mars: Diana Gould (with Elisabeth Schooling, Susette Morfield, Peggy van Praagh, Isobel Reynolds); "Neptune": Mortal Born under Neptune (The Mystic): Kyra Nijinska; The Planet Neptune: Antony Tudor (with Nan Hopkins, Joan Lendrum).

The Descent of Hebe: April 7, 1935; Ballet Club, Mercury Theatre, London.

Music: Ernest Bloch: Concerto Grosso no. 1 in b-minor

Decor and costumes: Nadia Benois

Cast: Hebe: Pearl Argyle; Mercury: Hugh Laing; Night: Maude Lloyd; Hercules: Antony Tudor.

Jardin aux Lilas: January 26, 1936; Ballet Club, Mercury Theatre, London.

Music: Ernest Chausson *Poème* for violin and orchestra

Decor and costumes: Hugh Stevenson

Cast: Caroline: Maude Lloyd; Her Lover: Hugh Laing; The Man She Must Marry: Antony Tudor; An Episode in His Past: Peggy van Praagh; The Sister: Elisabeth Schooling; The Sailor: Frank Staff; The Young Cousin: Ann Gee; The Soldier: Leslie Edwards; A Friend of the Family: Tamara Svetlova.

Dark Elegies: February 19, 1937; Ballet Rambert, Duchess Theatre, London.

Music: Gustav Mahler: *Kindertotenlieder*

Decor and costumes: Nadia Benois
Cast: First Song: Peggy van Praagh; Second Song: Maude Lloyd, Antony Tudor; Third Song: Walter Gore (with Antony Tudor, John Bryon); Fourth Song: Agnes de Mille; Fifth Song: Hugh Laing.

Gallant Assembly: June 14, 1937; Dance Theatre, Playhouse, Oxford.
Music: Giuseppe Tartini: *Cello Concerto in D*
Decor and costumes: Hugh Stevenson
Cast: Aristocrats in Love: Agnes de Mille, Peggy van Praagh, Phyllis Bidmead, Victoria Fenn, Antony Tudor, Hugh Stevenson; Hired Performers: Margaret Braithwaite, Hugh Laing.

Seven Intimate Dances: June 15, 1938; Westminster Theatre, London. Two dances given as part of seven dances in a curtain raiser to Gogol play *Marriage.* (Other five dances by Agnes de Mille.) *Hunting Scene* (music by J. C. Bach) and *Joie de Vivre* (music Jacques Offenbach and Johann Strauss).
Cast: Agnes de Mille; Antony Tudor; Hugh Laing; Charlotte Bidmead; Therese Langfield.

Judgment of Paris: June 15, 1938; London Ballet, Westminster Theatre, London (replacing *Seven Intimate Dances* as curtain raiser to Gogol play *Marriage*).
Scenario and costumes: Hugh Laing
Music: Kurt Weill: selections from *Dreigroschenoper*
Cast: Juno: Therese Langfield; Venus: Agnes de Mille; Minerva: Charlotte Bidmead; The Client: Antony Tudor; The Waiter: Hugh Laing.

Soirée Musicale: November 26, 1938: Palladium Theatre, London.
Music: Gioacchino Rossini, Benjamin Britten
Decor and costumes: Hugh Stevenson
Cast: Canzonetta: Gerd Larsen, Hugh Laing; Tirolese: Maude Lloyd, Antony Tudor; Bolero: Peggy van Praagh; Tarantella: Monica Boam, Guy Massey.

Gala Performance: December 5, 1938; London Ballet, Toynbee Hall Theatre, London.

Music: Serge Prokofiev: 1st movement of Piano Concerto no. 3 and *Classical Symphony*
Decor and costumes: Hugh Stevenson
Cast: La Reine de la Danse (from Moscow): Peggy van Praagh; La Déesse de la Danse (from Milan): Maude Lloyd; La Fille de Terpsichore (from Paris): Gerd Larsen; Cavaliers: Antony Tudor, Guy Massey, Hugh Laing; Choryphées: Monica Boam, Rosa Vernon, Sylvia Hayden, Charlotte Bidmead, Susan Reeves, Katherine Legris; Conductor: Richard Paul; Dresser: Therese Langfield.

Mercury *(New scene added to The Planets):* January 23, 1939; London Ballet, Toynbee Hall Threatre, London.
Music: Gustav Holst
Decor and costumes: Hugh Stevenson
Cast: Mortal Born under Mercury: Peggy van Praagh; The Planet Mercury: Guy Massey (with Monica Boam, Sylvia Hayden).

Goya Pastorale: August 1, 1940; Ballet Theatre, Lewisohn Stadium, New York.
Scenario: Nicholas de Molas
Music: Enrique Granados: piano pieces, orchestrated by Harold Byrns
Decor and costumes: Nicholas de Molas
Cast: Majas: Alicia Alonso, Nora Kaye; Escorts: Donald Saddler, Jerome Robbins; Marchesa: Lucia Chase; Young Man: Hugh Laing; Ladies in Waiting: Tania Dokoudovska, Miriam Golden, Maria Karnilova, Kirsten Valbor; Young Men: Fernando Alonso, John Kriza, David Nillo, Oreste Sergievsky; Fools: Leon Danielian, Dimitri Romanoff, Mimi Gomber, Olga Suarez; The Ass: Eugene Loring; Nobleman: Antony Tudor; Maiden Carrying a Basket of Grapes: Tilly Losch.

Time Table: May 29, 1941; The American Ballet, Little Theatre of Hunter College, New York.
Music: Aaron Copland: *Music for the Theatre*
Decor and costumes: James Morcom
Cast: The Station Master: Zachary Solov; The Girl: Gisela Caccialanza; Her Boyfriend: Lew Christensen; High School Girl: Lorna London; High School Boy: Charles Dickson; Three

Young Girls: Beatrice Tomkins, Ruth Gilbert, Ruth Sobotka; Two Marines: Walter Georgov, Jack Kauflin; Lady with Newspaper: Georgia Hide; Soldier: Edward Bigelow.

Pillar of Fire: April 8, 1942; Ballet Theatre, Metropolitan Opera House, New York.
Music: Arnold Schoenberg: *Verklärte Nacht*
Decor and costumes: Jo Mielziner
Cast: Eldest Sister: Lucia Chase; Hagar: Nora Kaye; Youngest Sister: Annabelle Lyon; The Friend: Antony Tudor; The Young Man from the House Opposite: Hugh Laing; Lovers in Innocence: Maria Karnilova, Charles Dickson, Jean Davidson, John Kriza, Virginia Wilcox, Wallace Seibert, Jean Hunt, Barbara Fallis; Lovers in Experience: Sono Osato, Rosella Hightower, Muriel Bentley, Jerome Robbins, Donald Saddler; Maiden Ladies out Walking: Galina Razoumova, Roszika Sabo.

The Tragedy of Romeo and Juliet: April 6, 1943 (incomplete); April 10, 1943 (complete); Ballet Theatre, Metropolitan Opera House, New York.
Music: Frederick Delius: *Eventyr, Over the Hills and Far Away, Brigg Fair,* and other orchestral pieces, arranged by Antal Dorati
Decor and costumes: Eugene Berman
Cast: Montague: Borislav Ruanine; Capulet: John Taras; Romeo: Hugh Laing; Mercutio: Nicolas Orloff; Benvolio: Jerome Robbins; Tybalt: Antony Tudor; Friar Lawrence: Dimitri Romanoff; Paris: Richard Reed; Lady Montague: Miriam Golden; Lady Capulet: Galina Razoumova; Juliet: Alicia Markova; Rosaline: Sono Osato; Nurse: Lucia Chase.

Dim Lustre: October 20, 1943; Ballet Theatre, Metropolitan Opera House, New York.
Music: Richard Strauss: *Burleske* for piano and orchestra
Decor and costumes: Motley
Cast: Waltzing Ladies and Their Partners: Barbara Fallis and Hugh Laing, June Morris and Kenneth Davis, Roszika Sabo and Fernando Alonso, Mimi Gomber and John Taras, Mary Heater and Alpheus Koon; The Lady with Him: Nora Kaye; The Gentleman with Her: Hugh Laing; A Reflection: Muriel Bentley; Another Reflection: Michael Kidd; It Was Spring: John

Kriza; Who Was She?: Janet Reed, Albia Kavan, Virginia Wilcox; She Wore a Perfume: Rosella Hightower; He Wore a White Tie: Antony Tudor.

Undertow: April 10, 1945; Ballet Theatre, Metropolitan Opera House, New York.
Scenario: Antony Tudor after a suggestion by John van Druten
Music: William Schuman
Decor: Raymond Breinin
Costumes: Hugh Laing
Cast: The Transgressor: Hugh Laing; Cybele: Diana Adams; Pollux: John Kriza; Volupia: Shirley Eckl; Aganippe: Patricia Barker; Sileni: Regis Powers, Stanley Herbert; Satyrisci: Michael Kidd, Fernando Alonso, Kenneth Davis, Roy Tobias; Nemesis: Roszika Sabo; Polyhymnia: Lucia Chase; Pudicitia: Cynthia Risely; Ate: Alicia Alonso; Hymen: Richard Beard; Hera: Janet Reed; Bacchantes: Maria Tallchief, June Morris, Mildred Ferguson; Medusa: Nana Gollner.

Shadow of the Wind: April 14, 1948; Ballet Theatre, Metropolitan Opera House, New York.
Music: Gustav Mahler: *Das Lied von der Erde*
Decor and costume: Jo Mielziner
Cast:
    I - Six Idlers of the Bamboo Valley: Igor Youskevitch; Hugh Laing; Dimitri Romanoff.
    II - The Abandoned Wife: Alicia Alonso; John Kriza; Mary Burr.
    III - My Lord Summons Me: Ruth Ann Koesun; Crandall Diel.
    IV - The Lotus Gatherers: Diana Adams.
    V - Conversation with Winepot and Bird: Hugh Laing.
    VI - Poem of the Guitar: Nana Gollner; Hugh Laing; Dimitri Romanoff; Muriel Bentley; Barbara Fallis; Igor Youskevitch.

The Dear Departed: July 15, 1949; Jacob's Pillow.
Music: Maurice Ravel
Cast: Diana Adams; Hugh Laing.

Nimbus: May 3, 1950; Ballet Theatre, Center Theatre, New York.
Music: Louis Gruenberg: Concerto for violin and orchestra
Decor: Oliver Smith
Costumes: "Saul Bolaski" (Hugh Laing)
Cast: The Dreamer: Nora Kaye; The Dream: Diana Adams; Dream Beau: Hugh Laing.

Lady of the Camellias: February 28, 1951; New York City Ballet, New York City Center of Music and Drama.
Scenario: after the novel by Alexandre Dumas fils
Music: Giuseppe Verdi: excerpts from the early operas Nabucco, I Vespri Siciliani, Macbetto and I Lombardi
Decor and costumes: Cecil Beaton
Cast: Marguerite Gautier: Diana Adams; Armand Duval: Hugh Laing; Armand's Father: "John Earle" (Antony Tudor); Prudence: Vida Brown; M. le Compte de N.: Brooke Jackson.

Les Mains Gauches: July 20, 1951; Resident company, Jacob's Pillow.
Music: Jacques Ibert
Cast: Sebra Nevins; Marc Hertsens; Sallie Wilson.

Ronde du Printemps: August 1, 1951; Resident company, Jacob's Pillow.
Music: Erik Satie
Cast: The Actress: Sallie Wilson.

La Gloire: February 26, 1952; New York City Ballet, New York City Center of Music and Drama.
Music: Ludwig van Beethoven: Overtures to Egmont, Coriolanus and Leonore no. 3
Decor: Gaston Longchamps
Costumes: Robert Fletcher
Cast: La Gloire (Lucretia, Phaedra, Hamlet): Nora Kaye; Sextus Tarquinius and Hamlet's Stepfather: Francisco Moncion; Hippolytus (Stepson to Phaedra) and Laertes: Hugh Laing; The Dancer in Gray: Diana Adams; Orion: Jacques d'Amboise; Artemia: Una Kai; Ophelia: Doris Breckenridge; Hamlet's Mother: Beatrice Tompkins.

Trio con Brio dances from *Ruslan and Ludmila*: June 27, 1952; Resident company, Jacob's Pillow.
Choreography: "Vispitin" (Antony Tudor)
Music: Mikhail Glinka
Costumes: Mario Nepo, Adelphine Rott
Cast: Tatiana Grantzova; Nicolas Polajenko; Ralph McWilliam.

Exercise Piece: May 7, 1953; students of Juilliard School of Music; Concert Hall of Juilliard School of Music, New York.
Music: Ariaga y Balzola: String quartet no. 2 in A Major
Cast: Juilliard dance students.

Little Improvisations *pas de deux:* August 28, 1953; Resident company, Jacob's Pillow
Music: Robert Schumann: *Kinderscenen*
Cast: Yvonne Chouteau; Gilbert Read.

Elizabethan Dances and Music: December 7, 1953; Juilliard dance students, Juilliard Concert Hall, New York. (Third evening of *A Festival of British Music.*)
Dancers: Lucille Badda; Donya Feuer; Sally Holroyd; Patricia Sparrow, Jerry Kurland, Vernon Long, Barrie Schenker, Charles Wadsworth.

LORD SALISBURY'S PAVAN AND GALLIARD
Music: Orlando Gibbons
LA RONDINELLA ("The Swallow")
Music: Thomas Morley
CORANTE SUITE
Music: Anonymous Elizabethan
LA VOLTA
Music: Thomas Morley, set to virginals by William Byrd
HEIGH HO FOR A HUSBAND
Music: John Gamble's Common Place Book
CANARIES
Music: Anonymous
WORSTERS BRAULE
Music: Thomas Tomkins

Britannia Triumphans: December 11, 1953 by Juilliard dance students as Fifth Evening of British Music at Juilliard Concert Hall, New York. (Masque rediscovered, adapted and edited by Murray Lefkowitz and devised and directed by Frederic Cohen; originally presented by Inigo Jones and William D'Avenant in 1637.)
Music: William Lawes
Scenery and lighting: Frederick Kiesler
Costumes and makeup: Leo van Witzen
Choreography: Antony Tudor

THE ANTI-MASQUES
Cast: Mock-Musick: Lucille Badda; Sally Holroyd; Jerry Kurland; Robert Moery; Charles Wadsworth; Ballad Singer: Karen Banner, Gene McDonald; Courtiers: Vernon Long, Barrie Schenker, Joel Schnee; Cats: Rena Gluck, Martha Schuh, Bruce Carlyle, John Coyle; Soldiers: Jerry Kurland, Vernon Long, Robert Moery, Barrie Schenker, Joel Schnee, Charles Wadsworth.
ENTRY AND DESCENT OF THE GRAND MASQUERS
Cast: Lucille Badda; Yvonne Brenner; Madeline Cantarella; Hazel Chung; Sally Holroyd; Patricia Sparrow; Elizabeth Stanley; Gail Valentine; Vernon Long; Gene McDonald (Britanocles); Robert Moery; Charles Wadsworth.

Offenbach in the Underworld or *Le Bar du Can-Can:* May 8, 1954; Philadelphia Ballet Company, Convention Hall, Philadelphia.
Music: Jacques Offenbach: *Gaité Parisienne*
Cast: Madame la Patronne: Ruth Anne Carr; Her Little Girl: Paula Mainwaring; The Painter (from Abroad): Michael Loposzanski; The Visiting Operetta Star (from Abroad): Viola Essen; Officer: Maurice Phillips; The Queen of the Carriage Trade: Elaine Wilson.

La Leyenda de José (*The Legend of Joseph*): August 19, 1958; Teatro Colon, Buenos Aires.
Music: Richard Strauss
Cast: Potiphar: Wladislaw Lesniewsky; Potiphar's Wife: Olga Francis; Joseph: Carlos Schiafino.

Hail and Farewell: March 22, 1959; Metropolitan Opera Ballet, Metropolitan Opera House, New York.
Music: Richard Strauss

FESTIVAL MARCH (op. 1)
Ensemble
SERENADE (op. 7)
Ensemble
FOUR LAST SONGS
Cast: Frühling: Lupe Serrano; September: Edith Jerell; Beim Schlafengehn: Audrey Keane (with ensemble); Im Abendrot: Nora Kaye.

A Choreographer Comments: April 9, 1960; Juilliard Dance Ensemble; Juilliard Concert Hall, New York.
Music: Franz Schubert: Octet in F Major
Lighting: Thomas de Gaetani

Gradus ad Parnassum: Dance Studies; March 8, 1962; Juilliard Dance ensemble, Juilliard Hall, New York. Tudor's new studies and revivals, new studies by Margaret Black, Alfred Corvino and Fiorella Keane, and an excerpt from Fokine's *Carnaval*.
New Tudor Studies:

BALLET I
PAZZAMEZZI
Music: Antonio Gardano: from Collection of Keyboard Pieces: *Intravolatura nova di varie sorte di balli*
Cast: Herman Campbell; Morris Donaldson; Lester Wilson.
FROM MUSICK'S HAND-MAID
Music: Henry Purcell
Cast: Margaret Goettelmann; Juanito Londono; Ellen Tittler; Martha Clarke; Margaret Cicierska.
(DANCE STUDIES LESS ORTHODOX)
Music: Elliott Carter: *Eight Etudes, A Fantasy for Woodwind Quartet*
Cast: Phyllis Edelmann; Diane Gray; Beatrice Lamb; Donna Lowe; Francesca Meunier; Francis Roxin; Linda Shoop; Susan Theobald; Martha van der Wijk; Dana Vass; Judith Wahl; Lawrence Berger; Hermann Campbell; Morris Donaldson; Steven Gross; Myron Nadel.

Fandango: March 26, 1963; dancers of Metropolitan Opera Ballet Studio, Town Hall, New York.
Music: Antonio Soler
Cast: Suzanne Ames; Ingrid Blecker; Nancy King; Carol Kroom; Iyako Ogawa.

Echoing of Trumpets*(Ekon av Trumpeter)*: September 28, 1963; Royal Swedish Ballet, Royal Theatre, Stockholm.
Music: Bohuslav Martinu: *Fantasies Symphoniques*
Decor and costumes: Birger Bergling
Cast: Gerd Andersson; Catharina Ericson; Viveka Ljung; Kerstin Dust; Hervor Sjostrand; Kari Sylwan; Annette Wiedersheim-Paul; Mario Menga elli; Jacques de Lisle; Eki Eriksson; Ulf Gadd; Nils Johensson; Nisse Winqvist; Richard Wolf; Svante Lindberg.

Concerning Oracles: March 27, 1966; Metropolitan Opera Ballet, Metropolitan Opera House, New York.
Music: Jacques Ibert: *Suite Elizabethaine, Capriccio, Divertissement*
Decor and costumes: Peter Harvey
Cast for all three sections: Teller of Fortune: Nira Paaz; Gypsies: Donald Mahler, Jan Mickens.

Shadowplay: January 25, 1967; Royal Ballet, Royal Opera House at Covent Garden, London.
Music: Charles Koechlin: *Les Bandarlog* and *La Course de Printemps*
Decor and costumes: Michael Ennals
Cast: The Boy with Matted Hair: Anthony Dowell.
(The Penumbra) Arboreals: Kenneth Mason; Lambert Cox; Keith Martin; Geoffrey Cauley; Peter O'Brien; Donald Kirkpatrick; Ann Howard; Marilyn Trounson; Frances Freeman.
(Aerials) Ann Jenner; Jennifer Penney; Deirdre O'Conaire; Christine Beckley; Rosalind Eyre; Diana Vere.
Terrestrial: Derek Rencher.
Celestials: Merle Park (with David Drew, Paul Brown).

Knight Errant: November 25, 1968; Royal Ballet touring company, Opera House, Manchester.
Music: Richard Strauss from *Le Bourgeois Gentilhomme* and the overture to *Ariadne auf Naxos*

Decor and costumes: Stefanos Lazaridis
Cast: Le Chevalier d'Amour (A Gentleman of Parts): Henrik Davel; A Woman of Consequence: Jane Landon; Ladies of Quality: Alfreda Thorogood; Margaret Barbieri, Elizabeth Anderton.

The Divine Horsemen: August 8, 1969; Australian Ballet, Her Majesty's Theatre, Sydney.
Music: Werner Egk: Variations on a Caribbean theme
Decor and costumes: Hugh Laing
Cast: Erzulie: Gail Stock; Ghede: Karl Welander; Damballah: Rex McNeill.

Sunflowers: May 27, 1971; students of the Juilliard Dance Division, Juilliard Theatre, New York.
Music: Leoš Janáček: String Quartet no. 1
Cast: Madeleine Rhew; Airi Hynninen; Pamela Knisel; Deborah Weaver; Anthony Salatino; Larry Grenier.

Cereus: May 27, 1971; students of the Juilliard Dance Division, Juilliard Theatre, New York.
Music: Geoffrey Grey: Quartet for Percussion *L'Inconsequenza*
Cast: Jerome Weiss; Sylvia Yamada; Larry Grenier; Lance Westergard; Marc Stevens; Bonnie Oda; Angeline Wolf.

Continuo: May 27, 1971; students of the Juilliard Dance Division, Juilliard Theatre, New York.
Music: Johann Pachelbel: *Canon* in D
Cast: Sirpa Jorasmaa; Anthony Salatino; Deborah Weaver; Raymond Clay; Madeleine Rhew; Blake Brown.

The Leaves Are Fading: July 19, 1975; American Ballet Theatre, New York State Theatre, New York.
Music: Antonín Dvořák: *The Cypresses* (string quartet) and other chamber music for strings
Decor: Ming Cho Lee
Costumes: Patricia Zipprodt
Lighting: Jennifer Tipton
Cast: (In order of appearance)
Mariana Tcherkassky; Amy Blaisdell; Nanette Glushak; Linda

Kuchera; Kristine Elliott; Hilda Morales; Elizabeth Ashton; Christine O'Neal; Michael Owen; Raymond Serrano; Charles Ward; Richard Schafer; Clark Tippet; Gelsey Kirkland; Jonas Kage.

Tiller in the Fields: December 13, 1978; American Ballet Theatre, Kennedy Center for the Performing Arts, Washington, D.C.
Music: Antonín Dvořák: *In Nature's Realm,* op. 91; from Symphony no. 6 in D Major (op. 60) and Adagio from Symphony no. 2
Decor: Ming Cho Lee
Costumes: Dunya Ramicova
Lighting: Thomas Skelton
Cast: Patrick Bissell; Nancy Collier; Cynthia Gast; Camille Izard; Lucette Katerndall; Chrisa Keramidas; Lisa Lockwood; Lisa Rinehart; Kristine Soleri; Brian Adams; John Gardner; Robert La Fosse; Danilo Radojevich; Johan Renvall; Raymond Serrano and Gelsey Kirkland.

DANCES IN OPERAS

Faust: September 28, 1933; Vic-Wells Opera, Sadler's Wells Theatre, London.
Music: Charles Gounod
Decor and costumes: O. P. Smith
Cast: Principal dancers: Freda Bamford; Antony Tudor; Pas de trois: Ailne Philips; Nadina Newhouse; Elizabeth Miller.

Castor and Pollux: 1934; Oxford University Ballet Club.
Music: Jean-Philippe Rameau

La Cenerentola: May 1, 1935; Royal Opera House, Covent Garden, London.
Music: Gioacchino Rossini
Cast: Alicia Markova; Walter Gore; Elisabeth Schooling; Peggy van Praagh; Antony Tudor.

Schwanda the Bagpiper: June 3, 1935; Royal Opera House, Covent Garden, London.

Music: Jaromíre Weinberger
Cast: Maude Lloyd; Antony Tudor; Elisabeth Schooling; Peggy van Praagh; Travis Kemp.

Carmen: June 4, 1935; Royal Opera House, Covent Garden, London.
Music: Georges Bizet
Cast: Maude Lloyd; Antony Tudor.

Koanga: September 23, 1935; Royal Opera House, Covent Garden, London.
Music: Frederick Delius
Cast: Maude Lloyd.

Die Fledermaus: January 6, 1937; Royal Opera House, Covent Garden, London.
Choreography: Antony Tudor, Madeleine Dinely
Music: Johann Strauss the Younger
Cast: Prudence Hyman.

Orfeo ed Euridice: February 1939; Toynbee Hall Theatre, London.
Music: Christoph Willibald Gluck
Cast: Gerd Larsen (with some members of the London Ballet).

The Bartered Bride: May 1, 1939; Royal Opera House, Covent Garden, London.
Music: Bedřich Smetana
Cast: The London Ballet.

La Traviata: May 2, 1939; Royal Opera House, Covent Garden, London.
Music: Giuseppe Verdi
Dancers: The London Ballet.

Aida: May 24, 1939; Royal Opera House, Covent Garden, London.
Music: Giuseppe Verdi
Cast: Margot Fonteyn (with the London Ballet).

La Traviata: November 11, 1950; Metropolitan Opera House, New York.

Dancers: Metropolitan Opera Ballet
Cast: Tilda Morse, Nana Gollner (with Metropolitan Opera Ballet).

Faust: December 12, 1950; Metropolitan Opera House, New York.
Music: Charles Gounod
Cast: Nana Gollner (with Metropolitan Opera Ballet).

Die Fledermaus: December 20, 1950; Metropolitan Opera House, New York.
Music: Johann Strauss the Younger
Decor and costume: Michael Manuel
Cast: Nana Gollner (with Metropolitan Opera Ballet).

Alcestis: December 6, 1960; Metropolitan Opera House, New York.
Music: C. W. Gluck
Cast: (Act II) Nancy King; Pina Bausch; Wally Adams; Jeremy Blanton; Richard Zelens;
(Act III) Edith Jerell; Bruce Marks.

Tannhäuser: December 17, 1960; Metropolitan Opera House, New York.
(Venusberg Scene)
Music: Richard Wagner
Decor and costumes: Rolf Gerard
Cast: Metropolitan Opera Ballet.

DANCES IN PLAYS, MUSICALS, REVUES AND FILMS

In a Monastery Garden: Film directed by Maurice Elvey, released early in 1932, including two dances by Tudor.
Dancers: Gina Malo, Harold Turner (with Marie Rambert Dancers).

The Happy Hypocrite: April 8, 1936; His Majesty's Theatre, London. Play with script by Clemence Dane (based on story by Max Beerbohm).
Music: Richard Addinsell

Decor and costumes: Motley
Dancers: Two lovers: Peggy van Praagh, Hugh Laing; The Fair Captive of Samarkand: Vivien Leigh; Aposchaz (her cruel father): Raymond Farrell; An Old Woman (her governess): Peggy van Praagh; Nissarah (her lover): Hugh Laing.

To and Fro: November 26, 1936; Comedy Theatre, London. Revue with ballets by Tudor, including *Prelude* with music by Lord Berners and *Symphonie Russe* with music by Prokofiev.
Dancers: Maude Lloyd; Hugh Laing and others.

Johnson over Jordan: February 22, 1939; New Theatre, London. Play by J. B. Priestley.
Music: Benjamin Britten, Ernest Irving
Principal dancer: Sophia Treble.

Hollywood Pinafore: May 31, 1945; Alvin Theatre, New York.
Music: Arthur Sullivan
Decor: Jo Mielziner
Costumes: Kathryn Kuhn, Mary Percy Schenk
Dancers: Viola Essen (with Helele Constantine, Barbara Heath, Ronny Chetwood).

The Day before Spring: November 22, 1945; National Theatre, New York. Musical with book by Alan Jay Lerner.
Music: Frederick Loewe
Decor: Robert Davison
Costumes: Miles White

DANCES FOR TELEVISION

Paleface: January 7, 1937. A floor show with Hermione Baddeley, Cyril Ritchard, Antony Tudor, Bobby Tranter's Girls.
BBC-TV.

Hooey: February 2, 1937. A floor show with Frances Day, Cyril Ritchard, Antony Tudor, Maude Lloyd, Bobby Tranter and His Girls.
BBC-TV.

Fugue for Four Cameras: March 2, 1937.
  Music: Johann Sebastian Bach: Fugue in D minor from "The Art of Fugue"
  Danced by Maude Lloyd.
  BBC-TV.

After Supper: March 2, 1937. A revue with Maude Lloyd, Antony Tudor and others.
  BBC-TV.

Dorset Garden: April 13, 1937. A miniature Restoration revue, designed "to recapture the atmosphere of a well-known London playhouse of the seventeenth century, Dorset Garden Theatre."
  BBC-TV.

Boulter's Lock, 1908–1912: June 29, 1937. Includes Antony Tudor, Maude Lloyd. "This revue has as a setting Boulter's Lock, a favorite haunt of boating enthusiasts on the upper reaches of the Thames."
  BBC-TV.

Douanes: July 5, 1937. A revue.
  Cast: Les Voyageurs: Valerie Hobson, Ernst and Lotte Berk, Eric Wild and his Tea-Timers; and *Un Douanier.*
  BBC-TV.

Excerpts from Relache: July 8, 1937. Ballet by Picabia.
  Music: Erik Satie
  Cast: Maude Lloyd, Antony Tudor.
  BBC-TV.

Siesta: September 6, 1937.
  Music: William Walton
  Decor and Costumes: Peter Bax
  BBC-TV.

Portsmouth Point: September 6, 1937.
  Music: William Walton
  Arrangement: Cyril Clarke

Decor and costumes: Peter Bax
BBC-TV.

High Yellow: September 14, 1937.
Music: Spike Hughes
BBC-TV.

Full Moon: October 25, 1937. Revue by Archie Harradine.
Music: Herbert Murrill
BBC-TV.

Tristan and Isolda (Act 2): January 24, 1938. A masque to the music
of Richard Wagner; mime arranged by Antony Tudor.
Decor and Costumes: Peter Bax
Cast: Tristan: Basil Bartlett (singer, John Wright); Isolda: Oriel
Ross (Isobel Baillie); Brangäne: Mary Alexander (Gladys Gar-
side); King Mark: Paul Jones (Robert Easton); Melot: Hugh
Laing (George Baker); Kurwenal: Peter Garoff (George Baker).
BBC-TV.

Wien: April 5, 1938. A Viennese entertainment.
BBC-TV.

The Emperor Jones: May 11, 1938. Play by Eugene O'Neill.
BBC-TV.

Master Peter's Puppet-Show: May 29, 1938.
Music: Manuel de Falla
BBC-TV.

Cinderella: December 13, 1938. Opera by Spike Hughes.
BBC-TV.

The Tempest: February 5, 1939. Play by William Shakespeare.
With members of The London Ballet.
BBC-TV.

The Pilgrim's Progress: April 7, 1939. *By* John Bunyan adapted for TV by H. D. C. Pepler.
Music: Collected from 16th and 17th century sources
Arrangements: Lionel Salter
BBC-TV.

INDEX